The Work of Recognition

THE WORK
OF RECOGNITION

Caribbean Colombia and the
Postemancipation Struggle for Citizenship

Jason McGraw

The University of North Carolina Press CHAPEL HILL

© 2014 The University of North Carolina Press
All rights reserved
Manufactured in the United States of America
Set in Miller by codeMantra, Inc.
The paper in this book meets the guidelines for permanence and durability of the
Committee on Production Guidelines for Book Longevity of the Council on Library
Resources. The University of North Carolina Press has been a member of the
Green Press Initiative since 2003.

Complete cataloging information for this title is available from the Library of Congress.
ISBN 978-1-4696-1786-2 (paper: alk. paper)
ISBN 978-1-4696-1787-9 (ebook)

18 17 16 15 14 5 4 3 2 1

Parts of this book have been reprinted in revised form from "Spectacles of Freedom:
Public Manumissions, Political Rhetoric, and Citizen Mobilisation in Mid-Nineteenth-
Century Colombia," *Slavery and Abolition* 32, no. 2 (June 2011): 269–88.

THIS BOOK WAS DIGITALLY PRINTED.

For Ellen, Paolo, and Augie

Contents

Map, Tables, and Illustrations

Acknowledgments

The Colombian expression *no dar papaya* means "Don't let anyone take advantage of you." Yet if the following institutions and individuals had not let me take advantage of *them*, repeatedly and over many years, this book would not exist today.

Financial support came from the Fulbright IIE Program; a University of Chicago Mellon Dissertation-Year Fellowship; the Tinker Foundation; and the Indiana University New Frontiers in the Arts & Humanities Program, College Arts and Humanities Institute, Summer Faculty Fellowship, and Center for Latin American and Caribbean Studies Faculty Travel Grant. In Colombia, I received institutional guidance from the Fulbright Commission, the Centro de Estudios Socioculturales e Internacionales at Universidad de los Andes, and the Instituto Colombiano de Antropología e Historia. I am deeply indebted to Jaime Jaramillo Uribe, Karl Henrik Langebaek, Adolfo Meisel Roca, Dolcey Romero Jaramillo, Sergio Paolo Solano, María Victoria Uribe Alarcón, Consuelo Valdivieso, and the Bogotá Fulbright office staff for all their help. At the University of Texas at Austin, generous support was provided by the Institute for Historical Studies of the Department of History and from the Teresa Lozano Long Institute for Latin American Studies. Many thanks to Susan Deans-Smith, Seth Garfield, Frank Guridy, Virginia Hagerty, Julie Hardwick, Charlie Hale, Juliet Hooker, Courtney Meador, and Carolyn Palaima. I also want to thank the archivists and librarians who helped me navigate collections in Colombia at the Biblioteca Nacional, Archivo del Congreso, Archivo General de la Nación, and Biblioteca Luis Ángel Arango; and in the United States at the National Archives and Records Administration, the Library of Congress, the University of Texas Benson Latin American Collection, the University of Chicago Regenstein Library, and the Indiana University Libraries. At Rutgers University, I owe a debt of gratitude to Paul Clemens, Ann Fabian, Aldo Lauria-Santiago, and Jan Lewis.

At the University of North Carolina Press, I have to thank Elaine Maisner, Alex Martin, Alison Shay, and Paula Wald for shepherding this work to fruition. Thanks go to Shirley Ospitia Hernández and Adriana Rodríguez Castañeda in Colombia and Dunstan McNutt in Bloomington for research assistance. This book would never have been finished without my children's teachers and care providers at St. Elizabeth's in Jersey City; the

Bloomington Developmental Learning Center; Wanda and Ricky Ewing; the University United Methodist Church Early Education Center in Austin; and the Monroe County Community School Corporation.

The influence of my University of Chicago professors is indelible in the following pages. I am still learning from my adviser, Thomas Holt, and his work all these years later. Dain Borges and Julie Saville have been generous with their thoughts and critiques for a long time. Ideas that Tom, Dain, and Julie planted in my mind more than a decade ago are only now bearing fruit. I hope they find this book a worthy tribute to their teaching and mentoring. A special thanks, finally, to Julie for her gracious permission to reference her book's title in my own.

I have benefitted from the advice, encouragement, and editorial comments of many scholars: Nancy Appelbaum, Karen Caplan, Meri Clark, Sharika Crawford, Robin Derby, Ann Farnsworth-Alvear, Seth Garfield, Peter Henderson, Catherine LeGrand, Claudio Lomnitz, Song On, Mary Roldán, David Sacks, Frank Safford, and Christopher Schmidt-Nowara. To Aline Helg and Eduardo Posada-Carbó I offer my deepest appreciation for their ongoing guidance and support.

At Indiana, thank you to my departmental chairs in history and American studies: Claude Clegg, Deborah Cohn, Peter Guardino, and Matt Guterl. Thanks as well to my Indiana colleagues Nick Cullather, Arlene Díaz, Vivian Halloran, John Hansen, Wendy Gamber, Shane Greene, Danny James, Javier León, Sarah Knott, Lara Kriegel, Alex Lichtenstein, John McDowell, Michael McGerr, Marissa Moorman, Khalil Muhammad, John Nieto-Phillips, Stephen Selka, and Dan Suslak. Karen Inouye, Michelle Moyd, and Stephen Selka deserve special praise for reading drafts of my work. Thank you to the staffs of the Departments of History and American Studies and the Center for Latin American and Caribbean Studies, with special appreciation to Becky Bryant. At IU, I owe much to my senior colleagues and mentors, Jeff Gould and Peter Guardino, for reading and commenting on my work and for guiding me through the tenure process. I can only hope down the line that they choose to quietly retire my debts without anyone noticing.

I am not ashamed to admit that I have taken advantage of a great number of friends and family. In Colombia, many people have made it feel like home over the years, including Andrés Carlos Barragán, Sharika Crawford, Santiago Giraldo, Francy Adriana González, Claudia Leal, Shirley Ospitia Hernández, Felipe Rivera Garzón, Abbey Steele, and Shawn Van Ausdel. And to my Colombian adoptive family—Fanny Suescún, Emperatriz Suescún, Diana and César Bocarejo, and Ximena Bocarejo—I hope I can make up for my deadbeat adopted child status someday. In Chicago, Portland, and beyond, I must pay my dues to Micah Anderson, Jessica Chi Nimjee, Corey Ciszek, Biella Coleman, Beth Cooper, Dana DeAno, Seth DeAvila, Susan DePaul, Teresa Ejanda, Jiro Feingold, Adam Geary, Kim Guinta, Chris Hallstrom, Moira Hinderer, Leslie Ito, Nicole Lee, Nora Leibowitz, Judy O'Gieblyn, Arissa Oh, Susan Palmer, Janeen Rojas, Talya Salant, Terri Schulte Scott, Mike Siswanto, Steve Tilden, Virginia Tilden, Candy Truong, Scott Wong, Khai Yang, and Rob Yang. In Bloomington, to Melanie Castillo-Cullather, Nick Cullather, Catherine Dyar, Matt Guterl, Deke Hager, Karen Inouye, Sandi Latcha, Jacob Lee, Jennifer Lee, Pedro Machado, Krista Maglen, the Malloy family, Marissa Moorman, Michelle Moyd, Don Rawe, Bret Rothstein, Jonathan Schlesinger, Christina Snyer, and Scot Wright. In Indianapolis, to the Chang, Chu, and Fu families. In California, Maryland, and Vancouver, to the Kwan, Wan, and Wu families, with a special shout out to Simon D. Wu. Last but not least, to the McGraws and Pattersons scattered about in Texas, New Mexico, and Colorado. This laundry list doesn't do anyone justice, but I hope you know how much I owe you all.

I have been acknowledging in print Steve Johnstone and Ellen Tilden across three decades now. Their love and friendship still sustain me.

My sons, Paolo and Augie, have given me the advantage of a day pass they continually stamp so I can visit the beautiful, weird world of childhood and escape from the academic rigmarole. And to Ellen Wu, exchanging draft after draft, punching the tenure clock at the same time, raising kids together, holding down a household, living a shared life . . . I think the papaya has been mutual.

The Work of Recognition

Introduction

> In return for my friendship
> I ask only a single thing of you,
> . . .
> You should say how citizens
> Are black, white, Indian
> . . .
> If someone wants
> To climb to the top,
> He should look for a ladder
> Somewhere else; . . . .
> The time of the slaves
> Is over;
> Today we are as free
> As the white. . . .
> —Candelario Obeso,
> *Cantos populares de mi tierra*, 1877

This is a historical study inspired by the work of a poet. Candelario Obeso was born free in 1849, on the eve of New Granada's slave emancipation, in the Magdalena River town of Mompós, in what would become the Caribbean region of Colombia. Raised and initially educated on the coast, Obeso eventually made his way to Bogotá, which afforded him access to higher learning, a flourishing print culture, and the political patronage that signaled his status as a lettered individual, a *letrado*. In the national capital during the decade before his death in 1884 he became a prolific writer of polemics, language manuals, legal documents, and poems, whose audience was a close-knit if fractious group of leading politicians and intellectuals. Obeso orbited at the social margins of his reading public, and while he sought various means of belonging in this lettered world, his decision to identify as *negro* was often taken as a provocation by the men from whom he sought respect. Of his extensive oeuvre one provocation in particular caught the eye of Obeso's readers, a small poetry collection from 1877, *Cantos populares de mi tierra* (Popular Songs of My Land), which secured his reputation and to a great degree defined his life.[1]

1

No Colombian in the generation after slavery articulated the problem of citizenship more trenchantly than Obeso. The thirteen brief poems of *Cantos*, written in Caribbean dialect, are spoken or sung by plebeian women and men who often call themselves black and who demand respect and rights. In "Epresion re mi amitá" (Expression of my Friendship), a "poor black man" offers allegiance to a "white" leader, but only if the latter first recognizes all citizens. The precondition for any politics, the man insists, must be equal standing for "black, white, Indian" citizens, or perhaps for citizens who are a mixture of the three. A universal sense of belonging undergirds this friendship, which in the poem is not a private relationship but a public bond of affection that does not abrogate differences between individuals. In another poem, "Seranata" (Serenade), another black man makes other demands, this time for an end to coercion and for his personal sacrifices in war not to serve merely as a "ladder" in the white man's bid for power. By invoking emancipation ("the time of the slaves / Is over"), the man extends freedom beyond the legal fiat of abolition to a meaningful independence and reciprocity between blacks and whites. Freedom for the speaker is not just the absence of black bondage but also the foundation, and the consequence, of social relationships between Colombian citizens.[2]

Although the two poems are remarkable for many reasons, their articulation of irreconcilable demands for recognition is particularly striking. The speaker of the first poem calls for, and calls into being, a universal if multihued citizenry. He petitions for a radical equivalence in which racial differences do not prevent parity in civil standing; on the contrary, differences require formal equality as an assurance of a meaningful public life. The speaker of the second poem claims something else entirely: regard for a collective "we" based on a particular experience of freedom not shared by the majority of that same multihued citizenry. Formal equivalence between defined groups, or of a citizenry sprung from once-defined groups, gives way to equality won through the historical struggle against slavery. If both speakers desire the similar outcome of a polity where racial difference does not preclude equalitarian citizenship, they nevertheless seek that goal by divergent paths and through different relationships with their fellow citizens.

The lettered rejection of Candelario Obeso's dual vision of citizenship as multiracial belonging and black freedom was widespread, and it was this general denial that informed the writing of subsequent narratives about Afro-Colombians. Despite the sizable national population of African descent, estimated at 10 million strong, they appear in most published histories as slaves, regardless of how few people were enslaved at any given time.[3] In part this fixation on slavery has coincided with the belief among intellectuals that former slaves failed to contribute to the nation. As Colombian historian Carlos Restrepo Canal proclaimed in the 1930s, "The most significant problem that appeared after [abolition] was this: the slaves, in general, were not prepared for civil life." Even scholarly rejections of Restrepo Canal's indictment have not overcome the low esteem for emancipation, which has reinforced an academic interest in the preabolition period.[4] The numerous conferences, edited volumes, and museum exhibitions commemorating the sesquicentennial of emancipation in 2001–2 reproduced the conflation between blacks and slaves by expanding knowledge of *slavery* and generating little new understanding about Afro-descended people *after* abolition. Emancipation concludes a story about black people in slavery whose aftermath is largely consigned to historical oblivion.[5]

Scholarly and political projects to overturn certain long-standing assumptions about Afro-descended people in Colombia have been a long time in the making. Newer histories treat Afro-Colombians as social actors in their own right, illuminating their participation in civic life since the independence era.[6] Anthropological approaches once focused on the recuperation of African cultures have shifted to analyses of blackness within dynamics of race mixing, multiculturalism, or governmentality.[7] Since the mid-twentieth century, a small but intellectually vibrant cadre of writers and activists of color has shaped this emergent field of Afro-Colombian studies, and because of their work the existence of people of African descent is no longer open to debate. Even so, these projects testify to the ways black visibility must contend with a sense of national unity imbued with powerful notions of color-blindness or *mestizaje*. In overt and tacit ways, Candelario Obeso's shadow looms over the challenges of imagining a multihued nation.[8]

Unlike recent scholarship's critical engagement with the problems of national unity and racial difference, the poet's competing message that emancipation was significant to the ongoing creation of citizenship has proved much more elusive. This outcome could not have been anticipated at the time, given how citizens defined the middle of the nineteenth century by liberating the republic's remaining slaves. "The legislators of 1850 could have done nothing more useful than to present the means in New Granada to extinguish slavery, that institution anomalous with our essentially liberal form," yearned the editors of one newspaper, reflecting a rising accord in favor of abolition. This desire bore fruit soon enough, and on the first day of 1852, the country's remaining 17,000 slaves left the state of bondage and joined the vast majority of the already free. Compared to the great slave societies of the Americas, where emancipation transformed the status of hundreds of thousands of souls, this change took place in what was a society-with-slaves. Still, abolishing slavery was championed as a pinnacle in the country's law and an emblem of national civilization, even if a legacy of pessimism toward emancipation left the fate of the former slaves unknown after the particularly festive New Year's celebrations of 1852.[9]

The stress on the legal fiat of abolition and disregard for its aftermath belie the transformative role of emancipation. Rivaling national independence in political and social significance, "the second liberation" of slave emancipation reshaped New Granada (soon to be renamed Colombia) in dramatic ways, not in spite of how few slaves won their freedom in 1852 but exactly because of it.[10] The power of emancipation in Colombia's society-with-slaves resided in the idea of freedom as the foundation of a new political compact of citizenship. The destruction of slavery made possible new modes of belonging for citizens who in turn fashioned practices and meanings for democratic life out of the belonging opened up by emancipation. Slave emancipation was not the progenitor of citizenship in Spanish America, where the concept of the citizen had originated during colonial times among a privileged few, only to be sanctioned and disseminated by the wars of independence and the first national constitutions after 1810.[11] Even so, it was the prospect for universal freedom that compelled Americans to rethink the questions of what citizens would look like, how they should act, and where they belonged. Alongside other political cultures of the nineteenth-century Atlantic world, including the hemisphere's former slave societies, the citizenship ideal rendered it unavoidable that Colombians would use slave emancipation to reflect on what kind of society and politics was desirable or even possible in its wake.[12]

Grounding citizenship in freedom, however, uncovered a profound lack of agreement over its meanings and relationship to democratic values. For Obeso, freedom prevented the strong from dominating society's more vulnerable citizens because all had attained equal footing in the republic. Whether derived from universal guarantees or local struggle, freedom offered Colombians personal independence and public belonging. Yet to lawyer and economist Aníbal Galindo, one of the letrados to whom Obeso dedicated his *Cantos*, freedom and equality were antithetical. "Choose then," Galindo demanded in an 1880 essay, "either inequality of income with liberty, or equality with servitude; and the decision cannot be equivocal." This stark choice was necessary because of "socialist" demands by "manual labor" to be treated the same as "the more noble categories of intelligent labor." He did not distinguish between economic and political freedom, and his specter of equality shrouded status differences based on work and on cultural attainment, yet his dichotomy was clear all the same. Unlike the political argument of the poetry collection that his name graces, Galindo worried that equal footing among citizens would destroy the liberty Colombians had worked hard to achieve.[13]

This book frames Colombia in the half century after 1850 as a poste-mancipation story in order to reveal citizenship as the problem of freedom. Ending slavery served the dual and contradictory purposes of signifying, on the one hand, universal notions of rights and belonging and, on the other hand, liberation for people of African descent. In this former society-with-slaves, emancipation destroyed legal barriers to citizenship for all adult men and evinced the fulfillment of venerable goals of national sovereignty and civil rule. Colombians turned to emancipation as the juridical precedent and philosophical ideal for a host of reforms in commercial policy, marriage law, education, and religious practice. This universalizing embrace of emancipation, however, made it all but impossible for Colombians of African descent to assert claims on their own behalf premised on the destruction of black slavery. As newly enfranchised citizens continued to engage in the kinds of activities that had undermined legal bondage, others regarded these behaviors as deficiencies that precluded the possibility for full and equal citizenship. And in moments when people of color and their allies presumed to defend the legacy of emancipation as an expression of political affinity, their opponents reckoned these actions as violations of the legacy itself. These competing worldviews, one universal and embodied by all and the other rooted in specific experiences of freedom, constituted a major struggle over citizenship in Colombia, one that continued into the twentieth century, long after the abolitionist impulse had faded.[14]

The paradox of emancipatory citizenship was acute in Candelario Obeso's native Caribbean region. Two groups stood out among the citizenry there: the *bogas* or boatmen who worked in the commercial economy, and the market women who ran local trade and provisioned coastal towns. As people of African descent who were already free at the time of emancipation, bogas and market women often formed kinship relations and together helped establish wider networks of Caribbean working people.[15] After slave emancipation recast citizenship, these networks transformed the meanings of local interactions—marketing goods, occupying land, founding families, and participating in politics—into assertions of their newfound status. In other moments they eschewed their provincial circumstances and differentials in vested rights to join ranks with fellow Colombians to defend the republic. Whether they embraced local ways of life or fought for the rights of all Colombians, Caribbean citizens often encountered lettered opponents who dismissed these efforts as affronts to universal notions of justice or morality. While conflicts rarely entailed two fixed and antagonistic groups, citizens nonetheless engaged each other in making war, law, faith, and wealth with unequal access to political and material resources. At stake in these struggles in Caribbean Colombia and elsewhere was the creation of a modern polity that could not be separated from the contested meanings of freedom.[16]

Colombians understood the essence of this contested citizenship to be recognition. The political and moral concept Nancy Fraser calls the "idiom of recognition" has strong philosophical currency in contemporary debates on identity politics, difference, and authenticity, in particular over the problem of reconciling universal human rights with cultural particularism. Charles Taylor has similarly noted how "democratic culture" since the Age of Revolution has introduced an individualized sense of "citizen dignity" and respect that have in turn undermined older hierarchical status markers. At the same time, according to Taylor, some advocates of egalitarian modes of belonging have interpreted modern political demands based on difference as a "betrayal" of the original universalist notions of citizen dignity. This sense of betrayal, however, has not prevented groups in power from withholding recognition from subordinate groups or perpetuating misrecognition through acts of discrimination and exclusion. In the Latin American context in particular, the politics of recognition has wrangled with the question of which racial ascriptions would be acknowledged and which suppressed in the public arena, or what anthropologist Peter Wade has posited as a tension between sameness and difference in national identity. The pervasive presence of this tension in Candelario Obeso's poetry shows that the origins of debates over recognition in Colombia are far from recent.[17]

This book argues that the majority of Colombians after slavery expressed and demanded recognition as part of the everyday practice of their citizenship. Recognition then was the social status and public habits through which individuals identified themselves and others as citizens. As a fundamental right of citizenship, Colombians continually insisted on being acknowledged and on being able to acknowledge others as individuals vested with rights and dignity. Constitutional principles influenced postemancipation citizenship in profound ways, and law had the power to level public distinctions or to erect new ones, as this book demonstrates. Yet in Colombia's preliterate society, where at most one person in ten could read and write, delineated guarantees were secondary to recognition based on daily social interactions among citizens, which engendered what Rebecca Scott calls vernacular understandings of rights and freedom.[18] Colombians joined political groups, enlisted in militias and armies, and joined crowds in civic ceremonies as expressions of vernacular citizenship. Their vibrant and often combative popular political cultures, like others in nations across the Americas, steered the crafting of formal rights and shaped the fate of constitutional orders.[19]

Vernacular citizenship was a decidedly public affair full of opportunity as well as peril for enfranchised and disenfranchised alike. Streets, plazas, work sites, voting tables, and marketplaces served as backdrops for Colombians to interact and mutually recognize or disavow each other as citizens. These publics had far-reaching implications for women as well as men. As slave emancipation expanded the rights of male adults, a masculine popular politics offered some possibilities for women to assert new forms of standing, and both privileged and humble women brought semiprivate activities into common places in attempts to claim respect and validation. One result of this vernacular cultural politics, detailed in chapters 5 and 6, was the movement led by Caribbean women to take control of church parishes as a pretext to expand religious belonging and proclaim the legitimacy of their children and families. Yet a dual sense of citizenship based in universal ideals and particular freedom struggles produced exclusions as well as inclusion. In public lettered groups sought to limit the formal participation of plebeian citizens and, more emphatically, validate new forms of private life for themselves in attempts to avoid the recognition demanded by the demographic majority. And in another sign of the circuitous and uneven development of citizenship, vernacular politics and public cultures sometimes outlasted the rescinding of formal rights, as this book details.[20]

Other politics was steadfastly cloistered from these vernacular social worlds, the most important being the burgeoning print culture that engendered a contentious public sphere by and for the erudite. This lettered republic overlapped with the personnel of the state, and letrados published opinion, poetry, and fiction that informed the writing of national law. The intersection of public writing and lawmaking held significance beyond the lives of the literate, since fictionalized sketches of popular culture in the genre known as *costumbrismo* offered meditations on the meaning of citizenship, especially true in the genre's depictions of people of color. As conduits for ideas about rights and culture, and of the limits of each, literary representations of the folk reflected letrados' deep ambivalence about the appropriate boundaries of democratic life. It was this ambivalence that Candelario Obeso challenged in *Cantos* through forceful displays of orality and illiteracy as tropes for postemancipation citizenship.[21]

The coexistence of vernacular and lettered publics became a major problem for the composition of citizenship. Emancipation required a new constitutional order that abolished legal exclusions based on property and literacy status and extended full political rights to all adult men. During debates over education and constitutional reform in ensuing decades, however, lettered Colombians repeatedly argued that literacy should be a standard for full political inclusion. Debates over formal rights and primary instruction amid unchanging rates of literacy (discussed in chapter 4) undergirded arguments for innate differences between the literate and illiterate. As the issue of education captivated the lettered republic, unlettered Caribbean citizens persisted in exercising a vernacular sense of rights and belonging, often misrecognized by letrados as behavior that proved their lack of fitness for full civil status. With no significant move toward mass literacy until well into the twentieth century, the contested cultural politics over popular and overeducated understandings of citizenship often proved insurmountable.[22]

Emancipation engendered other citizenship debates defined by the problem of labor in the market economy. The 1853 constitution's bill of rights, which abolished literacy requirements for manhood suffrage, also introduced the "liberty of industry and labor." With this single phrase, the charter demolished the monopoly of the slave masters and the monopoly of exclusive economic privileges, yet in conjoining opposed social relations— profit and labor—as a single freedom, it generated struggles over the economic development of the republic. As bogas, market women, and other working people sought independence from wages, employers and public officials looked to the coercive powers of the state and technology to subordinate labor to commercial interests. Before these disputes could be resolved, reforms in the 1880s concentrated the conflict anew by defining labor as a prerogative of the state. The ongoing problem of settling labor rights within market relations preoccupied political leaders, leading merchants, and working people across late nineteenth-century Colombia.[23]

The lack of resolution of these debates pointed to the problems of determining the boundaries of inclusion and exclusion in public life as much as to domination and resistance between groups. State officials, ecclesiastical leaders, and merchants discovered the limits to imposing their will on populations along the social and geographical margins. Bogas of the Magdalena River, discussed in chapter 3, famously held their ground against all three for centuries. Instead, letrados wielded an inordinate capacity to open or deny public access to law, literacy, and legitimacy. By suppressing or validating distinctions between illiterate and literate, countryside and town, barbarous and civilized, they regulated inclusion in and exclusion from the formal advantages of public life. Laboring people exercised their own capacities to include or exclude others, and quite often in agreement with political leaders and social institutions. Republican politics became the premier realm for multiclass interaction even as the inequalities between vernacular and lettered authority left populations vulnerable to misrecognition by ruling groups.[24]

Struggles within popular politics, the church, education, and the market economy also reflected a profound disagreement over the basic meanings of rights and duties. Caribbean citizens often parlayed civil and religious obligations into expressions of citizenship, and when they could not convert taxation, tithing, or military conscription into entitlements, they withdrew in protest from public activity.[25] For lettered observers, as university-trained lawyers, such actions proved an acute lack of fitness for civil standing. The disparities between understandings of obligations and rights only intensified at the turn of the century, when the imperatives of warfare, religious obedience, and a monetized economy began to transform the relationship between citizens and the state. In the midst of evolving civil, ecclesiastical, and commercial regimes, citizens relied on emancipation-era social practices to evade relations that smacked of unfree labor or subservience. The two senses of right—of authority to impose universal obligations on citizens and of citizens to remain independent from obligations—proved all but impossible to resolve.[26]

As constitutional orders remade the possibilities of citizenship, lettered Colombians reproduced racial ideologies that fixated on essentialized differences in order to deny their official validity.[27] Postemancipation civil equality generated a new democratic ethos that suppressed the public acknowledgement of racial differences toward named persons of public standing. This ethical practice guided behavior among citizens, and when pressed to articulate its nature, individuals commented that they no longer distinguished between black and white. In politics this ethos enabled and constrained certain interactions among elected representatives and their supporters, and in the lettered republic it informed the careers and reputation of lawyer-poets. This sense of racial democracy was grounded in beliefs about the country's liberal inheritance, which hinged on the boundaries of public life and did little to influence racial tolerance, mixing, or discrimination in private relations. Colombia after 1850 was then not unlike twentieth-century Cuba, where egalitarianism and racial discrimination often pivoted on similar distinctions between public and private.[28]

The flip side of Colombians' eschewing race in public relationships was their general acceptance of antiblack racism in private, against unnamed collectivities, and through the anonymous circulation of rumor. The logic of racial marking under conditions of anonymity was tied to gender, literacy, and other status differences, which allowed polemicists to reproduce racism even as they upheld democratic forms of nondiscrimination in the street and in the press. This was true when propaganda invoked savagery and rape to counter wartime mobilizations of plebeian men, or when commercial boosters impugned bogas as a feminized, and hence uncivilized, labor force.[29] Even if ethical restrictions and a racial etiquette complicated the production of antiblack racism, the license to circulate racialized language anonymously or against anonymous populations reproduced the inequality between lettered and vernacular publics.[30]

Racial ideology, guided by public-private distinctions, leveraged efforts to insulate politics, economy, and morality from popular control. As an agrarian society with scant wage labor and a market dependent on local trading, nineteenth-century Colombia harbored economic and political spheres of indistinct separation, which allowed citizens to introduce tradition-bound ideas into work and the public sphere. And for a time, the postemancipation expansion of citizenship rights further confounded the boundaries between morality, honor, commerce, and rights.[31] This was the case, as detailed in chapter 3, when bogas staged the country's first strike not just for better wages and working conditions but also for recognition as an honorable labor force. Coastal people's response to the period's bitter state-church conflicts likewise engaged with both new political rights and older demands for sexual honor. Yet by the 1880s, a new state and church order based on lettered authority, known as the Regeneration, worked to scale back political and economic rights for the propertyless majority. Prominent families and their political allies began simultaneous efforts to create private forms of belonging shielded from the boisterous public. Over time, the circulation of racialized denials of lower-class citizens and the splitting off from popular control of certain aspects of economic, political, and religious life transformed the experience of citizenship.[32]

Historicizing race compels some attention to terminology in the Latin American context. The problem of classification is acute because of the legal fiction and subsequent commonsense belief that emancipation abolished race as well as bondage. Following other scholars, I employ some terms ("of African descent," "Afro-descended") that acknowledge Colombia's place in the African Diaspora, as well as other terms from the time period (e.g., "of color") that are more inclusive if less exact. I also quote from historical sources whose racial ascriptions (*negro, zambo, mulato,* "*branco*") appear conditioned by differences in politics, region, gender, literacy, and public standing. The decision to use updated and period-specific terms does introduce problems of interpretation, and one caution this book offers is that we rarely know how individuals ascribed themselves. At the same time, the approach here offers possibilities for understanding how Colombians marked race in public, the realm of life where such differences were created and perpetuated and that had real effects on people's political lives.[33]

The language of social class obscured or overdetermined status in a similar fashion. Elite thought on class, as typified by Aníbal Galindo's plea to divorce freedom from equality, often slipped between understandings of the material conditions of labor and its cultural or moral attributes. Such was the case when letrados applied the term *boga* to the work performed by river boatmen but also to entire Caribbean families as a comment on region, gender, or race. Another instance was their use of the term *peón*, which was inflected by similar racialized and regional distinctions but always signified a status of social subordination or labor servility.[34] By far the decisive class status marker for most intellectuals was literacy, which often subsumed other cultural differences. A focus on literacy follows the linguistic turn in labor history, which no longer considers ideas and discourse reducible to material conditions but instead posits how language and the law shaped debates and struggles in the social world, often in sporadic and nonlinear ways.[35] To avoid the monolithic distinctions heightened by the measure of literacy, as well as to highlight moments when Colombians sought to actively create such monolithic social categories, this study historicizes the language of labor and class. Studying the politics of recognition requires us to analyze metalanguages of race and class while attempting to dodge the clutch of determinism.[36]

The contradictions of defining citizenship through recognition highlight societies-with-slaves as important locations for the historical study of freedom. The transition from plantation slave production to capitalist production that preoccupied freed people, former slaveholders, and abolitionists in the United States, Brazil, and the Caribbean was faintly perceived in New Granada. Like other early nineteenth-century Spanish

American republics, New Granada harbored some slavery and some plantations albeit without its economy, politics, or society being defined by either.[37] Studies of abolition in these American societies-with-slaves, for their part, often begin with the late colonial erosion of slavery, hastened by the wars of national independence, and conclude with the legal fiats of the mid-nineteenth century.[38] By looking beyond the plantation complex and beyond the moment of legal abolition, we can see how African-descended people expressed religious belief, mobilized in the face of dominant racial ideologies, and influenced national political cultures. Unlike the prominent struggle in former plantation slave societies over defining free labor, the issue of work in Colombia's market economy was "inescapably" tied to questions about the political fitness of workingmen and -women in civil life. Debates over freedom after the demise of the society-with-slaves, then, centered on race-making, morality, and popular politics as problems in the constitution of the national citizenry. The example of Colombia forcefully brings this perspective into view.[39]

A postemancipation perspective creates a powerful frame through which to view citizenship as the problem of freedom, but it still must admit to temporal borders whose end point scholars acknowledge is not self-evident.[40] This book establishes those borders as the five decades after final emancipation in 1851–52, which follows a certain chronology in the scholarship on Colombia. The first era's democratic experiments after final abolition align with the rise of the Liberals, a time noted by historians for the consolidation of the country's partisan politics, disestablishment of the Catholic Church, and early attempts at free trade. The second era corresponds to the Regeneration, beginning in the 1880s, years that they identify as crucial to state-building, church reinstitutionalization, and the origins of the coffee economy, ending with the devastating Thousand Days' War.[41] By examining change across two eras, this book considers ruptures as well as continuities in Colombia's development. The rescinding of formal rights and changes in relations of church and state authority in the 1880s, for instance, had dramatic effects on the lives of Caribbean citizens but did not curtail popular efforts to make good on earlier democratic experiments.[42]

The following chapters trace this broad sweep of struggle in Colombia. Chapter 1 examines how New Granada's citizens collectively rejected slavery, sanctioning the abolition of legal bondage at little political cost nationally as part of an effort to remake the democratic basis of the republic. Yet this consensus, whose force generated new possibilities for civil engagement and a new democratic ethos, quickly gave way to disagreement and uncertainties over the meaning of rights, equality, and freedom. These uncertainties only deepened after an 1854 military coup widely supported by Caribbean people and after the postcoup election under rules of universal manhood suffrage brought to power in 1857 a government at best indifferent to popular participation. Chapter 2 examines how fear of disenfranchisement after the election led many citizens to fight for a counter-republic and overthrow the national government in a civil war (1859–62) that became a referendum on the democratic legacy of emancipation. Through service in arms citizens created Colombia out of the ashes of New Granada, although the war also left in doubt the democratic legacy of emancipation.

Chapters 3 through 5 introduce the problems of labor, learning, and popular politics after emancipation and civil war. Chapter 3 assesses the creation of the single and irreconcilable constitutional freedom of labor and industry, which between the 1850s and 1870s pitted commercial capital against bogas and other Caribbean laboring people. New regimes for policing boatmen sparked the boga strike of 1857, which in turn inspired new technologies to discipline labor. Chapter 4 examines how letrados wrote their ambivalence toward democracy into the public sphere through distinctions of literacy, education, and barbarism, and how their depictions of the folk reaffirmed lettered authority over language and law. It was in this milieu that Candelario Obeso engaged his peers in an attempt to validate oral culture and to demand inclusion for black citizens. Chapter 5 reveals how, even as Obeso entered into public debates in Bogotá, democratic experiments in Caribbean public life became irrevocably tied to factional politics. People of color found opportunities to participate in local republican governance, and they used their public standing to demand significant alterations in property, religious, and sexual relations. As their appeals became increasingly radicalized, many political leaders joined the opposition, eventually fashioning a new alliance intent on undoing the democratic experiments that grew out of emancipation.

The sixth and seventh chapters examine the consequences of disenfranchisement, economic dispossession, and war after 1885. Chapter 6 looks at the political and cultural order known as the Regeneration, which reassembled state and church power along new authoritarian lines. Faced with the loss of economic, political, and spiritual sovereignty, Caribbean people responded in a mass messianic movement, El Enviado de Dios. The state suppression of this movement led to armed rebellion, which preceded and in many ways anticipated civil war. Chapter 7 reconsiders this war, now known as the Thousand Days' War (1899–1902), as a partisan conflict fought through regional, class, gender, and cultural distinctions. Disenfranchised citizens attempted to formulate new possibilities for public recognition even as deteriorating social conditions, violence, and the government's mass denial of their legitimate standing threatened livelihoods and basic existence.

THE CARIBBEAN CASE

The Work of Recognition is a Colombian story told from the vantage point of the Caribbean region, a place rarely mentioned in national histories though central to the country's creation. The geographical focus of this book is a zone extending along the Caribbean coastline from the city of Cartagena eastward to the city of Santa Marta and inland to the towns of Mompós and Magangué. Included in this zone are the other significant population centers of Barranquilla and Ciénaga, an area that in its entirety comprised the most heavily settled parts of the Caribbean coast. This book also highlights the connections and differences between the coast and other regions. The following section offers a very brief background on the Caribbean region, and the significance of its location and people in a national context.[43]

The most noteworthy geographical characteristics of the region were the Caribbean coastline itself and the Magdalena River, which runs south to north through the middle of the country before emptying into the sea. Until the mid-twentieth century, the coast-river axis provided the primary conduit to the world beyond for New Granada/Colombia. By facilitating communication and offering natural resources—albeit less than reliably— the region's navigable bodies of water and populated shorelines, artificial canals, marshlands, and floodplains gave rise to an "amphibian" human culture, according to one leading interpretation.[44] Much of the backlands away from the Magdalena River offered a more arid climate and more sparse population, in particular on the savannas of Bolívar, the grasslands south of Cartagena; to the east of Santa Marta toward the Guajira Peninsula and the Venezuelan border; and to the south and west of Barranquilla. The region's other remarkable physical feature is the isolated massif of the Sierra Nevada de Santa Marta, the highest coastal mountain in the world, which contains many distinct climates and arable lands at its lower elevations.

Geography conditioned demographic patterns. The region boasted some of the oldest European and African settlements in Spanish America, with the towns of Santa Marta, Cartagena, and Mompós dating from

Map 1.1. Caribbean Coast of Colombia

early colonial times. Still, the coast entered the independence era in demographic decline amid historically low population density. This decline reversed around the middle of the nineteenth century when the population of the Caribbean region began to rise at a much faster rate than that of Colombia as a whole (see table 1.1). The demographic decline and subsequent repopulation of the coast altered residential patterns as newer towns rose at the expense of older locales. The most dramatic example of this reallocation of population was the emptying of the walled colonial stronghold of Cartagena and the growth of the hamlet of Barranquilla to become the country's third-largest city. Population movements often exacerbated interurban rivalries between settlements old and new—not only between Cartagena and Barranquilla but also between Santa Marta and Ciénaga, and Mompós and Magangué, respectively—over demographic, political, and commercial supremacy.[45]

Despite the Caribbean setting, a semiarid climate and lack of capital frustrated large-scale plantation production, and it was trade instead that defined much of the regional economy in the nineteenth century. Given that nine-tenths of the country's imports and exports flowed through the Caribbean cities and along the Magdalena River, the port economies reigned over coastal populations, and all significant settlements of the period were ports. Many of the demographic movements after independence tracked market transformations or the changing state of communications, and the rivalries between Caribbean towns were tied to commercial ambitions in the boom-bust export economy. Only after the turn of the century did the cattle, banana, and sugar industries, with their attendant accumulations of vast stretches of coastal territory, begin to rival the economic dominance of navigation, shipping, and trade. Otherwise, outside the commercial sector productive relations took the form of small-scale agriculture and fishing oriented toward self-subsistence or local markets. Port towns were linked to their hinterlands largely through foodstuffs provisioned by peasant farmers, fishermen, and traders. The struggles around peasant proprietorship and land occupation amid an expanding market economy, first in commercial transportation and then in commercial agriculture, were central to the story of recognition.[46]

The coastal cities collectively monopolized Caribbean social life, interurban competition notwithstanding. The status of regional centers wielded by Cartagena, Barranquilla, Santa Marta, and to a lesser extent Mompós, Magangué, and Ciénaga, set them apart from their hinterlands. A few smaller towns were important in regional politics, and some rural areas were heavily populated and linked to cities through the circulation

Table I.1. Population of Caribbean Coast and Colombia, 1825–1918

	1825	1851	1870	1905	1918
Caribbean coast	177,983	129,121	323,959	528,351	826,950
Colombia	1,229,259	2,243,730	2,707,952	4,533,777	6,303,077

Sources: Urrutia and Arrubla, *Compendio de estadísticas históricas de Colombia*, 19–20; Posada–Carbó, *The Colombian Caribbean*, 29.

of food and labor, as noted in the following chapters. Still, the coastal cities amassed inordinate legal, political, and financial resources that often prevented rural populations from accessing the advantages associated with national civil life. Disparities between town and countryside were ongoing features of Caribbean society.[47]

What integrated otherwise dissimilar urban and rural areas was a population of African-descended majorities. In this respect the coast shared some demographic features with other regions of Colombia with large black populations, in particular the Cauca Valley, the Pacific coastal zone, the Chocó, and certain districts in Antioquia. Caribbean coastal slavery, however, tended to be urban, artisanal, or isolated on a few haciendas, with little of the concentrations of slaves found on Cauca sugar plantations and Antioqueño gold mining operations. The lack of plantation or mining economy left the Caribbean region after independence with a small absolute slave population living among a free majority of African descent. This dynamic was in part the legacy of the city of Cartagena, for two centuries a main port for African slaves entering Spain's American colonies. While contemporary observers reckoned southwestern Colombia's Cauca Valley to have the country's largest concentration of people they identified as black, they claimed the Caribbean as the only region with an African-descended majority. People hailed as *negros* but primarily as *mulatos* or *zambos*—of mixed African and European or African and indigenous ancestry, respectively—comprised the majority population in Caribbean towns and countryside alike (see table I.2).[48]

The Liberal Party dominated the Caribbean coast after 1850. Control of the national government between 1863 and 1885 often hinged on which Liberal faction carried the two coastal states of Bolívar and Magdalena, in particular their respective capitals of Cartagena and Santa Marta. Liberals owed their political success in no small part to the region's middling and lower-class populations. The up-and-coming port of Barranquilla, with its migrant working population of color and its cosmopolitan merchants, gained the reputation as the most Liberal city in Colombia. Before 1885,

Table I.2. "Population, Classified by Races and Castes, and Savages," [1853]

	White	Indigenous	Black	Mestizo	Mulatto & Zambo	Total
Caribbean coast	30,000	19,000	13,500	46,421	138,200	253,251
Colombia	450,003	421,000	80,000	1,029,051	383,000	2,363,054

Source: Mosquera, *Memoir on the Political and Physical Geography of New Granada*, 97.

Conservatives controlled some secondary Caribbean towns, but across the region they remained a minority in a political culture defined by habitually bitter rivalries within Liberal politics. Even after the mid-1880s, when Conservative or Nationalist factions controlled national and local politics, the Liberal sentiments of Caribbean citizens were never in doubt.[49]

This study telescopes between local, regional, and national contexts to tell the story of recognition after slavery. The purpose of this approach is to show new perspectives that the Caribbean element of Colombia offers on well-known national developments. Caribbean citizens played unique roles in civil wars, constitution-making, and economic reforms, and these broader changes in politics and society in turn affected the Caribbean coast in particular ways. The connections between the local, the regional, and the national were not a given, however; they had to be consciously considered and articulated. A case in point was Candelario Obeso's claim to represent the Caribbean coast in Bogotá's lettered republic as a pretext for his demands for citizenship based on universal belonging and black freedom. Throughout the following chapters, the intent is to offer local and regional perspectives on a national story while also accounting for national inflections of local change.[50]

Although a paucity of records frustrates attempts to name many non-literate Caribbean individuals who played identifiable public roles during this period, sources do allow us to reconstruct the dramatic and mundane consequences of their exploits in national life. Official documents and lettered publications that leave few traces of the life histories of uneducated men and women do offer a trove of heretofore little-known events in which coastal people were important actors. After emancipation they led the country's earliest labor strikes and only known mass millenarian movement. Caribbean citizens also played roles in the consecration of Colombia's patron saint—Cartagena's Pedro Claver, "el esclavo de los negros"—and in the naming of the republic itself. Evidence from the period reinforces laboring people's obscurity yet does not conceal their imprint on the making of modern Colombia. Even as many individual stories cannot be recovered, this book endorses an imperative in studies of the Black Atlantic world to acknowledge the central part played by people of African descent in the creation of their own societies. At the same time, the elite production of plebeian anonymity is a key facet to historicizing recognition.[51]

Old and new citizens embraced freedom to fashion novel political projects and to rethink social relations, even as the meaning of freedom remained contested. Laboring men and women, religious authorities, urban letrados, and commercial interests engaged in public life often without agreeing to the terms of that engagement. In his poetry, Candelario Obeso brooded over how Colombians had heralded an expansive sense of citizenship before resolving fundamental questions over the meaning of rights and obligations, labor and industry, faith and legitimacy. Obeso himself never resolved the work of recognition and instead left behind a vision of democratic affection colored by sorrow over its political prospects. The decisions by Obeso's contemporaries to misrecognize his vision and to abandon the emancipation legacy altogether, decisions that produced their own profound and unintended consequences, were part of the struggle that is the story of this book.

The Emancipatory Moment

The middle years of the nineteenth century brought to New Granada disease and death, turmoil and renewal. This much was known to the people "from the poorest class" of the Caribbean town of Sitionuevo, where they forced their mayor into flight one August day in 1849. The townsfolk, wracked by cholera, had demanded medicine to alleviate the distress of their families, and when they were met with official indifference, they flashed blades, broke into the homes of wealthy residents, and destroyed furniture. Men and women then turned to other targets, giving "machete blows to the doors of the tax collector's house" and ransacking the town's supply of tobacco, "shouting out that now it would be sold for one *real* per handful." Troops soon arrived from surrounding districts led by Pascual Gutiérrez, a local *jefe político*, who upon entering Sitionuevo hailed the first man he met, "a black youth named Eusebio 'La Pulga' García, native of that city." After Gutiérrez demanded that La Pulga submit to his authority, the youth allegedly attacked him with a machete, prompting the officer to shoot him in the leg. Although La Pulga and others were arrested, and a detachment of soldiers remained to help reinstate the ousted mayor, Pascual Gutiérrez remained apprehensive about the restoration of the old order. While the rioters had not physically harmed anyone, they had seized and destroyed a great deal of property. "If those in the uprising had had more time," the jefe político warned, "who knows how far they would have taken their projects."[1]

The protestors' willingness to upend property and authority in assertion of their right to live free from misery was one instance of the dramatic transformation that swept across New Granadan society in the decade after 1848. Just four months before the Sitionuevo protest, a new national government had come to power in Bogotá under José Hilario López, a general, diplomat, and former governor of the Caribbean province of Cartagena. In its bid to establish legitimacy, the López administration turned back to the provinces, where demands for political change flourished after the election and where new alliances between national leaders and local groups produced significant shifts. In the law, liberals (and, on occasion, moderates and conservatives) pushed through a host of reforms over suffrage, marriage and religious rights, jury trials, and local autonomy in the name of equality and liberty. The formal expansion of citizenship rights, culminating in the 1853 constitution, encouraged further protests like those in Sitionuevo. And although legal changes could not alleviate the immediate hardship underlying such protests, they did often validate projects far beyond the letter of the law.[2]

The conditions that enabled reforms and popular mobilization under López and his successors were fortified by the imminent destruction of slavery. In New Granada, *cimarrones* (fugitive slaves) hollowed out institutionalized bondage through flight into the country's backlands. By the time Congress passed the final emancipation act in May 1851, which went into effect on 1 January 1852, slavery was all but a dead letter, the political costs diminished by a national antislavery consensus and by the actions of the slaves themselves. Even as slaveholding faltered, liberal and democratic reformers of the López administration staged public manumission ceremonies before mass audiences to disseminate egalitarian citizenship and promote their faction's legitimacy. The significance of these spectacles—freeing slaves to promote the López administration and its role in abolishing slavery—went beyond partisan calculus. The libertarian and egalitarian impulse behind slave emancipation became the basis of a new ethos that shaped law, governmental administration, and public interactions between citizens. The fusing of liberal citizenship to slave emancipation stamped the decade with a host of experiments in democracy, as citizens used legal freedom to challenge prevailing ideas of racial, marital, and economic status.[3]

Yet despite the consensus to end slavery, New Granadans reached little agreement over the consequences of legal freedom and civil equality. The attempt to sculpt citizenship out of emancipation quickly ran into disagreements over its content and beneficiaries. The mass mobilizations and ethos against discrimination built from abolitionism soon disrupted the tenuous compromise between the progovernment Liberals, their Conservative opponents, artisans, and enfranchised plebeians in the provinces. While some groups were apprehensive about the scope of change, many Caribbean citizens pushed for fundamental redefinitions of equality and authority not always anticipated by political leaders.[4] Provincial protests that the López faction had sought to channel for political support were not easily contained. In April 1854, a military coup supported by many coastal citizens overthrew the national government. The Melista coup, as it was known, became a major contest for democratic citizenship, and its resolution—in particular, the first vote under rules of universal manhood suffrage, held in 1856—left behind more uncertainty over recognition for those who had helped create that citizenship in the first place.

FREEDOM'S BURDENS

Emancipation came to New Granada gradually and principally through the efforts of individuals who fled their enslavement. Some slaves sought liberation through self-purchase, although barriers to such efforts were formidable, and economic decline after independence constrained their opportunities for earning freedom wages. Instead, many more escaped into the forests and remote valleys of the Caribbean and Pacific coastal frontiers, a steady movement of population beginning in the colonial era that accelerated under the social disruptions of the wars of independence and succeeding years of unrest.[5] In the first half of the nineteenth century, as the older Caribbean population centers of Cartagena, Santa Marta, and Mompós endured hard economic times and outmigration, to the benefit of the younger and more commercially dynamic settlement of Barranquilla, urban and hacienda slaves also found opportunities for escape and mobility in newly opened terrain.[6]

One consequence of flight was the rise of new settlements in the coastal backlands. Smallholdings dotted the landscape where individuals and families built simple huts and developed garden plots on which men felled trees, fished, hunted, and raised livestock; while women and children tended fields of corn, bananas, manioc, sugarcane, and rice. Travelers often witnessed women and men along waterways guiding boats full of produce on the way to local markets, and they noted that women maintained independent livelihoods and sustained families by making straw hats, reed mats, and other handicrafts. Women's active and visible role in marketplaces allowed families to acquire essentials that could not be self-produced and bolstered relations between widely dispersed settlements.[7] Exploiting land, water, and forest for subsistence or barter minimized the reach of outside employers, former slaveholders, and urban government. As part of a hemispheric movement of people out of bondage, escaped slaves in New Granada looked to a hardscrabble existence on the land to fashion new forms of kinship and labor.[8]

The movement toward freedom by means of individual flight and physical resistance deepened already tangled relations between slave and free in the Caribbean region. After independence, the few remaining people in bondage lived in both coastal towns and countryside among a vast free population of African descent. In Minca and San Pedro in the foothills of the Sierra Nevada, "blacks and slaves" worked together on haciendas owned in the 1830s by Joaquín de Mier, "the wealthiest merchant of Santa Marta." The seeming ease with which laborers could flee these locales, at times absconding with slaveholders' animals and other movable property in the process, may have dampened abolitionist calls.[9] At other moments, slave resistance inspired free people to agitate alongside bondmen and -women, as in July 1833, when individuals on a hacienda near Cartagena hacked to death their English slaveholder, his wife, and his son. After the bodies were taken to the city, an "immense multitude . . . composed of slaves and persons of color of the lowest class" rioted on Cartagena's wharf and prevented officials from removing or even inspecting them. In these moments democratic rhetoric in circulation since independence may have raised expectations of further change, encouraging slaves and free people separately or collectively to challenge myriad forms of social domination.[10]

The relationship between the enslaved minority and free majority was further complicated by flight as a movement by and large of the already-free. Squatters and fugitives were in the majority not escaped slaves, yet they all followed similar paths into the coastal backlands to establish settlements or inhabit existing ones often founded by earlier generations of escaped slaves. Despite penalties in the early republic for the "mulatto or black who harbors a runaway slave," keeping them apart proved impossible once individuals reached the backlands.[11] In the rural hideaways, remarked one foreign diplomat, status distinctions blurred, as nearby de Mier's Sierra Nevada haciendas were communities of "poor Indians" and "lazy blacks" that were otherwise similar in being "little stimulated by the needs of material life."[12] By the middle of the century, entire swaths of the countryside were in the hands of motley groups of runaways. One jefe político along the Dique Canal southeast of Cartagena warned his superiors about this social world in early 1850, when he reported on two haciendas abandoned by their owners that "are today *rochelas* for other escaped slaves, deserters, fugitives, etc., on which they do not cease to commit scenes that cannot be stopped because only with armed force would it be possible to assault and capture them without risk."[13]

Slaves joined the free in mass flight because the country's political leadership in the three decades after independence expressed general reluctance over emancipation. New Granadan officials defined abolition as a gradual process to be controlled by governors or, better yet, by the slaveholders themselves. In the earliest abolitionist measure, the Congress of Cúcuta passed the 1821 law of free birth and manumission, which raised expectations of freedom without providing it.[14] The law established manumission juntas that functioned only intermittently, freed few slaves, and suffered significant financial and political constraints.[15] Belated legislative efforts to stem the hemorrhaging of the slave population due to marronage and civil war only produced more fugitives. Reforms passed in the early 1840s that required former slaves to submit to an apprenticeship system under former slaveholders were an attempt to counter the accelerating pace of self-liberation, yet only those individuals with enslaved kin were likely bound by this unfree status.[16] Between 1843 and 1849, when manumissions all but ceased and apprenticeship was the law, Cartagena's and Santa Marta's slave populations shrank by half. Whether New Granadan governments paid lip service to abolition or directly opposed ending slavery, the onus of emancipation fell to the slaves themselves.[17]

By 1850, only 17,000 slaves remained, comprising less than 1 percent of the national population, down from roughly 4 percent in 1825 (see table 1.1). In all but the sugar plantation zone of the Cauca Valley in southwestern New Granada, slaves made up a minute fraction of the total population. In some districts of the Caribbean coast where people of color had long predominated, slavery had disappeared altogether, and many rural districts were de facto free regions. Already in the late 1840s, slaves from Brazil were fleeing into New Granada, given the republic's reputation, with some justification, as a sanctuary of freedom.[18]

If slaveholders and their allies wished to stanch self-liberation and flight, the midcentury mobilizations in the political arena, epitomized by the growth of the democratic societies, helped thwart such efforts. The democratic societies, with origins among Bogotá's artisans in the 1830s, were revived and spread across the country in the late 1840s and early 1850s to provide men with little prior experience the means to participate in public affairs. The sudden popularity of these groups coincided with arrival of news of the 1848 revolutions in Europe, upheavals that inspired New Granadans across the political spectrum.[19] In the dozen or more Caribbean cities and towns where citizens formed new societies, these groups tended to be composed of university-educated men, artisans, and landless laborers—peacetime forums unprecedented in their social diversity. One of Cartagena's first such societies, founded in early 1850 by lawyers, military officers, and merchants, met at night to allow workingmen to attend, since its "objective" was "to moralize and instruct [the people]." The democratic society in Chinú, a savanna town south of Cartagena, similarly aimed to "serve as a political school for instructing the people in their duties and rights."[20] The intent of educating men on their citizenship began in society meetings but soon spread to the nascent

Table 1.1. Slave Population of New Granada, 1825–1851

	1825		1843		1851	
	Number of Slaves	Percentage of Population	Number of Slaves	Percentage of Population	Number of Slaves	Percentage of Population
Caribbean coast	7,120	4.0	4,507	1.8	2,555	0.9
New Granada	46,829	3.8	26,778	1.4	16,468	0.7

Source: Fernando Gómez, "Los censos en Colombia," tables 2, 7, 8, in Urrutia and Arrubla, *Compendio de estadísticas históricas*.

public sphere. "Cobblers, as artisans, tend to your shoes," exhorted a February 1850 editorial in a Cartagena newspaper, "but as citizens, tend to your rights and observe your duties."[21]

The democratic societies also performed a practical function as the political clubs to mobilize support for the presidential administration of José Hilario López. Although his candidacy was popular among many New Granadans, López did not win a clear electoral majority, and his eventual victory in March 1849 came under the cloud of a disputed vote by a deeply divided Congress. Subsequent reforms early on in his presidency, like the expulsion of the Jesuits, further galvanized conservative opponents, which compelled followers of the president to enlist popular sectors to shore up their faction's political viability. As a shadow organization for López, the democratic societies issued broadsides and editorials to appeal to voters in Cartagena, and their leadership recruited adherents by horseback in Santa Marta.[22] The societies' noisy street rallies and clashes with political rivals, moreover, transformed their relatively poor members into the backbone of the ruling party. Conservatives in Santa Marta, in Mompós, in Cartagena, and throughout the country soon founded their own groups, known as popular societies, although on the coast they were never more than a fraction of the size of the pro-López democratic clubs.[23]

Even as the largest democratic societies attracted hundreds of dedicated attendees, López supporters found it necessary to broaden their influence even further beyond their formal organizations. In the 1850s, national, provincial, and municipal elections fell at different times throughout the year, making campaigning and voting an almost constant feature of public life.[24] On the Caribbean coast, Juan José Nieto, Francisco Troncoso, José María Obando and other presidential appointees sought to capture electoral majorities, and as they gave political speeches during the frequent rallies, their subordinates registered laborers and other illiterate men to vote, well ahead of any constitutional expansion of suffrage.[25]

"The November elections for the municipal council of this city are very heated," wrote conservative leader Juan Antonio Calvo from Cartagena in 1849, with "the recent night meeting [where] the *rojos* [liberals] took to the streets with military bands shouting *vivas* and *mueras*."[26] Music was a common sight and sound during rallies, like the January 1851 fandangos in Cartagena's plazas, during which hundreds of city residents danced and sang in parties that doubled as nighttime political gatherings. Organizers in Mompós used a similar mix of processions and music to convert the town's lower-class *barrio de arriba* into a López stronghold.[27]

The illiterate and poor recruits of the democratic societies were in the main free men of African descent, making the multiclass organizations implicitly, and often explicitly, multiracial. The composition of the López faction reflected local demographic patterns noticed by many contemporaries. Foreign and native travelers remarked on the correlation between class and color in the region, how in Santa Marta the "preeminent" inhabitants were "of the white race" and "the lowest occupations" comprised only "those of color," according to one European. Liberal intellectual and abolitionist José María Samper, passing through Mompós in the late 1850s, observed the town's overlapping social, racial, and geographical divisions, with *barrio de arriba* "inhabited by the laboring classes, all of color" and *barrio de abajo* along the riverfront reserved for the "wealthy classes." Descriptions of Cartagena, Barranquilla, and other coastal communities left similar impressions.[28] As another indication of the new administration's appeal to people of color, the López-aligned democratic societies appeared to attract members from neighborhoods that had once sustained religious institutions organized by men of African descent. The festive processions and music of the coastal political campaigns may have served similar social ends as the slave *cabildos de nación* and African and multiracial Catholic *cofradías*, once robust colonial-era institutions, especially in Cartagena and Mompós, that had disappeared after independence.[29]

A more likely reason men of color joined the local democratic societies with enthusiasm was their political promotion of individuals from familiar backgrounds. Cartagena's municipal elections in late 1849 were heated in part because "the list of candidates of the dominant [López] party . . . is made up, in general, of zambos and blacks." Candidates of color ran for local office with the full support of Obando in Cartagena and Troncoso in Santa Marta, and governors appointed some plebeian citizens to district mayorships and judgeships. And Nieto, as Cartagena's jefe político under Obando, chose as his deputy Manuel Antúñez, a Cuban-born man of African descent, who drummed up backers among people of color.[30] A similar dynamic to that reshaping Caribbean political cultures was noticed in the Cauca Valley, where former slaves and free men of color joined the democratic societies to combat the political strength of the region's slaveholding class.[31]

The alliance of laboring people and prominent men, many of whom were inspired by libertarian and revolutionary ideas emerging from Europe, initiated new calls for slave emancipation. Cartagena's *El Ciudadano* newspaper in August 1850 appealed for an end to "the contradictory spectacle of a Republic with slavery," an "institution anomalous with our essentially liberal form [of government]."[32] Caribbean artisans, although fewer in number compared to Bogotá's guilds, often took the initiative on abolition. On the day that craftsmen and López officials founded the Santa Marta democratic society in March 1850, they circulated two resolutions, one calling for the end to church tithes and debtors' prison, and the other demanding the immediate end of slavery.[33] Artisans in Mompós, Lorica, Chinú, and Riohacha broadcast abolitionist sentiments by pooling their resources to purchase the freedom of slaves "as the most dignified pledge" of civic duty. These acts of charity propped up destitute manumission juntas while also sending a message to elected leaders that they had tied the antislavery cause to their new role in public.[34]

The demand for immediate emancipation marked a shift in the political culture. After a generation of gradual abolitionist policies and a decade of conservative ministerial governments that favored slaveholder interests, the two years after López took office in April 1849 saw a surge in public appeals for an end to slavery. Nevertheless, this was not a sustained or autonomous abolitionist movement like those witnessed in Great Britain and the United States; by 1850 there was a broad antislavery consensus across the political spectrum in New Granada. The development of the proemancipation position in public debate more than through a freestanding pressure group allowed any number of citizens to join what by all appearances had become the majority opinion. According to the vocal majority of artisans, intellectuals, students, and laborers, to be a citizen meant to advocate for freedom from bondage. This new consensus also reversed the political calculus in place since independence by lowering the stakes for elected leaders willing to push for an end to slavery and raising them for those who continued to advocate for a gradualist approach to abolition. Public opinion could still be ignored, but perhaps only at a political cost.[35]

Provincial officials of the governing faction reacted quickly to the change in public opinion, often because they were intimately involved in shaping it. In early 1850, Francisco Troncoso, the nationally appointed governor of Santa Marta and president of the abolitionist Sociedad Filantrópica, petitioned Congress to end slavery immediately because "times have changed, the world civilized, equality of rights recognized, [hence] the law of slavery is a stain of injustice that reveals ancient barbarity and present inconsequence." Although he respected property rights, Troncoso insisted that questions of slaveholder compensation must not delay emancipation.[36] Other Caribbean governors and prominent individuals seconded Troncoso's views in their own petitions, and given the rapid decline of the slave population on the coast and in some other regions of the country, an abolitionist stance only redounded to their benefit. The appointees of President López, who since taking office had hesitated to embrace final emancipation, began to press him to take more substantive action.[37]

As abolitionist petitions and editorials reached Bogotá from provincial cities, otherwise reluctant congressional leaders also felt the pressure to enact new legislation. Their initial response was a May 1850 law, the first congressional act related to slavery in eight years, that reestablished provincial manumission juntas and disposed more public funds to pay for the freeing of slaves.[38] During debates on the bill, abolitionists Agustín Núñez, José María Rojas Garrido, and Juan José Nieto—who had recently arrived in the national capital as Cartagena's newest congressman—offered draft amendments to grant freedom to fugitive slaves, to set a definite date for ending slavery, and to impose a low ceiling on financial compensation for slaveholders. Opponents struck down the first two amendments and doubled the proposed compensation rate, marking the finished draft with a conservatism that antislavery advocates had hoped to surpass. Nevertheless, public opinion had helped end official inaction on the subject.[39]

By early 1851, democrats and liberals returned to Congress prepared to push for a final emancipation act. They dominated the Cámara (presided over by Francisco Troncoso, Santa Marta's abolitionist former governor) and entered a Senate evenly split with conservatives, although even the upper chamber generally agreed on a resolution to end slavery. After resisting appeals for immediate emancipation for two years, López himself guided the consensus along by indicating his willingness to sign the bill. He used his annual address to the opening of Congress in March 1851 to claim the issue for his faction. "It is time, then, to give the ultimate blow to this institution," in the name of "the philosophy of the century in which we live and to the Christian fraternity that with so much emphasis the liberal party of the world proclaims."[40] After two months of draft legislation, Congress passed the final emancipation act on 21 May. The law guaranteed an end to slavery on the first day of 1852 and decreed that, "As a consequence, from that day they [former slaves] will gain the same rights and will have the same obligations that the Constitution and the laws guarantee and impose on other Granadans." Forty years of ineffectual measures were over, and slavery was coming to a legal conclusion.[41]

As word of the May 1851 law reached beyond the capital, government officials and López propagandists trumpeted imminent slave emancipation. Santa Marta's governor posted copies of the law across the province, which was "received with the greatest enthusiasm, not only from the wretches whom it sets free, but also by the majority of those who have been able to cease calling themselves owners of slaves."[42] In Mompós, the governor ruled that execution of the law "must be decided in favor of liberty according to very sweeping principles such as those generally recognized as universal justice," and he blocked local legislative efforts to force freedpeople to financially compensate former slaveholders.[43] Newspaper editors and other polemicists backed emancipation by labeling the new law an emblem of the modern liberal polity, "this immense movement of progress among us."[44] They rarely hesitated to remark how freeing the slaves was essential to the march toward democracy, or how New Granada was taking moral leadership among American republics, with often pointed comparisons to the slavocracy of the United States. An 1853 essay reprinted in newspapers across the country detailed four years of reforms enacted by Congress and the López administration and highlighted, lest there be any uncertainty in the matter, "THE BLACK RACE LIBERATED!!"[45]

LIBERATION SPECTACLES

Political clubs and petitions were only one method New Granadans used to fashion an emancipation consensus as a function of their citizenship. The López administration also elaborated a project of political education by freeing slaves before large audiences in symbolically charged manumission ceremonies, events that rose in a crescendo in the months around congressional passage of the law of emancipation.[46] Between January 1850 and December 1851, manumission juntas and local governments across the country staged more than fifty manumission ceremonies, freeing hundreds of slaves in front of tens of thousands of citizens, in a renewed burst of public liberations first witnessed in the independence era.[47] By joining religious and patriotic elements—manumitting slaves during Christmastime or the Feast of the Immaculate Conception in festivities "recalling the glorious days of our political history"—officials fashioned a civil religion around the ostensibly shared values of participants. The import of these acts, which national law required be held in public, weighed on liberators and slaves alike.[48] In 1851, the junta in Mompós planned two months in advance the freeing of José María Otero, and "the day of 6 August was assigned for the act of his manumission, with the intent of honoring better the anniversary of independence that annually is celebrated in this city." Otero's freedom had to wait for a day that delivered the appropriate patriotic register for such an occasion.[49]

The public manumissions infused civic culture with even more dynamism, as crowds of prominent individuals and common folk thronged to town plazas to witness the freeing of a few slaves. Unlike the democratic societies, whose membership was limited to men and in some cases to craftsmen, students, and lawyers, the spectacles transmitted civic ideals to men, women, and children from all walks of life—a reliable medium directed to a populace often without direct access to newspapers or legal codes.[50] The spectacles for Cartagena's 11 November Independence Day commemoration in 1851 were representative of this movement, as local officials festooned balconies with banners, read the public proclamation with the names of the individuals being freed, and led a procession of the manumittees through the streets with marching bands and "followed by a packed and enthusiastic multitude." The combination of popular entertainments and daylong reunions ensured the widespread appeal of these civic engagements.[51]

The freeing of the remaining slaves on 1 January 1852 allowed political leaders to stage even grander versions of the manumission spectacles carried out over the previous two years. On that day in Barranquilla, members of the local junta and a large crowd attended mass before gathering for the reading of the names of the sixty-one women and men being emancipated. In Popayán in southwestern New Granada, the day was given over to parades, political speeches, and high mass. Medellín began the "great national fiesta" on New Year's Eve with music and festive lights, followed on 1 January by mass, a twenty-one-gun salute, numerous speeches, and a "brilliant and numerous procession on horseback with music [that ran] through the streets and plazas of the city."[52] Antislavery advocate Juan José Nieto returned from Congress to Cartagena as the presidentially appointed provincial governor and manumission junta leader in time to stage three days of music, fireworks, and speeches in January 1852.[53] Even small towns and villages held elaborate, multiday emancipation observances to free their few remaining slaves.[54]

The diversity of participants in this spectacular movement fostered competing political messages. Manumitted men and women wearing red Phrygian caps, that "ancient emblem of liberty," evoked Spanish American independence, the freeing of Roman slaves, or even the French Revolution's more radical phase.[55] The display of liberty caps and the process of manumissions often conveyed hierarchical notions of republican virtue and masculine citizenship that ran counter to other, more egalitarian sentiments. In a reversal of historical trends toward manumitting women and the aged, the public ceremonies after 1848 freed young men at rates equal to women from a slave population that was three-fifths female.[56] The spectacles reinforced the privileged representation of young (black) men by offering white women the symbolic roles of adorning slaves with liberty caps or decorating manumission pavilions. In many ways, young privileged women's activities in the spectacles shadowed that of the manumittees, since their festive part also epitomized social change without granting them the authority to bring about that change.[57] Within the rhetorical reach of the ceremonies, governors and manumission juntas also offered plaudits to "honorable" or "humanitarian" slaveholders. This parading of tyrannical power before the public was permissible so long as slaveholders embraced the language of republicanism and, importantly, foreswore financial compensation for the slaves.[58]

In even more potent political symbolism, officials used the spectacles to project their authority in ways that mirrored the relationship between former masters and freed slaves. The public events functioned not unlike private manumissions that slaveholders imagined as a gift exchange, by which freed slaves remained forever indebted to their former masters for the granting of freedom.[59] Governmental juntas and provincial leaders used President Tomás C. Mosquera's national seizure of the right of manumission in 1848, which ended the process as a private act of slaveholders and required its public function, to generalize the terms of debt obligation to the citizenry as a whole. Obedience to authority and respect for the law were due from all in attendance because citizenship was offered as a gift through the releasing of slaves into the free majority.[60] During the 11 November 1850 celebrations in Cartagena, the Nieto and López loyalist Vicente García made this new political relationship clear by enjoining the crowds, "And you, slaves yesterday, citizens today, never forget that it was the munificence of the Government to which you owe the inestimable benefit of your liberty." García directed his closing words to all in attendance: "Without the Republic, you would be nothing. You would be slaves." García's epigrammatic oration collapsed the real freeing of men and women from bondage with political manumission, a gifting of rights to the already free in exchange for their adhesion to the current order.[61] Audience members may have fathomed various meanings from these acts, but the latter conveyed an overarching message that citizens who demonstrated virtue, behaved honorably, and obeyed authority would be guaranteed their rights.

Even as Nieto, García, and other local leaders assumed sole authority over liberating slaves, they continued to rely on individuals to free themselves, as evidenced by the glacial pace of manumissions before the end of legal slavery. The province of Cartagena freed a total of 16 of its 1,200 slaves in 1849, and Santa Marta manumitted only 28 of the more than 800 people in bondage during the height of abolitionist sentiment between June 1850 and May 1851.[62] National statistics for the early 1850s reveal a similar trend in which 4 percent or less of the slave population received letters of freedom annually, a rate that mirrored worldwide private manumissions and showed that the juntas earned the widespread discredit into which their name fell.[63] Officials with the political will to free more individuals could do little to change public penury, which required that they shift the onus to slaves themselves. Amid constant appeals to republican liberty and governmental control of the process, manumission still remained the least likely path out of slavery, and the burden continued to rest on those with the least means but the greatest desire for freedom.

The continued reliance on the slaves to free themselves allowed the López government to employ manumissions for political ends. The constant cycle of freeing slaves on holidays in authoritarian spectacles allowed the president's delegates to monopolize the rhetoric of freedom and citizenship, which essentially turned manumittees into partisan propaganda.[64] Campaigners freed slaves across the country, in locales as distinct as the Chocó, Popayán, Neiva, and Panama, to celebrate José Hilario López "for his democratic principles and in honor of his progressive Administration."[65] The democratic society in the Caribbean town of Lorica celebrated the second anniversary of López's 7 March 1849 election victory by purchasing the freedom of seven slaves. And in Cartagena, Governor Nieto converted 1 January into a mass political rally, ending the ceremonies with a rousing, "Viva New Granada! Viva the Legislature of 1851! Viva the savior of the Seventh of March 1849!"[66] This ploy not only trumpeted the López faction but also excluded claims to an antislavery patriotism by the president's political opponents, precisely because all parties, including conservative ones, had joined the emancipation consensus by 1850. Such unabashedly partisan appeals within quasi-official civic rituals offered the citizenry new possibilities for social belonging while simultaneously promoting political divisions.[67]

The symbolism of the spectacles was potent enough that on at least one occasion long after final emancipation Caribbean leaders again staged a public manumission. In June 1856, after being alerted to the presence of a slave aboard a Dutch ship anchored in Cartagena's bay, city officials boarded the vessel and apprehended a bondman from Curaçao named Antenor Dovale. Instead of a summary execution of a legal writ—invoking the 1853 constitution's prohibition against slavery within the republic and simply liberating him—they reenacted the ceremonies from earlier in the decade. Before a gathered crowd, Cartagena's mayor proclaimed that Dovale had been granted both his freedom and full national citizenship status, a patriotic and egalitarian act gifted to the people. The choice of the spectacle over a perfunctory official act may have had to do with the national election to be held just two months later, which would be the first presidential contest under rules of universal manhood suffrage, with the votes of men in attendance already being actively courted.[68]

Politicians outside the López alliance were not alone in being denied a voice in the manumission spectacles, which also averted acknowledgment of the slaves who had undermined slavery. Manumittees stood as mute symbols of the free majority's preoccupations, allowing elected and appointed leaders to appear as the republic's liberators. Subsequent legislative inaction only affirmed this legend. Three years after final emancipation, abolitionists and liberal reformers in Congress introduced a bill to grant letters of freedom to slaves who had been fugitives on 1 January 1852. The bill was a seemingly modest gesture to their individual struggles for freedom and, more significant, a formal extension of citizenship for an unknown number of New Granadans and their direct descendants whose standing had been left in doubt by emancipation. Former slaveholders and their allies, however, defeated the measure in the first hearing. The refusal to extend legal status to cimarrones codified the silence around their central role in destroying slavery, which was reinforced by their flight to the countryside far from the centers of civil life. With fugitive slaves denied legal standing, the manumission spectacles' message of lettered leaders' gifting of freedom slid into place as the dominant story of emancipation.[69]

A NEW ETHOS

Republican leaders who freed a few slaves in public while quietly relying on the rest to free themselves used the spectacles to articulate and shape powerful egalitarian ideals. In a ceremony in Neiva on 20 July 1850, abolitionist and manumission junta leader José María Rojas Garrido proclaimed that "today two members of our family have entered the democratic communion of Granadans, have bridged the boundaries of slavery and for the first time walked in the land of equality."[70] The assertion that equal rights and national citizenship sprang forth at the moment of freedom was not mere rhetorical flourish. Unlike neighboring plantation societies, where manumitted slaves were denied suffrage, forced to move, or liberated only after the posting of bonds in their names, freed adults in New Granada joined the general population without a residual slave status or fear that they would be deemed public charges. The lack of distinction for emancipated slaves may have signaled official disinterest in their fate as a group, yet the manumission ceremonies converted individuals like Antenor Dovale and hundreds of others into persons with full citizenship rights who thereby joined an egalitarian national belonging through formal freedom. The date of 1 January 1852 had done the same for the remaining 17,000 slaves.[71]

The conflation of antislavery, citizenship, and equality by Rojas Garrido and other abolitionist leaders laid the foundation of a new democratic ethos. For many liberal reformers in the López administration, these attitudes and behaviors centered on the suppression of race or color in the law and the equal treatment in public of individual citizens. They looked on emancipation as not only the end of slavery but also the conversion of slaves into citizens and the final demolition of colonial-era social distinctions, the May 1851 law serving as the embodiment and guiding spirit of a public life free from discrimination. Writers defined the new ethos in language shot through with anticolonial rhetoric. "Hereditary or blood nobility, life-long appointments, primogeniture, distinction of social classes before the law," according to leading jacobin Manuel Murillo Toro, "had to disappear before the sacred dogmas of equality and liberty that make a single family of all humankind." Murillo's was the consensus view on egalitarianism, supported by radical democrats, moderates, adherents of laissez-faire economic philosophy, and Bogotá artisans who despised free trade.[72] These ideas were far from novel at midcentury, and their roots lay in a color-blind republicanism fermented during independence, only to combine with a universal liberal individualism as the century progressed. What had changed was emancipation itself, which not only freed the remaining slaves but also abolished race as a category in the law. For many liberals of Murillo's generation, ending slavery was the necessary path to full citizenship for all.[73]

Within months of emancipation, Congress codified the ethos in the new national political charter of 1853, which guaranteed "equality of all individual rights; no distinctions based on birth, and [that] no titles of nobility, profession, privilege, or class shall be recognized." Many educated New Granadans looked to the law as the perfect instrument to end these distinctions, whether they manifested between black and white, master and servant, or even national and foreigner, which were all to be replaced by a single category of civil standing. The constitution fulfilled this ideal by consecrating suffrage for all men, which for many utopian thinkers extended civil equality in order to preempt social inequality.[74] In this circular reasoning, equal rights both begot equality and derived from it, leading Murillo Toro to defend universal manhood suffrage as having "recognized a right that was indisputable," a self-evident state of affairs manifested in the knowledge that "the essence of suffrage perfects itself through its use." For liberals, egalitarian constitutional guarantees were made possible by legal freedom, and the new political charter's bill of rights concluded with a necessary restatement of the extinction of slavery.[75]

In the ethical association of slave emancipation with manhood suffrage, New Granada's reformers fashioned citizenship that denied the legal weight of status differences between men even as it reinforced other distinctions between men and women. As a legal counterpart to the manumission ceremonies, where increasingly conspicuous male slaves were transformed into undifferentiated members of the citizenry, the 1853 constitution extended a self-evident egalitarianism to men of color and impoverished males in explicit ways. Civil equality obliterated exclusions based on literacy or property, and even male beggars and husbands whose livelihoods were dependent on women's labor, groups once denied citizenship status, found all legal barriers removed to their exercise of the vote and public standing. This change was evident to leaders at the time, as in an August 1853 speech by José María Obando, who praised the new constitution for returning "to the citizen of this Republic the sublime majesty of manhood, restoring to him his natural dignity and the rights with which his Divine Creator had endowed him." A facet of the era's utopian expectations, what Murillo Toro claimed as an indisputable state of affairs, was a public life created by and for an undifferentiated male citizenry.[76]

The power of the emancipatory ethos, beyond creating the legal conditions for a republican brotherhood, resided in its ability to permeate other, seemingly unrelated reforms. The 1853 constitution also granted equal rights to marriage and divorce for men and women, making New Granada only the second American republic to do so, which the framers grounded in the a priori fact of slave emancipation. The unfettered capacity to engage in or to annul marriage contracts presupposed the absence of "force and fear that would be sufficient to obligate one to work without freedom." This freedom that derived from slave emancipation extended contractual relations in marriage and divorce to women without distinction or impediment.[77] The right to divorce at will horrified conservatives and the Catholic Church and dismayed many liberals, yet still its successful passage spurred some lawmakers and political groups to push other equally controversial proposals by linking them to slave emancipation. Educational standards, titles of honor and address, and economic privileges all were abolished in the name of human emancipation. In the push for social change in the law, the extinction of slavery was the touchstone for reform.[78]

Emancipation's legal sanction of a homogeneous masculine citizenship was insufficient without its civic enactment, and egalitarian practice began to reshape public culture through the contravention of informal social barriers. At the height of the abolitionist consensus, lettered and propertied individuals began consorting in overt ways with the folk, in particular when women were involved. In 1850, José María Guerrero attended a public dance in Santa Marta where he allowed his "pretty niece of alabaster color" to mingle freely with men "who seemed coarsest and of worst exterior." Not to be outdone, local conservatives also attended dances as a part of the same "practical lesson of social equality [and] class leveling."[79] The manumission spectacles also provided an important setting for these performances of public race mixing. In an April 1851 ceremony in Bucaramanga, where forty slaves were manumitted, the governor "directed himself to the most timid [freedwoman] and invited her to dance," prompting an "explosion of applause that demonstrated how suddenly everyone had comprehended his idea" of mixing whites and blacks, citizens old and new. For people of color who witnessed these acts, the willingness of influential men to socialize with the newly free perhaps signaled that their own rights and standing were more than guaranteed.[80]

Already at the moment of its ebullient conception, the ethos against discrimination was put to the administrative test. In a December 1851 petition to Governor Nieto, a merchant from the United States, Henry Sears, claimed he had been detained at Cartagena's main gate by Bernardo Roa, a soldier stationed at the city walls. Sears protested having been "assaulted by a black soldier who had the presumption of seizing the head of my horse, while spewing the most insulting expressions." While "no civilized guard would ever be permitted to insult a foreigner with impunity," on the contrary, "the deed frequently occurs here as a pastime." Sears may have assumed preferential treatment as a foreigner and white man, and in his official response Nieto did promise to investigate the incident fully. At the same time, the governor assumed an ethical standpoint that undermined the racist assumptions of the merchant's complaint. "Mr. Sears must understand that in New Granada the distinction between black soldiers and white soldiers is not recognized," Nieto observed, "as all Granadans are servants of the Republic."[81] Nieto played on patriotic sentiments, rekindling comparisons between a democratic New Granada and a slaveholding United States, yet written just days before final emancipation, his words also anticipated the new outlook that would forbid any regard for the color or race of a publicly named individual. The governor asserted the right to protect Bernardo Roa's status as a citizen in ways that did not also acknowledge the weight of racial status. While Nieto's invocation of a black-white dichotomy in order to deny its validity was by then a familiar rhetorical gesture, his statement went beyond an older color-blind republicanism to claim a new form of democratic governance.

The ethos and policy of disregarding color entailed no substantive change in positive law. Besides removing legal barriers that might inhibit people of color from public activity, governments had no program to carry out. The law had equated blackness with the status of slavery, and to emancipate the remaining slaves was to abolish race as a social category that defined a state of subjugation. Nieto and other reformist López supporters sought to obliterate similar forms of social dependence and shed other potential wards of the state who could be marked by racial difference. Civil standing, as attained by propertyless men under the 1853 constitution and by Bernardo Roa and his fellow soldiers through the actions of public officials, freed citizens from racially ascribed forms of dependence.[82] For individual citizens, the ethos established a vague code of conduct primarily by dictating what not to say or do. Activity and status free from discrimination meant the suppression of any mention of race when addressing public men or men in public, but it did not direct New Granadans toward particular kinds of interactions or toward private expressions of social acceptance. If some citizens were emboldened to mingle publicly in the name of democratic belonging, just as many perhaps offered only tacit acceptance of the ethos that mandated no change in their private lives.

Many newly enfranchised citizens, however, were not content with a passive legal equality, and they actively challenged existing forms of social discrimination, with the criminal justice system as a primary target.

Among its reforms, the 1853 constitution consecrated jury trials, which plebeian New Granadans embraced less as obligation than as fundamental right. Liberal reforms also abolished political crimes and the crime of disrespect for authority, the latter a catchall offense often levied against the poor. Even before the constitution's ratification, Caribbean citizens appropriated civil equality to renounce punishment for crimes against property and authority.[83] In February 1850, the cabildo of Cartagena had abolished incarceration fees because many impoverished convicts who could not pay for their own upkeep found themselves trapped in a form of debtors' prison.[84] And in taking up duties as trial juries, propertyless and illiterate men began to oppose the harsh penalties of the legal codes and judicial system. In Cartagena's tribunals they "resisted the cruelty and disproportion of the law with an almost absolute leniency," rebuffing any criminal sentencing that included the death penalty, ten years' imprisonment, or sixteen years' forced labor.[85] Jurors showed mercy because they lacked confidence in criminal statutes and because, as intellectual and public servant Salvador Camacho Roldán observed in 1852, convicts were incarcerated in insalubrious prisons that represented a hateful "social power" redolent of slavery.[86] Out of a sense of "justice," Cartagena juries acquitted most defendants, in particular those who had already served time in the city's presidio. In submitting acquittals for men accused of property crimes, juries appeared to take their cues from liberal lawyers and artisan public opinion, which demanded an end to debtors' prison as a fulfillment of the ideals embodied in slave emancipation. By early 1853, the anti-incarceration advocates made this connection explicit by calling themselves "abolitionists."[87]

In the citizen-led revolt against criminalization, juries and sympathetic officials agreed that the vast majority of individuals sent to trial were innocent.[88] This belief led to the reversal of the steady rise in criminal conviction rates during the 1840s, until acquittals soared to more than 70 percent of all court cases by 1852. Mass exoneration effected other changes in the system of justice during the same period, as total criminal trials plummeted by 75 percent; prosecutions of property crime dropped from their 1848 peak of over 1,000 to just over 200 in 1852; and convictions for "disrespect to authority" fell by half. With acquittals all but assured in jury trials, Julián Ponce, the democratic reformist governor of coastal Sabanilla, informed President López in July 1852 that he had suspended the pursuit of fugitives convicted of property crimes.[89] Some commentators lamented a lack of effective "repression" for wrongdoing, but their voices were drowned out by the calls of Caribbean liberals and jurors to end debtors' prison and introduce what Santa Marta's governor called "radical reform of the penitentiary system" ahead of similar nationwide efforts.[90]

As popular juries gained the reputation of handing out blanket exonerations, the López faction had little incentive to curb efforts that could serve partisan ends. Even Nieto, who believed in capital punishment and sought more convict labor for Cartagena, appeared to understand the need to pay lip service to "penal reform that public opinion and philosophy demand with ardor, a reform in which the public works and the gallows must be abolished."[91] He perhaps realized that, as with partisan control of the manumission spectacles, any political dividends derived from decriminalization favored his faction, in particular with the anticipated expansion of suffrage. This was especially clear on the Caribbean coast, where majorities supported López, as evinced during the reactionary uprising to stop passage of the law of emancipation in 1851. Unlike the armed conflict in southwestern New Granada, where the army had to put down a rebellion of slaveholders and their allies, the Caribbean region remained calm. Otherwise, popular agitation favored democratic demands and, hence, appointees and elected officials tied to the López camp.[92]

Conservative opponents of the ruling party, before and after the failed attempt to stop slave emancipation, cautioned that the Liberals' promotion of egalitarian measures would have deleterious political and moral consequences. In the wake of the López electoral victory in 1849, Mariano Ospina Rodríguez and José Eusebio Caro had organized intellectuals, landowners, and merchants into a Conservative caucus to counterbalance the Liberal alliance and defend the Catholic Church. Unlike conservative and moderate strength in the western province of Antioquia or southwestern Popayán (where many former slaveholders dominated local politics), their Caribbean allies faced an engaged populace and a potentially enduring minority status. During the 1848 presidential election, under rules of indirect and restricted suffrage, conservative ministerial candidates had taken a majority of ballots on the coast except in Santa Marta, where they won a plurality. After the vast expansion of suffrage in the 1850s, they never came close to repeating that success.[93]

Placed on the defensive, coastal Conservatives articulated ideas of innate social differences, in particular as the poor appeared ready to gain the most from civil equality. During the 1849 cholera epidemic, some argued that the potter's fields with their thousands of corpses (in Cartagena and other coastal towns upward of 20 percent of the population died) were the fault of the poor. One doctor in Santa Marta argued that bile caused the disease and that "the poor generally are those that secrete more bilious humor." Antipoor attitudes and the inaction of wealthy Caribbean families, many of whom fled the lowlands for higher elevations during the epidemic, contrasted with the philanthropy of former president Tomás C. Mosquera, a Cauca native who won widespread respect among the region's popular classes for traveling to Barranquilla in July 1849 to help with cholera relief efforts. Elite Caribbean opinion also praised Mosquera while accusing impoverished people of bringing death to New Granada.[94]

Antipoor sentiments stemmed from the belief among some Conservatives that social behavior expressed ineradicable distinctions that legal reforms, far from resolving, only exacerbated. José Eusebio Caro posited the religious iteration of this argument shortly before his death in Santa Marta in 1853, when he asserted that blacks, whites, Jews, and Christians were equal in the eyes of God but that the works of man on earth left them unequal.[95] Other commentators modified Caro's interpretation in their insistence that morally suspect conduct expressed the inferiority of individuals, a claim that appeared a direct rejoinder to the emerging ethical code between individual citizens in public settings. New proscriptions against acknowledging differences in public, in other words, did not preempt self-incrimination of one's low status through objectionable public habits. After Obando and Nieto had taken control of Cartagena's provincial government in 1849, Juan Antonio Calvo confessed, "I believe that the moral scandals will continue unabated, because it is not the first time that they remained unpunished, and because it is well known in this country of *Equality* that the laws are not made for those who wear shoes." For Calvo, the problem was less innate difference than a legal equalitarianism that enabled the poor to put their lesser worth on display. This focus on moral substance expressed through behavior, moreover, may have also been a direct response to mass decriminalization.[96]

Some advocates for highland artisans, who had joined the emancipation consensus at midcentury, propagated similar arguments that formal equality encouraged public expressions of innate inequalities. In the early 1850s, one polemicist appealed to Bogotá's politically influential craftsmen by asking whether they could ever receive a fair trial without control over jury selection. "If the accused holds the belief . . . that men of *black color* are barbarous, of evil heart, mortal enemies of whites and inclined to murder, and has been left in the hands, disgracefully, of two or more *blacks* as jurors who must sentence him . . . will the unfortunate man have any confidence in the trial?"[97] This fearmongering was at odds with Bogotá's demographic realities, which made it unlikely to find men of color on juries. The specter of the black juror, however, shadowed political attacks by artisans against their rivals, the university students and lawyers of the liberal Gólgota faction. The smearing of the Gólgotas as the party of blacks implied they organized followers along the lines of discredited legal and social categories. The polemical assertion of artisans' moral authority, made by invoking a sense of black inferiority, furthermore cast doubt on the workings of the entire jury system. Like Calvo's warnings, it argued that legal equality put too much faith in the wrong population. At the same time, these published diatribes against imaginary men of color skirted the charge of discrimination by not naming actual individuals.

For Caribbean officials the possibility of jurors of color was not hypothetical, and one jefe político in Cartagena province was scandalized in late 1852 when a jury acquitted men charged with rioting, an outcome that "has left authority mocked and soon will corrupt public morality." He claimed that since the province had begun authorizing jury trials, "criminals of the worst degree" were being freed by their peers among the poor. While committed to the ideal of the jury, Cartagena's attorney general concurred that "the lowest class of society, of its most ignorant and vicious part," lacked the moral or intellectual capacity to judge the law and warned that disaster awaited full implementation of random selection of jurors. Judicial leniency exemplified the belief that civil equality opened the door to displays of innate inferiority.[98] These statements came not from ministerial holdovers but from appointees of José Hilario López and Juan José Nieto, and their views were in line with those of the governor himself. "We must realize the truth," Nieto had proclaimed in his Emancipation Day speech eleven months earlier. "Hierarchies will always exist as created by nature and society against whose order . . . one has no power to resist because there is no power more forceful than nature nor law more infallible than public sanction." Not even the "civil equality" he had trumpeted in the Henry Sears case could deny this truth.[99]

New Granadans who embraced the belief that behaviors expressed an unchangeable social inequality helped circulate fictionalized narratives of Caribbean public race mixing. In one version published in a liberal Bogotá newspaper two weeks after final emancipation, a white woman at a dance in Cartagena rebuffs "a liberal artisan, one of those of the dark race," who believed new legal guarantees had ended all distinctions between citizens. "Soon enough artisans *of color* had learned the proper difference between political questions and social questions," the story intoned, "a difference that did away with the disharmony between whites and blacks of the same political stripes." The lesson served the new citizens well, because "after always learning only about their *rights*, without ever coming to the chapter on their *obligations*, it was not expected that they would be subjected docilely to the latter." For liberal reformers and confirmed antiegalitarians alike, obligations of citizenship entailed social deference first, constitutional duties second. Yet the story clarified the problem as one less of color than social class, since any man of color invited to such a fete would be educated and hence welcomed by lettered society. To the extent that color mattered, black skin only confirmed the lowly rank of manual occupations.[100] For elite New Granadans, the real and fictional Caribbean dance floors became locales for working out the murky boundaries of social inclusion—and policing the role of white women in that process. In no case, however, did this process imply an end to distinctions or a rethinking of the racialized terms of decency that precipitated such reflection in the first place.[101]

Alongside lettered and artisan articulations of inequality came the concurrent circulation of new legends that blamed slave emancipation for the country's economic and social woes. New Granadans and foreigners spied abandoned or decaying Caribbean haciendas and suspected the culprit was abolition itself. The governor of Cartagena before Obando took power in June 1849 remarked that "the bad condition of rural estates of this province is well known since slavery, which was the key to development, has disappeared." The story of haciendas in decline persisted despite the very few slaves freed on the coast before or during January 1852.[102] It also appeared alongside a more polemical legend of the *zurriago*, that before and during passage of the emancipation act in 1851 slaves had risen up and flogged slaveholders in the Cauca Valley. The narratives of ruined estates in the Caribbean region and violent former slaves in southwestern New Granada expressed a deep pessimism for postemancipation politics, and together they indicted an illegitimate equality assumed by freedpeople and their allies as the cause of national backwardness.[103]

The variety of antiegalitarian arguments appeared to anticipate the code of universal manhood suffrage enacted under the 1853 constitution, and some New Granadans may have wanted to disabuse newly enfranchised citizens of the idea that political inclusion would eradicate social distinctions. Neither Juan José Nieto nor José Eusebio Caro appeared to conceive of the new ethos as applying to informal or personal acts of discrimination, and once the public dances ended—assuming white women and men of color observed the rules of proper mixing—democratic revelers returned to their respective social worlds without any change in fundamental distinctions. As with the manumission spectacles, prominent men used the dances to broadcast democratic ideals in ways that did not imply a surrender of status or authority. Within these political horizons, full citizenship rights did not address social or economic conditions, and Manuel Murillo Toro's tautology that equal civil standing created equality could be used to preempt challenges to private forms of discrimination. The law did not address poverty or informal barriers to public life; on the contrary, a self-evident and official equality precluded further discussion of the matter.[104]

UPRISING OF 1854

A major trial for the nature of emancipation-bequeathed equality came with the extended events around the 1852 presidential contest to succeed José Hilario López. In the election López loyalist, military general, and congressional leader José María Obando faced two rivals from the Liberals' lettered and civilian Gólgota faction. During campaigning, the Obando camp circulated rumors that his opponents, if elected, would reinstate slavery. Although audiences unlikely inferred the literal return of legalized bondage from this rumor, it may have sent a message that Gólgotas condoned the kinds of discrimination and dependence that slave emancipation had ostensibly eradicated.[105] The López administration's gifting of freedom through the manumission spectacles, which had cast doubt on Conservatives' ability to rule, now fell over their Liberal adversaries as well. At the same time, the uses of race in this fearmongering campaign were complex. By the time of the 1852 election, some of Obando's artisan supporters had issued antiblack polemics against the jury system, accusing Gólgotas of organizing followers based on discredited racial categories. Arguments against social equality that came from some lettered quarters appeared to support the Obando campaign's allegation. Yet Obando himself had once faced condemnation for mobilizing slaves and free blacks against whites during the 1839–42 conflict known as the War of the Supremes, for which he endured a decade of political exile until granted amnesty by López. Obando won the 1852 presidential election, including a lopsided share of the expanded (although not universal) Caribbean vote. His showing on the coast owed something to his time as governor of Cartagena in 1849, immediately after returning from exile, but also perhaps from his reputation as both a defender of the democratic ethos and a leader of people of color.[106]

Obando's presidential inauguration in April 1853, just weeks before ratification of the new constitution, helped the López faction consolidate power, albeit amid growing social turmoil. In Bogotá, letrados and artisans clashed over issues of foreign trade and the size of the army. On the Caribbean coast, with few university-trained leaders or craftsmen and with a weakened Conservative opposition, the main tension lay in continued plebeian demands for political change. Since the cholera epidemic, the region's impoverished populations had shown a willingness to confront leaders who did not live up to popular notions of justice. Just weeks after final emancipation in 1852, Francisco Carmona, a Venezuelan-born officer who had served under Bolívar and Páez during the wars of independence, was killed during Carnival in the coastal town of Ciénaga. Competing rumors circulated that Carmona had murdered a local democratic leader, assaulted an individual, or even merely disrespected "a man of the pueblo" during the celebrations. In response to these rumors, an armed crowd broke into his home and killed the former general, horrifying prominent New Granadans throughout the country. In response to this perceived breakdown in the social order, and out of concern about the growing influence of artisans and other laboring people in the incoming Obando administration, many Conservative and Liberal letrados sought common ground across the partisan divide. To many lettered observers the particular motive for Carmona's murder, which remained unsolved, mattered less than a "rising popular furor" that no longer shied away from attacks on the respectable classes.[107]

They did not have to wait long to experience the force of this popular furor. A year into Obando's presidency, General José María Melo, the officer in charge of Bogotá's garrison, staged a coup and overthrew the government. The immediate cause of Melo's actions in April 1854 was the decision by Congress to eliminate the military leadership and reduce the size of the standing army. Civilian leaders and government officials who escaped arrest by Melo's forces regrouped outside the capital. In the eight-month civil war that ensued, artisans and other plebeian citizens joined soldiers against the combined forces of the so-called constitutionalist establishment, which included letrados of all factions and former presidents Tomás C. Mosquera and José Hilario López, who together led the military effort against Melo.[108]

The uprising took a distinct turn on the coast, one of the main regions outside Bogotá to back the coup. When word of Melo's actions arrived in May, Governors Juan José Nieto in Cartagena and Juan Manuel Pérez in Santa Marta, along with local military units and employees of the national government in Barranquilla, declared their support for him. The motivations of men like Nieto, a López and Obando loyalist, were not made public, nor is it clear how joining the coup furthered his political aspirations. It is possible that the fifty-year-old Nieto considered a Melo victory conducive to his long-held goal of regional autonomy from the central government.[109] In response to the coastal rebellion, the constitutionalists declared Nieto and Pérez "enemies of the Government" for their "chicanery and disloyalty" and dismissed them and national employees from their positions.[110]

Mosquera's arrival on the coast to banish procoup officials, however, did not quash popular unrest. When the former president attempted to lead troops from Cartagena into the interior to join the other constitutionalist columns in the assault against Melo, bogas and porters began "seizing the *bongos* [large dugouts] that were carrying the baggage train" to prevent their departure. Mosquera was forced to march overland, greatly slowing his progress. In the town of Ciénaga, hundreds of men led the procoup uprising, fanning out across the region to block river traffic and gather more followers. And to the south in Mompós, the town's inhabitants spent months under threat of an invasion from the surrounding countryside, leading Mosquera to declare a state of siege over the entire coast. The removal of prominent leaders like Nieto and Pérez, far from halting locals' protests, had instead seemed to spur them to claim territory as their own.[111]

The enthusiastic participation of working people gave the uprising a strong element of social conflict. Evidence suggests that on the Caribbean coast it was the landless, like the urban bogas of Cartagena and perhaps some on the Magdalena River, who supported the overthrow of the government. Countering them was an alliance of merchants and prominent men, in the main from the new Conservative Party. This class divide appeared in the worst fighting on the coast, when in July 1854 hundreds of plebeian men from Ciénaga invaded Santa Marta, where they waged street battles against the city's "sons of the notable families," who had been organized as a self-defense force by Conservatives. The conflict also appeared to some observers to exacerbate a racial divide. In Mompós, José María Samper recalled how people of color "of that vigorous and proud race" had served valiantly in the wars of independence but after Melo's coup became the "fearful combatants in the disgraced civil conflicts of the Magdalena."[112] And from Cartagena, Juan A. Gutiérrez de Piñeres, a coastal native, hero of independence, and a leader of local Conservatives, rallied wealthy citizens. In a broadside issued during the conflict, Gutiérrez quoted from one of Simón Bolívar's dismal assessments of Spanish American democracy, that "these countries would fall inevitably into the hands of the uncontrolled multitude, to pass almost imperceptibly to little tyrants of all colors and races, that devoured by all crimes and extinguished by ferocity, the Europeans would not dignify themselves to conquer us." Only the aristocratic Conservatives could save New Granada from this social malady.[113]

Yet despite the "popularity" of Melo on the coast (according to one chronicler), his Caribbean confederates often appeared at odds with the coup's highland leaders. Years of political mobilization, appointment or election of men of color to local posts, and assertions of popular jury control had created a recognizable strain of regional popular sovereignty. Since the rise of the liberals and democrats, agitation had forced out old-guard officials, and "even constables are abandoning their positions, and the common people are behaving more impudently every day," wrote a disgusted Calvo in 1849.[114] In Ciénaga alone in the two years after the murder of Francisco Carmona in 1852, crowds had driven out mayors, civil servants, and prominent men of every partisan stripe. Citizens in Barranquilla had attempted similar actions in the months before the coup, albeit with less success.[115] Rural populations and smaller towns offered some of the fiercest challenges to authority, such as in the Magdalena River village of Plato, where crowds produced "an enormous disorder" in protest of new provincial taxes in early 1854. "I have never seen a people as insolent and bold as these people," protested the deposed mayor, who remained powerless until "honorable" residents and national troops arrived in March "to make the rebels respect authority and enter into their duties."[116] Under these circumstances, some citizens may have interpreted Mosquera's removal of Nieto and Pérez in June as a sign that popular control was close at hand. This antiauthoritarian sensibility, however, largely ran counter to General Melo's demands for expanded public powers and an enlarged military. Caribbean citizens, moreover, had expected more concrete gains from legal equality, yet Melo had suspended the 1853 constitution soon after seizing control. Along with the impugning of black jurors by artisan sympathizers in Bogotá, these measures communicated a different political direction than the actions taken by protestors on the coast.[117]

By September 1854, Mosquera and his constitutionalist allies had suffocated much of the Caribbean uprising. In its wake, Juan José Nieto was forced out of public life, and in Barranquilla and Santa Marta numerous pro-Melo judges, government secretaries, provincial legislators, and civil servants were purged from office.[118] Replacing them was a united group of lawmakers and officials who set aside partisan differences to reestablish the legitimist government. In the year after the rebellion, Cartagena's provincial government transitioned from Nieto's secretary, Rafael Núñez, to a Mosquera loyalist, and finally to Conservative leader Juan Bernardo

Calvo, an opponent of popular suffrage and the street politics favored by many local citizens. In Santa Marta, a power-sharing agreement let Conservatives control the province while anti-Melo Liberals retained the municipal government.[119] After defeating Melo's troops in Bogotá in December 1854, constitutionalist forces there adopted a similar strategy of political purges, forced exile of coup leaders, and coalition rule already underway on the Caribbean coast. Obando, who took no active part in the coup but remained suspect because of his ties to artisans, the democratic societies, and the military, was forced to renounce the remainder of his presidential term.[120]

AN UNCERTAIN THERMIDOR

The nascent Conservative Party gained the most from the coup and its immediate aftermath. In the interim before new national elections in mid-1856, Conservatives controlled the Senate for the first time in five years, which enabled them to appoint one of their own, Manuel María Mallarino, as acting president of the republic. Much of their newfound influence owed to the backing of Gólgota Liberals who controlled the lower house and who cast their lot with Mallarino's Conservatives against Obando and the democratic societies. This Conservative-Liberal alliance had originally exhibited its political might during the first national election under rules of universal manhood suffrage, held to select the country's attorney general in October 1853. In that election, Conservatives had won with their candidate Florentino González, a former finance minister and the leading laissez-faire liberal of the era. González's pronouncements likely resonated with lettered men of many factions, including his desire to live in a "learned democracy, in which intelligence and property direct the destiny of the people," which would overcome "a barbarian democracy in which equalitarianism and ignorance . . . bring disorder and confusion to society."[121] With this early victory in hand, prominent Conservatives and Liberals remained unified throughout the struggle against Melo and into the postcoup political order. Yet as abolitionists José Hilario López and Manuel Murillo Toro joined together with former slaveholders like Julio and Sergio Arboleda, it was not immediately clear where plebeian citizens fit in the reclamation of constitutional authority.[122]

The reestablishment of civilian government under a lettered alliance led not to the wholesale rescinding of democratic reforms but instead to a mix of legal reversals in some areas of political rights and new advances in others. Congress again limited the size of the army, the act that had precipitated Melo's coup, to a total of 500 soldiers and with a drastically reduced budget. And in April 1856, three years after legalizing civil marriage and divorce with equal rights for women, a majority in Congress repealed divorce altogether. Even this setback for liberal equality struck down other forms of social exclusion, as the law repealing divorce also carried provisions that expressly strengthened of the rights of illiterate citizens to contract civil marriage.[123] Although the military and marriage reforms seemed disparate, they shared the quality of the reassertion of learned authority over the law. Legally trained men such as Attorney General Florentino González insisted on dominion over political affairs, and the repeal of the standing army and divorce along with the expansion of legal guarantees over those seeking civil marriage strengthened their hand in each case.[124]

Conservatives did not prevent the period's most sweeping liberal reforms. After the coup, provincial leaders pressed for increased decentralization of governmental powers, a process begun under the López administration. By the middle of the decade, this demand had developed into calls for a federal system not unlike that of the United States. The desire for federalism came largely from the Gólgotas, although it held such wide acclaim that Conservative office holders chose not to oppose it. Unlike the ousted Nieto forces, many Caribbean populations were lukewarm or even hostile to the proposed federal system, and the city of Barranquilla, capital of the province of Sabanilla, objected to being subordinated to Cartagena in a new state structure. Federalism won out, however, and by 1857, eight federated states replaced the patchwork of thirty-six provinces, with the six Caribbean provincial jurisdictions collapsed into the states of Bolívar and Magdalena. Conservatives' retention of the other significant democratic reform of the era, suffrage for all men over twenty-one years of age, was to be expected. Educated New Granadans remained divided over the popular vote, a mood captured by a newspaper editor who stated in September 1856, "I would be disgusted to find myself supported by 100 savages and opposed by 80 civilized men." Yet given the electoral success of Florentino González in 1853 and the opposition to wide suffrage by Obando, Conservatives and their lettered Liberal allies chose to reaffirm their commitment to universal manhood voting rights.[125]

What bipartisan unity had been achieved during and after the coup, however, rapidly dissolved amid the campaigning to choose the next national president. Three candidates vied in the August 1856 election—founding Conservative Mariano Ospina Rodríguez, Tomás C. Mosquera, and Manuel Murillo Toro—all with extensive political credentials who had joined the constitutionalist fight against Melo. On the coast, only Mosquera and Murillo, who already harbored a mutual enmity, proved viable in the popular voting, in part a reflection of their long-standing relations with citizens of the region. During a sojourn in Santa Marta in the late 1840s, Murillo had established political and commercial networks and had come to embrace slave emancipation, while Mosquera was still admired for aiding cholera victims in Barranquilla. Ospina, with his ties to former slaveholders, public hostility to direct elections, and lack of personal acquaintance with the Caribbean region, fared poorly there.[126]

The first presidential election under full suffrage for all male citizens animated Caribbean voters, and the region demonstrated one of the highest turnouts in the country. In Cartagena 57 percent of eligible voters cast ballots, in Mompós 50 percent, and in Santa Marta 63 percent. Even Barranquilla's 39 percent participation rate was in line with the national average of 40 percent and ahead of Bogotá's count. Vote suppression and manipulation distorted the outcome in some districts, most likely for the candidates already favored locally, yet even fraud could not obscure the election's propulsion of a massive expansion of the franchise.[127] No one candidate held sway over the electorate, with majorities voting for Mosquera in Mompós and Sabanilla and for Murillo in Santa Marta, while Cartagena split its vote, garnering Mosquera a plurality there. Caribbean voters supplied a large share of the overall returns for non-Conservative candidates and helped deny Ospina an outright majority nationally—the Conservatives took less than 18 percent of the region's vote, compared to winning more than 46 percent across the republic. The splitting of votes on the coast between Murillo and Mosquera, however, worked in favor of Ospina, who ultimately won the national count.[128]

The democratic legacy of emancipation appeared uncertain in the immediate wake of the Conservatives' election victory. Upon assuming the presidency in April 1857, Ospina promised to preside over "the reunion of all Granadans, whichever be their origin, their profession, their religion, their race, and their opinion." New Granada, once a colony where "the conquered race was the servant tied to the land, the imported race from Africa dragged chains of domestic slavery, the mixed races excluded from all participation in the exercise of power and in social considerations," was now a "democratic representative republic" based on "equality." In private, however, Ospina confided less sanguine views about the prospects for democracy. "The miserable and ignorant classes have never exercised power and will never exercise power," he wrote, "because they cannot do it."[129] Although opposed to popular involvement in public life, his Conservative faction had gained the most from the expansion of voting rolls—the so-called barbarian democracy serving the ends of the learned democracy. For Ospina's coup-era allies among the reformist Liberals, especially those of Manuel Murillo Toro's camp, civil equality and universal manhood suffrage remained premier legacies of emancipation, and the disappointing election returns had to be abided so that the franchise could correct itself over time through use. No political faction spoke openly of dismantling wholesale the legal changes enacted since 1848, although many leaders were adamant that those changes not be equated with social equality.

Beyond the election's visible expression of formal democratic rights, with their unclear prospects under the incoming administration, there were other ongoing social transformations that breathed life into the letter of the law. Traveling through New Granada in the mid-1850s, French geographer and anarchist Élisée Reclus alleged that Caribbean people of color had successfully struggled for equal status in public life. On conditions in Santa Marta, he reported that "blacks in America are not more respected in principle, but in effect due to the abolition of slavery and mixing of whites and blacks (to form mulattoes), . . . while the Indians have continued living isolated in the mountains, blacks and mulattoes little by little . . . with the presumption and spirit of assimilation which characterizes them, have affiliated with *the human* and left to the Indian the qualification of being *nobody*." Within Reclus's overgeneralizations and fixation on race mixing can be glimpsed the dynamic by which people of color had used emancipation to push for more substantive recognition, even how these social interactions had helped fashion citizenship itself. This was a process far from concluded with the freeing of the slaves in 1852 or with the passage of the new constitution in 1853. People in the coastal backlands and towns continued to protest taxes, confront authority, and demand respect after Melo's defeat and Ospina's victory. How many of these protestors came from the fugitive settlements of former slaves and the already free that still dotted the landscape was unknown, and deposed mayors and judges were only sure that with their presence "the immorality of some of the people will increase and crimes will go unpunished."[130] The Conservatives around President Ospina could discredit these as the actions of the miserable and ignorant classes, but like earlier administrations they soon discovered that they could not ignore them and could do little to contain them.

CHAPTER TWO

Revolution of the People, War of the Races

The republican spirit has quite entered into our soldiers. None of them assumes to have privileges or to form a distinct class within society; and everyone knows that only they can claim the honor of defending the liberties and dignity of the country on the front line.
— President Manuel Murillo Toro, Message to Congress, February 1865

Africans are the born enemies of the Caucasian race. . . . They are automatons that work only for the destruction of society. . . . I hope that you come to the coast to see the world's most horrible debauchery within the African class; here liberty is not the rights that the laws permit one to exercise, but is whatever each one wants to do; *I am free* is the favorite phrase heard from the mouths of these infernal people.
— Anonymous writer to Tomás C. Mosquera, Barranquilla, October 1861

They say of our form of government
That it is republican:
They tell us we are free,
Like the slaves in the backlands.
— "El 20 de julio de 1810 i el de 1874," *El Chino de Bogotá*, August 1874

The movements around emancipation carried the promise of a flourishing democratic culture and the perils of inflamed hatreds. A consensus to end slavery and advance liberty and equality as universal ideals of the republic had not curtailed political ambitions or the recourse to arms in the pursuit of power. This tension was borne out by events subsequent to the Conservative victory in the 1856 presidential elections. The popular vote, far from resolving questions over the political sentiments of enfranchised New Granadans, instead aroused resentments and new aspirations among defeated factions. Protests against Mariano Ospina Rodríguez began soon after he assumed the presidency in 1857, a time of unrest further complicated by the federalist system called the Granadine Confederation, which was just then being installed, as well as by a trade recession and rising unemployment. Conservatives soon enacted measures in attempts to stymie the opposition, and in this atmosphere of partisan contention and economic contraction warfare erupted as a continuation of politics by other means.

The civil war of 1859–62 was not the republic's first internal conflict, but it was the most significant. Unlike the failed insurrection of the early 1840s or Melo's defeated coup in 1854, this new civil war led to long-term transformations in the political culture. With their military successes and the eventual alliance between Juan José Nieto on the Caribbean coast and Tomás C. Mosquera in the Cauca Valley, Liberals won newfound legitimacy. Their victory over the Conservatives in 1862 ensured the party's dominance for two decades and sharpened partisan differences that were still inchoate at the war's commencement. This aftermath also marked the transition in leadership from the independence-era generation to younger letrados, many of whom had served in the López administration and were disciples of future national president Manuel Murillo Toro. These legally trained civilians would eventually outflank Mosquera, Nieto, and the war's other military leaders to ratify a new national constitution in 1863 that heralded their ascension. From the conflict's beginnings on the Caribbean coast (as Liberal intellectual and publisher Felipe Pérez wrote at the time), the armed rebellion culminated in a national revolution.[1]

In part what conveyed the war's revolutionary character was its role in the struggle over the legacy of emancipation. The Ospina administration, which included former slaveholders, represented for many New Granadans the possible reversal of the rights and public voice won over the previous decade. The Mosquera-Nieto alliance exploited these fears in order to counter Conservatives like Governor Juan Antonio Calvo in the new federal state of Bolívar, and Caribbean Liberals portrayed their rebellion in 1859 as a fight to protect popular suffrage and the democratic ethos against racial discrimination. Plebeian women and men of the coast responded by joining Nieto in large numbers, as did their counterparts with Mosquera in the Cauca. Liberal rebels not only cast the Ospina-led Granadine Confederation as aristocratic and reactionary, but over the course of the war they also erected within its borders an alternate political regime, the Pacto de Unión, which would soon be renamed the United States of Colombia. As Liberals transformed Colombia into the legitimate state through warfare and the law, citizen-soldiers fashioned their own new meanings and practices around national citizenship.

For common folk who supported the rebellion military and political success came at a price, however. While Conservatives attempted to defend their crumbling authority, they also waged a campaign to discredit soldiers of color, exactly because of the latter's central place in the ranks of the rebellion. The circulation of antiblack rhetoric, anonymous rumors of race war, and the image of disreputable Caribbean *macheteros* cast a pall over plebeian soldiering. Ultimately, wartime propaganda on both sides framed the conflict with competing narratives about its participants: one of citizen-soldiers defending emancipation, and the other of rapacious hordes attacking honorable families and civilization itself. Colombians who fought with the Liberals in a war that was defined as a referendum on the status of rights, race, and freedom remained vulnerable to competing interpretations of the same struggle. With the hardening of partisan and social hatreds, as well as other customary but no less grievous wartime coercions and expropriations, Caribbean people experienced myriad new possibilities and dangers in the recognition of citizenship.

A VIOLENT PRELUDE

In September 1857, Caribbean people began to stage heated protests as new governors and presidentially appointed prefects took up their posts and as the new federal states came into being. Mompós in the state of Bolívar and Santa Marta, capital of the state of Magdalena, became early knots of unrest. In Mompós, demonstrators armed with machetes menaced wealthy residents of barrio de abajo until the municipal guard turned its guns on them, driving many into the surrounding countryside. In the following months, gangs repeatedly entered town to attack local Conservatives, and even after Governor Juan Antonio Calvo sent national troops in December to begin making mass arrests, men "without shirts" managed to assault the prefect.[2] Conservatives organized their own militias armed from government stockpiles, which included a cannon, and they made raids into the lower-class barrio de arriba, during which they attacked and killed several individuals. During clashes "citizens of worth" saw their "homes attacked by the frenetic mob" and their belongings looted or demolished. Most of the town's prominent families fled to other provinces and did not return until January.[3]

Two weeks after the beginning of protests in Mompós, a dispute over state assembly elections in Magdalena led Santa Marta into political turmoil. Liberals took the majority of new state assembly but remained divided between the pro-Melo democratic societies and followers of the national lettered Gólgotas. When both groups attempted to install their representatives for the same assembly seats, armed henchmen stormed the meeting hall and shut down the proceedings. Fearing the Conservative governor would use the discord to assume full control of the state, the

Liberals reunited, helped along by crowds that laid siege to the city. "In gatherings of the democratic mob," reported one eyewitness, "they roam the streets, without leaders, threatening honorable men. . . . Every night there are warlike demonstrations, the city is in military campaign." In late September, after weeks of constant protest, the Conservative governor, the party's leadership, and several leading families fled the city.[4]

The political crises in Mompós and Santa Marta were fueled by overlaying problems of popular suffrage, partisanship, and federalism. Advocates of a federal system had argued that the states would represent homogeneous customs and interests, yet that system was not fully in place at the time of the 1856 election, in which Caribbean citizens had voted overwhelmingly against Conservatives. Despite the vote, the continued unity among lettered New Granadans and the interim appointment powers wielded by president Ospina allowed Conservatives to assume the governorship of Magdalena and to control the government and assembly of Bolívar. By the fall of 1858, with the new federalist states relieving Bogotá of administrative responsibilities, the political position of Caribbean Conservatives became untenable. While Governor Calvo blamed "liberal institutions" for the "revolutions and disorders" in Bolívar, a Conservative observer in Magdalena admitted just days before the Santa Marta revolt in September 1857 that "in the end this state will be Liberal, because this is the dominant opinion."[5] Nor could Conservative national dominance alter the outcome of the new state constitutions, which like the new federal constitution of 1858 reiterated all of the most liberal provisions of the 1853 political charter.[6]

Local class divisions exacerbated the political turmoil on the coast. While Conservatives recruited their own local followers—and in Magdalena leaders had many clients among the indigenous Guajiro people of Riohacha and the Guajira Peninsula—Caribbean people of African descent overwhelmingly developed ties with Liberal factions. In Mompós, this partisanship broke largely along neighborhood lines, with Conservatives inhabiting the wealthier streets along the river and Liberals the middling and plebeian barrios further inland. The violence there thus took on both social and partisan qualities. For the town's laboring majority, the exclusivity of the barrio de arriba and its influence in the state and national Conservative governments may have created the perception of looming political disenfranchisement. A similar overdetermined aspect of class and partisanship was at work in Santa Marta, where political cleavages had survived the defeat of the Melo uprising three years before. When street conflict erupted in September 1857, Liberal leaders appeared to have little command over armed crowds that occupied the town. In this case, social antagonisms and partisan affinities appeared mutually beneficial, as the toppling of the Conservative government allowed Liberals to install a governor who had supported Melo's coup.[7]

Any hope of overcoming these class resentments collapsed with the economic recession that began in early 1858. What started out as a bank panic in the United States soon rippled across world markets, and by 1858–59, New Granada's exports and imports had plummeted 53 percent and 27 percent, respectively, from their 1857 peak. Diarist José Manuel Restrepo observed in July 1858 that "in the provinces there is a general misery and commerce is found in a bad state."[8] Bogas, haulers, and other port workers on the Caribbean coast and Magdalena River felt the adverse effects of slackening trade unevenly. Laborers with recourse to garden plots and other self-subsistence strategies may have endured the recession with less trouble, although the constriction in money circulation may have prevented marketers from selling surplus produce. People without access to land were likely buffeted by the effects of the recession, and after a decade of witnessing their earning power weakened by money inflation during the local tobacco boom, many residents of coastal cities suffered a sharp contraction in wage labor. As early as February 1858, newspapers reported that numerous employees had been dismissed from businesses, their "lack of work" leaving them in "dejection." Coastal consumers, moreover, failed to benefit from falling prices of staples like North American wheat because of the curtailment in international shipping.[9]

Economic hardship deepened the sense of political crisis on the coast, leaving "the traces of rebellion, discontent, and moral disorder that promise infinite problems for the future." When wealthy families that had fled Mompós in September began returning in early 1858, "blacks and mulattoes gathered at the shore of the Magdalena to direct rude insults and threats at [them]." Rising unemployment compounded partisan hatreds, since locals who heaped abuse on returnees were in many cases laborers dismissed from recession-affected enterprises, a good number run by Conservatives attempting to return to their Mompós homes.[10] The concentration of merchant wealth in the barrio de abajo and the idling of working people from the barrio de arriba were mixing with preexisting racial and partisan tensions in explosive ways. Revelations in 1858 that coastal governments still resorted to debtors' prison and capital punishment, five years after the constitution had abolished both practices, may have incited more impoverished citizens to protest.[11]

Faced with financial and political uncertainty, the Conservatives passed new national legislation meant to expand their authority, but this only aggravated unrest. The federal government also suffered financially during the recession, since the growing trade imbalance and overall reduction in commerce disrupted the ability of the customs-dependent treasury to cover the costs of public administration.[12] Although hobbled by the economy, or perhaps fearing worse consequences from it, the Conservative-controlled Congress in early 1859 passed a series of laws authorizing national intervention in state elections, presidential removal of state executives, and appointment of new state-level officials accountable solely to the president. At least one law singled out the coast by expanding Bogotá's jurisdiction over the income from the customshouses of Cartagena, Sabanilla, and Santa Marta. Felipe Pérez tersely summarized these legislative measures as, "The Constitution: suffrage for all. The law: *effective* suffrage only for Conservatives."[13] Even significant democratic reforms passed by Congress that year over commutation of the death penalty and amnesty for political crimes did little to prevent political disaffection. For Liberals, the problem was no longer a few local appointees but the national government itself, which had begun to preempt the authority of the states before the ink was even dry on the federal system.[14]

The new powers granted to the national executive made little headway on the coast, however. In February 1859, Pedro Navas Azuero, the new superintendent of the customs service and Ospina's highest-placed official in the region, witnessed the installation of a new municipal government in Santa Marta. This was not a regularly scheduled election but one demanded by hundreds of petitioners because the existing officeholders had not been chosen by popular vote and thus constituted an "antidemocratic" regime.[15] After hours of live music and street rallies, "a great gathering of citizens met, and they proclaimed the candidacy of those who were to replace the others [chosen under the defunct provincial constitution], proceeding to their election in a popular junta." While the outcome was peaceful, Azuero felt the event "very lamentable for the precedent that is established," that is, elections by public and popular will.[16] Two months later, Azuero found himself the target of that popular will. In Cartagena the superintendent, a national officer whose authority Liberals considered "ad hoc," was assaulted on the street by an employee of the customs service. Immediately afterward, a "group of people passed by [Azuero] . . . a tumultuous crowd of the scum of society, adding to the event they shouted out at Sr. Superintendent Azuero in a hostile manner, saying, 'Down with the Superintendent!,' 'Out with the Superintendent!' and other vituperations truly degrading to even the degraded." Azuero's assailant was eventually convicted of assault and inciting mob action, even though court depositions described the crowds that day as spontaneous.[17]

A PEOPLE'S COUP

Of the partisans who sought advantage from the unrest and faltering legitimacy of the national government, none scored greater than Juan José Nieto. During the first half of 1859, Conservatives and Liberals along the coast published propaganda, hired street musicians, set off fireworks, and organized followers into gangs in anticipation of a political showdown.[18] Amid this agitation and with President Ospina preoccupied by a military intervention against Governor Manuel Murillo Toro in the state of Santander, Nieto regained his leadership position by plotting a coup against Bolívar's Juan Antonio Calvo. Although the Liberals controlled Cartagena's municipal government, they had little in the way of materiel, and Nieto himself confided (or boasted) that the conspirators possessed only 150 pesos and a small cache of sidearms.[19] He did possess, however, local support from artisans in the state militia and laborers from his own hacienda mustered into a unit he named the Glorious Battalion.[20] In late July 1859, coup forces overwhelmed Cartagena's state police and loyalist soldiers without firing a shot, sending the deposed Governor Calvo into internal exile. Liberals set about arresting and replacing government functionaries and issued a manifesto directed to Ospina demanding that he recognize their legitimacy.[21] Soon after taking control, Nieto imprisoned Pedro Navas Azuero for conspiring "against the omnipotent will of the people, the only sovereign," which capped off a year of ignominy for the customs service superintendent.[22]

If toppling Calvo's government came easily, the Liberals recognized that they needed to mobilize and arm the populace to maintain control. Alongside the Glorious Battalion, Nieto organized other laboring men into companies he called the Zouaves, the Hunters of Vincennes, and the Hunters of Africa. "I explained to them the meaning of such names from the French army, so celebrated in the war [in Crimea]," Nieto wrote in 1862, names that were "inspired to awaken enthusiasm and encouragement." He likely did not relay the history of the Chasseurs d'Afrique as a white regiment in France's colonial wars and may have instead intended the name to conjure a black martial tradition, albeit one conforming to the democratic ethos he also communicated by telling the men, "So long as there is glory, all are equal."[23] Liberal forces grew as individuals wrote to Nieto "to assure you that if you had sufficient arms, it would be easy . . . to call to service 600 men, all volunteers."[24] With this corps of supporters, the Liberals soon overwhelmed Conservatives camped on the savanna south of Cartagena, forced Calvo out of Mompós, and finally defeated the remaining opposition in Barranquilla in December 1859. Civilians behind Conservative lines in Mompós and Barranquilla played a decisive role in the Liberal victories by staging frequent protests against Calvo's presence and refusing to provide aid to his forces. Calvo himself admitted that he found it impossible to recruit volunteers because the majority of the state was "committed" to Nieto.[25]

After Nieto's coup in Bolívar, Liberals in Magdalena joined the revolt and soon bore the brunt of the war in the region. The state's leadership attempted to maneuver between the "liberal mob" and increasingly organized Conservative militias. In October 1859, demonstrations called for the state's secession from the Granadine Confederation, yet the Magdalena assembly defeated the motion. Angered by the failed vote, prosecession crowds in the long-standing "points of rebellion" of Santa Marta and Ciénaga once more occupied the streets and agitated for independence. Protests continued to swell even after progovernment gangs dispersed crowds, and in December Santa Marta's Conservatives abstained from elections out of concerns over violence.[26] With election strategies closed off and perhaps sensing advantage from the internal struggle within Liberal ranks, Conservatives from Riohacha invaded and occupied Santa Marta in July 1860, touching off some of the deadliest fighting in the war. Only in December 1860, after months of bloody combat in which hundreds died, were Liberals able to retake Magdalena's destroyed capital.[27]

Liberals experienced less difficulty consolidating their hold over Bolívar than did their counterparts in Magdalena, in part because they renewed the kinds of relations between leaders and citizens that had sustained them during the emancipation era. The ideological instrument they chose to reach out to a wider swath of the citizenry was the published proclamation. Like similar documents issued throughout Spanish America since independence, these proclamations functioned as written communication across distances and as a way to produce local forms of political consent.[28] In terms of content and production, Nieto's followers justified rebellion by combining the language of constitutional legalism with the practices of popular democracy. The night before the July 1859 coup, hundreds of men gathered in Cartagena's municipal palace to sign a declaration stating that they "formally disavow[ed] the political authorities that currently are at the service of the State," and that they acted for "the majority of the pueblos of the State" in order "to make effective the right of suffrage of all citizens" and to realize a new constituent assembly "chosen by the people."[29]

In the following weeks, like-minded declarations poured into Cartagena from more than a dozen towns across Bolívar. Each one contained hundreds of signatories, in some cases with a majority who could not sign for themselves, whose names always appeared below those of men who could write. If the documents visibly produced a hierarchy, the deliberate inclusion of illiterate men, or their demand to be included, nevertheless bolstered the coup's legitimacy by more than doubling the number of its publicly identified supporters. They also reproduced the "patriotic offerings" earlier in the decade sent by the democratic societies to López signed by thousands of men of all social ranks. These displays of social diversity acted as a moral counterweight to recent Conservative electoral victories under the regime of universal manhood suffrage.[30]

The proclamations also served to justify Juan José Nieto's return to influence in the Caribbean Liberal Party. The former governor and abolitionist member of Congress had been drummed out of public life for endorsing the Melo uprising in Cartagena against the constitutionalists led by Tomás C. Mosquera.[31] After years in the political wilderness, Nieto sought through a leading role in the 1859 coup to ensure his return to the political fold. This time popular support led to renewed credibility, with full vindication coming in early 1860 when, as expected, Bolívar's revolutionary assembly chose him to be governor. More extraordinary still was the decision by President Ospina to sanction Nieto's power in March— over howls of protest from coastal Conservatives—and Nieto's reconciliation with Mosquera, who looked to him as an ally in the overthrow of the same president who had just blessed his authority.[32]

THE COUNTERREPUBLIC OF COLOMBIA

Guided by victories on the coast, Nieto led Caribbean rebels into an alliance with Mosquera's forces, who went into revolt in southwest Popayán in May 1860, and in the process they transformed separate uprisings into a national movement. As Liberals joined forces, their local leaders declared themselves in mutiny against Ospina's government, and in quick succession between May and August 1860, the states of Cauca, Bolívar, Magdalena, and Santander seceded from the Granadine Confederation. The Liberals of Bolívar led the early stages of the secessionist movement and the formation of a new republic by authorizing Nieto in June 1860 to create a provisional national government for the rebellion.[33] In Cartagena that September, delegates from the states of Bolívar and Cauca signed a treaty, the Pacto de Unión. Twelve months later, Liberal delegates from the Granadine Confederation's other six states signed the pact, and the treaty took on the appearance of a constitution.[34] Under the pact, Supreme Director of the War Mosquera implemented a bureaucratic apparatus that included departments of war, foreign relations, justice, public works, interior, and treasury. He and his ministers issued executive decrees, laws, and accords dealing with subjects from property rights to postage rates, presuming them to carry full legal weight in all parts of the national territory. They reinforced their legitimacy by having official measures codified and published while the war was still being fought. Once Liberal armies took Bogotá in July 1861 and the civilian Liberals who had opposed the war began to voice their support for it, Mosquera's counterrepublic looked less like an insurgency and more like the legitimate government.[35]

As Liberal military officers and lawyers projected the appearance of a functioning state, it fell to ordinary soldiers and civilians to sustain the Pacto de Unión. Because we lack written traces left by the illiterate majorities, and hence have severely circumscribed notions of their motivations, some scholars have argued that foot soldiers were mere cannon fodder for elite interests or, at best, fought for purely material gain, in contrast to leaders' well-honed political goals.[36] Certainly the timing of the civil war during a recession lends itself to an interpretation of bifurcated motivations based on economic or status differences. Yet much of the evidence portrays widespread enthusiasm for the Liberal revolt among ordinary citizens, and public shows of loyalty both extraordinary and mundane validated the endeavors of war leaders. By 1860, thousands of volunteers had joined armies of the Caribbean, Cauca, and Santander to fight against the forces of the Ospina government. On the coast, the turnout for the Liberals made it a lopsided affair, where "a thousand men, with machetes," in Magdalena and perhaps twice that many in Bolívar overwhelmed the few hundred Conservatives in arms. The likelihood of material gain for soldiers was minimal, in particular on the recession-wracked coast. Like the 1859 proclamations for Nieto's coup, which literate and illiterate men signed jointly, Liberal leaders relied on popular political fervor to gain military advantage against the Conservatives.[37]

Civilians also played a role in bolstering the rebellion, even if their actions blurred the lines between combatants and noncombatants. Those who did not join standing armies staged street protests and other noisy demonstrations that eroded Conservative authority. The president's brother and archbishop of Bogotá, Pastor Ospina, arrested by Liberal forces and sent to the coast in September 1861, experienced the force of this popular agitation firsthand. During a stopover in Mompós on his way to prison in Cartagena, "some 200 persons of the liberal mob conducted us through the street" led by "four black men of democratic appearance, many more women in rags and some youths." Other locals flanked the archbishop's route to throw mud, trash, and rocks at him, and crowds gathered outside the window of his jail cell to chant and taunt him throughout the night.[38] Through such militant displays, citizens created a daily existence for the republic-in-formation separate from the legal trappings of public administration.

For these actions to be politically meaningful, citizens demanded that revolutionary leaders reciprocate by acknowledging their sacrifices. Military officers complied by giving postbattle speeches that praised soldiers and noncombatants alike. After his forces took Mompós in October 1859, Nieto declared before his troops and the local populace, "You, sustained by law and opinion, have fulfilled your duty as brave people. . . . You come not as mercenaries, but as armed citizens, to defend guarantees and the law." Nieto and other leaders fastened onto honorifics like "armed citizens" and "valiant soldiers," which they used in speeches and propaganda to hail all troops without regard to their social origins.[39] The occasional Liberal commander publicly acknowledged women, too, and after a victory in El Banco, General Antonio González Carazo proclaimed "the enthusiasm, decisiveness, and valor of the daughters of this town, facing the dangers of combat in the trenches. . . . For this they are owed the same considerations as the most courageous men of the army."[40]

It may have been young men of color who received the most significant portion of this wartime recognition. In an effort to win over volunteers and create a semblance of organized force after the post-Melo decimation of the standing army, Nieto and Mosquera promoted plebeian youths from the Caribbean and Cauca into officer and subaltern positions. In Nieto's junior officer corps "all were youths" because, he averred, "the call of youth is to promote the progress of this epoch." Although little is known about these men, he did remark that among his subordinates were individuals from "poor artisan" backgrounds.[41] Some of the new officer class were men of African descent, the most renowned being the thirty-year-old general in the Cauca army, Manuel María "el Negro" Victoria, who some claimed was the child of slaves and others called a mulatto.[42] There were other lesser-known men of color at all ranks whose promotions advanced the democratic fraternity of emancipation even as they served the practical ends of installing leaders who looked like the majorities of both the armies and the populations of the regions where they operated. During his incarceration in Mompós, Pastor Ospina noted this camaraderie on the coast, where "officials demonstrated friendship and consideration" to "black youth" who served as guards and police.[43] And yet the ethos against singling out public individuals based on race required leaders to appoint men without publicly acknowledging their backgrounds. Like Nieto's Hunters of Africa, it appeared best to be indirect about the intentions behind even antiracist or inclusive promotions.

In other public relations the Liberals were less equivocal, and they engaged in the active production of symbols necessary to project governmental authority. While it is doubtful that rank-and-file troops knew of many decrees passed by the revolutionary government, they did witness the awarding of ribbons and medals, honors that helped project the image of the troops as a national army. Like the French revolutionaries with their tricolor cockades after 1789, Nieto improvised these traditions in the field as the war unfolded. "When I saw so many good servants more worthy still, who could not be rewarded with promotions in rank," he reported in early 1862, "I had the happy inspiration of creating two decorations, the 'Military Merit' and 'Civil Merit' of the State of Bolívar." Soon he also created the Military Star of Bolívar for acts of bravery in combat. While liberty caps worn by manumitted slaves had merely signified the citizenship of the spectacles' audiences, these new accouterments acknowledged the active sacrifices of the citizens themselves.[44]

The Liberals' most momentous and lasting symbolic act of the war occurred in 1861, when the Pacto de Unión was rechristened the United States of Colombia. The new name for the republic gained traction after Mosquera's forces defeated Ospina's government at Bogotá in July and Liberal leaders from the remaining states signed the pact in September. In November 1861, Mosquera designed a new flag, still in use, for the Colombian republic.[45] The reclaiming of the name *Colombia*, with its independence-era and Bolivarian associations, brought familiarity and historical weight to the Liberal cause while also being original enough to assert claims to a new order. As the name caught hold, citizens who continued to embrace New Granada or the Granadine Confederation became associated with the politics of reaction and a regime of exclusion — despite the multifactional consensus over democratic emancipations of the 1850s. As Conservatives, including many former slaveholders, rallied to the defense of the Granadine Confederation, however, the Colombian counterrepublic accrued a popular democratic appearance. Mosquera's and Nieto's conscious if oblique mobilization of citizens of color, moreover, helped strengthen their title to the emancipation legacy.[46]

In other ways the new Colombia reproduced exclusions, in particular around gender. The wartime rhetoric of the armed citizen was masculine, as epitomized in Francisco Paula de Borda's reminiscence that Liberal soldiers dignified the conflict with "virile courage." Despite women's active roles as camp followers, messengers, and soldiers, the language of armed citizenship reinforced the fraternal equality that had shaped political change after 1850.[47] Leaders on both sides maintained distinctions between men and women in the ranks by fixating on behavior. Mosquera blamed the lack of morality and discipline among his troops in part on female camp followers and decreed the removal of scandalous ones. One Bogotá Conservative recalled the militancy of the city's female population against Liberal forces in early 1861 yet smeared women who picked over bodies on battlefields as "vultures."[48] Gender differences worked their way into wartime lawmaking, as when legislators in Bolívar, hoping to shape the postwar political regime, passed an expansive civil code in early 1862 that reaffirmed equal rights among all men while denying them to women. The earlier public statements from Antonio González Carazo that female soldiers were owed the same considerations as male ones did not extend beyond these moments of postcombat appreciation.[49]

Even though men received the armed citizenship ideal with enthusiasm, the actions of some civilians and soldiers set limits on the Liberals' assumption of authority. The war did not end Caribbean people's tradition of protest against officials who showed a lack of proper deference or popular justice but may have magnified it. Perhaps fearing that multiple armies within a single territory might double their obligations to the state, locals resisted taxes, property confiscations, and conscription decreed by Nieto. Riots in Conservative-voting coastal towns were frequent after Nieto's July 1859 coup, and Liberals could secure some districts only with the permanent stationing of troops.[50] Yet Liberal towns proved just as defiant, with El Carmen's pro-Nieto mayor reporting "the *pueblos* view with repugnance the contributions that weigh over them—and if the governors do not have sufficient forces with which to make them respect and obey, they will fall into an abyss." The mayor himself witnessed that abyss during his rounds to collect contributions, when "great groups" surrounded his house and had to be dispersed by militia units. Constant threats against his life soon forced him to flee the region.[51] Volunteer soldiers, for their part, refused to fight when doing so made them appear coerced. Late in the war, an officer in the Caribbean town of Lorica warned of a possible mutiny among his troops, not because the men harbored Conservative sympathies but be-cause "individuals of this Province resist marching anywhere unarmed for fear of being mistaken for [forced] recruits." The growing financial strains that led Liberals to conduct confiscations and impressment late in the war conflicted with the rebellion's rhetoric of honoring citizen volunteers. This contradiction may have fueled more resistance against the Liberals, and some men deserted from Nieto's own Glorious Battalion, perhaps exactly because their *patrón* had compelled them to fight.[52]

RACE WAR

The Conservatives, thrown on the defensive, devised a campaign of pro-paganda and rumor in an attempt to gut the rising legitimacy of the coun-terrepublic. Their main target was Liberal foot soldiers, men often called *macheteros* (machete wielders) no matter what weapons they carried into battle.[53] The machete took on multiple meanings as a symbol of plebeian visibility, a weapon of retribution, and for lettered observers, a sign of the irregular nature of combat and the presence of ill-equipped and ill-trained troops. Conservatives, moreover, exploited the image of the machetero to confirm the low status of Liberals, in the process converting Caribbean people's enthusiasm into a fanaticism that connoted a lack of either mar-tial skill or political reason.[54] As Ospina appointee Juan Gutiérrez de Pi-ñeres reported from Cartagena after the coup, the Liberals, despite their early successes, "are now paying for their inexperience and weakness, the ridiculous actions of one and the shameful acts of another." His counter-parts in Santa Marta accused Bolívar's Liberal leaders of being puppets of the macheteros. While Gutiérrez's military judgment was not borne out by the Liberal victories in subsequent years, his accusations of fanaticism may have encouraged Nieto and his officers to introduce the image of the honorable armed citizen into postbattle speeches.[55]

Conservative diatribes against plebeian soldiers soon slid into invoca-tions of race war. Gutiérrez de Piñeres had remained at his post after the July coup but experienced the quick deterioration of his authority in the face of public protests. "Bands of black men armed with machetes were passing through the streets of the city making displays of their insolence," he wrote in November 1859, "as their theme is always long live democracy and death to the whites." Gutiérrez also pleaded for help from Ospina to preserve "the lives and properties of the disgraced inhabitants" of Carta-gena. "You can have no idea of all that we suffer here and of the outrages that are committed by a brutal and savage common people who today dominate this city," he insisted. "The constant insult in word and deed, the threats of slitting the throats of whites and of looting, are the repeated chants that we are witnessing." Gutiérrez then quoted Simón Bolívar's prophecy of the coming despotism of the multiracial rabble, as he had also done during the Melo uprising five years earlier.[56]

The slogan "Death to the Whites" raises certain political implications as well as interpretive problems. Although "whites" may have stood in for all oligarchic propertied groups, usage of the word during the war was attributed to crowds of the Caribbean and Cauca that ostensibly chanted racial epithets to create a sense of majority power, however ephemeral, over nonblack elites.[57] Yet because knowledge of the slogan's use derived from lettered men who believed themselves its intended victims, reports describing its public invocation were also racial ascriptions of the groups purported to have chanted it. As in other nineteenth-century Spanish American wars, the assignation of racial meanings to popular action heightened a sense of imminent threat to ruling groups and simultaneously reduced diverse populations to a homogeneous other status.[58] Coming so soon after emancipation, the phrase may have elicited more contempt for than fear of what opponents regarded as Liberals' racist violations of the democratic ethos, in particular given the perception that their armies were composed entirely of black men.[59]

While accusing Liberals of engaging in race war, Conservatives also laid claim to emancipation's egalitarian rhetoric. In the months after Nieto's coup, one progovernment newspaper in Santa Marta appealed to the coastal populace by informing them, "We do not make distinctions between blacks and whites," a phrase familiar from the proclamations of Nieto and other abolitionists. The same Conservative paper sought to turn the tables on its enemies by suggesting that Liberals supported a U.S.-style federalism, with its slavocracy and racial hierarchies, where "the sons of the people, those who have black skin, cannot occupy the same place in the church, in the theater, or in any of the public activities." It concluded with a promise to citizens to "work with tireless interest for the disappearance of those stale and ridiculous ideas of nobility and hierarchy." Through such contradictory messages—claiming to have overcome racial discrimination yet willing to work for its eradication; speaking to and for the people, equating the people with both whites and blacks, then reiterating the low status of blackness—Conservatives staked their legitimacy in the same color-blind rhetoric that proved so thorny when Liberals wrangled with it.[60]

These antiracist appeals were fleeting, however, because Conservatives saturated much of their wartime discourse with the specters of savagery and rape. During the Liberal assault on Calvo in Mompós in October 1859, Santa Marta's *La Reforma* accused Nieto's men—"all . . . macheteros"—of looting shops and of raping "many virgins and honorable mothers," although one Conservative eyewitness to the battle admitted privately that both armies had committed "a thousand scandalous crimes."[61] Calvo's forces in Barranquilla prepared their defense by publishing a broadside warning locals of "the hordes of Nieto" that in Mompós had "for five hours given themselves over to the insatiable greed and brutal instincts that characterize them." Immediately after Liberals took the town, rumors circulated that rebel soldiers had butchered government troops and perpetrated other "atrocious acts to instill terror" in the population. Similar rumors spread in Santa Marta after Liberals occupied the city. As Caribbean revolutionaries amassed other military victories, propagandists intensified their allegations of Liberal looting, rape, and, especially, machete attacks against innocent civilians. To Conservatives, the Caribbean *machetazo* characterized those "who practice democratic doctrines in all their extreme forms" as one of the gravest threats to the republic.[62]

Only on occasion did this propaganda have a direct effect on events, its long-term consequences notwithstanding. Three months after the July 1859 coup, rumors throughout Cartagena spoke of a machetero conspiracy against the city's prominent families, and the protests and pleas by locals compelled Nieto to return from the military campaign to assume direct control of his revolutionary government. The rumor achieved little more than a temporary diversion of the Liberal onslaught, which continually "swelled with many volunteers." Even before the Caribbean rebels' victory in Santa Marta in December 1860, some Conservative military leaders had concluded that "it was well known that little good could be done there."[63] Although the rhetoric of uncontrolled macheteros could not turn back the Liberals, it did reinforce Juan Gutiérrez de Piñeres's image of a widening gulf between political legitimacy and popular participation.[64]

As local uprisings coalesced into a national war, propagandists braided racial and regional hatreds to galvanize support for the Conservatives. In the 1861 invasion of the state of Antioquia by Nieto's army, editorials and broadsides painted the conflict as civilized Antioqueños defending against encroaching *costeño* animals, a moment of dehumanization that also obscured the actions by people of color in Antioquia who rallied to the side of the invading Liberals.[65] According to Felipe Pérez, the same rhetoric trailed Mosquera, "the caudillo of the savage hordes of the Cauca, as the shameful legitimists said and wrote." President Ospina himself invoked the language of Liberal savagery and rape as Mosquera's army approached

Bogotá in mid-1861, when he called on the population to defend the capital against the "rapacious hordes that have desolated the Cauca and Magdalena Valleys and a few days ago fixed their eyes eagerly upon the capital of the Republic." If Bogotanos did not respond, the invaders would "satiate their greed, their ferocity and their brutal instincts on the wealth and on the inhabitants of this beautiful city." Just seven years earlier, soldiers of color from the lowlands had been lauded for joining constitutionalist forces in the assault on Bogotá to overthrow Melo and restore civilian rule, yet with his own government under siege, Ospina fused regional and racial antagonisms to galvanize the local populace. The capital fell to Mosquera's troops a few weeks later.[66]

The rumors that black Liberals raped white women had dubious military value, although like the fears of the macheteros they did assault the standing of citizens of color. After the collapse of the Conservative effort in the Cauca, the returning officers tried to reassure Ospina that "the federalist [Liberal] army was composed of demoralized drunkards and black Africans, bandits, rapists, and cowards." In his 1862 published account of the war, Felipe Pérez captured the spirit of Conservative propaganda in a single phrase: "rapists of the Cauca."[67] Like the stories of sexually aggressive black men that appeared in the weeks after slave emancipation, the translation of political action by men of color into a criminal sexuality transpired at a moment when they commanded a public presence.[68] Conservatives who interpreted the struggle as prominent men's defense of female honor not only obscured women's active roles in the war but also reinforced their own whiteness.

Conservatives eluded charges of perpetuating racism by arguing self-defense against the racist actions of their opponents. If their enemies called for death to the whites or preyed on honorable women, they by default renounced the right to equal treatment. Rumors circulating in Bogotá against "the mulatto Nieto" transposed the blackness of common soldiers onto their leader in an attempt to discredit him, yet even this slur could be justified as a correct response to his presumed promotion of race war.[69] This double standard that penalized democratic appeals to citizens as more socially divisive than antiblack racism appeared in an anonymous warning sent to Tomás C. Mosquera from Barranquilla in October 1861. "Africans are the born enemies of the Caucasian race. . . . They are automatons that work only for the destruction of society." The writer attacked citizens' struggles as "horrible debauchery" and mere license, which marked them with a foreign blackness beyond the bounds of the republic. "*I am free* is the favorite phrase heard from the mouths of these infernal people," he concluded. While such a condemnation of black freedom ten years after emancipation indicated the dire stakes faced by citizens of color, the writer adhered to the basic ethical tenets against discrimination by naming no individuals and by remaining anonymous.[70]

Liberals, constrained from organizing along explicit lines of race, turned to the propaganda ploy used by José María Obando in his 1852 presidential campaign. In Magdalena, they spread rumors that "the Illustrious Arboleda proclaims legalized slavery in Santa Marta." Julio Arboleda, a former slaveholder and "scourge of humanity" who had opposed emancipation in 1851 and was poised to succeed Ospina as president of the Granadine Confederation, arrived on the coast in 1860 to take command of the Conservative forces. As during the Obando campaign, the rumor's audiences likely understood the threat of reenslavement figuratively as the new imposition of exclusionary (white) minority rule.[71] Arboleda's debarking in Santa Marta with a company of black Panamanian soldiers (as well as leading local "savages of the Goajira") did not undermine these allegations; indeed, Liberals turned their shock into new attacks on his racism. "An incredible thing!" wrote a Liberal veteran soon after the Caribbean campaign. "The decided friend of slavery, the fervent and cruel enemy of the black race, counted few, very few individuals in his ranks who were not of color." Within months of entering Santa Marta, Arboleda abandoned the city to Nieto's troops.[72]

PYRRHIC VICTORY

The last Conservatives surrendered on the Caribbean coast in late 1862, ending the three-year conflict, although the war of words persisted for decades afterward. Writers of the vanquished party often retold tales of wartime depredations by Liberals against virgins and priests, and at least one newspaper reprinted Ospina's June 1861 warning to the inhabitants of Bogotá about the approaching invasion of Mosquera's lowland hordes. Intimately related to the cultivation of these memories was the perpetuation of emancipation-era slander that Caribbean Liberals were "so wise a herald to trick the blacks" to vote for them, a message that rendered men of color both perpetrators and victims of political crimes.[73] Many more Conservatives embraced the metaphor of political slavery to explain their situation, claiming that the Catholic Church, honorable women, and respectable families lived as a "colony of slaves" under a postwar Liberal regime of terror and tyranny. Polemicists also made a foil of actual human bondage. "Oh sweet independence! For you black slaves are free; and while many white men have become slaves, it is not your fault!" went one 1864 commemoration for 20 July.[74] The language of Liberal slavery filtered into local politics, where petitioners from one Bolívar town in early 1865 denounced the policies of Juan José Nieto as attempting to "enslave" coastal citizens. Throughout the following years, Conservative political discourse denied their opponents exclusive domain over the language of democracy and emancipation.[75]

Many Liberal leaders tried to avoid this increasing political polarization by working toward reconciliation with prominent Conservatives. As the war was ending in 1862, Nieto gave a speech in Cartagena that predicted how the "few hands that still carry rifles, will surrender them in order to take part in the attainment of so many benefits," which he intended to include former "enemies of the people," because "all are equal" in a system of "legality and progress." No matter how tenuous his commitment to bipartisanship in practice, Nieto's appeal for reunion among the partisan leadership stretched to include Julio Arboleda. His incorporation of former slaveholders and other possible reactionaries in a proposed peacetime *convivencia*, however, left in doubt the political role of the armed citizens who had fought for the new Colombian republic.[76]

Some intellectuals on the margins of the conflict crafted their own arguments for elite reunion as they tried to make sense of the war. One such reckoning came from Cartagena's Manuel María Madiedo, a newspaper editor and liberal-minded Conservative, who argued that the causes of the war lay in the inability of the democratic movements and reforms born of emancipation to fully eradicate the country's colonial legacy. In a January 1862 public letter to Rafael Núñez, a fellow Caribbean native, Nieto's secretary during emancipation, and a government minister in Obando's presidential administration, Madiedo blamed the war on their Spanish forebears' sin of enslaving indigenous and black peoples. "Yes, we will pay for the blood of the innocent Indian and the liberty and life of the wretched African, torn from his native shores, come here to die as a human beast, under the bloodied whip of greed and ferocity." In divining the contradictions between democracy and slavery as the root of Colombia's problems, Madiedo also evoked the contemporaneous "revolution" tearing apart the United States, whose significance he and other intellectuals probed in attempts to make sense of their own civil war. At the same time, Madiedo's analysis cast people of color outside the republic—he depicted them as either physically or socially dead—and he accorded them no visible role in the war. Despite his call for a new political order based on representative democracy, his own political thought left in doubt the place of black and indigenous citizens in that system.[77]

Madiedo and others did not have to wait long for the unveiling of the postwar order. The 1863 Rionegro Constitution was heavily influenced by the Mosquera-Nieto Pacto de Unión, including ratification of the provisional United States of Colombia as the official name of the republic. Nevertheless, at the Liberal-only constitutional convention the party's lettered civilian leadership, many of whose members had not joined the war effort until Mosquera's army took Bogotá in July 1861, outmaneuvered the military officers to wield final say over the drafting of the document. Distrustful of Mosquera and the army, the lawyers wrote a constitution characterized by a limited central government, a minimal public force, expansive individual liberties, and robust sovereignty for the states. As it had in 1854, the lettered political faction once known as the Gólgotas again pushed back a popular military movement during the postwar peace process.[78]

In terms of the formal and informal citizenship rights that had characterized republican life for more than a decade, the outcome of the war and constitutional change proved more complex. Whereas Rionegro's denial of active rights for women echoed earlier gendered political exclusions, its delineation of rights for men was not so straightforward. The charter enunciated civil guarantees within a rigid federalist framework, which left their final status to the discretion of the individual states. It did not mention suffrage rights at all. As a consequence, within a few years half of the states instituted literacy and property qualifications for voting, effectively limiting suffrage to a small minority of the adult male population. These central or eastern highland states were the home of the lettered Liberals in control of the Rionegro convention who worried primarily about the political pull of the Catholic Church and the machinations of priests among their parishioners at election time. In an attempt to simultaneously ensure civilian, partisan, and elite control, the drafters had placed sovereignty of the states before popular rights. After a war fought in part over protection of suffrage, this was an outcome few had anticipated.[79]

The men of the Caribbean coast and the Cauca who had sustained the Liberal war effort experienced other ambiguous outcomes of the new constitutional order. Unlike the letrados of central Colombia, Liberals in the states of Magdalena, Bolívar, Panama, and the Cauca, along with Conservatives who controlled Antioquia, affirmed soldiers' sacrifices by preserving universal manhood suffrage. In practice, coastal voters experienced widespread electoral manipulation in the years after 1863, and even where popular suffrage survived, many citizens engaged in partisan politics through their continuing recourse to arms. On the coast, violent politicking became formulaic, conditioned by legalized private arms trading, the near abolition of the standing army, and in particular, the Liberals' success in overthrowing the national government in 1861.[80] During elections in the 1860s and 1870s, every faction recruited men into gangs and "guerrilla units" to engage in rough-and-tumble street politics. They distributed alcohol to followers, clashed with rivals at the ballot urns, and protected their districts from armed parties that haunted the countryside in most election cycles.[81] Under Rionegro, the one state–one vote method of selecting national presidents (with a simple majority of five out of nine states needed to secure a victory) raised the stakes of local control, and with Caribbean politics dictated by popular suffrage and intra-Liberal rivalries, the goal of factional dominance only increased the standing of young men with weapons. The divergence in local political cultures was great. Whereas Caribbean bosses relied on ballot tampering and violence in the context of universal manhood suffrage, their lettered counterparts in the country's central highlands had chosen mass disenfranchisement to maintain control.[82]

Political violence after the war rarely led to the ultimate sacrifice because many men expressed service in arms not as a duty but as an entitlement. The democratic Liberal Manuel Murillo Toro, as the first national president elected under Rionegro, captured this political sensibility in his 1865 address to Congress, when he noted how the "republican spirit has quite entered into our soldiers." And while they did not assume special privileges, "everyone knows that only they can claim the honor of defending the liberties and dignity of the country on the front line." José María Samper was more specific on the issue when he reminded readers, "The sons of the Magdalena are notable for their warlike bravery," which was especially true for "the terrible machetero."[83] As an entitlement, men of the coast demanded to fight, as witnessed during the 1876 Conservative uprising in western Colombia, when thousands volunteered over the objections of local leaders. Of this significant Caribbean force, only one in five owned a rifle, the rest arriving to recruitment points carrying machetes. Military officers tried to turn away individuals "whose services we do not accept for their not having munitions," but many macheteros persevered, refusing to be taken for granted.[84]

These armed actions by ordinary citizens complicated Liberal politics in other ways as well. The sense of entitlement to a combative public role led Caribbean Liberals to avoid fighting when it appeared unnecessary, counterproductive, or dangerous. On numerous occasions, they abandoned leaders in the middle of street clashes, prompting charges of acting with cowardice or as "undisciplined troops"—censure that obscured how plebeian men regarded the authority of individual leaders as provisional at best.[85] The precarious nature of leadership for a combative citizenry eventually undid the political careers of Nieto and Mosquera. Soon after the war, the commanders of the counterrepublic had a new falling out, after which the Cauca leader's Caribbean allies organized the overthrow of Nieto's state government in late 1864. Nieto blamed the coup on the "ignorant masses" that five years earlier had brought him back to power, a sign that he had squandered the trust of locals.[86] Mosquera was next in line when opponents waged a similar struggle against him in the name of the people he had once led into battle. In 1867, during his last turn as national president, Mosquera shuttered an intransigent Congress and jailed several of its leaders, prompting Bogotá's letrados to depose him in the name of the macheteros "who won the battles of the revolution." Congress's democratic rhetoric, however, did not prevent it from removing the Liberal Party's most popular leader and dismantling the standing army. Like the dynamics of the war itself, partisan machinations and popular action remade peacetime politics in ever changing ways.[87]

By winning the battles of the revolution, citizens of the Caribbean and Cauca had transformed the republic into Colombia, yet the challenges that followed the war proved as formidable as those that came before it. Diverging political regimes meant that men formally retained the franchise in the states with the largest populations of African descent, while illiterate and propertyless men lost the right to vote in states where lettered Liberals had once allied themselves with Conservatives. It was typically the leadership of the elite factions of the central highland states that controlled the national government over the following generation, in particular after Mosquera's ouster in 1867. The national movement that had won the war for the Liberals quickly fragmented into local and often mutually antagonistic regimes. Within the country's changing political, commercial, and cultural landscapes, citizens of the laboring classes endured myriad new challenges to their role in public life.

CHAPTER THREE

The Freedom of Industry and Labor

Aquileo Parra, petty merchant from Santander and president of Colombia after the civil war, endured many trials in his public life, but by his own account nothing approached the ignominies of his 1845 journey on the Magdalena River to conduct trade at the Magangué fair. In Mompós, Parra hired a *champán* (a large covered dugout) and its crew, which entailed paying for the rental of the boat, the wages of the boat's *patrón*, half-wages for the *bogas* (as the men who worked the *champanes* were called), and enough provisions for all the men's meals during the trip. Despite assurances from the patrón of a prompt departure, on the scheduled day some of the crew failed to appear. In response to Parra's query about when they would be able to leave, the patrón shrugged, "Who knows, white man; we're missing two men, but maybe they will arrive soon." By the time the tardy bogas showed up, the rest had abandoned their stations, with the situation repeating itself the following morning. After the boat finally embarked on the third day, it took Parra's plying of alcohol and tobacco to coax the drunken men into steady work. Nevertheless, along the way the bogas "made cause to declare themselves on strike for three or four days in any old miserable hamlet on the shores of the Magdalena," circumstances the hapless merchant was powerless to change.[1]

The confrontation between Parra and the Magdalena bogas played out in miniature a larger struggle in the country's market economy. Few of Parra's contemporaries shied away from blaming environmental, political, or technical conditions for what they considered to be Colombia's backwardness, yet they fixated on boatmen's dominion over navigation as a major obstacle to commercial progress. Reforms passed soon after Parra's trip designed to foster economic development also pitted boatmen and other laborers against merchants and public officials. Nowhere was this confrontation more intense than along the Caribbean coast-Magdalena River axis, the country's gateway to the outside world. Once it became clear that men of the coastal lowlands were the primary force in the movement of exports and imports—the crux of national wealth and public revenue—questions about highland artisans in the market economy ceased to be germane.[2]

73

Midcentury reforms exacerbated these struggles by conjoining labor and industry as a single freedom, which served as the legal embodiment and guiding spirit of slave emancipation. Advocates of laissez-faire expected that the abolition of monopolies in all forms would liberate men from the tyranny of masters and capital from the tyranny of labor, yet market relations came up against the same ways of life that had ensured emancipation in the first place. Merchants, intellectuals, and civil servants understood the fragility of the contract in an environment where many working people had continuing recourse to land, which encouraged state action to subordinate labor to commerce. Against the coercions of industrial freedom, transport workers employed old strategies to defend their independent livelihoods against wage servitude. The conflation of labor and industry as a single constitutional precept, with all its intrinsic paradoxes, thus became a major test of emancipation's legacy.

The free-trade era after 1850 was punctuated by significant turns and flashpoints as citizens wrangled over economic priorities. In the crafting of commercial policies, business advocates also defined labor in a manner that classified bogas as a principal problem of market capitalism. Commercial rhetoric soon instigated a new national regulatory system, the *inspección de bogas*, which rendered boatmen the country's most heavily policed workforce. As new regulations bore down on their lives, however, bogas staged a strike to demand higher wages and recognition for their role in the economy. With the limitations of state power exposed, merchants and government officials looked to steam power as a means to displace bogas' dominion. By the end of the free-trade era in the early 1880s, industrialized navigation had encouraged economic development yet had proved ambiguous in its disciplinary power over labor. In the "coming of the steamboats, to which [the bogas] have offered impassioned and systematic opposition," according to Antioqueño author and politician Juan de Dios Restrepo in 1852, the era witnessed no clear resolution. Nevertheless, letrados and merchants, who frequently clashed over partisan politics, had united in the effort to free industry from the working people aboard boats, in canals, and along Caribbean waterfronts.[3]

FREE LABOR, ENCHAINED CAPITAL

Improving transportation and expanding trade, internally but particularly outward to world markets, was long a goal of leading Colombians. The tobacco export boom that got underway in the 1840s validated this thinking, and previous state-led economic reforms inspired efforts to create effective communications to serve this industry.[4] Even as commercial boosters envisioned a lacework of railroads to tie the republic to the modern age, from the midcentury onward governments and merchants concentrated on the effective development of the Magdalena River. Since early colonial times the Magdalena had served as the country's highway, flowing to the Caribbean Sea near major urban centers and agricultural zones and bearing a succession of goods to world markets: gold, tobacco, hides, cinchona bark, coffee.[5] River navigation won a privileged place in governmental policy through reduced taxation and government subsidies, and in the early 1850s Congress declared the Magdalena the country's first *vía nacional*, leaving it free and open to all navigation, even by ships flying flags of foreign powers. Subsequent legislation abolished customs and tolls and extended vía nacional status to other waterways, all in the name of promoting the export trade.[6]

Men of business tempered their enthusiasm for the transformative power of markets by expressing doubts about the position of bogas in a system of free trade. During the sixteenth century, Africans had largely replaced indigenous men on the river, and by the independence era they constituted a substantial force of free men of all colors. One foreign traveler in the 1820s claimed there were 10,000 bogas in the Magdalena Valley, a figure that may have underestimated their ranks.[7] The bogas worked canoes, skiffs, and large dugout *bongos*, with the mainstay of human-powered transportation being the champán, a boat 40 to 150 feet long and 6 to 8 feet wide, with a thatched bamboo canopy to protect passengers and goods and a displacement of up to fifteen tons.[8] The champán was operated by crews of ten to twenty-five men and conducted by a patrón, a boga who had achieved a degree of prestige and craft-like skill, enough to pilot and provision the boat, recruit and supervise bogas, and arrange contracts with merchants. Patrones and bogas tended to work together as regular teams, resembling labor gangs that hired themselves out as porters and haulers in ports around the Atlantic littoral.[9] To be a patrón conferred to the boga some status among merchants, and an otherwise humiliated Aquileo Parra even praised his boat's master. While the patrón was akin to a boss, earning roughly double the wage of the common boga, travelers frequently noted the camaraderie among all boatmen.[10]

Rowing and pushing boats in the tropical heat were grueling and dangerous tasks, alleviated only by nightly respites and the men's own self-made entertainment. Bogas propelled the champán forward by wedging a long forked pole into the river bottom and walking the length of the canopy with the butt of the pole planted on their exposed chests, which often

Ramón Torres Méndez, Champán en el Río Magdalena, *color lithograph, 1878.*
Photo © Museo Nacional de Colombia/Ángela Gómez Cely.

caused bleeding, massive scar tissue formation, and permanent physical disability.[11] On upriver trips they worked twelve-hour days, stopping only for a brief repast of plantain, rice, or fish, sometimes seasoned with onion and salt. Day and night boatmen suffered exposure to the elements, slept on open boats or riverbanks, and endured attacks from insects, snakes, and caimans. Drowning, while perhaps not frequent, was known to happen in rough waters.[12] Bogas synchronized their labor and relieved the tedium by singing call-and-response work songs, praying at the beginning of their day, engaging in verbal duels with rival champán crews, and offering advice to peasant farmers passed along the way.[13] After the fatigue of pushing against the current they let the river do the work on the return trip to the coast, whose days were filled with tobacco, rest, song, and play—a stark contrast that led one traveler to remark, "Bogas lead either the most indolent or the most laborious life." One trip by champán from the coast to Honda, Bogotá's river port, lasted three months, with another month needed for downriver travel. Such were the pains and pleasures of human-powered travel, which remained the primary means of commerce and communications well into the nineteenth century.[14]

As the dominant force in transportation, bogas required passengers and merchants to abide by long-cherished habits. Work was arduous but also task-oriented and given over to the rhythms of nature and custom, with boats embarking at no specified times and routine stoppages along the river for purposes of leisure. Boat work typically involved alcohol consumption as well, and most travelers complained that Magdalena bogas poled while inebriated. Nevertheless, merchants and government officials often set aside cash, liquor, and tobacco as incentives to guarantee that the men worked until the task was completed.[15] Demands by boatmen for more goods to finish work contracted beforehand were a sign that they controlled not only the timing of their labor but to a certain extent their compensation. Seemingly spontaneous stoppages may have been in part eruptions of preindustrial work habits with their blurred boundaries between labor and leisure, although they were gauged to exact increased payments in specie or in kind from stranded and desperate passengers. Bogas' control of their labor meant that the merchants who were their ostensible employers "had no more authority over them than I," harrumphed one foreigner submitted to a leisure strike, "neither has an alcalde, nor any other person."[16]

This control extended through long-distance transport networks and set the tempo of the nation's commerce. Bogas from Barranquilla refused to take their boats above Mompós, and those from farther upriver equally declined to row below that town, confirming either a dislike for travel too far from their homes or a proprietorship over distinct sections of the river. Frustrated merchants entering Mompós or Magangué were required to transfer from one champán to another, enter into new contracts, or hire other crews. In some cases, employers could compel the continuation of their boats if not their employees. The champán *Cuatro Hermanos* began its journey in Santa Marta in February 1852, yet the patrón and bogas debarked at Mompós, where merchants had to hire Juan Miranda and his men to take the vessel upriver. Even less geographically mobile employees, like the rowers for Cartagena's customs service, "resist continuous work," which held up the inspection of incoming trade.[17] "No task is more disagreeable than to negotiate with bogas," lamented one foreign traveler, who added that such a task required "great diplomacy." With boatmen's control of labor all but assured, however, there was often little negotiation to be had. The movement of armies depended on them, and their decisions about when or whether to row determined military strategy in times of war. During the midcentury cholera epidemics commerce declined because "no boga wants to embark until the news improves." Boatmen often abandoned the river as a matter of collective security or in solidarity with ill crew members, which left military commanders and merchants in the lurch.[18]

Bogas' independence was predicated on the exploitation of land and water resources as part of the movement of free people to the Caribbean countryside. "These unhealthy shores," explained a French visitor in the 1820s, "are peopled with old bogas who, tired of navigating the rivers, without a doubt want to leave to their children the fruit of their painful work; manumitted slaves, deserters of all races or, rather, of all colors." Bogas who, alongside other rural folk, occupied provision grounds and fisheries for their own consumption or to sell as surplus at market reduced their earnings from poling boats to a supplemental wage. Fifty years later the Magdalena River settlements looked much the same to a Swiss traveler who described the region's bogas and other smallholders as "truly Rousseauian" individuals who lived in a state of nature "not subject to authority."[19]

European cultural impositions aside, boatmen maintained their independence not through isolation but through relations with laboring women, men, and children. Their extreme mobility, which carried them over hundreds of miles for months at a time, was tempered by connections to specific plots of land occupied by kin. Although many merchant-employers retained part of each boga's pay to dispense directly to his family, in the main it was the pole man who relied on the activities of those he left behind. In some remote riverside warehouses entire families loaded boats alongside stevedores, even if the more common sights were the settlements in the countryside where women farmed, fished, sold produce at market, or ran *chicherías* and dry goods shops frequented by boat crews.[20] Living around the old fugitive rural communities meant an avoidance of the dependence and potential abuse endured by some women who hired themselves out in coastal cities—women including "a dear old black, 'Natividad' by name," who worked as a cook and servant for British agents in Barranquilla in the 1860s. While riverside villages proliferated, still a majority of Caribbean wage laborers chose the major transportation hubs of Cartagena, Barranquilla, Calamar, and Mompós, where bogas sought crew work and women drudged in foreign and local households as domestics. Female labor was significant enough that national governments in the 1850s and 1860s argued that "seamstresses, ironers, washerwomen and women who exercise other occupations without belonging to a designated house must be classified" as "artisans" for census purposes.[21]

Caribbean family networks extended to the women and children who joined men on the champanes. Patrones traveling with their families marked the indistinct boundaries between work and nonwork lives, their independence from employers, and their elevated status vis-à-vis common bogas.[22] During the semiannual *feria* at Magangué, attended by tens of thousands of merchants and laborers, champanes clogged the Magdalena River halfway across to form a "floating city where numerous families live." On some boats groups of women cooked and cleaned, yet the most typical arrangement was the solitary presence of the patrón's wife, not unlike the "fierce black woman dressed in fabrics of vivid colors" aboard the boat in Felipe Pérez's novel *Imina*. Mealtimes during trips embodied the social dynamics of the patrón's commonality with, yet elevated status above, pole men, given that all ate from the same pot even as the boat's master took his meals aft, either alone or with his female companion.[23] Traveling with children sometimes bore the practical function of ensuring the regularity of written contracts. In the 1850s, Juan Miranda made a place on the champán *Elisa* for his son, Ensermo, who could read and write—vital aptitudes when negotiating with merchants. Indeed, the presence of literate children like the younger Miranda, who signed pay sheets and shipping manifests "for the patrón my father Juan Miranda," may have indicated some boatmen's lack of trust in businessmen.[24]

By far most expressions of this distrust, however, originated from business merchants and their supporters, who with numbing uniformity repeated colonial-era opprobrium against the "boga of the lower Magdalena . . . a strange, primitive, and savage animal." In 1865, Felipe Pérez complained that bogas showed "the insolence of the proud races" for demanding more pay to carry luggage from the boats into towns, which left travelers "at the mercy of those bedouins of the water." Writers contrasted the behavior of Caribbean men with indigenous and mestizo *peones* of highland regions, who displayed deference by addressing their social betters as *patrón* or *amo* in typical Andean fashion. Although wage-earning men of the coast were often defined as peons, they exhibited none of the social subordination associated with the category.[25] In his early 1850s essay "True Bogas and Apocryphal Bogas," Juan de Dios Restrepo argued that bogas of the upper Magdalena River in the country's interior were apocryphal because of their deference, unlike the true bogas of the river's Caribbean sector. This was an undesirable authenticity, of course, derived from their unruliness and morally suspect behavior, which stood as "the symbol of our primitive epoch." Such oppositions—between merchant and labor, citizen and animal, national advance and colonial stagnation—weighed on the minds of the men of progress.[26]

The antiboga rhetoric at midcentury drew on the language of old chronicles in order to articulate the new commercial priorities. When José María Samper admonished "the boga family, that lives off fish, in torpor, inertia, and corruption, that will not be regenerated except after many years of civilizing work," he was expressing more than his own contempt for Caribbean people. Intrinsic to Samper's ascription of coastal inferiority was an attempt to measure groups based on economic performance, with bogas' independence a sign of low productivity.[27] For many liberal thinkers, the division of labor within the region's families was a problem. Manuel Ancízar, in his 1853 travel account written as part of a government geographical survey, rebuked the "lazy black men" he encountered "who will forever reign over the Magdalena" by subsisting off the work of their artisan wives. He felt certain that "the future fortunes of these villages depend on economic activity and river traffic to pull them out of the semibarbarous state that paralyzes them."[28] To Ancízar, Samper, and other business advocates, men's dependence on female labor rendered them unproductive, and allegedly sedentary activities like the selling of goods were "petty trades [that] must be abandoned to the women." They desired instead manly exertions and the eradication of feminizing idleness among lowland inhabitants through wage labor and the accumulation of profit. These ideas coincided with emancipation's extension of full citizenship status to all men yet appeared to trump political rights when individual economic activities fell short in their measurement of industrial progress. Moreover, free trade advocates did not consider the labor of women of color to be valuable but interpreted it instead as artisanal and therefore another symbol of commercial paralysis.[29]

The logic of liberals' renovation of centuries-old stereotypes of the boga derived from the belief that their control of the labor process was a discredited colonial legacy. The merchant paper *El Vapor* explained the problem: "These savages have been the law in the navigation of the Magdalena because, having been exclusive in its exercise, they have constituted to their advantage a species of monopoly." This was a serious charge given the justifications made in support of slave emancipation as part of the legal destruction of the colonial vestiges of monopoly power. After slavery came to an end, economic monopolies carried no standing before the law, and yet from government reports to poetry the alarm rang out that commercial capital was the victim of boatmen's exclusive powers and privileges. Monopolies on gold, tobacco, salt, and transportation had been swept away by midcentury reforms, and merchants demanded that the "abolition of these classes" of boga labor be next.[30]

The call to eradicate labor monopolies exposed the inherent tensions in the legal reforms of emancipation. The 1853 constitution enshrined "the liberty of industry and labor" in its bill of rights, hence conflating disparate activities into a single freedom. At the time, New Granada's political leaders comprehended the freedom of industry as the (manly) right to trade, invest, engage in contracts, and farm commercially, with factory production perceived dimly on the horizon. The constitutional freedom of labor, a seemingly self-evident consecration of slave emancipation, had been in fact a political compromise. An earlier draft of the political charter had defined this freedom as "proprietorship over the fruit of one's labor," a more fundamental right that convention delegates rejected because it granted sovereignty to artisanal and noncommodified production and because it might reproduce labor monopolies.[31] The subsequent national constitutions of 1858 and 1863, instead of fully disentangling the two guarantees, shielded industry from labor monopolies by offering specific protections only to those engaged in profit-oriented business or trade. Over time constitutional protections for commercial industry over labor monopolies took the form of an implicit boga clause. The 1865 Bolívar state constitution offered one such boga clause, as it permitted "freedom to exercise all industry, and to labor" so long as it did not "obstruct the avenues of communication." The solution to the conundrum of emancipation's legally entwined freedom of industry and labor, then, was to subordinate the latter in order to safeguard the former.[32]

As antimonopoly doctrine raised expectations for commercial growth, merchants and journalists began demanding policies to curtail bogas' independence. Joaquín Acosta's 1850 report on the difficulties of communication between the Magdalena River and the Caribbean Sea along the route called the Piña Channel laid the blame squarely at the feet of the area's laborers. In an analysis that presaged the boga clause, Acosta insisted that obstructions in the Piña Channel were human-made, since "the bogas are content with passing through dragging their boats over [the mangrove roots], making them each time more compact," which increased the expense of removal. He proposed that Congress decree the Piña a vía nacional, that the government contract its dredging in exchange for the "exclusive use of the channel by steamboat," and that all bogas to be banned from the waterway.[33] Acosta's proposals were remarkable given the laissez-faire sentiments of the era, although they meshed well with concurrent antilabor diatribes in the press and numerous petitions sent to Bogotá by Magdalena River merchants demanding regulation of boatmen. In government *informes*, newspaper editorials, and travel accounts, the commercial consensus argued that a market economy was impossible so long as bogas controlled the industry.[34]

INSPECCIÓN DE BOGAS

The mounting published attacks against boatmen drove national and local administrations to reinstitute the police force known as the *inspección de bogas*. In response to public opinion, Tomás C. Mosquera's first presidential administration in the late 1840s nationalized the nearly defunct inspection service, expanded its jurisdiction, and raised it to the status of a permanent government agency. Mosquera based his reforms on an 1843 law that empowered the executive to monitor boatmen, grant work permits only to those with a permanent home, issue manifests of merchandise to prevent theft, regulate the hours of departure, set wage rates, and punish men with prison sentences for deserting their boats. Further rulings established the patrón as the supervisor and source of discipline aboard the champán — despite the fact that patrones and bogas came from the same social milieu, or perhaps because of this.[35] The inspection service sent to river and coastal ports officials who issued passports, work rolls, and payment sheets to prevent crews from cheating merchants. The inspectors answered directly to Mosquera's minister of foreign relations, a measure intended to circumvent the authority of local alcaldes of unknown qualities or loyalties.[36]

Within these broad regulatory powers, the inspectors' primary task was to standardize wages and expenses, which in previous decades had been hammered out by bogas and merchants in a makeshift manner, much to the chagrin of commercial enterprises. Inspector Plácido Barrera carried out this duty as detailed in the rolls for the champán *Joaquín Antonio Mier*: pay of eighty pesos (round trip) for patrón José Mantaño, and twenty-three pesos for each of the boat's twenty-three bogas for the trip from Barranquilla to Honda, sixteen pesos of which had been paid up front, four pesos paid by inspector Barrera in Mompós, and the remaining three pesos to be paid upon completion of the trip. Along with enforcing a standardized pay and ration scale for commercial trips, Barrera also reviewed receipts and supplies to guarantee that patrones were not misappropriating provisioning budgets. To facilitate the regulation of pay and discretionary spending, Bogotá sent inspectors preprinted wage and ration receipts to be issued to boatmen.[37]

The criteria for these wage rates are unclear, as is the larger story of wages in the nineteenth century, where a lack of data prevents discussion beyond generalities. Pay varied across the Caribbean region and between the coast and various parts of the country's interior, while any variations occurred within an overall monetary system of silver shortages and of wages that experienced a secular decline in value over the second half of the century.[38] Comparing wages in transportation to other occupations with any specificity is further complicated by a per-trip schema of payment, as opposed to the daily rates of most manual labor. With these caveats in mind, evidence for the 1850s and 1860s suggests that patrones earned about 10–15 percent more than the average pay of manual laborers employed by municipal governments, whereas common bogas earned about half that average. The more noteworthy story about pay, however, may be the inspection's attempts to regularize rates across the coast and valley, perhaps raising wages for some rural bogas with access to land and depressing them for some urban bogas subject to higher living costs. And most significant, the inspection's pay scale revealed an unprecedented state intervention in the contracting of labor for private enterprise.[39]

Beyond regulating labor contracts and payments, the boga inspection kept watch against theft, desertion, and delays. Officials recorded on shipping manifests and passports the dates of departure, the marks of the merchandise, and the number and names of men on board.[40] The frequent loss of cargo from boats that capsized in rough waters triggered investigations into whether boatmen, often presumed guilty, had been negligent or had engaged in criminal fraud. Inspectors were motivated to enforce penalties for disruptions and delays by rules that held them responsible for finding replacements when bogas deserted.[41] Plácido Barrera typically inscribed in the passports carried by champanes, "In order to protect commerce, authorities along the route will not permit this boat to be detained anywhere by the bogas without just cause, in whose case the patrón will request the necessary help." In one case, he made further notation that "the bogas are obligated to depart without delay the morning of Monday, 21 June, and if they do not they will receive a reduction of three reales from the three pesos each one is to receive in Honda." Five months later, the ever diligent inspector, citing national laws, noted in the passport of Silvestre Castro of the champán *Susana* that he had "advised both the patrón and the bogas of the punishments they would incur if they fail in their duties."[42] Merchants ensured that monitoring for desertions remained a primary task of the service, as had Aquileo Parra in 1845, when his complaints had led a Mompós inspector under the old system to intervene, which allowed him finally to embark on his trip.[43]

The inspection's public powers overshadowed the meager influence of merchants who could do little more than cajole boatmen. The popularity of the service in the business community and the antilabor sentiments of the press provided officials latitude when intervening in employment relations. An inspector of Mompós demonstrated his authority in 1848 by condemning boatmen Jacinto Rivera and José del Rosario Rodríguez—each a "laborer" of "light mulatto color"—to the presidio in Cartagena for six months, respectively, "for the offense of deserting their boat." The following year, another official hauled to jail José María Ortiz, ostensibly for desertion, despite the patrón's insistence that Ortiz was taking care of his ill mother and that, besides, the boats rarely if ever left port on time. Even with testimony from the boga's chief, the inspector remained unconvinced, and although eventually compelled to release Ortiz, he informed the governor that the boga's "few days in prison would serve as correction for the offense."[44] Writers Eugenio Díaz Castro and Manuel María Madiedo memorialized in their fiction these daily confrontations between boatmen and inspectors to the apparent fascination of the reading public of the 1850s.[45]

Before it could make its way into literature, the national inspection service fell victim to the abolitionist movement. Just two days after passing the final slave emancipation act in May 1851, liberals and radicals in Congress dismantled the national policing of Magdalena River boatmen. For some legislators the measure may have expressed the same expansive libertarian values that had impelled the ending of legal bondage, although a more likely motivation came from the desire to enact administrative decentralization and to make good on a general ambition to scale back governmental power. Unlike the widespread approval of slave emancipation, some observers criticized the ending of the inspection. Conservative Joaquín Posada Gutiérrez complained that the combination of reforms, in particular the concurrent loosening of workplace regulation and abolition of debtors' prison—which he considered the only effective check on physically mobile labor—reinforced bogas' monopoly and sanctioned a "vile theft" of merchant property.[46]

Yet administrative devolution once more to local governments engendered more not less surveillance, as provinces and municipalities regained the authority to regulate bogas abrogated by Mosquera's 1848 decree, only to be joined by the new federal states after 1856. In the Magdalena town of Puebloviejo, a customary stop for champanes, the council voted to resume inspections in 1858 with sweeping provisions that touched on every aspect of boga labor: the time at which they must report to work, rates and schedules of their pay, their relationship with their "superiors and supervisors on the embarkation," jail time for those who refused to work after receiving wages, and the right of creditors to reclaim debts owed by bogas who had received pay.[47] It was not surprising that Puebloviejo's ordinance read much like previous legislation, given the administrative redundancies that decentralization created. Budget-conscious administrators failed to persuade elected officials to eliminate overlapping jurisdictions in the boga inspection, and federal states such as Magdalena created their regulatory structure by adopting word-for-word national law over transportation labor. Inspectors employed by the national government disappeared for a time, but policing continued to impinge on boatmen's lives through rulings formulated from Congress down to the smallest cabildo.[48]

Although this diffuse policing effected little immediate or uniform change in working conditions, new public powers expanded the range of official activity and conditioned boga responses to authority. Labor regulations far from extended into the innumerable waterways outside major ports of call, and public penury often hampered inspections in these locations as well. Even where the service functioned with any regularity, merchants continued to pay bonuses to boatmen above official pay scales—despite legal prohibitions—to guarantee that they would complete trips or load or unload champanes in a timely manner. This continued upward pressure on wages was another sign that once boats left port, the inspector's authority was nil.[49] Even within their jurisdictions, officials could do little about bogas' access to land or the marketing activities of their female kin, which freed them from the compulsion to sell their labor on a steady basis. Nonetheless, since this was a national policy aligned with commerce, officials at all levels of administration could invoke a panoply of laws in their dealings with boatmen. Governmental authority expanded, and bogas faced public officials as well as merchants in their attempts to maintain control of their work.

THE BOGA STRIKE OF 1857

Bogas could not stop the expansion of public policing but they could block its intrusion into their lives, often with great effectiveness. Within the postal service in particular, tensions around regulation increased after decentralization led to wage reductions. As national postal administrator in the early 1850s, Salvador Camacho Roldán admitted that the government did not even consider "the laziness of the bogas" as a factor in delays of the mails, which arrived "with all the regularity that could be desired, given all that is possible to expect from the bogas." Yet his plan of cash incentives to speed up service belied the government's general unwillingness to pay wages the boatmen considered just.[50] In 1856, Caribbean officials were reprimanded by national overseers for not adhering to national rules on wages and rations and for conceding to boga demands for better pay. In defending the actions of his subordinates, Cartagena's governor, Juan Antonio Calvo, insisted that the men "do not offer their canoes willingly, and some have opposed with great resistance furnishing what is required of them for the postal service for the miserable sum of 3.20 pesos for each trip that takes the span of one month." Postal administrators on the coast had been caught for years between insufficient budgets and employee pressure to double their per trip earnings. Warnings of future delays went unheeded in the national capital, where in February 1857, out of concern for costs, federal officials rejected a last-ditch effort to move the growing backlog of mail upriver.[51]

After these negotiations failed, the bogas of the lower Magdalena River went on strike. In mid-February, patrones Pedro Fifa, Rudecindo Marco, D. G. Hernández, Pedro Moreno Pupo, Simón Pino, and Francisco Queto sent a written petition to the postal administrator at Calamar, an entrepôt fifty miles above Barranquilla where the Dique Canal joins the river. With their petition, the patrones demanded more pay, increased benefits, and better working conditions for their continued conveyance of the post. "Since remote times," they declared, "the residents of this region have been charged with conducting the National mails due to their knowledge in navigation, exactitude, and honor, and because it is proved that they are the ones disposed to suffer with resignation the hardships of a consecutive and rough journey, despite the long distance and dangers that present themselves at each turn." As a consequence of such hardships, they and their crews, who were making their own demands "in justice," protested that current pay was so low they could not cover their basic living expenses on the long trips upriver to Honda and back. They requested, "within our rights," wage increases for each patrón and boga, an increase in the rations allotment, continued rental fees of their canoes, and new leather boat coverings for each trip. They hoped for a swift acceptance of their conditions, warning, "if not, both we and all the conductors and bogas are disposed not to offer our services for any amount of money." They ended their petition by reiterating their determination to prevail, "in the conviction of being just what we express."[52]

For days all boats on the lower Magdalena stood idle, the mails and commercial trade did not move, and with Calamar as the transshipment point for all coastal routes, the country's transportation system was in effect shut down. Bogas in the region refused to row upriver until the strike was settled, which severed the Caribbean from the interior and the country's three main maritime ports from each other. Local officials realized that the action represented something more than a customary work stoppage, and they acknowledged the demands by offering a compromise. In taking the lead in the negotiations, an obsequious Governor Calvo admitted that "the bogas cannot be obligated to give their services for less salary than they demand," and proposed a per trip pay increase of 500 percent for all men. With communications paralyzed, no local administrator dared oppose the proposal, and Calamar's postal official concurred that the pay increase was "very just" by noting, in language taken from the patrones' own petition, the dangers of work on the river.[53]

Officials made hasty concessions because they lacked the means to make men work. Although relatively few individuals were employed in the postal service at any given time, they lived within a community of hundreds if not thousands of boatmen who were not directly part of the strike. Despite so many bogas in the immediate vicinity, the government's inability to bring in strikebreakers resulted from the pressures of full employment at the height of the tobacco export boom as well as, significantly, a demonstrated unity among river workers. The decision to carry the mails by canoe for speed's sake, moreover, required the postal service to hire men who owned their own watercraft, which afforded them greater leverage and further limited the government's options in breaking the strike.[54] The petitioners had highlighted social distinctions by taking the leading role in making demands, even as they acted in unison with bogas in ways that muted differences. The boatmen's ability to strike in the first place, moreover, testified to their occupation of land in the countryside and the possible backing of workingwomen. The patrones who signed the petition lived in Barrancanueva, a rural hamlet ten miles upriver from Calamar, where land was plentiful and, perhaps, just far enough from inspectors and other government officials. Settling remotely on smallholdings that they and their families farmed diminished their need to settle the strike quickly.[55]

At the time of the negotiations, patrones and bogas apparently accepted the governor's compromise, since there was no permanent work stoppage, even though conflict over wages remained for some time. Four months after the strike settlement, Calvo admitted that he remained subject to "the will and caprice of the pilots and bogas, and the more urgent and critical a service is, the greater the obstacles that appear in offering it, and the greater the remuneration that they demand." In September 1857, he reported that labor relations were still "very bad," and as a sign of bipartisan unity against labor unrest, the Conservative governor recommended that President Ospina reappoint Liberal Ricardo Núñez as local postal administrator because "Sr. Núñez has a certain power over them that will make them work." Coastal functionaries also spent months after the strike appealing for larger remittances from national customs receipts to pay increased wages.[56]

To all appearances, the strike was a fundamental departure from typical boga behavior, in part because the bogas made an emancipation-era demand for recognition. Unlike customary work stoppages, the Calamar bogas went on strike neither for the sake of leisure nor for an ad hoc renegotiation of wages but instead to create a permanent change in the just price for labor. Increasing consumer prices caused by the tobacco export boom—the recession of 1858 was still months away—may have necessitated an adjustment in wages beyond what was possible through informal action.[57] At the same time, amid what seemed to be a modern strike for economic interests, the bogas invoked honor and justice that, irrespective of wages, demanded dignified work free from both state interference and peon status. Even the patrones' means served their ends, since the formal petition was itself a claim to legitimacy that distinguished the strike from customary boga behavior and that justified the boatmen's role in the economy. Recognition of their demands implied sanctioning their control of the river, where the formal strike remained merely one option for maintaining independence. Given the absence of a subsequent wave of work stoppages among bogas, it appears likely that boatmen regarded other activities as sufficient defense of their status and livelihoods.[58]

After the strike, public officials who perhaps feared that the wage concessions would be understood as capitulation to bogas began to implement increasingly repressive measures. The 1858–60 economic recession and decline in tobacco exports encouraged attempts to rein in labor, while the boga clause provided legal cover for reintroducing punishment for the recently abolished crime of disrespect to authority. Boatmen in the customs and postal services were the first to feel the effects of these changes, since their status as public employees justified coercion in the national interest. In late 1858, a no-longer-deferential Governor Calvo demanded stricter labor discipline, and subsequent Liberal administrations followed suit with mandatory licenses and stringent schedules for boatmen.[59] National, state, and municipal governments meted out severe punishments against violations of poststrike regulations, firing some bogas for being "incorrigible" employees or for causing "great scandal" during their hours of leisure, and jailing others for absenteeism or for "various punishable acts." In the decade after the strike, dozens of bogas in coastal cities were fined, dismissed, or imprisoned "for the damages that they cause with their resistance or desertion of their work," despite the unconstitutionality of incarceration in certain cases.[60] Local officials also curtailed patrones' ability to make contracts and ordered the construction of government boats to end the renting of their canoes and to reduce them to wage-labor status. New legal measures backed these efforts. The same year drafters inserted the boga clause into the Bolívar state constitution, Congress mandated that "all inhabitants of the shores of the Magdalena . . . have an obligation to offer help to the boats or canoes that carry the national mails"—a measure intended for emergencies on the water that could just as easily apply to a labor strike.[61]

Liberals joined the assault on transportation workers' independence even as bogas came to the party's defense. During the civil war, hundreds of boatmen volunteered to serve the counterrepublic of Colombia, where they formed a vital link as conveyors of soldiers, munitions, and information between the nonadjacent Liberal-occupied territories of the Cauca and Caribbean coast. In 1862, Supreme Director of the War Mosquera, who had implemented the national inspection service during his presidency in the late 1840s, decreed awards and incentives for bogas who served in a military role. Juan José Nieto obliged Mosquera's decree with his Military Merit and Civil Merit decorations, "extending them with equal consideration to the troops and the boatmen."[62] Nevertheless, the wartime political alliance between bogas and Liberal leaders did not reverse rising antilabor sentiments. On the first anniversary of the strike, the merchant paper El Vapor lashed out against those "brainless machines for moving the watercraft: without more patria than the boat itself." To José María Samper in 1859, "the donkeys of Calamar seemed . . . more rational than the bogas."[63] The repeated descriptions of subhuman boatmen endorsed coercive measures, which could prove lethal. Just weeks after Nieto's July 1859 coup in Cartagena, the revolutionary government was presented with the case of José Ciolo, a local boga patrón accused of killing two French merchants. Despite Nieto's lament at being unable to fulfill "the bright and dominant ideas of the century around the abolition of the death penalty," and regardless of the lack of evidence against the boga, Ciolo was publicly hanged in Cartagena. Nieto's abolitionist credentials did not supersede his continuing endorsement of capital punishment, nor did his disapproval of laissez-faire policies keep him from defending commercial interests over those of labor. Six months later the Bolívar state assembly abolished the death penalty, a measure ratified nationally by the 1863 constitution, making Ciolo the last citizen executed by the republic.[64]

As postwar Colombian governments reasserted control over navigation, local administrators carried out disciplinary measures against bogas in the name of the national state. By the 1870s, vía nacional status had been extended to other waterways, a state monopoly controlled significant spheres of transportation, and laissez-faire was all but a dead letter. The growing demands for coordinated commercial policy reestablished Bogotá as arbiter of labor relations as well. Boatmen worked in disparate conditions the lengths of the coast and river, yet the leeway Governor Juan Antonio Calvo enjoyed to negotiate labor disputes in 1857 had been whittled away by the national government.[65] Instead, bogas faced a reunified regime of labor discipline. Bolívar officials in June 1865 dragged to jail Dionisio González, a patrón of a government launch, for "highly reprehensible and harmful conduct." In the following years, other bogas and pilots of the Cartagena customshouse faced reprimand, dismissal, and incarceration for dereliction of duty.[66] Barranquilla's boatmen fared little better. Harsh punishment for presumed infractions befell the patrón and bogas of a bongo robbed while carrying the mails in the Ciénaga Grande in March 1871. When the postal employees returned to the city, officials arrested them and, despite his protests of innocence, submitted the boat's master "three times to the horrific torture known by the name of *soga llanera* [bullwhip] and the terrible mock firing squad." A few weeks later, men in Santa Marta unconnected to the bogas confessed to the crime.[67]

Only rarely did officials acknowledge that wage reductions exacerbated these continuing confrontations between laborers and authorities. Cyclical fiscal difficulties for local and national governments led to delays in wage payments for men in the customs service, transport, and public works.[68] The secretary general of Magdalena admitted in 1869 that many low-level state employees had not been paid for some time, and the bogas in the customs service were often forced to sell their wage promissory notes to speculators at a 20 percent discount. Neighboring Bolívar faced similar retrenchment a decade later, and the state superintendent confided that bogas and other public works employees did not receive regular pay. Given their subsistence-level wages, the delay in payment proved detrimental to the livelihood of men living in cities or without access to garden plots.[69]

Governmental repression and diminishing wages combined in a double assault on bogas' control after the 1857 strike.

STEAM'S IMPASSIONED AND SYSTEMATIC OPPOSITION

Business leaders, not content to wait for the unfolding of the state's regulatory power, turned to technology to demolish labor's monopoly. Permanent steam navigation on the Magdalena River appeared during the first Mosquera presidency and soon dramatically reoriented commercial and political affairs. The *vapores* were far fewer in number but superior to champanes in carrying capacity, even though the latter remained competitive for decades to come. Still, steamboats helped push down shipping rates, which began to dip below those of human-powered craft in the late 1850s, and which dropped more than 20 percent across the transportation industry in the three decades after 1845. More critical than its role in reducing freight costs was the steamboat's potential for massive profits and increased exports, particularly with the initiation of large-scale coffee production. Steam-powered ships also quickened the pace of commerce and communications, slashing times in the Barranquilla-Honda round trip from four months to two weeks and literally leaving the champán in their wake. The rate of change brought by industrial transportation was felt most directly in the coastal lowlands, which became more integrated into foreign markets and less economically dependent on the country's Andean highlands.[70]

Expansion in shipping capacity came not from mechanical crafts supplanting their predecessors but from their fraught complementarity. The frailty of the steamboats led shipping companies to pull outfitted champanes in case they ran aground or foundered, and early in the steamboat's career this arrangement was required by law.[71] Mishaps of the larger vessels led to new contestations with the bogas on the towed champanes. When one vapor did run aground on river shallows in the mid-1850s, a foreign passenger reported that the ship's crew labored for hours to maneuver it off the sandbar while the bogas, who understood the predicament to be outside their duties, remained "idle." A decade later Conservative letrado and future president José Manuel Marroquín referred to the champán towed behind the steamboat *Antioquia* as a "useless tail" that served no other purpose than to impede the steamer's ascent.[72]

The role of both classes of boats in facilitating exports before and after the recession of 1858–60 had the unintended effect of expanding local markets in labor and goods. The hum of activity was noticeable in

Calamar, Magangué, Honda, and points in between, where hundreds of stevedores loaded and unloaded boats of all sizes. Many other laborers in the Caribbean ports of Cartagena, Salgar, Santa Marta, and Riohacha shifted merchandise between carts, canoes, and ocean-going vessels: tobacco, hides, and coffee outbound; finished European goods and North American wheat inbound. The relative low cost of hiring large numbers of casually employed men (whom national law defined as peons) to haul goods on their backs compensated for the shortage of docks or wharfs.[73] With geography and governmental policy on its side, the village of Barranquilla grew after 1850 to become the country's commercial hub, its waterfront thronged with people and commodities from all parts into a veritable "tower of Babel." Visitors arriving in Colombia noted that alongside the "incessant movement" of "blacks and Indians, stevedores of the port" arose a larger "floating population" of men, women, and children selling produce, wares, and their labor at the waterfront.[74]

Marketing activities predated steamboats, but the arrival of the new technology provided new opportunities to engage in trade. Female vendors boarded anchored boats as a "semi-African mob" (sneered José María Samper) to sell foodstuffs to passengers and crew.[75] The delicate yet voracious steamboats stipulated arrangements with a range of specialized and nonspecialized labor, from artisans and mechanics in the urban shipyards of Cartagena and Barranquilla to canal diggers in dredging works, in particular in the Dique Canal, to woodcutters at fueling stations along the river. Within this diversification of local markets for goods and services, woodcutters were of particular importance, given that steamboats burned anywhere from 85 to 500 kilograms of wood per hour, leading to frequent stops at leñateos (wood stations) and daily outlays of up to 200 pesos for fuel. In this new occupation, men worked either alone on land they occupied or in itinerant gangs that traveled between stations along the river.[76]

Steam power's ostensible role in stimulating economic activity, which obscured the continuing importance of the champanes, led observers to duck the ships' functional difficulties in order to paint stark differences between progressive technology and the irredeemable backwardness of native labor. "Steamboats mean industry and commerce, speed and comfort, progress and civilization," assured Juan de Dios Restrepo, whereas the "damned champanes, with their discomfort and slowness, frighten the traveler and cause the man of business to lose hope." Traveling by steam in 1859, José María Samper called his boat "the child of the republic and instrument of liberty," which seemed to "protest against the barbarity" of its tropical surroundings, whereas bogas in passing champanes were "like a legion of savages." Lettered Caribbean opinion ratified the sentiments of its national counterpart when it complained of steamboat passengers' surprise "at finding here something better than black bogas and palm-covered huts."[77] In this intellectual environment, few writers abided Manuel Murillo Toro's critiques of laissez-faire and technology. "It is necessary to take care that the new discoveries, the conquests made in the field of industry, would be beneficial for all and not for the few," Murillo cautioned in an 1853 published letter. "Do you not think that the great step of substituting steam for human power in the navigation of the Magdalena would come to very little good if all do not benefit from it?" Most educated liberals and trade boosters rebuffed Murillo's caveats in their hope of submitting Caribbean labor to technological progress as part of a commercial consensus.[78]

The civilizing power of technology was also specifically envisioned as the solution to the bogas of Calamar. Just months after the strike, and with labor tensions still running high, *El Vapor* advocated "the advantageous revolution" of steam reducing not only "transport costs" but also of "finishing with the damned race of bogas and with the lamentable navigation of the champanes."[79] Government officials agreed, and a year after the strike the finance ministry dismissed out of hand "the resistance that [the bogas] offer to continue for what is currently paid to them." With the "conduction of mails between Calamar and Honda currently being made by steamboats," it continued, "the need has ceased for adopting the measure" of wage concessions negotiated by Calvo. Government ministers in Bogotá were so confident that they had found the cure for "the disorders of the State of Bolívar" that they suspended delivery of the mail, "except when the service could be had by means of steamboats." After the anti-boga boycott began, some individuals warned that "disorder continues to cover the mails from the Atlantic coast," although officials persevered out of the belief that technology would succeed where their own policing had failed.[80]

This belief hinged on the shift from labor-intensive to capital-intensive steam transportation, commanding a new social structure composed of skilled and unskilled labor. After the captain, engineer, and purser came the *contramaestre* (crew chief), a position typically filled by a retired military subaltern. Next was the pilot, who was often a former champán patrón with reduced responsibilities yet with the skills to guide steamboats without maps or instruments through the river's maze-like channels and shallows. One traveler maintained that pilots were "usually old men, and are treated with great respect by the rest of the crew," while also retaining sufficient standing to be held legally responsible, along with ship captains, for passenger deaths.[81] Following the pilot were the thirty to forty men of the service and common crews, who were called *marineros* as well as *bogas*—a relic of their old profession and a sign that changes in technology had not altered social status. José María Samper hailed marineros as "the aristocracy of navigators," and one North American argued in 1857 that bogas made "capital deckhands." Whichever name travelers gave them, "the bogas or marineros" performed the most menial tasks, loading cargo, stoking the boilers, and guarding ships during stopovers along the riverbank. These alleged labor aristocrats, moreover, were exposed to the intense heat and danger of the ship's lower deck, where they took their meals, slept atop cargo and amid animal carcasses carried to supply meat for passenger and crew meals, and, except for servants, maintained little contact with passengers.[82]

Within these new working relations, steamboats raised expectations of intensified domination of labor by joining the hierarchy of large maritime ships to a factory-like routine. Unlike champán bogas subjected to inspectors, early vapor deck hands endured no public policing, out of a belief in the restraining powers of foreign ship captains or the technology itself. When regulation extended to mechanized watercraft in 1871, officials continued to tread lightly on employers' prerogatives in their dealings with boat crews.[83] Limitations in government action stirred wary transportation companies to continue the practice of hiring former noncommissioned officers in an echo of the militarization of the boga inspection after the civil war. That only captains and contramaestres were permitted to carry guns testified to the unofficial, though brutal, mechanisms of control aboard steamboats.[84] In terms of mechanization, the shipboard differentiation of tasks and skills and the crews' physical removal from passengers contrasted with the champán's human propulsion and face-to-face and often tense negotiations. And since each crewmember was contracted individually on a per-trip basis, the *boga marinero* had less latitude in setting wages than the champán labor gangs had enjoyed.[85]

The new social relations of mechanized transport notwithstanding, crews brought onto the steamboats the folkways of the champán. Like pole men, marineros ate communal meals, sang together after completing their day's work, and engaged in word play with rival crews. They also found camaraderie from kin, and sometimes entire communities came to waterfronts to welcome or see off vessels.[86] Other traditions appeared invented as part of the arrival of steam navigation, perhaps to give meaning to changed working lives or to express unity among laboring men where it might otherwise have been lacking. In a ritual reminiscent of Atlantic mariners in the age of sail, crews insisted that captains halt the boats to officiate a drunken, raucous "parody of the ancient and traditional baptism of the line" for first-time boatmen crossing from the lower to the upper reaches of the river.[87] Such customs did not scandalize refined sensibilities as did other behaviors, like the "bogas" of one steamboat in 1863 who worked "without scruples toward the nuns" on board—that is, they performed their duties "without pants" on.[88]

It was not blasphemous behavior but steamboat workers' lack of social deference that generated conflicts with merchants and passengers. Men handled cargo haphazardly, loading ships in a "most frightful disorder," and piling goods into riverfront warehouses with a "terrible confusion." The service crew—"all . . . black," and whose "untidiness is legendary"— drank from travelers' glasses, used their utensils, and ate food from their plates before serving them. "Against such disgusting habits, there is no remedy," cried one foreigner. "Those rogues are incorrigible." Perhaps the contested site of the passengers' dinner table encouraged travelers in the common practice of packing their own food.[89] Not to be outdone by censorious outsiders, Colombian nationals ranted in equal tones against "the insubordination of the lazy crew," sounding in the process as if they were describing champanes. They may as well have been, as when Liberal writer and former abolitionist Medardo Rivas lambasted the "barbaric bogas" who shoved him off one steamboat gangplank. The ship's Caribbean servants, for their part, were "insolent, lazy, foul-mouthed, dazed, rowdy, and useless," according to Rivas.[90]

Laborers and marketers onshore who were linked in some way to steam transport expressed their own determination against social subordination. Coastal canal dredging in the 1860s and 1870s was hamstrung each year "when the days of Carnival presented such attractions to the men we had employed," according to one engineer, "that both crews were obligated to suspend their work and return to Ciénaga and Barranquilla, and two weeks of favorable time were lost." Canal diggers on government projects also demanded and received allotments of land adjacent to work sites to be used for growing crops, which lessened their dependence on wages and all but guaranteed subsequent work stoppages.[91] And woodcutters, who like bogas and canal diggers tended gardens and raised animals alongside their leñateos, refused to sell wood below prices they set, so that steamboat captains were required either to pay "exorbitant" rates for fuel or to send out deckhands to cut their own.[92]

Market women similarly exploited the arrival of steamboats while still controlling the terms of trade. The "black, mulatto, and Indian women" of the Magdalena Valley approached negotiations with steamboat passengers over wares and produce in a style many foreigners found particularly defiant. Like other rural inhabitants with access to land, their autonomous economic activities allowed them to halt transactions when exchanges with outsiders smacked of servility.[93] Some observers discerned the logic of withholding food from passengers desperate for gastronomic variety. According to a published history of Colombian steam navigation from 1884, "The inhabitants of the shores, enemies of an enterprise that said it was going to impoverish them, resisted selling the most necessary foodstuffs, and these things could only be secured by paying for them in gold." The steamboat may have fostered local markets, but it also bolstered the independence of the local populations in charge of them.[94]

Such affronts to commercial interests were not simple holdovers from the presteam era but were also in many cases responses to the new technology. Like the bogas who commanded more money from Felipe Pérez to carry his luggage ashore, the deckhands' haphazard stacking of merchandise could have signaled efforts not to be taken for subjugated and low-status peons. But perhaps the clearest gauge of marineros' determination against mechanized transport was their championing of collective safety over personal gain or compliance with ship regulations. Crews refused to work when presented with the possibility of steamboat boiler explosions, like the blast aboard the *Magdalena* in 1848 that killed most of the lower-deck hands but harmed none of the cargo. As word of work-related deaths and injury spread, men abandoned en masse ships considered dangerous. Following an explosion on the *Isabel* in Barranquilla in 1877, no crew would work on it, despite the captain's offer of two pesos gold per day, four to five times the going wage. So unfailingly did deckhands avoid work after boiler explosions that in 1881 the government criminalized crews' abandonment of damaged ships.[95]

Even where steamboats overcame their frailty and managed to establish themselves, they facilitated certain forms of work evasion. Much like the champanes they sought to replace, the mechanized craft followed capricious diurnal rhythms due to the perils of night travel and the need for constant refueling. They were, in effect, inefficient clocks that required constant resetting by the same men who took advantage of these pauses for rest and play. In what appeared to be informal pacts among crewmembers, men dragged out the time needed for loading wood. One boat traveling through the Dique Canal in 1879 "lost" four hours at a single leñateo that typically

Waiting to sell on the banks of the Magdalena. From Albert Millican,
Travels and Adventures of an Orchid Hunter *(London, 1891).*

took one-quarter the amount of time.[96] On many occasions, crews refused to handle wood when commonplace dangers of wild animals presented themselves, although whether these "stops . . . of interminable length" always corresponded to imminent threats or instead constituted variations of boga leisure strikes was difficult to determine. And even under the eye of armed captains and contramaestres, crews were notorious for waking late and starting up the boilers long after scheduled departure times.[97]

If the steamboats proved to be inefficient clocks, the relentless drive of machinery nevertheless eroded marineros' ability to choose the timing and pace of labor or leisure. According to one traveler, crews worked "ceaselessly," first loading ships and then stoking boilers with tons of wood daily, a punishing routine that encouraged malingering on their part. Other than certain unavoidable interruptions, they could not hold up the advance of the ships for more than a few hours—a sharp departure from the three- and four-day strikes that idled the champanes. The ritualized work stoppage of the human-powered craft manifested itself among steamboat crews as little more than a work slowdown. According to Barranquilla chronicler Julio H. Palacio, marineros in the 1870s and 1880s called the steamboat *Confianza* the *perra brava* (fierce bitch) exactly because its speed and range limited leisure time.[98]

In the decades after Manuel Murillo Toro's critique of steam technology, one of the few lettered Colombians to question the racial assumptions underlying industrial freedom was Bogotá law professor and Liberal Party boss Ramón Gómez. Traveling through the Caribbean region in 1880, Gómez refuted the supposition that "on the shores of the Magdalena none can survive but the black race, and progress does not follow this race, nor does any industry extend its roots within it." To Gómez, the "error and laziness [attributed to] the blacks and mulattoes who inhabit the lower Magdalena, we believe, are incorrect." To see a boga laboring on a ship's lower deck or a *leñador* with his own stack of steamboat fuel was to present a "black man who will display agility in caring for what is his and in augmenting his income." Bogas belonged to a possible future of commercial development, not to a preindustrial past doomed by civilizing technology. Most of Gómez's peers refused to follow his analysis of postemancipation labor and race relations, and by the time he published his account they had joined the consensus forged by antiboga critics.[99]

When free trade was officially repealed during the early 1880s presidency of Rafael Núñez, labor and industry alike could declare preeminence over commerce. The exertions of bogas and other workingmen and -women had linked the republic to world markets at the same time that they had bested every attempt by business interests to extinguish local ways of life. Champanes still plied the waterways, perhaps in record numbers. Still, the first generation of industrial labor in Colombia—the men who worked the steamboats of the Magdalena, and soon thereafter, the crews of the country's few railroads, which were initiated on the coast in the 1870s—had witnessed a loss of ability to determine wages, time, and workplace conditions. Moreover, their lack of voice in labor regulations formulated by distant and hostile legislatures or commercial consortiums denied them the recognition as honorable labor demanded by the striking bogas in 1857. Even as Ramón Gómez praised the accomplishments of Caribbean working people, ongoing transformations in letters and politics were remaking the possibilities for regarding their position in public life.

CHAPTER FOUR

The Lettered Republic

Because you see me the skin
The color of ink
Perhaps you believe that
My soul is also black?
—Candelario Obeso, *Cantos populares de mi tierra*, 1877

All the others are sickly and of an ambiguous race. Their endeavor is to be white and *pretty*. For me, it is an honor to be black and my ugliness delights me. Human regeneration is in my race. Science has already said this.
—Candelario Obeso, *Lecturas para ti*, 1878

Obeso was an Othello without a Desdemona who would love him.
—José María Rivas Groot, *La lira nueva*, 1886

The bogas' absence from the crafting of policies that impinged on their lives reflected their physical and above all social distance from the world of men who monopolized the writing of law and the written word itself. While illiteracy denied most plebeian citizens firsthand knowledge of legal codes, the learned minority cultivated intellectual and cultural distinctions to explain the existence of a republic with a vast unlearned majority. The midcentury social struggles did compel discussions of rights in the generation after the civil war, a period when Liberal letrados consolidated influence over Colombian law and letters. As political debate was driven by an expanding print medium, the very venue for public engagement intensified differences between literate national leaders and nonliterate provincials. Educated men assumed stewardship of the legacy of emancipation with ambivalence, their hold on power complicated by the preservation of a gulf between cultural exclusions and universal citizenship.[1]

The paradox of the national Liberal leadership's simultaneous promotion of social distinctions and democratic values testified to the strength of Colombia's lettered republic. Less a physical location than a social network, with Bogotá as its universally acknowledged base, the lettered republic encompassed men who converted their erudition into public stature, active citizenship, and administrative élan. The university-trained letrados practiced reading and writing as modes of cultural attainment in a society without vast disparities of wealth albeit one where literacy touched as few as one person in ten and primary schooling reached only one in fifty.[2] They assumed the reins of the republic despite their concentration in Bogotá exactly because this physical isolation ensured their position, according to José María Samper, as "great agents of democratic civilization" over the unlettered populations of the lowland provinces. Inspired by European and North American ideas of progress, these agents universalized their customs in part by downplaying the status of the ubiquitous oral cultures in their midst. In their attempts to remake national life, Samper and his contemporaries, including a few provincial brethren, saw their role not as direct emissaries but as models for the majority of citizens to emulate.[3]

If most letrados understood the need for economic development, they nonetheless preferred to preoccupy themselves with the major institutions of their democratic civilization, education and print culture. After 1850, they passed several significant reforms over public instruction, from the freedom of learning during emancipation to the major reform of 1870 known as the Organic Decree over universal primary education. Each systemic change in schooling embodied particular features of liberal civilization, and while letrados understood basic instruction as a precondition for citizenship, their adherence to sophisticated learning often trumped the attempts to promote literacy. By framing education reform as a moralizing emulation of literate culture and the eradication of barbarism, letrados shored up their own authority at the expense of constitutional rights and guarantees.

Debates over education appeared in the newspapers and books that proliferated as vehicles for the political rhetoric many literate men considered the preeminent form of public action.[4] In the largely unregulated press, writers of every political faction and partisan persuasion expressed ambivalence over how to reconcile a privileged erudition with democratic governance, the refinement of the minority with the coarseness of the majority. As a consequence of this ambivalence, prose, poetry, political philosophy, and legal thought appeared in the public sphere alongside costumbrismo stories filled with racial stereotypes of the same lowland populations expected to emulate lettered culture. Liberal policies engendered fierce opposition and counterreform, yet even when education efforts and print culture fueled partisan antagonisms, they nonetheless helped ensure bipartisan lettered supremacy, one written for a time in the language of liberty and rights.[5]

As the church and Conservative opposition asserted its influence in the 1870s and early 1880s, Candelario Obeso offered his own challenge to the contradictions of the lettered republic. Obeso, an educated man of color from the Caribbean region, was an outsider to Bogotá, the city where he spent most of his civil service and literary career. Other than Luis A. Robles, a contemporary and fellow letrado also of coastal origins, Obeso was the only individual to attain national stature as a man of African descent. Unlike Robles, who did not address issues of race in public, Obeso used his standing to critique the racism of liberal civilization and to demand recognition for citizens of color. In a series of published racial, sexual, and linguistic provocations, he presented black men (including bogas) as lead actors in social life, a premise rooted in republican manhood and freedom. His call for the expansion of rights and representation for citizens of color came at a moment when many letrados had begun to reconsider the democratic legacy of emancipation. Even as Conservative politics and culture gained ground, Obeso continued to dispute the exclusions within citizenship and to offer an alternative vision of national belonging.

EDUCATING CIVILIZATION AND BARBARISM

Changes in education were the product of the same social movements and legal reforms that brought about emancipation. Between 1850 and 1852, Congress and the López administration decentralized primary and secondary instruction and abolished national education standards, which allowed provincial schools to create curricula free from the previous oversight by Bogotá. Congressional radicals pushed further still by eliminating university degree requirements for entry to most professions and de jure extinguishing the universities, all as part of an effort to establish free thought, liberate instruction, and destroy social hierarchies they believed were products of higher education.[6] This same libertarian impulse inspired legislators to end national public financing for schools and, at the height of anticlericalism in the early 1860s, to dismantle Catholic instruction, actions that essentially abolished the country's educational system. Taken together, these changes engendered a double freedom of learning, in which students were free to receive instruction as they saw fit and free from any support to do so, which liberal reformers justified by citing slave emancipation and the constitutional freedom of industry and labor. "The efforts of the friends of liberty triumphed; slavery and ignorance disappeared," recalled one advocate of the reforms. Under this double freedom, families that found instruction for their children did so by dint of personal initiative, which reaffirmed the liberal thought that imbued the reform.[7]

The student careers of Luis A. Robles and Candelario Obeso, both born in 1849, developed within this environment. The double freedom of learning notwithstanding, both men began their studies in a place where any education reform departed from inauspicious beginnings. On the coast, few schools could be found in rural areas, and in the cities private and public academies operated precariously through a combination of fees, government disbursements, and charitable donations. Even the commercial center of Barranquilla lacked a public school before 1849, and the one opened that year remained its only learning facility for almost twenty years.[8] Liberal reforms and public penury caused a contraction in access to instruction at a time when already less than 1 percent of school-age children matriculated. One foreign traveler described the poor quality of schools across New Granada but claimed they were worst on the coast, with their dirt floors, lack of instructional equipment, and teachers not much older than their naked and shoeless students. Local officials tended to neglect primary schooling and augment secondary education, which guaranteed instruction for literate children from families of means, since any funding for schools under the double freedom of learning meant de facto support for exclusive quasi-private instruction. In response to the disestablishment of the already paltry education system, in 1852 diarist José Manuel Restrepo asked, "Where will the poor who cannot pay study?" The answer was self-evident: whether learning remained in the hands of tutors or municipalities, it was typically reserved for an entitled few.[9]

In the era of double freedom, many lettered men expressed disenchantment with the state of instruction through contempt for the uneducated, whose illiteracy forfeited entitlements to civic life. According to one member of Congress during debates over education reform in 1862, learning formed "useful citizens," while its absence "makes democracy impossible," an assessment seemingly at variance with the constitutional guarantee of equal civil rights for all men. Ideas about the unlettered were not new, although the presumption that all were free to instruct themselves rendered ignorance a choice that might leave one unfit for full citizenship. This logic reinforced the doubt of many leading Liberals and Conservatives over the continued existence of the jury system and the political voice of illiterate citizens who exercised the constitutional right to petition.[10] It also led letrados to reserve special scorn for *tinterillos* (pettifoggers) who represented illiterate individuals before the law, and for local political bosses whose failure to properly educate themselves left them incapable of

Candelario Obeso. Courtesy of Biblioteca Luis Ángel Arango, Bogotá.

serving as models for the citizenry. This hostility toward the intermediaries for illiterate citizens did not inspire university-trained lawyers to represent plebeian litigants themselves, which would have troubled carefully drawn distinctions between lettered leadership and marginal provincials.[11]

To receive a formal education under these conditions required young Caribbean men to travel and to expend financial or political resources. The Robles family exhausted an inheritance to send their son Luis away from Camarones for primary instruction in Riohacha and then to Cartagena to attend the region's most reputable *colegio*. Candelario Obeso's father, a Mompós lawyer who collaborated with Juan José Nieto in 1860, tutored his son at home before sending him to colegio, only to return him to private tutors after armies occupied the school as a makeshift barracks during the civil war.[12] Private instruction offered the youths advanced literacy in Romance languages and the ability to interpret a range of written works—a far cry from Caribbean democratic societies that started Sunday schools to teach basic literacy or the "labouring classes" that relied on Protestant missionaries who "secured for the children and poor artisans that gratuitous instruction." Along with creating cultural distinctions from the unlettered

Luis A. Robles. Courtesy of Biblioteca Luis Ángel Arango, Bogotá.

and semilettered majority, colegios and tutors afforded Robles and Obeso access to learned men with ties to partisan politics beyond the coast.[13]

Divergences in the two men's postsecondary careers reflected personal circumstances and the influence of broader political changes under the Rionegro Constitution. After finishing colegio in Cartagena, Robles was sent to Bogotá to study under leading jurist Manuel Ancízar and received a law degree from the private Universidad del Rosario in 1872. Eugenio Obeso used his Liberal Party ties to obtain a scholarship for his son to attend Mosquera's Colegio Militar in Bogotá. The civilian coup that removed Mosquera from the presidency in May 1867 and closed the Colegio Militar compelled Candelario Obeso to continue his studies in the newly established public National University. His command of oratory and political contacts on occasion led to public speaking engagements, including his address before a crowd of thousands gathered in Bogotá's Plaza Bolívar during one 20 July Independence Day celebration. Obeso eventually left university before earning a degree, perhaps due to lack of personal funds, yet like Robles he had enhanced his classical and legal training, expanded his connections to Bogotá officials, and learned a valuable lesson about the vagaries of patronage.[14]

Financial straits did not impede Obeso from careers in education and civil administration, which underscored his intellectual capacities and continuing relationship to influential men. After leaving university, Obeso returned to the Caribbean coast to teach in a rural school, a typical role for a lettered provincial. His lack of university credentials was no hindrance to employment, given the abolition of prerequisites for the teaching profession in the 1850s reforms and the extent of his formal training, which distinguished him as the area's most learned individual. While on the coast, he received an appointment from President Manuel Murillo Toro as national interpreter in Panama, where his knowledge of English and French proved invaluable.[15] In the early 1870s, Obeso returned to Bogotá to begin his literary career in earnest, surviving off government contracts attained through university connections. His primary civil service position during the second Murillo presidency was instructor of the National Guard, which had him "Turning the barracks into lyceums / And teaching knowledge to your soldiers." Part of that knowledge included the *Republican Catechism for Popular Instruction*, penned shortly after the civil war, which conveyed constitutional rights in homilies and plainspoken language. By translating his received learning for men of the laboring classes, Obeso reinserted himself into the capital's academic circles, if through a decidedly low-status position.[16]

The years around Obeso's peripatetic teaching experiences coincided with the 1870 Organic Decree on Public Instruction, the era's most important change in educational policy. The Organic Decree annulled the double freedom of learning by making education universal and compulsory for all children ages six to fourteen, a measure explicitly designed to "form men sound in body and spirit, decent and capable of being citizens and magistrates of a free and republican society."[17] One of its explicit directives related to citizenship, and a leading impetus for literacy instruction was to form future citizens capable of serving as jurors. "The jury being one of the most effective guarantees of civil liberty and public security, the teachers will instruct their students continually over the practice of this institution, making them understand the attributes of justice, the magnitude of the duties of judges, and the moral responsibility that they wield." Although it set no deadline for achieving these goals, the Organic Decree did reestablish after a twenty-year hiatus national funding for primary schools, quintupling education spending in 1870 alone and quadrupling it again over the next decade. It also created a bureaucracy to set learning standards and appoint functionaries to the individual states, which along with commercial and transportation labor policies produced the farthest-reaching efforts of state centralization during the federalist era.[18]

The Organic Decree had demonstrable effects, and guided by the democratic ethos against discrimination, it provided learning to many middling and poor children, especially girls. By 1875, numerous villages and towns had opened their first schools, cities expanded their educational opportunities, and national primary enrollments tripled to nearly 80,000 students, representing roughly 2 percent of the population. By definition, the free public primary schools served families with few financial means, either in bereft rural districts or cities that hosted only exclusive colegios. The reform also authorized the government to confiscate certain private academies to serve as tuition-free institutions with open admissions, whereby some formerly selective secondary schools began to enroll children of color for the first time.[19] In absolute and relative terms, female students from all backgrounds gained the most from the Organic Decree's egalitarian framework. No longer limited to private tutors, female students in schools increased in number from fewer than 2,000 in 1869 to more than 30,000 by the early 1880s, or roughly 35 percent of the national student body. The growth of institutions instructing girls followed this trend. Although matriculation rates did not reach parity under the decree, the new focus on teaching children regardless of color or sex instantiated the reform's universal and democratic objectives.[20]

The goal of a secular and literate citizenry signaled liberal ideals, yet the new teaching standards managed from Bogotá required provincial students to emulate refined learning and civility. The Organic Decree mandated that school directors "make the greatest efforts to elevate the moral sentiments of the children and youth" and teach "the principles of piety, justice, respect for virtue, love of country, humanity and universal benevolence, tolerance, sobriety, industry and frugality, purity, moderation and temperance," to name just a few. It licensed the General Directory to expel students on scholarship who were not apt for learning, and children could not apply for subventions without official documentation of "good moral conduct."[21] The expectation that students on the social and geographical peripheries would imitate the values of bureaucrats in the national capital transformed Samper's adage that letrados were agents of democratic civilization into official policy. The linking of literacy to morality and a presumably measurable aptness for learning, moreover, trumped the proviso against discrimination in school admissions and raised a new extralegal bar for inclusion. Regardless of the democratic intent behind the exceedingly detailed decree, which ran to three times the length of the national constitution, the exclusions based on behavior revealed its drafters' willingness to supersede the same political guarantees they had recently established.[22]

According to the Organic Decree, "purity and correction of language and style" guided this universalizing morality by excluding dialects as expressions of a deficient particularism. The centrality of language in the reform was no accident. Erudite men who demanded linguistic homogeneity in education also monitored their own social world for malapropisms they took as signs of outsider status or a discredited politics or both.[23] Manuel Murillo Toro, twice president of the republic despite his humble provincial origins and education, endured rumors that he loathed reading, and he was openly mocked in Congress for inelegance with language. Candelario Obeso, as Murillo's client, published attacks on the president's opponents that noted their own imprecision with legal prose. It was within the highbrow language politics of the 1870s that poet, professor, and future national president José Manuel Marroquín demanded remedy for "The speech of the plainsmen / Or that of the lowlanders / Or the Indians or the blacks." This anticipated demolition of vernaculars validated the mandate for universal compulsory instruction as well as national leaders' faraway control of it.[24]

The principal institution for the emulation of refined citizenship was not the primary school itself but the new system of normal training. As an admission of the lack of qualified instructors, the Organic Decree inaugurated teacher preparation programs housed in confiscated church properties in every state and conducted for the national government by professors from Germany.[25] Normal schools instructed poor men and, significantly, poor women from every region, yet to partake in this opportunity for advanced learning and prestige these students, like their future primary school charges, also had to imitate grammatical correctness and civility or else face expulsion for lack of "intelligence, energy, good character, morality, and aspiration."[26] Proper edification and comportment were necessary given normal graduates' social role as local liaisons for letrados, which made them, unlike uneducated political bosses, model citizens and sources of emulation for school children. To enhance the cultured stewardship of the republic, the decree proclaimed each normal school director "the principal official of the District," with his urbanity overruling the authority of local elected leaders on issues of education. And given the reputation of Prussians as preeminent secular nation builders during the Kulturkampf, Colombian reformers were willing to entrust the integrity of their beloved Castilian to foreigners who could scarcely communicate in the idiom.[27]

Bureaucratic growth under the Organic Decree came to define the early career of Luis A. Robles. After receiving his law degree, Robles traveled to Santa Marta to become Magdalena's first director of public instruction,

Table 4.1. Primary Instruction, Nationwide and Coastal States, 1848–1895

	1848		1872		1876	
	Schools	*Enrollment*	*Schools*	*Enrollment*	*Schools*	*Enrollment*
Colombia	474	20,352	1,319	51,946	1,646	79,123
Bolívar	N/A	3,808	119	N/A	67	4,465
Magdalena	N/A	2,501	28	1,028	40	2,479

Sources: Loy, "Modernization and Educational Reform in Colombia," 243, 252, 259; Colombia, *Memoria del Ministro de Instrucción Pública al Congreso* (1881), 51, 81; Colombia, *Informe que el Ministro de Instrucción Pública presenta al Congreso* (1896), xlvi, 214; Ramírez and Salazar, "The Emergence of Education in the Republic of Colombia in the Nineteenth Century," 29, 35, 67.
[1] Enrollment rate for 1894.

an appointment made by President Murillo. As director he opened new schools, organized normal training, collected education statistics, and tried to implement national instructional standards, even when the state's penury and unwillingness to abide certain mandates frustrated his efforts. He continued to promote education after assuming other administrative positions in the state, eventually helping to double the number of primary schools and triple enrollments. By 1875, Magdalena ranked third in terms of new student enrollments behind the much wealthier and more populous states of Antioquia and Cundinamarca, led the republic in matriculation rates for girls, and prevailed as the only state with an equal number schools for each sex. With his help, Robles's birthplace, the seaside hamlet of Camarones, committed its first public school to female instruction.[28]

Robles and Obeso worked in different aspects of education, yet each framed his promotion of popular learning in terms of the lettered consensus. In a report to the Magdalena state assembly on the difficulties in expanding the public system, Robles noted a lack of resources and qualified instructors, but he primarily blamed illiterate parents' resistance to the civilizing force of schooling.[29] And while he taught soldiers how to read, Obeso published opinions that reinforced a similar exclusionary sense of progress. In an 1874 pamphlet intended to influence an ongoing debate over federalism and national intervention in the states, he introduced positivist notions of the perfectibility of humankind and the historical movement away from "barbarization." Obeso went on to argue that the national government's only legitimate role in the federal states was "to establish schools and foment industry to debarbarize the people," a defense of his patrons' views and the Organic Decree, just then beginning to bear results. Like the model citizens in the normal schools, Robles and Obeso

1880		1883		1895	
Schools	Enrollment	Schools	Enrollment	Schools	Enrollment
1,395	80,091	1,297	74,744	1,612	95,498
75	5,241	N/A	N/A	115	6,771
59	2,383	N/A	N/A	91	1,973[1]

advocated education through a commitment to competence and substantiated their public status by imitating the forms of knowledge necessary for maintaining the political order.[30]

Despite the initial enthusiasm among the Liberals, the Organic Decree was soon a dead letter, its demise due in large part to a lack of funds that made primary instruction universal in name only. Student enrollments nationwide peaked at 80,000 between 1876 and 1880, but by 1883 dropped to less than 75,000, and in certain districts fell below rates of schooling at the beginning of the reform. Primary schools nationwide suffered a similar fate, declining in number over the same years by more than 20 percent. The record was more mixed on the coast, where Bolívar closed one-third of its primary schools without a decline in enrollments, while Magdalena under Robles doubled its schools but witnessed a slight decrease in student numbers (see table 4.1). And yet, for all the advances on the coast, at the height of the reform not a single public school existed on the Magdalena River for 100 miles south of Barranquilla.[31] The normal schools fared little better, producing only a miniscule percentage of the national corps of primary teachers, thanks to the myriad difficulties in enrolling students and obtaining finances. By the early 1880s, several professors had returned to Germany, a fatal blow to the training of teachers.[32] The continuing limitations under an ostensibly compulsory regime did end up reproducing one feature of the double freedom it had replaced: the mandate that the majority of families rely on their own means to teach their children.

Violent Conservative opposition also helped stall the Organic Decree even as the party adopted the same civilization-barbarism dichotomy that was Liberal article of faith. Intense hostility from bishops and from the state of Antioquia, as well as the 1876 armed uprising in western

Colombia against compulsory secularization, shuttered many schools and sapped enthusiasm for the reform. At issue was the Conservatives' demand for religious instruction in public institutions, to which the national government under Aquileo Parra consented just days before the uprising, to no avail. This concession only animated Conservatives to seek more church oversight of schools lest "Colombia retrocede . . . to something very similar to barbarism." Religion was not the only point of contention, however. Conservatives also blamed the Organic Decree's "spirit of emulation" in teaching the poor to disrespect women, while the newspaper *El Chino de Bogotá* blared in June 1874 that students "study immorality" and that

> The distinguished families
> Are surrounded by dirt
> When the *mulattoes, Indians, and blacks*
> Form the *aristocracy.*[33]

To fight back against emulation and social equality, dialect-hating poet José Manuel Marroquín and other Conservative grammarians founded the philology-driven Colombian Academy of Language just months after passage of the Organic Decree. Advocacy for language purity allowed them to mock normal students as linguistically deficient and hence unfit to be considered their social peers. "If freedom is kind to them," quipped one poet, "then why do they have to enslave themselves to grammar?" Emboldened by political successes against education reform, Conservatives began touting their party as the standard-bearer of liberty of instruction, freedom of industry, and slave emancipation.[34]

Beyond Bogotá, lettered groups subverted popular instruction by rebuilding elite schooling, in particular for girls. Prominent Caribbean families responded to the state takeover of colegios by secluding their children in new private institutions, whose numbers expanded quickly under the Organic Decree. By 1877, Barranquilla boasted four public secondary institutes but seven colegios, the latter forming a significant branch of Bolívar state's private system of 28 schools with nearly 1,200 students. In Magdalena, the German professor contracted to direct the government-run normal school founded the Catholic, grammatically oriented, and socially exclusive Colegio Ribón in 1881.[35] Secondary education concentrated scarce resources away from basic instruction and reinforced "an inequality for the youth of the state," according to one anonymous critic in Cartagena in 1878, by not being "accessible to the poor classes." Upper-level schooling, moreover, still rarely reached beyond larger towns. Coastal bishops and their supporters, in the name of civilization and women's emancipation, did come to embrace female education, yet private or public colegios continued to teach only the literate few, and with primary school enrollments in decline by 1880, qualified students of either sex from impoverished backgrounds proved more difficult to come by.[36]

Proreform intellectuals lampooned the resistance to secular public education, yet they also embraced the same penchant for the quality of learning adhered to by Conservative grammarians. While the national directorate and its supporters proclaimed the success of normal training, they did not deny a preference for scholarly sophistication or the problems caused by those who lacked it. "The Liberals with the greatest good faith of all have wanted to organize a Government founded on absolute equality of citizens and on the principal of freedom," went one 1878 assessment of the failures of the Organic Decree. "For their part they have done all that was possible to do; but their ideal has been obstructed by the lack of learning in the masses and by the difficulties posed by the Conservatives."[37] An unmentioned but palpable problem in expanding instruction was the concurrent demand for lettered tutelage, which led Liberals in Congress to increase funding for the National University at a much faster pace than for primary schools, and even before the 1876 armed uprising universities were absorbing more than one-third of the entire national budget for education. The channeling of public funds away from primary schools toward higher education followed the reestablishment of private universities in the 1860s, which Liberals had sanctioned despite arguments by radical democrats that these institutions reinforced social inequalities. In approaching instruction as a reflection of their own cultural significance, writers and lawmakers did little to address the ongoing lack of basic learning for the majority of citizens.[38]

Unlike in other nation-building projects of the nineteenth century, Colombian education reformers trumpeted codified written language and disparaged local vernaculars as less a tool for national unification than a means of social distinction. The expectation that plebeian students would emulate literate culture and morality was a function of elite disdain for unlettered cultures, and so long as emulation remained the approved mode of learning, the emphasis on normal training guaranteed that this cultured citizenship would not extend to the majority. Leaders of all factions reacted to the shortfall in universal instruction, moreover, with a new focus on erudition and philology as discernible markers of belonging, which left uneducated citizens subject to a double exclusion based on their illiteracy and a diminished public status that derived from it. Even as universal instruction failed to materialize, contention over its fate had engendered intense debate about the relationship of education to citizenship, with some of its shortcomings attributed to those without direct access to the written word.[39]

THE REPRESENTED FOLK

Letrados deliberated over school reform through a rapidly expanding public sphere that, like education reform, developed as part of the liberal political culture and as an appendage to the lettered republic. Absolute freedom of the press and the abolition of libel, first attempted in the 1850s and finally sanctioned in the 1863 constitution, fueled a publications boom in Bogotá and to a lesser extent in other cities. By the early 1880s, more than 100 periodicals and untold numbers of books, pamphlets, and broadsides circulated amid a population of perhaps a quarter million readers.[40] The print medium proved to deliver little economic independence, and many writers relied on civil service positions for their income. Politically connected men with printing presses such as Medardo Rivas received government contracts for producing official publications, and the Organic Decree offered assistance on this front by authorizing funds for a dozen newspapers dedicated to instruction.[41] The close relationship between journalism and government kept publishing in the hands of perhaps a few hundred individuals. And while newspapers offered varied political viewpoints, there were few signs that their readership expanded in the nineteenth century. To influence law and policy through published debates required a reading ability and level of rhetoric that inhibited participation by individuals without university training, and use of the press for patronage limited access for those without personal or partisan connections.[42]

Press freedom encouraged writers to explore a number of contentious and even taboo subjects, including race. As an analogue to arguments for linguistic purity, published opinion underlined distinctions between white civilization and black barbarism. While Manuel Ancízar's published 1853 travelogue had simply condemned the black family of the Magdalena Valley as living "in an indecisive state between civilization and barbarism," José María Samper offered a more convoluted defense of racial hierarchy.[43] In his highly regarded 1861 *Essay on Political Revolutions*, the stalwart abolitionist of the early 1850s defended slavery, despite its unfortunate legacy of black demographic expansion. The growth of the black masses was due to a "fecundity" that ensued "when intelligence and morality are depressed . . . as with all the barbarous races." Race mixing had not solved this problem as Samper had once hoped but had produced instead "mulattoes who are of the habit of making revolutions, or at least they find support among them." In Samper's opinion, the "mulatto is turbulent because he is mulatto," not because of racial discrimination but because he lacked "the double break of education and well-consolidated interests." To the extent that mulattoes were a positive social force it was by way of "moral qualities infinitely more white than black." Manuel María Madiedo reiterated Samper's universalizing scheme of white civilization by demanding that people of color give up their "racial pride" and join with white people "of recognizably superior origin."[44]

The ethos against discrimination enabled authors to promulgate antiblack statements so long as they followed rules of etiquette that forbade mention of public individuals. In his 1871 textbook, Cartagena colegio rector D. H. Araújo described his Caribbean contemporaries with unreconstructed colonial caste terminology (*mulato*, *negro*, *zambo*, but also *tercerón*, *cuaterón*) yet claimed that "reason and justice universally reject [these categories]: under a republican system virtue alone has titles: the Constitution guarantees to all equality of rights without distinction of classes." Araújo's textbook taught children both the outmoded language of racial hierarchy and the emancipation-era dictate against regard for distinctions between citizens, in effect scolding students for the racial prejudice they learned from his textbook. Such an apology was perhaps a necessary rationalization for Araújo, Samper, Madiedo, and others to be able to write about people of color as a problem while simultaneously celebrating Colombia's civilized democracy. The sociological pretext of their writing also highlighted a disjunction between blanket ascriptions of nameless collectivities and silence with regard to the race or color of named living individuals. Letrados became enthusiastic proponents of this racial etiquette because it confirmed their position as stewards of the law. For lettered men, public standing presupposed literacy, and universal guarantees of rights without distinction belonged to those with the reason and justice to comprehend those rights.[45]

The consensus over how to address race in print shaped opinion throughout the public sphere. Some editors did banish racist language from their newspapers, and on rare occasions Bogotá artisans and other political outsiders criticized the upper classes for racial discrimination. Otherwise, Araújo's logic of promoting racial etiquette and the democratic ethos while adhering to white superiority prevailed.[46] This logic framed the era's debates over proposals to bring to Colombia slaves freed during the U.S. civil war. Some Colombian writers responded positively to colonization because African Americans would be "equal to citizens of the country in personal and real rights without difference or restriction of any kind." Publicists advanced colonization during the more democratic political climate of the 1860s presidential administrations of Mosquera and Murillo, yet this seemingly inclusive project, which was never pursued, perpetuated black marginality by proposing to seclude refugees on the Caribbean coast and Magdalena Valley. The idea of settling tens of thousands of people of African descent in Bogotá was not considered.[47]

A free press that affirmed narrow ideas of civilization created openings for the opinions of some privileged but otherwise marginalized individuals. The career of feminist Soledad Acosta de Samper was a case in point. As a prolific writer, newspaper publisher, and foremost advocate for girls' education, Acosta demanded a place for learned women in national discussions in part by comparing their subordination to that of blacks.[48] More fundamentally, in several publications Acosta contrasted white women's progress to the unchanging and ruinous nature of men of color. In "Mercedes," the female protagonist is seduced by the mulatto Santiago, a freed slave from the lowlands who has inherited his dead master's property and now seeks status by marrying into a respectable Bogotá family. Over the objections of her parents, Mercedes weds Santiago, only to discover that he leads a drunken, dissipated life that leaves her "the slave of the master of the house." With the theme of impossible love between whites and blacks came an even bleaker message of the diametrically opposed struggles of white women and men of African descent.[49] Acosta returned repeatedly to this message with stories of black men as abject slaves, as traitors in the independence struggle, as "lawless men" who "committed murders in cold blood" during civil wars, and as lazy and unruly bogas. Her erudition constituted a claim to the public sphere, and her oeuvre argued for white women's public status by denying the same to black men.[50]

Racial etiquette among letrados also opened access to the public sphere to the two men from the coast. During the 1870s and early 1880s, Bogotá papers supported Robles in his political campaigns and Obeso in his literary endeavors, an esteem that, as with Soledad Acosta de Samper, presumed their high scholarly attainments and emulation of accepted cultural standards. Unlike Acosta, whose gender was both unavoidable (when not veiled by pseudonyms) and central to her political positions, the public stature of Robles and Obeso dictated that editors disregard mention of their color, even as they filled their periodicals with antiblack and anti-Caribbean screeds. The same issues of *El Relator* that included positive reports on Robles also ran editor Felipe Pérez's attacks on former slaves, bogas, and other people of African descent. *El Elector Popular* similarly published articles on black Caribbean degeneracy alongside encouragements of Robles in his Magdalena political career.[51] Obeso also received sponsorship from editor Manuel María Madiedo, who was concurrently formulating his arguments for white civilization, and Adriano Páez published Obeso's work while inveighing against Caribbean citizens who "vegetate in poverty and darkness, and while you enjoy political liberties and live under the Republic, you are still slaves of ignorance and superstition." The standing of these letrados of color entitled them to be publicly identified as individuals of merit free from any association with race, a freedom that separated them from illiterate populations still tainted by blackness.[52]

The main literary genre mediating the gulf between overeducated minority and unlettered majority was *costumbrismo*. Through costumbrismo, whose popularity rose in conjunction with print culture, writers crafted moralistic and self-consciously national prose that fictionalized ordinary life of various social classes and regions, beginning with the Magdalena River boga.[53] "His defects are for the most part inherent in the race from which he originates and the climate in which he lives," opined lawyer Rufino Cuervo in one of the genre's formative texts. "Superstitious like the Spaniard and pugnacious like the African . . . without education, without family, because the boga almost never knows his father, he is an isolated being, ignorant, careless, and full of bad habits." Cuervo's oft-republished 1840 sketch inspired subsequent depictions of boatmen by Eugenio Díaz Castro (*Manuela*, 1858), Jorge Isaacs (*María*, 1867), and Manuel María Madiedo (*Nuestro siglo XIX*, 1868), as well as those in the writings of José María Samper, Felipe Pérez, José Manuel Marroquín, and many others. The influence of Cuervo's portrait reached even into governmental labor and commercial policies.[54] Those who followed Cuervo's literary pursuits found outlets for their writing in numerous weekly newspapers and book anthologies, many of them joint efforts by Conservatives and Liberals. In publications and salon readings, costumbrista writers adumbrated social types (*tipos*) to represent Colombia—the impoverished artisan, the acculturated Indian, the bootlegger—even as Magdalena bogas provided the sine qua non of nationalist literature for decades. The paradoxical power of racial etiquette in defining the possibilities of recognition meant that letrados, who over the decades wrote scores of stories about their experiences on the river living for months at a time in close quarters with the bogas, never once published the name of an actual boatman.[55]

Representations of tipos validated lettered culture in part by translating local speech into standard written Castilian. Unlike the contemporaneous vogue of dialect literature in other American contexts, Colombian authors depicted vernacular language in only the most attenuated form.[56] The black slaves in Isaacs's *María* speak in refined Castilian, and dialect makes only an occasional appearance through interpolated text. In *Manuela*, characters also speak through orthographically standardized dialogue, although Díaz Castro identified and mocked provincials by inserting "*ñor*" as a bastardized democratic honorific, a device that Isaacs adopted for *María*, as did others for their own depictions of local life.[57] The numerous costumbrista sketches of bogas contained the most developed plebeian speech in print, while even these interludes reduced it to linguistic minima that signaled the boatmen's lack of formal learning without letting cultural difference overwhelm fine writing. If costumbrismo did not annihilate popular voices, as wished by the conservative founders of the Academy of Language, the genre did render these voices eminently legible. It was this legibility that provided authors with a claim to stand as interpreters of folk culture for a national readership.[58]

Whether fictional characters spoke in a vernacular or standard tongue, the enhanced authenticity of their folk status led authors to articulate political views through their voices. Much like contemporaneous publications from Puerto Rico's creoles, whose *jíbaro* masquerades adorned nationalist polemics with the invented speech of the island's rustics, costumbrismo writers fashioned illiterate tipos as mouthpieces.[59] Eugenio Díaz Castro perfected this technique in *Manuela* through lowland characters who verbalize jeremiads against liberal democracy and provincial politics. In one scene, the wizened muleteer *ñor* Dimas derides the young Bogotá lawyer Demóstenes for his naive faith in republican equality. Later in the novel, Demóstenes listens in horror as a "black woman" describes the brutal work on a plantation owned by a "captain, who was a black man of the most severe kind, who seemed very much a friend of slavery, because he wanted to treat everyone as slaves."[60] Tales of bogas followed this mold with characters that verbally mock the pretensions of letrados even as their speech reinforces the pervasive image of boatmen's extreme ignorance. Later writers addressed specific policies, and in the 1870s costumbrista peasants, parish priests, and caciques criticized German normal professors and the Organic Decree. Unsigned newspaper columns of the era invented black dialect to attack political rivals over issues of free trade, public finances, and education.[61]

By engaging each other in political debates by way of fictional characters from marginal groups, speaking for the people by sometimes speaking as the people, letrados forged a lettered republic through social difference and cultural hierarchy. Unlike their Antillean counterparts, Colombian authors attempted not authentic portrayals of the folk but sketches whose very superficiality authenticated their own public role based on distance from and ambivalence toward provincial oral cultures. These practices took root in costumbrismo's presumption that persistent illiteracy was a defect that prevented its sufferers from any active participation in public on their own behalf. Widespread ambivalence led university-educated men to switch between reforming legal codes and writing depictions of provincials who were incapable of enacting those codes. The defect of illiteracy that prevented competence over the law and denied its sufferers public standing, moreover, licensed racialized representations of the folk. Or in the dichotomy laid out by Conservative Manuel Briceño in 1878, "The educated black man tries to rise up from the prostration of his race; the savage black man is the worst instrument of barbarism." Whether writers condemned illiterate citizens or created them as interlocutors to condemn their literate rivals, rarely did they discuss how the equivocal growth rates in education and literacy continued to produce exclusions at the heart of the public sphere.[62]

POPULAR SONGS AS POLITICAL CRITIQUE

Candelario Obeso chose to stake his literary reputation by challenging not his opponents or their party factions but the lettered republic itself. In *Cantos populares de mi tierra* (1877), he hewed closely to certain costumbrista conventions by depicting an unschooled Caribbean speaker or singer to narrate each poem. Whereas characters in sketches by contemporary writers were rarely more than political mouthpieces, Obeso's narrators are also social actors in the world, individuals who work the land, build homes, make (and break up) families, tell stories, dance, have sex, go off to war. The book's transcendence derives not only, and not mainly, from its portrayal of more believable characters of color but from its wholesale violation of the conventions of white civilization, racial etiquette, and lettered authority. Likewise, by spinning narratives out of imbricated sexual and political metaphors, *Cantos* posited an antiracist republican politics that demanded specific recognition for black men's freedom.

Obeso's challenge to his readers began with verse composed entirely in a Caribbean vernacular, an unprecedented and perilous approach that disrupted distinctions between high and low language. By presenting the "everyday speech and the customs of the people," he countered the typical diminution of dialects and exhibited his skills as a translator.[63] Aware of the likely negative response to this demotic speech, Obeso included introductory remarks to defend his orthography and commissioned the linguistic scholar and former general director of public instruction under the Organic Decree, Venancio G. Manrique, to offer his letrado bona fides. Calling the collection "a kind of poetry entirely new in the country, and perhaps in the Spanish language," which painted "the faithful portrait . . . of the uneducated people of the State of Bolívar," Manrique set out to pre-empt critics who might "admonish the exaggerated form of their expression." Such caveats obscured Obeso's self-referential fashioning of black speech to claim standing for people of color and his own position in the public sphere. One poem, "Cancion der boga ausente" (Song of the Absent Boga), is partially plagiarized from Jorge Isaacs's *María*, a sign that Obeso was not simply transcribing coastal dialect, and that like his contemporaries he represented the folk as his interlocutors in public debate.[64]

Beyond the poetry's challenging form and language, Obeso showcased his political critique by constructing his poems around three distinct social relationships: between men and women of color; between black men and white men; and between a black man and a white woman. Each pairing comprises a dialectic of affection (*cariño*) and sorrows (*pesares, penas*), two conflicting sentiments that reappear throughout the book, in which the speaker/singer demands the former in order to alleviate the latter. When the appropriate affection is not returned, as is the case in many of the poems, black men are threatened with economic insecurity, isolation, coercion, and even death. As the poems unfold the argument becomes clear: proper familial, sexual, and patronage relations must be maintained by individuals and, by extrapolation, by the social order itself, so that men of color might gain a recognized role as full citizens.

The most frequent and fundamental relationship in the poems is that between men and women of color, a kind of domesticity at once familiar and novel that forms the point of reference for understanding the book's subsequent political relationships. Obeso prized the domestic ideal in the opening poem, "Lo palomos" (The Doves), where the animals work toward a common goal by dividing their labors ("Marvel at the decency of being together; / The little straw and leaves for the house / He brings them and she makes it!"). The male then demands sexual exclusivity to the female, and she reciprocates with "an effective sign of affection," in which she "never gives us a wicked grimace." In this and other poems, Obeso proclaimed as desirable women of color—doves stand in for black people throughout the book—and he recognized their beauty as equal to that of white women.[65] Their desirability flowers within their own homes, a circumscription that countered costumbrista stories of women of color as long-suffering servants preyed on by white men, yet it also prioritized black men's sexual prerogative and a division of labor, with female obedience as a primary expectation.[66]

The significance of domesticity is heightened by its failure in subsequent poems, which threatens black men's livelihood and public status. In "Cancion der boga ausente," the boatman sings about an unfaithful woman who, "While I struggle on the sea . . . perhaps she does not remember me." Throughout the collection physical absence and exile arise from an inability to establish appropriate relationships—in the case of the boga, due to the infidelity of the "*negra* of my life"—although the man's desire for *cariño* depends on a woman not for sentimental or sexual reasons alone.[67] Obeso's domestic ideal captured the efforts of Caribbean families to maintain independent livelihoods free from outside control, and his poetic households share the labor as if to reject invectives against lazy bogas or black men living off the earnings of black women. "Cancion" and other poems may have also been direct rejoinders to diatribes published in the mid-1870s by Liberals like journalist Felipe Pérez and education reformer Enrique Cortés, who portrayed vice-ridden and ignorant Magdalena boatmen as "animal life" to explain Colombia's failure to become a republic of laws.[68] In response, Obeso offered a reflection on republican manhood in which male heads of household assert their status as equals, which nullified his contemporaries' racial and class determinism. Still, such assertions shifted the onus to women of color, whose subordination in the poems forms a precondition for masculine independence.[69]

Closely shadowing heterosexual domesticity in the poems is the relationship between black men and white male leaders, a bond originating in some idealized patronage but whose unfavorable manifestations are imminently contestable. In "Epresion re mi Amitá" (Expression of my Friendship), "a poor black man" and foot soldier in an impending war offers to sacrifice himself "for a handsome Liberal, / And moreover beautifully educated," but then abruptly dispenses with praise and hails the letrado ("Listen to me, white man") in order to set out the terms under which he will fight:

I have regard for none
But two things, to wit:
My beloved woman and my free will.
Of her, not even to God Eternal
Would I give a single little piece;
Of the latter I am of the habit

Of surrendering a little to any friend;
Though never ever by force
Because I am my own king.

Having established his sovereignty as a head of household, the black man can demand that military service be voluntary—even a form of entitlement, perhaps—and that the white leader return an appropriate amount of *cariño*. "Very rare was the person," he tells the letrado, "to whom I gave so much affection!" His status as a free man traverses any feelings of political obligation or fraternal love, and potential sacrifices on his part require a substantive public recognition of multiracial democracy: "In return for my friendship / . . . You should say how citizens / Are black, white, Indian."[70]

"Epresion" and other poems contained autobiographical details that furthered Obeso's ambivalence over military experience for men of color. The poet had served in the national armies during the 1876 Conservative uprising to halt the Organic Decree, fighting alongside Luis A. Robles at Garrapata, and he was still on active duty at the rank of captain when *Cantos* was published.[71] In his 1878 translation of a French-language military manual, he called the conflict a "fecund revolution" for the victorious Liberals, while *Cantos* and subsequent literary works dwelled on the futility of war in general and the "death and terror" of Garrapata in particular.[72] Obeso's disillusionment derived in part from propaganda that circulated during the uprising denigrating foot soldiers as undisciplined looters or simply as "those blacks" in need of a white man's control, and more palpably, from the lack of proper gratitude he had received for his own military service.[73] In response, another interlocutor, the black veteran of "Seranata" (Serenade), ruminates on the senseless death of the battlefield without any apparent gain for men of color:

I know many,
Poor cripples
Who have died of hunger
Next to the handsome ones.

Since his service in arms would result only in more of the same domination, the man refuses to fight again, a decision he grounds in the continuing import of emancipation. "The time of the slaves / Is over," the man states. "Today we are as free / As the white." Ending the destructive political relationships between leaders and men of color, or their literate intermediaries, meant embracing a more robust notion of freedom than that offered by the lettered republic.[74]

Other poems impart similar *pesares* caused by the breakdown of black-white relations, which leave in their stead coercion and the renunciation of public obligations. The peasant speaker of "Canto rel Montará" (Song of the Wild) leads a "solitary life" and refuses to "trade it for the life / Of the *pueblos*." Here Obeso rejects his earlier embrace of civilization by invoking a positive Lockean state of nature, with man's natural rights existing prior and superordinate to the social compact. Much like the veteran of "Seranata," aggravated by "the commotions" of partisan conflict, the peasant's solitude in the wild is the outcome of a conscious political choice to remain independent in the face of illegitimate public force:

Here no one bothers me;
The prefect
And the troops of the commissioner
Live far away.

Whereas he can fend off venomous animals, "If there is something with no known antidote / It is for Government." Without *cariño* to guide black-white relations, official power turned predatory, reduced to armed tax squads and military impressment. This antistatist position resonated with Obeso's *Proposed Law over Public Order* (1874), in which he argued that the best defense for people of color against social domination was a limited state, given the little they gained from actually existing institutions. Unlike the earlier polemic's ideological commitment to lettered civilization and constitutional law, the poem praised the Caribbean traditions of emancipatory flight and rural usufruct as the republic's bulwark against barbarism.[75]

The final relationship in the poems, that between a black man and a white woman, which has long been understood literally as a manifestation of Obeso's proclivity for interracial sex, can be read more significantly as a demand for inclusive citizenship pushed to its metaphorical conclusion. In "Lucha i conquijta" (Struggle and Conquest), a black man seduces a "beautiful white woman," urging her to "come closer and do not fear." Understood as autobiographical, the poem then transcribes Obeso's desire to confront opinions against race mixing and propaganda that smeared black men's military service with allegations of rape and, more generally, to disrupt lettered society's ramified social exclusions. His projection of interracial sex into the public sphere perhaps offered a riposte to the antiblack writings of Soledad Acosta de Samper, whom Obeso had engaged in published debates over the status of women during the early 1870s.[76]

There are clear indications within the poem, however, that the woman symbolizes the republic, whereas her seducer performs the metonymic function as its true political actor. Obeso signified these racialized and gendered allegories through the black man's description of himself, which directly references writing. "Because you see me the skin / The color of ink," he asks, "Perhaps you believe that / My soul is also black?" The lines conflate phenotypic blackness with letrado practice while simultaneously protesting racist ascription—arguing for an essential public role for men of color but seeking to avoid the double consciousness of an essentialized blackness. The speaker wants to join with the object of his desire as the fulfillment of emancipation's ideals, as ink to parchment, as black men to the white nation. At the same time he demands that the republic show respect, for once, by approaching him and accepting him on his own terms.[77]

Read more literally as a real or desired sexual encounter between Obeso and a white woman, "Lucha i conquijta" still functioned as a quasi-autobiographical analogue to the period's national romances, one that subverted the racial and sexual violence that stalked some costumbrista novels. In these contemporary romances, love was supposed to be a "reconciliation" and "amalgamation," a project of nation-building through the depiction of heterosexual unions.[78] Unlike *Manuela* and *María*, in which amalgamation fails to occur, or Conservative opinion in the 1870s that posited race mixing as the cause of racial hatreds, Obeso inverted racial and gender hierarchies in order to portray the black man as civilizer and mixing as an alternative, triumphant vision of democratic national belonging. He similarly discarded the domination and rape of costumbrismo, although he ironically referenced them in the poem's title. He instead allowed that the white woman must come freely and willingly to him, pledging that

> In exchange for your affection,
> I promise you on my life,
> That with my demeanor
> I will never cause you harm.[79]

As a good letrado, Obeso used not physical force but words—notably, still in dialect—in order to seduce the white woman. With the highly anticipated coupling, which is consummated in the poem's final lines, he reworked the national allegory into one based on racial equality and erotic affinity.

Obeso indicated that he was under no illusions as to the likely reception of his proposals and anticipated how his peers might neutralize the critical content and vernacular language of his poems through the power of translation. In "Epropiacion re uno corigos" (Expropriation of Some Codes), the poem at the center of *Cantos*, a Caribbean peasant presents himself before his lawyer patron after having failed to deliver six bound volumes of the eponymous codes. The peasant begins by acknowledging the asymmetries in their relationship, which he nonetheless affirms to be one as fundamental as the domestic ideal:

Each being in the world has,
Apart from one's wife,
Another being that since stronger
Is the support of his life.
. . .
I, white man, I have you;
In you my sorrows
Always found comfort
And quick remedy.[80]

The peasant, however, shows little remorse for absconding with the codes, which he has used as stuffing for the "holes and cracks of my hut." Obeso extended this picaresque ridiculing of the letrado tradition by gently signifying Liberal university professor Manuel Ancízar. "If this [expropriation] seems horrible to you, / I will go right now to Doctor Ancízar," the peasant says to the white man. "He has mountains of paper / If you need paper." This affront to literacy—belittling paper, the law, the written word—is not the result of the peasant's unschooled country ways but is instead a conscious protest against the white lawyer's failure to treat the peasant with respect.[81] The differences between them are transitory, and the white man's power does not sanction his prejudice or annul their equal status:

That deep down the dove
Is equal to the hen. . . .
All that, white man, I will know,
But I will stay the same:
For all the disappointments that I receive
I will always be who I am.

And if the lawyer fails to understand this equality, the peasant intimates his ability and willingness to end lettered rule once and for all.[82]

To emphasize the ease with which the lettered republic withstood vocalized protest, Obeso followed the peasant's warning with "Versión caztisa," a prose translation of "Epropiacion."[83] In essence the white listener's (or reader's) interpretation of the peasant's speech, it is the only poem in the book rendered in this way, and its effect on the message and meaning of the original is devastating. Besides the elimination of Caribbean sayings, this version redacts *branco* (white man), a word that connoted spoken dialect and that lettered Colombians understood as coastal people's (in particular bogas') nondeferential and racial etiquette–defying term for whites.[84] More profoundly, the peasant's criticisms are neutralized through an elegant translation that willfully manipulates their meaning in order to establish him as the problem. Whereas in the original poem the lawyer's racist slights brought "confusion," in the prose version the peasant's attempts at "explaining it . . . have made it more confusing." More-over, the translation produces a more pervasive sense of the elite power of misrecognition, with the peasant's existence now hanging on the whim of white men. Obeso also reasserts the antidemocratic nature of language politics by ironically subtitling the *castiza* version "(Model)," whereas the peasant's spoken verse, the original version, is merely the "(Paraphrase)." The peasant's protest has been nullified, the codes expropriated no longer the written laws but the peasant's words, used to stuff the holes and cracks of the lettered republic.[85]

Cantos can be read strictly for its literary value, and Obeso's "Author's Preface" avers that "the Nations can found a true positive literature" based on popular culture that "will calm the furor of imitation, so sad, that has held back the widening of Hispano-American letters so much." But even this nationalist appeal belied his invention of a regional black vernacular to critique letrado politics while simultaneously showcasing his own authorial merits. Obeso staked his reputation on a rejection of foreign styles and his political standing on an advocacy of multiracial citizenship and black masculine freedom. His readers would not have denied the entangled nature of poetry and politics, since their own oeuvres issued similar public pronouncements through verse. What distinguished *Cantos* from its contemporaries, along with its relentless demotic language, was its call for a more inclusive republic—a "widening" of citizenship—as a precondition for a more authentic national culture.[86]

REMEMBERING AND FORGETTING OBESO

After *Cantos*, Obeso's changing relationship to public writing and to national politics, as well as the many published eulogies after his death in 1884, proved correct his premonition that "expropriation" and willful interpretation could annul critique. With his next project, *Lecturas para ti* (Readings for You, 1878), Obeso proved himself at once more and less willing to compromise with fellow letrados. Written in graceful Castilian, the collection comprises original poems and translations from English,

French, and the Latin Vulgate as demonstrations of his multilingual talents and imitative abilities.[87] His motifs of imitation, formal writing, and translation—the popular songs replaced by readings of foreign literary masters—also responded directly to the slights Obeso had received for *Cantos*. One insult had come in a terse published note whose sole comment about the poetry collection was that it included "a prologue perfectly written by señor Venancio G. Manrique." Antonio José Restrepo had followed with "To Candelario Obeso," a poem that began, "No more songs, no more!" confirming Obeso's expectation of the literati's resistance to the vernacular. His response was the major original verse poem of *Lecturas*, "Sotto voce," which ruminates on the "atrocious scorn that I have endured" for writing in dialect, and whose title suggests an awareness that lowering his voice and changing his tone might gain him the audience he desired.[88]

Obeso may have conformed to prevailing literary standards, but *Lecturas* also issues a more defiant stance against white civilization. After recapitulating his belief in equality and women's public honor as a function of domesticity, he avows that any "disgraces" he received (ostensibly for *Cantos*) had been due to racism and snobbery, not because of any inherent inferiority on his part. If there were social inadequacies, they existed among "our aristocracy . . . sickly and of an ambiguous race. . . . Their endeavor is to be white and *pretty*." Upending racial hierarchies, Obeso asserts, "For me, it is an honor to be black and my ugliness delights me. Human regeneration is in my race. Science has already said this." He then ironizes the Faustian bargain by which public stature required an acceptance of universalizing exclusion: "I was a child and now I am a man. . . . Today I hate the selfishness of the common peoples. . . . I judged the small grand and cursed my fate."[89]

Even as his statements against racism and for black pride would frustrate attempts to pin him with a presumed obsession with upper-class Bogotá women, Obeso went further by gesturing that the woman to whom he dedicated *Lecturas* ("A B—") was the lettered republic itself. The scarce evidence suggests that his desire was not for elite women but for elite men of Bogotá with whom he formed life-long, if fraught, homosocial relations. He had indicated this desire in part by dedicating *Cantos* to more than forty public men, Liberals and Conservatives alike.[90] Like his earlier work, *Lecturas* invokes sexual conquest as a metaphor for literary fame and social inclusion, although Obeso had come to consider himself a better writer than his peers who were now unworthy of *his* love. "You must not follow me," he tells his "sickly" whitish readers. "Wait for me below, at the foot of the mountain." If *Cantos* had demanded recognition for black men like Obeso, *Lecturas* proffered that white men, who were perhaps not really all that white, did not deserve acknowledgment alongside him.[91]

With the three-act *Secundino el zapatero* (Secundino the Cobbler, 1880), Obeso projected an even stronger ambivalence toward the lettered republic and national politics. In the play, Don Secundino attempts to shed his artisan past and lowly upbringing by providing a classical education for his daughter, Aniceta, and by buying a seat for himself in the Senate. His efforts produce only a haughty child mesmerized by European literature and a coterie of liberal philosophy-espousing sycophants who leave him in financial ruin. In the play's climax, Secundino is saved by Félix Tapia, an artisan in love with Aniceta who prevents the family's eviction from their home. The play's ridiculing of letrado politics coincided with the arrival of the Independents, the Liberal faction opposed to many of the commercial, education, and religious policies enacted since the 1850s. Just months before the play was published, the Independents had assumed control of the national government under Cartagena native Rafael Núñez, a one-time deputy of Juan José Nieto and the most influential Caribbean Liberal of the 1870s. The play's bland praise for artisans and its lampooning of free trade and the 1863 Rionegro Constitution fit well with the new political mood in the capital, and Obeso even dedicated the work to Núñez, whom he identified as "so great a teacher. . . . You cried *excelsior!* and held out a generous hand to me."[92]

Secundino responded to political changes while also restating Obeso's criticisms of the self-proclaimed national intelligentsia. The play fashions a kind of countercostumbrismo in which the lives of erudite and aspirant men are held up for scorn, its depictions of drunken and parasitic letrados who "carry a great deal of body stench" appropriating the imagery of innumerable sketches of hard-drinking, foul-smelling bogas.[93] Obeso returned to his critique of the civilization-barbarism dichotomy by depicting the character Facundo's attempts to shed his peasant past through university training, only to have his brutishness reassert itself in his public behavior. In its references to Domingo Sarmiento's portrait of the Argentine tyrant, Obeso's Facundo similarly embodies the struggle between urbanity and the untamed, yet unlike either Sarmiento's work or much of Colombian costumbrismo, the play locates barbarism in the city. Facundo stands in contrast to the artisan Félix, who demonstrates honor not through his occupation—which is unspecified, although possibly alluded to by his surname—but through the unaffected elegance of his writing.[94] With Félix, Obeso restated a belief in the intellectual abilities of common folk as equal if not superior to his own learned peers. And perhaps recalling his old debate with Soledad Acosta de Samper or indicting the Conservative movement against the Organic Decree, which had successfully promoted instruction for girls from privileged backgrounds, Obeso used the play to critique young women's learning as sterile when it engendered social distance from the poor. Given his own dependence on patronage and formal training, this seemed a highly ambiguous message.[95]

The play makes no mention of race, and Obeso's avoidance of his earlier critiques of whiteness and discrimination corresponded to a new vogue for authority in public opinion. By the early 1880s, Conservative, Liberal, and Independent opinion makers had begun to advance challenges against the constitutional principles of federalism, pluralism, and popular suffrage. The new authoritarian view opened the field to many targets. Conservative Sergio Arboleda attacked the "diverse morality" in jurisprudence as the cause of social unrest, while Panamanian letrado Justo Arosemena demonized caciques and argued for contested local elections to be decided by Congress or the Supreme Court.[96] Liberal economist Aníbal Galindo offered more sweeping indictments of the legal and social failures of the same democratic institutions. In the mid-1870s, Galindo had informed the U.S. consul in Bogotá that, although he lacked evidence to support the claim, he was certain Colombia was experiencing an "extraordinary yearly increase in the offenses against life and property, the reason being the impunity with which crime can be committed." He later remarked that the preservation of freedom required social inequality, to be maintained through enhanced forms of political power.[97]

In line with this iteration of elite power, former Liberals Rafael Núñez, José María Samper, and others attempted to make peace with Conservatives. Together they advocated for literacy and authority as overriding the interests of democracy and equality, a view that sanctioned a rethinking of emancipation's democratic ethos.[98] In rejecting the status quo that rendered racial differences invalid in law and public life, this tentative new alliance indicted emancipation (as guided by the Liberals) as a primary social problem. According to Manuel Briceño in 1878, "the liberal party expedited the law that abolished slavery and launched the blacks against their masters, and if it is certain that they cured that cancer in a single blow it is also certain that they unleashed hatred between the two races." The Liberal inheritance was "the savage hatred of the blacks" and "the ignorance of the Indians." Against the failures of that party's stewardship of freedom and racial harmony, some intellectuals began to contemplate a new regime whose basis of citizenship would not be grounded in the emancipation legacy.[99]

Obeso weathered the first years of the new politics by rededicating himself to letrado practice. Throughout the early 1880s, he collaborated with his old apologist, Venancio G. Manrique, to publish manuals for French-, English-, and Italian-language instruction. His good relations with the Núñez administration and Liberals in Congress offered him ongoing access to patronage: a lump-sum payment for his translation services, a clerkship in the Colombian Senate, and a posting to the military command in Panama. In each case he exchanged for a meager livelihood his language abilities, intellectual skills, and social connections—forms of distinction about which he expressed much ambivalence in print. At the same time that he scraped for work, he attempted to make his own writing more palatable to potential readers.[100]

One marked change in Obeso's work during these years was a rising tone of nostalgia, albeit one that continued to argue for a socially inclusive lettered republic. In *Lucha de la vida* (Struggle for Life, 1882), the cash nexus threatens Colombia's high and low cultures, which are portrayed through a multivocality of countless characters from across the social strata and through Latin phrases, popular songs, and street slang.[101] The poem play's main character, Gabriel, searches for meaning in a world of corruption, prostitution, and misery, fatally succumbing to alcohol in the end. As a black poet from Mompós and veteran of the 1876 Battle of Garrapata, Gabriel was an easily recognizable, if once again fictionalized Obeso. Yet Gabriel does not struggle against racial discrimination, which is dismissed early in the play. Not only does he have a casually observed history of romantic liaisons with several white women, but an oblique reference to Luis A. Robles—"That black Minister? He is detestable!"—is uttered as an aside so brusque that it emphasizes the otherwise near total disregard for race in the play. Greed and money, not racial discrimination, produce an insurmountable social bar, and they appear as manifestations of a new morality engulfing the country. *Lucha's* critique of Darwinian commercial capitalism, however, is overshadowed by its paean to a lost liberal bohemia, a sophisticated and hierarchical if still polyglot world that succumbs to the new and more powerful market society. Obeso evoked this self-referential and nostalgic mood through the interpolation of his *Cantos* poem "Cancion der boga ausente," sung by an offstage voice, which when heard by Gabriel induces in him sorrow for his own past.[102]

Obeso's apparent willingness after *Cantos* to write sotto voce achieved mixed results at best. Critics in Colombia and abroad did comment positively on his oeuvre and identified him along with Jorge Isaacs as one of the promising young "standouts" of Colombia's literary culture.[103] Some

Conservatives, however, used his presence in lettered circles to resuscitate the legends of Mosquera's hordes and their alleged rampage in Bogotá during the civil war. One sketch published in 1883 laments the undesirable types of a plebeian district of Bogotá who were serenaded by "the popular verses sung in time with an awful guitar, by an almost indigent mulatto, a precious . . . relic of the conquering armies of 18 July [1861]." Readers of the sketch may have recognized the references to Obeso, his *Cantos*, and the patronage of Mosquera that had originally brought him to the national capital. Reduced to a costumbrista caricature, one that preserved etiquette by not mentioning names, Obeso became a cipher for the political opposition and a symbol for the Liberal Party's decline. Instead of the vibrant intellectual who continued to reflect on his relationship to public life, the sketch portrayed him as a social isolate, racial outsider, and holdover from an old political crime.[104]

Candelario Obeso's death in July 1884 by self-inflicted gunshot wound led to a flurry of commemorations from a bipartisan clique of eulogists that reinforced his image as an outsider. In noting his military service, many writers recalled him as a lieutenant or sergeant major, and none correctly noted that he had attained the rank of captain. Several described him as having lived in perpetual poverty and financially dependent on prominent men, and when loaned money to retire outstanding debts appeared "almost white." Others claimed he was a drunkard.[105] Having never been accused of improper comportment in life, Obeso's death exposed his reputation to idiosyncrasies that painted him as a pathetic outcast. Editors anthologized "Cancion der boga ausente," whose imagery of loneliness added pathos to their eulogies and transformed his critique of the limits of citizenship into an allusion to suicide.[106]

Many of the same eulogists ascribed to Obeso an inescapable blackness and self-hatred as explanation for his pathetic nature and early demise. José María Rivas Groot did not refer to him by his full name and repeatedly called him simply "el negro," and he reiterated the message of the 1883 costumbrista sketch that linked the poet to the racist legend of the Liberal soldiers of 1861. Another eulogist called him his "beloved black" and compared him to a manumitted slave. One newspaper editor identified him as a former boga.[107] Writers accentuated their racial ascriptions by claiming Obeso had harbored a complex about his color. This mythical self-hatred, which Obeso himself had anticipated in his critiques of double consciousness, was most strongly evoked by Juan de Dios Uribe and Antonio José Restrepo in their copublished 1886 eulogy. Uribe obsessed over the poet's "black body" and "black skin that burned like a bath of fire," and he claimed that Obeso "viewed sadly his skin in hours of anguish" as his "disgrace." The poet Restrepo, who years earlier had demanded that Obeso cease his songs, followed Uribe's fabrications by claiming pride had been his downfall, a pride that was product of the same fixation on color. "He was not of the nobles and masters," Restrepo intoned. "And the comparison of races and colors / Was his constant and accursed punishment." This castiza version of Obeso's work and life willfully interpreted his ideas as the outgrowth of a racial defect that reinforced his posthumous status as a social outsider.[108]

In their sexualizing of Obeso, moreover, writers reinscribed lettered taboos against race mixing and beliefs about black inferiority that Obeso had spent his career challenging. "My poor friend had the innocent vanity of believing himself very loved by the women," lamented Juan de Dios Uribe in the opening line of his 1886 eulogy, "and this preoccupation occasioned in him the most painful setbacks." His "erotic fantasies" and sexual obsessions involved white women and "marriage projects almost always unlikely." Eulogists did not read the sexual metaphors of Cantos as political allegory and instead yoked his writing to autobiography, thus reducing to literalism and personal tragedy the possible interpretations of his work. As Rivas Groot quipped, "Obeso was an Othello without a Desdemona who would love him." He became a tragic negro, tragic because of his blackness and his pathetic attempts to exceed the limits of his color in the arms of white women who rightfully spurned him. By reducing Obeso to sex and race, which would have been an unconscionable act against a living public man, eulogists exposed their ambivalence toward the inclusion of men of color as full members of the republic. The possibility for a broadening of both literary culture and citizenship was denied by a bipartisan group of men who claimed to love Obeso most.[109]

Candelario Obeso's funeral in Bogotá was attended by hundreds of leading Liberals, Independents, and Conservatives who chose the occasion to attempt conciliation at a time of rising partisan hatreds. However heartfelt their grief, one eulogist predicted that memory of Obeso would relegate him to "only rumor from the wings of Oblivion."[110] His forceful reminder to lettered leaders that citizens of color sustained them in power was forgotten, and his writings on freedom were reimagined as self-hatred or as violations of racial and sexual etiquette. Without an alternative mode of public address to foster critique and generate livelihood, Obeso depended on the same political and publishing relations as other university-trained men, some of whom controlled his posthumous reputation. Obeso had earned public esteem, but commemorations revealed the provisional nature of his acceptance. Factions opposed to compulsory primary education were at the time of his death wielding new influence in national affairs, which cast doubt over the likelihood that individuals from similar backgrounds would follow Obeso and Robles into the lettered republic. Instead, it was the citizenry of Obeso's Caribbean land, far removed from that rarified social world, who attempted to sustain the country's increasingly fragmented political cultures.

CHAPTER FIVE

The Rise and Fall of Popular Politics

After a day out drinking in late October 1874, Étienne Cassez arrived at his home in the coastal tobacco province of El Carmen only to be arrested by the district alcalde, taken to the municipal jail, and placed in the stocks. Upon his release Cassez fled to Barranquilla, where he reported the incident to the French consul, whose formal complaint to national and Bolívar state officials prompted Alcalde Ignacio Mendoza's summary removal from office and initiated an investigation into the incident. The investigative commission recorded testimonials about the episode from merchants, farmers, and day laborers, including one tobacco grower who confided that Cassez was a "provocative and perverse drunkard," who, if not for the graciousness of the pueblo, "would have been taught a lesson long before now." Others clarified that the Frenchman had been arrested not for drunkenness but for assault, which directed investigators to a deposition previously taken from the victim, an illiterate laborer named Casimir Valencia. The deposition asserted that Étienne Cassez, "completely intoxicated on liquor," had attacked Señor Valencia, "and that according to what was expressed, when he was carrying out the beating, did it only because Valencia was black." Valencia and two eyewitnesses had then reported the racist attack to the alcalde, instigating the lesson from which the pueblo had restrained itself for so long.[1]

The fragmentary records do not divulge the outcome of the investigation or what became of Étienne Cassez, Ignacio Mendoza, and Casimir Valencia, but they do evince something of the politics of a Caribbean community at the height of the Rionegro constitutional era. Alcalde Mendoza had etched the local boundaries of belonging by punishing a "perverse" foreigner, and perhaps aware of where his power lay, he had taken action based on the word of unlettered men whom official documents accorded the same title of respect as literate merchants. The alcalde had also meted out justice in the name of fighting racial discrimination and in doing so, notably, had violated etiquette by publicly identifying a citizen by color. If Mendoza's hand in producing Valencia's deposition led its veracity to be questioned, he nevertheless justified official action through the will of the populace. Local determinations, however, had not ensured the alcalde's position in the eyes of political superiors, and the events in El Carmen demonstrated how authority established in the name of the people was easily undone by competing sources of rule.

The milieu of the Cassez incident contrasted with the lettered republic and the commercial sphere, as Caribbean citizens joined civic cultures that nurtured many emancipation-era popular practices. Unlike the exclusions built into national law and letters or the expanding state coercion to enforce industrial freedom, coastal politics in the two decades after passage of the postwar Rionegro Constitution in 1863 offered citizens opportunities to demand and receive representation, validation, and on occasions, material concessions. Public life developed boisterous and even violent procedures—what Candelario Obeso called "commotions"—that provoked national costumbrista writers to depict ungovernable pueblos or the provincial death of citizenship. Contrary to these fictionalized versions of local politics, however, actual bosses like Ignacio Mendoza did not control all aspects of civil affairs, and at times plebeian citizens pushed them toward more substantive and responsive forms of recognition. Throughout the 1860s and 1870s, the coast witnessed tax revolts, land occupations, the parishioner takeover of church parishes, and plebeians' demands for public legitimacy of their families. Many civil and church officials who refused to acknowledge the standing of the local populace met with mass repudiations of their authority.

Yet as the alcalde and other regional leaders also discovered, these commotions contained a generative force that could be channeled toward personal or partisan ends. By the late 1870s, Caribbean cliques led by Luis A. Robles in Magdalena and Rafael Núñez in Bolívar struggled for control of the Liberal Party. This factional rivalry, which occurred amid Liberal supremacy in the region, opened politics to new participants at the same time that it tied the legacy of the 1850s reforms to the party's fate. Ultimately, the particular mix of partisanship and popular politics proved unstable. Caribbean citizens who exacted tangible and intangible gains from their role in public life provoked a growing chorus of national leaders to call for an end to political mobilizations, yet not until coastal Liberal leaders joined with Bogotá letrados did serious prospects appear for countering local movements. With the rise of Rafael Núñez from regional influence to national power in the early 1880s came new challenges to coastal public cultures and the constitutional regime they sustained.[2]

VOTES AND FETES

The popular vote prevailed as a central paradox of Liberal supremacy under the Rionegro Constitution, an era when Magdalena, Bolívar, Panama, the Cauca, and Antioquia retained universal manhood suffrage, while the country's interior highland states repealed voting rights for illiterate and propertyless men. Control of the national executive, which in turn ensured national dominance, required command over a majority of the nine states, each with its own party leadership, rules for the franchise, and political culture. On the coast, Liberals appeared to be in agreement that the benefits of popular suffrage outweighed its perceived drawbacks. Cartagena letrados who opposed "the pure democracy . . . the civil equality" of uneducated men's voting attempted three times in the decade after the civil war to pass literacy restrictions for suffrage, but majorities in the Bolívar state assembly refused them a hearing on each occasion. Faced with similar calls to repeal universal manhood suffrage in order to stop "election frauds," Magdalena's state executive in the early 1870s reminded critics that fraud existed "not due to a defect of the law, but in spite of it." His solution for vote manipulation was a system of ballot counting "in a manner for which the population of the State would be represented with more equality" and for expanded primary instruction under the Organic Decree, to be carried out by the state's new director of schools, Luis A. Robles.[3]

The preservation of the popular vote did not ensure all male citizens a public voice, however. Ruling groups manipulated local administrations to perpetuate their control, mainly through bosses who selected candidates and, as Magdalena's executive admitted, doctored ballots or stuffed election urns. Powerful families aligned with statewide factions ran some small Caribbean towns as personal fiefdoms, like the Palacio clan's four-decade reign over Tubará near Barranquilla, where the populace was typically excluded from any part in civic affairs.[4] Even in the more fractious cities, municipal leaders could dispense with representative government in moments of exigency. After Barranquilla's mayor was assassinated in August 1867, four dozen prominent men, all with ties to national commerce and politics, chose a new executive from their ranks, a decision never submitted to public referendum.[5]

The ability of ruling groups to sway, if not outright rig, elections created a quilt-like pattern of factional control. Notwithstanding one astonished Venezuelan visitor's 1861 report that the Caribbean coast "is not a liberal majority, it is a unanimity," the region hosted multiple political circles. Both locally and nationally, the foremost intra-Liberal rivalry remained the one between lettered civilian Gólgotas and the Mosquera-Nieto popular alliance, commonly referred to after the war as the Radicals and the Nationals, respectively.[6] In the late 1860s and early 1870s, the

Nationals controlled Cartagena, Barranquilla, Lorica, Corozal, Magangué, Mompós, Valledupar, and the "riverside pueblos," while the Radicals held Santa Marta, Sabanalarga, Chinú, and Ciénaga. Party splits at the local level, which at times also reflected commercial competition between towns, reappeared as statewide political cultures, with Bolívar becoming a stronghold of the Mosquera Nationals and Magdalena controlled by Radicals who supported Manuel Murillo Toro. Under the one state–one vote system of choosing national executives, the coastal states cast ballots for rival presidential candidates in the 1869 and 1875 elections, as they had in 1857.[7] While at times Liberal leaders divvied up assembly seats and state posts, factional antagonism was so great that the region's Mosquera supporters, like their national counterparts, would occasionally back unelected Conservative mayors rather than permit Radical "imposters" to assume control of municipalities.[8]

In Cartagena, Liberal unanimity bolstered the dominant prewar faction and the rising star of Rafael Núñez. As a native of the city, Núñez had advocated for the local democratic societies, slave emancipation, and the presidential candidacy of José Hilario López, which earned him positions as secretary to Governors José María Obando and Juan José Nieto and his own brief tenure as governor after the defeat of José María Melo in 1854. At entering national politics through election to Congress, Núñez displayed an uncanny ability to work with all party factions, which led to cabinet posts in the administrations of José María Obando, Manuel M. Mallarino, and Tomás C. Mosquera. It was as Mosquera's secretary of the treasury that Núñez, then an adherent to federalism, laissez-faire, and secularization, carried out the state expropriation of church properties at the end of the civil war. Soon after serving as a delegate to the Rionegro convention in 1863, he departed Colombia for a decade in the United States and Europe as a diplomat and expatriate letrado, although his influence in Bolívar state politics remained strong even in his absence.[9]

With elections rarely competitive where leaders like Núñez exerted control, enfranchised men and wider nonvoting communities steeped partisan politics with meaning through festivity and debate. Street parades, fireworks, and orations by politicians, female students, and even children transformed older traditions of democratic spectacle into demonstrative Liberal partisanship.[10] Civic engagement in Cartagena and Barranquilla was a facet of city affairs for "all social classes" in which receptions for visiting dignitaries and funerals of prominent locals were attended by thousands. One memoirist similarly recalled 1870s Santa Marta, where "men and women of different social classes, including women cooks and servants, discussed the laws, things, and persons" of public life.[11] The circulation of peasants, bogas, artisans, ranchers, and merchants between hinterland and town fostered even more social mixing in urban marketplaces or streets. Little if any of this was an innovation of the post-1863 constitutional order; López-era democratic societies and manumission ceremonies had harnessed much the same popular energy. What changed was the civil war's consolidation of the political parties and, for the coast, the preservation of manhood suffrage and frequent voting days throughout the year, which obliged party officials to mingle with unlettered citizens in elections they engineered as a refraction of the public culture.[12] In all but the few Conservative coastal towns, this culture of controlled popular electioneering ensured a Liberal consensus as a building block of party supremacy for two decades under the Rionegro charter.[13]

Perhaps not wanting to leave voting outcomes to chance, local ruling groups frequently mobilized men to resume their role as armed citizens. After the war, martial civic practices continued to embolden some plebeian individuals to enhance their own public visibility by denying guarantees to others, even leading to the use of force against men of higher social rank. On other occasions recruitment reproduced the egalitarian spirit of emancipation, such as the 600-strong peacetime civil militia in early-1860s Barranquilla that mingled merchants, artisans, bogas, and domestic servants "so that the service would be well provided for and the individuals of the rounds would inspire trust."[14] Coastal political practices hence opened access to formally enfranchised (and some nonenfranchised) persons who relied on masculine bravado and fighting skills to control access to the public realm. By enforcing manipulations of the vote or by defending against them, armed citizens exercised the informal right to grant or deny the formal rights of others. This pattern reflected the larger paradox of popular suffrage in the Liberal era, which gave Caribbean party leaders a firm hand over local governments while tempering their ability to exclude broader participation by the public.[15]

By joining in demonstrative Liberal politics, coastal populations sustained new manifestations of emancipation's antiracist ethos. In orations and newspaper editorials reminiscent of the manumission spectacles' messages, politicians, writers, and editors offered democratic or patriotic rhetoric that might resonate with local populations. Mompós native Isaac Ribón proclaimed with his Independence Day "Hymn" in 1869 that Colombia would be a land of "neither slaves nor tyrants." Other Liberals joined Ribón in the attempt to prevent Conservatives from monopolizing the metaphor of political slavery after the war. "A pueblo that only yesterday ceased to be a slave, today counts the most beautiful catalog of public liberties known," proclaimed the organizer of the 1878 Independence Day festivities in Sabanalarga, Bolívar, noting that these liberties did not favor "the privileged classes."[16] Some Liberals offered more explicit encouragement to citizens of color in language that skirted the constraints of racial etiquette. In legislatures and broadsides, party officials promised "the descendants of Ham, populator and civilizer of Africa," that only Liberals guaranteed "the extinction of those hateful distinctions" formerly imposed on "negros, zambos, mulatos," and the like.[17]

In the postwar Liberal hegemony, audiences for these democratic pronouncements injected their own symbolic and vernacular expressions. By far the largest and most enduring popular contribution to the era's festive politics was "those three days of license and madness" during Carnival. Since the 1852 murder of Francisco Carmona in Ciénaga, Caribbean lettered opinion had come to praise Carnival's "popular aspiration to equality and liberty," with "social barriers considerably flattened between rich and poor, masters and footmen, señores and pueblo."[18] Yet not until the codification of Barranquilla's Carnival in the 1860s, when municipal officials and plebeian revelers turned scattered pre-Lenten celebrations into the town's most significant annual event, was this popular aspiration hitched to partisan politics. New city ordinances required that a mayoral proclamation start the festivities and that the title of Carnival president (the honorary king of past years giving way to a republican spirit) be conferred on a local artisan or day laborer. Government endorsement of slave-era *comparsas* and drumming, just then combining with *cumbiamba* dances brought by migrants from the countryside — or by canal diggers abandoning dredging projects in extended leisure strikes — further inflated the event's profane significance.[19]

Popular participation in Liberal politics also changed the complexion of officialdom, as the strategy first developed by Obando and Nieto in Cartagena in 1849 carried over into the Rionegro era. Even as patronage networks safeguarded the more influential public positions for a few educated men from well-connected families, men of color won civil service posts or election as "small politicians" on the coast, in the Cauca, and in other regions.[20] The U.S. consul's claim in 1866 about the multiracial makeup of the Supreme Court and presidential cabinet can be dismissed, yet his general remark that "many mulattoes hold office, also a few negroes and Indians," was seconded by other observers. According to one foreign resident in the early 1880s, individuals from the "intelligent race" of mulattoes "have risen to managing positions in public life."[21] For Colombian writers comfortable with conflating *mulato* with *Liberal* when speaking of the coast, this politics was as much about social class as color. Bogotá's artisans in the 1860s expressed wonder as their Caribbean brethren regularly won seats in state assemblies, and given local demographics, their election meant the de facto inclusion of men of color. This overlap between class and color perhaps explains why in the late 1870s Barranquilla's governor, Julián Ponce, who had served in the same position during emancipation, scandalized his "white" peers by entrusting the organizing of a ceremony in honor of the arrival of French engineer Ferdinand de Lesseps to laborers "who did not give the guarantee of culture."[22]

Yet like Candelario Obeso in lettered circles, in general individuals served in local administrations under a polite silence about race or color. The men and women from impoverished backgrounds who studied in the coastal normal schools and afterward earned teaching posts may have been African-descended, but the prohibition against race as a criterion in governmental policy frustrates attempts to confirm this. Even critics of persistent racial discrimination restrained themselves from discussing specifics. One artisan editorialist accused aristocratic men in the 1860s of abandoning the clergy and military "because their personnel had been much *democratized* . . . having chosen among their officials some men of color," although he did not name these appointees. Foreigners who noted the "negroid" men in power with equal parts fascination and horror similarly passed along these findings as vague anecdotes.[23] For Caribbean Liberals from Nieto onward, this prohibition likely complicated political organizing. Given the ethical constraints, they focused on proclaiming the sanctity of equality or speaking of (if not to) the children of Ham at the same time that they promoted men of color in unacknowledged fashion. Officials who made these connections more explicit, like Barranquilla's Julián Ponce and El Carmen's Ignacio Mendoza, ran the risk of violating the code that penalized public appeals based on race or color as socially divisive and politically invalid.

The paradox of opening politics to citizens of color while disavowing the role of race shaped the career of Luis A. Robles. After his presidential appointment as Magdalena's education director, Robles began a rapid ascent through subsequent administrative posts before entering state and national electoral politics in the 1870s. As he gained influence in lettered Liberal circles, including winning a seat in Congress and being selected as treasury secretary under President Aquileo Parra in 1876, his opponents in the capital charged the Radicals with the nepotistic promotion of an unqualified man, denunciations that focused on his youth but perhaps insinuated race.[24] Robles's identification with civilian politics did not prevent him from volunteering alongside Obeso for military service to fight the 1876 Conservative uprising, during which he was appointed second-in-command of the battalion of the Caribbean coast. While the specifics of his selection are not known, his commission did reproduce the unspoken strategy of recruiting local men by providing them with an officer of color under whom they could fight.[25] After the uprising, the twenty-eight-year-old Robles was elected state executive of Magdalena, a victory assisted by his networks of national letrados and prominent Santa Marta families as well as, perhaps implicitly, popular support from local citizens of color. In becoming the most politically influential Colombian of African descent, Robles buttressed the Radicals' national control, which had been weakened by the 1876 uprising, even as his success personified the more socially inclusive local politics of the Liberal era.[26]

The same rules that dissuaded leaders from acknowledging their enlistment of men of color did not apply to their depictions of rivals in the heat of political battle. Like the antiblack propaganda and rumor of the civil war, the Rionegro era's armed electioneering led polemicists to invoke racist rhetoric in attempts to smear opponents. Rafael Núñez discovered this legacy of the war after his return to Colombia to stand as the National candidate against Radical leader Aquileo Parra in the 1875 presidential race. From his seat in Bolívar, Núñez waged a campaign in the name of popular democracy, claiming to fight a lettered Radical oligarchy that taxed "the poor people more than the rich" and comparing his effort to a rebellion against slaveholders. He also curried support among artisans who joined with him as "men of all races, all beliefs, and all ages."[27] The Bogotá letrados around Parra (his days as a merchant confronting bogas behind him) ridiculed the possibility of a Caribbean president with caricatures of Núñez as a *gamonal* of blacks and the choice of ignorant *costeña* women, reducing the veteran of liberal law and letters to a shady, unmanly Cartagena barrio boss.[28] As partisan leaders recruited armed followers and Caribbean men fought for both factions in the run up to the vote, Radicals published antiblack jokes and circulated rumors about "the black rebels of the coast." Despite the National faction's securing the votes of Bolívar and Panama, their defeat in combat, Radical control of the national government, and the perception that Núñez represented only the coast (and only people of color) prevented him from gaining traction in national balloting, sealing Núñez's image as a marginal provincial leader.[29]

The concentration of the election's armed combat on the coast, and in Magdalena in particular, exposed the paradoxes of the era's popular politics.

Rafael Núñez and Luis A. Robles in neighboring states and opposing factions mobilized workingmen, yet these alliances opened each to rhetorical attack. As Aquileo Parra's main Caribbean ally, Robles led his followers against Núñez supporters among Magdalena's population—a multiclass pluralism on both sides that belied letrado racist insults of the Nationals' political base. The Radicals who deployed antiblack propaganda against enfranchised coastal citizens hailed from Santander, Cundinamarca, and Boyacá, states that had already repealed universal manhood suffrage. Pro-Núñez polemicists, for their part, depicted their opponents as *cachaco* (Bogotano) outsiders "imposing the candidacy of Señor Parra on the pueblos of the coast by means of bayonet" and refused to admit that most Radical combatants were also local men. Both Liberal factions, moreover, relied on wartime Conservative propaganda to portray their opponents as rampaging macheteros for supporting their party in one of the more substantive public roles granted to plebeian men during the Rionegro era.[30]

HAVES AND HAVE-NOTS

Armed with the machetes, ballots, or petitions that so offended letrados, illiterate citizens compelled local officials to respond to their demands for the distribution of resources. The abolition of many taxes after 1850 and the confiscation of most church property after 1860 excited expectations that Liberal governments might sanction some further transfer of wealth, yet subsequent policies tended to be haphazard and politically motivated. When the Mosquera administration abolished the salt tax in 1863, out of concern for poor people's access to the mineral—and despite its constituting one-third of government revenues—some coastal officials followed his lead by exempting laborers from public contributions.[31] As acts of financial grace, these measures were often undone during moments of pressing financial need: Congress revised Mosquera-era price controls on salt on an annual basis, and coastal jurisdictions enacted or abolished taxes on a district-by-district basis, leaving behind a patchwork of levies.[32] Inconsistencies in taxation reached as well to Luis A. Robles as Magdalena's executive in the late 1870s. Robles repealed the stamp taxes required to file legal documents, a reform that expanded access to the courts and stood alongside his promotion of public education as a hallmark of civil inclusion. Yet he also eliminated state-funded public defenders that helped illiterate and poor litigants navigate the legal system. The combination of governmental penury and popular politics did not create an easy route to an equitable distribution of public goods.[33]

If there was a general pattern in these inconsistencies, then merchant and landowner resistance to taxation led administrators to enact a greater number of regressive taxes in piecemeal fashion.[34] Without calculations from the period it is difficult to assess the actual distribution of the tax burden, although anecdotal information reveals the pattern at a local level. In 1870s Barranquilla, shops selling foreign merchandise paid the municipality one peso, market stalls provisioning local produce paid three pesos, and higglers pushing hand-drawn carts paid one peso for a one-time use of public roads.[35] Coastal officials also passed a host of sumptuary taxes that collected fees from card games, cumbiamba dances, and aguardiente in order to boost petty receipts and to correct "the decline of customs of the greater part of the habitants."[36] Outside the towns armed roving tax squads targeted the catches of commercial and subsistence fishermen alike, threatening to burn down the huts and crops of those who refused to pay.[37] Whether these levies added up to a burden above the customary top rate of 10 percent is unknown, although tax codes that compelled generally impoverished rural districts to collect the same fixed amount as cities and towns did lead one governor to note, "the poor have no rights because the poor have no money." Perhaps in part because of these policy measures the Caribbean coast was believed to have the highest tax burden in the country.[38]

The legal category of the deserving poor (*pobre de solemnidad*) distilled the regressive trend in taxation. Citizens who qualified as deserving poor relief gained exemptions from stamped paper and court fees, the financial instruments that enabled officially recognized representation in public and legal affairs. Whereas the national government conferred the most lenient eligibility requirements for poor relief, which expanded during the Mosquera and Murillo administrations of the 1860s, the Liberal-controlled states of the Caribbean coast and the Cauca maintained the highest thresholds for eligibility in the country. Although Bolívar state law protected qualified individuals from state-imposed liability, nonetheless it also allowed litigants, including the state, to contest defendants' tax exemption status. The states may have pleaded insolvency as the justification for these measures, yet they still proved willing to raise financial barriers to legal representation to the same sectors of the population that supported them politically. (Robles's abolition of Magdalena's stamp taxes did not occur until the late 1870s and proved short-lived.) Moreover, the liberality of national eligibility requirements, intended as a model for the states, made little difference to impoverished Caribbean citizens with no direct legal dealings with Bogotá.[39]

Liberal governments that espoused democratic rhetoric and passed regressive taxes exposed the contested meanings of discrimination and equity, which derived in part from an earlier failure to enact a direct progressive income tax, "the most hateful contribution." Since the late 1840s, Manuel Murillo Toro, Juan José Nieto, Rafael Núñez, and other liberal reformers had advocated a generalized system of income tax only to face opposition from wealthy and poor citizens alike.[40] In lieu of a universal measure they had sanctioned a hodgepodge of levies with no agreement over fairness, as revealed in the 1878 Retiro case. In this case, Bolívar's attorney general petitioned the state supreme court to overturn a tax ordinance from the town of Retiro near Magangué that exempted day laborers, bogas, fishermen, and the deserving poor, arguing that the ordinance amounted to "inequality," since it "makes the contribution neither general nor even equitable, because it concedes privileges and distinctions." The obligation to contribute to the state "derived from the condition of citizenship and not from the occupation or profession that we would take up." Unconvinced by the state's arguments, the court ruled that exempting the working poor "does not sin against the guarantee of equality." Yet despite the legal victory for impoverished citizens in Retiro, taxation remained a patchwork, and Liberal state officials had marshaled universalist egalitarian language in attempts to impose a larger financial burden on the poor.[41]

Perhaps due to the financial barriers in access of the courts, plebeian citizens normally took to the public arena to protest arbitrary policies. Coastal fishermen, long impugned by local administrators as tax cheats, led one extended effort to demand exemptions and an end to the boga inspection–like registries and armed tax gangs. Isolated fishing communities might send one of their own to hand signed and unstamped affidavits to officials, while in cities and towns they appeared en masse to present their petitions to elected leaders.[42] On several occasions in the 1870s, fishermen went before Barranquilla's municipal council with petitions to contest the system of imposing multiple fees on the same catch. They argued that "petty capital, then, carries on this industry, and it is directed only by poor persons who are resigned to a meager income," and in invoking the interests of all working people stated that the levy "on the principal food of the greater part of this numerous population . . . does not proceed in agreement with the state of poverty." The protestors may have had in mind national laws that exempted fishermen and other food provisioners from financial obligations, since as the bogas of Calamar had demonstrated and as letrados failed to recognize, illiteracy was no bar to an articulate defense of rights and interests.[43]

When public officials failed to acknowledge petitioners, laboring people could cease to accept their authority by responding with violence or flight. The tax officer for Sabanalarga reported in 1866 that the "greater part of inhabitants seem to be discontented with that tributary system," leading to "inconveniences" in regional rule. Ten years later little had changed, and administrators could only collect revenues in outlying districts by stationing armed squads there. In a sign that they also understood the political rules, crowds appeared on tax days with "recourse to arms in order to intimidate the employees of the revenue collection," prompting some local bosses to forego their official duties to state governments.[44] If confrontation did not discourage tax collectors, plebeian families relied on older traditions of escape into the backlands. In the 1870s, scores of fishermen abandoned their homes in jurisdictions on the Magdalena River to found Nueva Venecia, a community on stilts in the middle of the waters of the Ciénaga Grande. This mass tax evasion by way of migration inspired locals to establish other villages on the same waters, leaving municipal authorities clambering to devise a means to force collections on them.[45]

The general refusal to pay taxes expressed a larger divergence in how Colombians defined citizenship. Some may have conceived taxes as a civic obligation, but the system was roundly contested because of a lack of agreement over their distribution. More important, working people rejected taxation because, unlike the taking up of arms, it was difficult to turn financial support to the state into an entitlement. As communicated through written petitions and mass migrations, the customary right to *not* pay taxes was seen as a duty of citizenship, and individuals who submitted to the abusive tax farming that targeted the poor appeared to renounce their claims to full public standing. Under an arbitrary and violent system that defied law and democratic virtues, their civic obligation was to resist state levies.

For many coastal inhabitants at or near a subsistence existence, the issue of taxation was perhaps secondary to preserving access to lands, waterways, and the livelihoods they sustained. Families outside Cartagena appealed to the public for help when in the late 1870s the state threatened to sell their customary salt-drying beds at El Hatillo, and in the savanna town of Corozal peasants menaced surveyors demarcating boundaries for proposed land auctions.[46] Nor were the cities exempt from property disputes. Barranquilla's *ejidos* (commons) on the floodplain of La Loma had descended into "anarchy," riddled by overlapping claims to title and usufruct, yet peasants and small ranchers joined together in the early 1870s to protest their wholesale adjudication to the Bolívar Railway.[47] On the outskirts of Santa Marta, where cattle rustling on estates had been rampant in the 1860s, peasants invaded the former slave hacienda of San Pedro Alejandrino, where Simón Bolívar had died, destroying irrigation ditches and redirecting water to their lands. Hacendado Manuel Julián de Mier sued the trespassers and won a court settlement in 1871, but they refused to pay restitution and badly wounded de Mier in an ambush that persuaded him to abandon the property to the occupiers.[48] In the same years, smallholders in nearby Gaira occupied the lands of an absentee landlord and former Liberal mayor of Santa Marta, who demanded governmental intervention and received from Luis A. Robles the promise that the peasants would be detained and his property restored to him.[49]

As sporadic occupations hit coastal towns and haciendas, a gathering movement against large landholdings in the lower Magdalena Valley region of Piñon near Calamar threatened to dismantle the property regime altogether. In October 1878, Benigno Ballestas, an old political hand and Rafael Núñez supporter, closed off lands and waters of customary usage on his vast estate. Soon after, a crowd arrived to cut fences, drive off his hired laborers, and burn his house to the ground. The invaders enjoined the fishermen who worked the lagoons to confiscate the launches and to cease paying rents to Ballestas. They then proceeded to the Magdalena River to clog it with felled trees before continuing on to other enclosures. Men and women "armed to resist and to mock authority" followed a common rite of peasant land invasions, arriving at haciendas chanting a "war cry," and "after the triumph they depart[ed] by drum beat and with banners flying, shouting vivas." Despite his political connections Ballestas could do little to stop the protestors, and at the time their reassertion of the common right to use the lands stood.[50]

The concentration of these conflicts in the 1870s was a response to the inconsistencies of Liberal law and governance at a time of new economic retrenchment. After 1874, a trade recession and the collapse of tobacco exports restricted currency circulation, sending more individuals to farming and fishing yet also inducing governments to lean heavily on regressive levies.[51] Many of the coastal tax and land protests in these years took place near cities, where population movements and property accumulations by politically connected families and commercial houses—some of which refused to pay taxes as well—put new pressure on land use. At the same time, proximity to the hubs of civic life afforded protestors access to valuable legal and political information. Some land occupiers perhaps learned that in 1878, as invasions of haciendas near Santa Marta and in the Magdalena Valley were intensifying, Luis A. Robles had secured from

Bogotá the promise of 100,000 hectares of untitled national lands to allocate to foreign immigrants and to the exclusion of citizens of the state. Peasants in Bolívar who could navigate the law may have ascertained that some of their state's edicts privileged foreign ownership, some defended local rights, and one from the Nieto years authorized expropriations of privately held lands for the creation of a new network of ejidos.[52] Other coastal peasants may have been aware of Manuel Murillo Toro's long-standing belief in breaking up large landholdings, a cause taken up during his second presidential administration by Treasury Secretary Salvador Camacho Roldán, or of an 1874 national law Murillo helped pass that defended settlers' rights to till unoccupied lands. The ability of cattle ranchers, land speculators, and influential families to neutralize the impact of pro-smallholder laws, along with financial barriers to adjudicating land disputes, led rural laborers to attempt these extralegal efforts at reapportioning resources.[53]

PRIESTS AND PARISHIONERS

The most significant contest over popular governance on the coast took place outside civil government, where Catholic faithful assumed the right to control the material and spiritual resources of the church. National religious conflicts under the Liberals invigorated this local struggle. President López's expulsion of the Jesuits in 1850, the Obando administration's separation of church and state in 1853, the confiscation of church property after 1860, and the Organic Decree's compulsory secular education fueled anticlericalism in the Caribbean region. In the years of Liberal consolidation over the coast, young lettered men openly mocked sacred practices, soldiers urinated in churches, and crowds physically attacked priests. Congregations in Cartagena, the region's ecclesiastical stronghold, verbally challenged bishops who used their sermons to accuse individual Liberals of heresy.[54] National politics fostered this popular movement even as the region propped up the policies of the national government. Church authority had been thin on the ground locally since colonial times, which made the Caribbean coast the republic's anticlerical sanctuary in the Rionegro era. Presidents Mosquera and Parra imprisoned bishops there in the 1860s and 1870s under the presumption that they had few local supporters who would come to their aid.[55]

Antiecclesiastical actions, which some Liberals justified by noting priestly involvement in partisan politics, did not erode Catholic faith but instead allowed parishioners to introduce vernacular expressions into their public religion. Worshippers transformed the sabbath into "fiesta days" with dancing and "carnival games," diversions often indistinguishable from the festive class mingling during trade fairs or political campaigns.[56] Drummers and *comparsas de diablitos* joined the procession of the sacraments through the streets of Ciénaga without waiting for the priest's approval, and the February pageants of La Candelaria in Cartagena included solemn mass followed by drinking, gambling, flirting, and *cumbiamba* dances.[57] The profane activities of religious crowds reflected certain venerable traditions but also innovations that redounded to the benefit of Liberals. Social mixing broke down the racially stratified religious observances of the colonial era, although not necessarily by creating social harmony. In Cartagena, "religious exaltation" during festivities gave way to frequent brawls between plebeian men of the Chambacú district and their counterparts from the more prestigious San Diego parish. After years of fighting during religious processions, fishermen took over planning for the "noisy festival" of La Candelaria in the 1870s, much to the dismay of Cartagena's lettered Catholics.[58]

These popular expressions were a sign that religious practitioners tied their public faith to the disavowal of social distinctions and the demand for regard from religious authorities. Caribbean Catholics had extended the emancipation ethos to religious disestablishment beginning in the early 1850s, when local democratic societies made simultaneous appeals for the abolition of slavery and church tithing, and when people of color during mass began to occupy pews previously held for the exclusive benefit of leading families.[59] Plebeian parishioners who insisted on receiving public blessings from clergy, moreover, echoed the kinds of relations they had developed in the political arena. In streets and plazas, "waves of people" witnessed the arrival of new clerics or blocked the passage of traveling bishops to demand blessings. They participated in these acts of mutual recognition while rejecting automatic obedience to the church, in particular when bishops admonished them for supporting the Liberals. The abuse heaped on archbishop Pastor Ospina during his passage through Mompós in 1861 may have been a manifestation of anticlericalism or of wartime hatred for his brother's presidential administration, yet for coastal populations his status as a prisoner unable to perform public blessings likely also rendered him unworthy of their pious regard.[60]

Parishioner petitions to religious officials transmitted this sense of popular entitlement over matters of the faith. Of the extant written petitions from the late nineteenth-century Caribbean coast, roughly half are directed not to elected civil leaders but to bishops, many of them sent by artisans, women, or illiterate Catholics requesting official visits to their parishes. Far from rejecting clerical authority, they demanded its local performance.[61] Parishioner petitioning was nourished by early 1850s legal constructions of a quasi-Catholic citizenship, which defined *vecinos católicos* as those who lived and worshipped in parishes and consequently had a right to a voice in parish-level affairs. From this legal scaffolding, however tenuous, Caribbean Catholics pushed for political legitimacy from the church, and given Liberal anticlericalism, some bishops validated popular demands in exchange for parishioner acknowledgement of ecclesiastical authority.[62]

Like tax resisters and militia members, vecinos católicos esteemed entitlements over obligations by withholding contributions from church officials they considered aloof. Freed from mandatory tithing by legal reforms and anticlerical propaganda, churchgoers gave little to the church, inciting Santa Marta's bishop in 1875 to complain that "those who make up the People are impious and have neither faith nor belief in the Religion which they profess," despite full attendance during mass and public festivities. What bishops took as lack of faith Caribbean worshippers expressed by providing material support for their home parishes, as measured by their monetary collections and donations of labor to build local churches.[63] In the mid-1870s, a half-dozen parishes refused to remit tithes to the diocese of Cartagena, and despite their bishop's plea of poverty, they instead retained the funds for the upkeep of local institutions. Many of these parishioners willingly took the communion wafer but refused to pay for what they considered their right to the sacraments.[64]

The challenge to traditional priestly authority also generated local struggles over parish cemeteries. Caribbean populations exploited the municipal takeover of churchyards to create vibrant cultures of midnight burials, Nine-Nights vigils, and celebratory wakes for deceased children—syncretic practices hemispheric in scope that gained new urgency in Colombia as matters of popular citizenship.[65] While many priests accommodated vernacular expressions, like drumming during the ministration of burial rites or even the call to dispense with liturgy altogether, others bitterly complained that parishioners were burying their dead without sacerdotal consent.[66] Some Catholics turned to foreign missionaries, as had families seeking literacy instruction, in order to circumvent exclusions from Catholic cemeteries. In Cartagena in the late 1850s, artisans and day laborers protested their bishop's proclamation that unbaptized children belonged in the potter's field by joining Protestants to build a nondenominational cemetery. Artisans constructing Barranquilla's universal cemetery in 1865 assented to the curate's pleas to erect walls between Catholic graves and those of Protestants and Jews, although, inspired by freemason and Liberal rhetoric or by a new state laws sanctioning local control of cemeteries, they later tore down the partitions.[67]

Many coastal priests in the direct path of this popular movement chose to side with parishioners. Clergy distributed food and clothes to the poor, maintained public processions, and rejuvenated defunct *cofradías*, even paying for them from their own meager government wages, because people demanded them.[68] Bishops who reprimanded priests for dereliction of duty, one of the worst offenses being the failure to preach on Sundays, often exposed sacerdotal accommodation of folk practices. Parish curates disobeyed orders by performing nighttime marriages and baptisms, by allowing dancing in the church, or by refusing to read the bishop's circulars to their congregations.[69] With their ancient privileges abolished and moral authority challenged by freemasons, Protestant missionaries, and their own congregants, many clergy adjusted accordingly. Even the occasional bishop was willing to excuse the priest who had "broken the Canonical laws and precepts of the Prelate" or "abandoned the Church to anarchy" when parishioners had forced him to do so.[70]

Conflicts over tithes or cemeteries were the visible manifestations of new questions over religious inclusion. Foreign Protestant missionaries to the coast who rejoiced at seeing "hundreds of the sons of Columbia who preach [the Gospel] in the streets and in their houses" misconstrued the actions of Caribbean Catholics long used to guiding their own devotion.[71] The church's disestablishment had unlocked a new uncertainty over how to conduct and whom to include in that devotion, and plebeian faithful often answered by sanctioning openness and pluralism in religious practice. Control of parishes promised the validation of expressive cultures or the right to a respectable death, each of which introduced new forms of spiritual and social life. Whether the move to make the church more inclusive was inspired by democratic rhetoric or the historical weakness of the region's hierarchy, it cultivated a sense of lay superiority over religious practice. One foreign visitor noted this sensibility in 1860s Barranquilla, where everyone, rich and poor, ladies and bogas, considered themselves "better Christians than the Priest and the Bishop."[72]

When religious authorities proved intransigent, Caribbean Catholics asserted their understanding of vecino católico citizenship by expelling priests from their parishes. "Much care for religious functions is noted in all the pueblos of the Province; but this cannot be blamed on [Conservative] fanatics," relayed the governor of Mompós in 1867, "because in almost all of the districts and at different times it has been observed that they have made the parish priest depart . . . when it seemed to them that he was very distant from his ministry."[73] This "great disobedience," complained Cartagena's bishop, occurred when parishioners in Simití forced out the priest in 1866. Two years later in Santo Tomás, crowds carried out an expulsion because "a part of the people, if not all, was discontented with the conduct of its priest and principally for the fiestas he called for holy week." After the priest refused to hear their protests, parishioners gathered at his house and threatened him with violent removal, prompting him to abandon the parish and to return only when requested for baptisms.[74] Even if political leaders who lamented these actions did not comprehend how vernacular understandings of *vecindad católica* legitimated expulsions, they could not deny that their party's banishments of the religious orders or armed mobilization to defend secular education only strengthened citizens' say over church affairs.[75]

Parishioners across the coast who wished to establish sovereignty over parishes may have taken inspiration from the upheaval that yielded Barranquilla's San Roque church. In 1852, after the bishop refused to recognize a new congregation to serve the bogas, stevedores, and artisans of the city's waterfront district, town residents headed by the priest Rafael Ruiz built San Roque without authorization, an act of defiance that disturbed elite Catholics nationwide and prompted the parishioners' excommunication.[76] For fifteen years, Ruiz remained a renegade spiritual and political leader, elected to Barranquilla's provincial assembly while still in charge of "this holy parish church, erected by the people, in virtue of the opposition from the . . . Bishop of Cartagena," as he inscribed in baptismal records.[77] Even when Ruiz renounced his insubordination and sought absolution from the ecclesiastical hierarchy in 1867, the thousand-strong congregation rejected diocesan control and pushed Barranquilla into general rebellion. Soon after the priest's departure, frustrated Catholics across the city, encouraged by San Roque's stance, petitioned the Vatican for separation from Cartagena, a plea that was granted in 1873. By founding and maintaining San Roque on their own, parishioners had rearranged the institutional organization of the Caribbean church.[78]

SEX AND RESPECTABILITY

The influence of popular Liberalism on parishioner sovereignty and religious pluralism positioned the coast in the middle of a national debate over marriage and legitimacy. Caribbean Liberals deviated further from the legal customs of other parts of Colombia—already pronounced given the priest expulsions and syncretic folk practices in Catholic observance— by erecting their own traditions around civil marriage and divorce status.[79] Colombians and foreigners alike conjectured that civil marriage in the region promoted racial mixing, and circumstantial evidence may suggest that it did promote some legal unions between people of different social backgrounds. "Negroes are more common, but the mixed compose the great body of the population," reported Protestant missionaries on the coast in the 1850s. "This would seem to indicate a great disparity of morals, but the case is not so bad, as it seems mixed marriages are as common as any other."[80] Legalized divorce only widened the regional variance from the rest of the country. When Congress repealed the right to divorce in 1856, the coastal states along with the state of Santander retained it, which Salvador Camacho Roldán argued was a greater affront to the Catholic hierarchy than the separation of state and church.[81] Yet as Bolívar conservatives discovered in the 1870s, efforts to recriminalize divorce met with the same rebuff from elected majorities that Cartagena letrados experienced in their attempts to overturn universal manhood suffrage.[82]

Caribbean popular customs may have sanctioned the liberalization of marriage and divorce law, even though formalizing unions did not appear of vital interest to many plebeian families. The coast contained some of Colombia's lowest rates of marriage and highest percentages of unbaptized children, with some two-thirds of all offspring born to unwed parents. These free unions may have reflected the region's material poverty or strength of popular sovereignty more than its irreligious sentiments, given the coincident lack of interest in the civil ceremony.[83] Barranquilla witnessed an average of just over fifty-eight civil marriages annually between 1863 and 1880, and in some years church marriages were on par with civil ones—hardly a groundswell of marriage secularization in the most Liberal city in the republic.[84] As Candelario Obeso depicted in his poetry, Caribbean families formed beyond the strictures of civil and ecclesiastical codes altogether, and couples may have inferred that to marry before either state or church meant subordination to norms maintained by lettered officials who frequently questioned the morality of people of color.[85] Still, parishioners used marriage as a weapon against the church by rejecting its authority over the matter when clergy refused to acknowledge them. After priest Rafael Ruiz abandoned Barranquilla in 1867, his former congregants renounced church marriage, a practice that did not resume in San Roque until Santa Marta's bishop offered to grant them the status of legitimate parish in 1881.[86]

The issue of legitimate civil status appeared to matter most in the local marriage debate. Coastal states moved beyond emancipation-era reforms that legalized civil marriage and divorce by establishing a series of constitutional guarantees that plebeian families may have interpreted as legalizing local forms of kinship. The same 1860s Bolívar state codes that sanctioned divorce equality also extended some rights in property and civil standing to cohabitating adults but not to unmarried singles or to women married before the church or state. Buttressing the sense that the codes favored those not formally married was their offering of civil status to children born outside of marriage (*hijos naturales*), who could qualify by "various means," including "extrajudicial recognition of the parents." These guarantees were inclusive in ways granted by neither church nor national state and could benefit the poor as well as those who rejected formal marriage relations for any reason.[87]

In seeking public and hence legal validation of their unions, coastal plebeian families took advantage of the combined effects of dismantled church privileges, civil control of parishes, and liberalized legitimacy laws. After disestablishment, women and men began to bury unbaptized children in parish cemeteries, which flouted clerical authority but also blessed their offspring and the unions that produced them.[88] There also appeared to have been a mass effort by poor women to baptize children from unions not sanctioned by either the church or state. Although data are limited, parish records from Cartagena suggest that unmarried women without male partners began to demand baptisms in greater numbers beginning in the 1850s. Baptism of children born to married parents (*legítimos*) as a share of total baptisms remained unchanged in the three decades before and three decades after 1852 (27.9% and 27.2%, respectively). Baptism of hijos naturales as a share of the total, however, jumped from 57.4 percent to 69.3 percent over the same periods. More significant, baptism of children from female-headed households increased from 25.5 percent to 32.7 percent of the total. Unwed parents had begun to use baptism as the extrajudicial recognition needed for their children's civil standing. Single mothers, moreover, who accounted for a significant rise in the share of baptisms of hijos naturales, compelled embattled parish priests to legitimate their children and households in the years after 1852.[89]

Reeling from the popular onslaught, defenders of the ecclesiastical hierarchy worked to prop up its debilitated status through a campaign against Liberal marriage and divorce. After the 1853 legalization of civil marriage and equal rights in divorce, Conservative opinion conflated both with adultery, fornication, polygamy, and in particular, "criminal concubinage."

According to one polemicist, civil marriage permitted "women of bad life" to assume the status of "legitimate mothers," while it also undermined the civilization-barbarism distinction and the Spanish language itself.[90] The claim to lettered Catholic respectability, which painted Liberals as promoters of sexual deviancy (accusing them, in fact, of the same deviancy for which they censured the bogas), was aimed less at regulating behavior within society than at rebuilding the Catholic hierarchy's own internal patriarchal authority.[91] This reassertion of clerical prerogatives over morality fell in line with Conservative opinion of the 1870s that blamed Liberal policies for illicit social mixing and attempted to conflate a generalized moral illegitimacy with political fallacy.[92]

The anticoncubinage campaign on the coast entailed a new cooperation between the church hierarchy and women from prominent families. In the mid-1870s, as plebeian faithful fought for control of the parishes, the diocese of Cartagena initiated the Society for the Daughters of the Sacred Heart to organize processions, publish prochurch editorials by young women and their mothers, and fight "anticlericalism" on the coast.[93] In return for women's support, bishops and their advocates committed themselves to Catholic education for elite girls and to "woman's emancipation," whose invocation sounded much like their denunciations of civil marriage. With a Catholic women's emancipation, "marriage will replace polygamy," since one "who avoids [Christian] marriage loves idleness or libertinage" that leads to ruin for women's honor.[94] The language of morality validated the sexual mores of lettered Caribbean women, who already consecrated their marriages in the church and stood to lose from the region's brush with illegitimacy. Many of their peers already refused to accept civil marriage and divorce—making an exception for bigamist Rafael Núñez, who married one woman before the law and another in the church—and they construed the existence of these civil guarantees as reducing their status to the level of the pueblo.[95]

As a sign of the continuing power of emancipation's democratic ethos to frame myriad debates, Conservatives paired their anticoncubinage rhetoric with Catholic disavowals of racial discrimination. Even while attacking Liberalism for promoting social mixing, they proclaimed that in their religion "there are no races, privileges, or nations," and that only the universal Christian Church bestowed freedom, justice, and racial equality. According to former slaveholder Sergio Arboleda in 1880, only the clergy could "relieve the indigene of the tribute and the African of slavery, procuring to make them both equal to the white man, through education and the influence of the priest, who, with his educational mission, was the only teacher capable of inculcating them, and many whites as well, with the duties . . . of citizens."[96] To demonstrate their stewardship of the democratic ethos, Catholic letrados joined their brethren on the coast in petitioning the Vatican to grant sainthood status to Pedro Claver, a seventeenth-century Spanish Jesuit who had ministered to "poor blacks" in Cartagena. In promoting Claver, defenders of the church perhaps had learned from Liberal office holders that the political stakes were too high not to make explicit appeals to enfranchised and mobilized Caribbean parishioners. This populist and problack appeal, however, did not supplant bishops' commitment to church-sanctioned marriage as the primary means to moral and social legitimacy.[97]

As prochurch forces gained influence in the 1870s, many lettered Liberals began to embrace a version of the Conservatives' anticoncubinage campaign in their defense of national institutions and norms. The Liberal Party's leading thinkers had long contrasted Andean highland peasant obedience to priestly authority over marriage with the sexual practices of lowland black populations.[98] And after twenty years of Conservative attacks, they attempted to bolster civil marriage by sharpening its legal distinction from unsanctioned cohabitation. Their main instrument in this effort was the 1873 national civil code, which defined the latter as a form of volunteer slavery: the "force or fear . . . sufficient to obligate someone to work without freedom," conditions that rendered null the civil contract in marriage, were not applicable to judgments rendered over "cohabitation between consorts." In the careful wording of the code, the original logic that slave emancipation had embodied a universal freedom as the necessary prerequisite for the establishment of civil marriage could not extend to authorizing other kinds of sexual unions or kinship relations. Along with the boga's labor monopoly, unmarried cohabitation came to be seen as an affront to freedom.[99]

Within a few years of the civil code's ratification, some Radical leaders showed a willingness to align church marriage with state marriage in order to defend both against new guarantees for plebeian citizens. The 1877 law over pensions for men who had served in national armies during the antisecularization uprising the previous year offered payments to veterans' widows who "could not prove that they were married civilly" but who nonetheless "lived matrimonially."[100] President Aquileo Parra, perhaps seeking to avoid new public obligations brought on by recognition of "true concubinage, rejected by social morality," demanded revisions in the law so that widows without state marriage licenses instead had to demonstrate that they had married in the church. Congress ultimately rejected

Parra's conditions, yet the national executive did not offer guarantees of the law's enforcement, and his conflation of civil with religious marriage legitimacy against unmarried cohabitation threatened the standing of many Caribbean and Caucano veterans and their families.[101]

The joining of lettered and religious interests eventually allowed national leaders to wrest control of the marriage issue from coastal legal cultures. In 1870, just eight years after passing state codes, Bolívar legislators overturned equal rights for hijos naturales and, worse, made their restrictions retroactive. From Barranquilla, Liberal leader Julián Ponce tried to reinstate the 1862 civil status for children of plebeian families by pressing for congressional action. In 1880, a bipartisan coalition in the Senate, claiming that "the civil state of persons is simply a mutable condition at the mercy of the legislator," overruled their Caribbean colleagues and endorsed the stripping of rights from Bolívar's unmarried couples and their offspring.[102] Reformers who relied on emancipation's democratic values to frame freedom of religion and marriage status had lost ground. Equal civil standing in marriage, argued Congressman (and boga defender) Ramón Gómez in 1878, derived from the legal fact that the "Constitution makes no distinction of races, and the lawmaker cannot ask anyone if he is white or black in order to permit himself to execute a civil act." Yet defining family legitimacy through priest-conducted marriage, as canon law required, and introducing new legal exclusions in marital status, as letrados had begun to demand, weakened the ethos in its application to sexual unions and families. At the time of the Senate's 1880 decision to uphold Bolívar's overturning of equal rights for hijos naturales, civil marriage remained legal, yet taken together with the Organic Decree's extraconstitutional emphasis on literate citizenship, the new restrictions surrounding marriage status narrowed the public standing of plebeian citizens.[103]

REALIGNMENT AND COLLAPSE

By the late 1870s, few observers of the political scene doubted that Rafael Núñez would again seek the presidency, speculation he encouraged by cultivating his regional base of support and by establishing new national alliances. Two years after his loss to Aquileo Parra in the 1875 election, Núñez won the race for state executive of Bolívar, which boosted his political profile, and from Cartagena, he began to assemble the old civil war leadership. Already endorsed by Tomás C. Mosquera, he then rallied former Nieto lieutenants Antonio González Carazo, Joaquín Riascos, José M. Campo Serrano, Miguel Cotes, and Pablo Arosemena, many of whom had grown disaffected with Liberal policies on religion, secular education, and reduced military spending.[104] Núñez also appealed once more to artisans, going so far as to proclaim them the republic's only legitimate working people, a stance in line with his recent rejection of free trade. In the Cauca and on the Caribbean coast, his campaign vowed to fight for the "oppressed" against Bogotá's political monopoly, which may have struck some as advocacy for local commercial interests and others as a challenge to lettered exclusions in national life.[105] Núñez demonstrated the multivalent meanings if not outright ambiguity of his positions as Bolívar's executive. In Cartagena, he renewed his relations with voters through Independence Day spectacles and by opening the governmental palace to fetes for all citizens, even as he sought to overturn local tax relief for impoverished laborers. He also protested for state sovereignty against the national Supreme Court, which had ruled that Bolívar's granting of local commercial monopolies was unconstitutional because it violated the freedom of industry and labor.[106]

To shore up Núñez's second national campaign, Caribbean Independents (as the successor faction to Mosquera's Nationals came to be known) moved to take over the political machinery of Magdalena controlled by the Radicals under Luis A. Robles. In the combats of 1875, Liberals in the state had defeated the Núñez faction to block his presidential bid. Four years later, however, social and political unrest worked against Robles, who faced a hostile national administration, neighboring Bolívar run by Núñez, and Magdalena's largest town in the hands of former allies now aligned with the Independents.[107] Robles found it difficult to rally supporters outside Santa Marta, where the Independents exploited the disruptions caused by peasant land invasions to arm antigovernment gangs throughout the state. He was also frustrated in his efforts to gather basic financial and military resources by functionaries of the national government on the coast who ceased to recognize his mandate. In June 1879, after more than a year of agitation and threats, militias from Ciénaga and Barranquilla, backed by National Guard troops, encircled the Radicals in Santa Marta and swiftly toppled Robles's government.[108]

Because Robles had been elected by popular vote and still enjoyed widespread backing, the Independents worked to establish their legitimacy with editorials and broadsides that portrayed Núñez as the true champion of justice.[109] While making democratic appeals, they also sealed a pact with local Conservatives, whose unelected representatives helped write a new state constitution and held statewide offices for the first time since the civil war.[110] From exile Robles protested that he alone represented the will of the people, although the moral force of his argument waned as Independents repeated their strategy across the country, overthrowing Radical governments and seeking rapprochement with Conservatives in Panama, Cauca, and other states. By Election Day, Independents dominated seven of the nine state regimes to guarantee Rafael Núñez a presidential victory.[111]

Independents waged a national campaign through armed combat and balloting while at the same time winning over a "defection" of Radicals with deep reservations about popular politics. Núñez supporter Miguel Samper criticized "the preservation of universal suffrage" for giving "the fundamental power of election of rulers to the illiterate masses." His brother, José María Samper, had left the Liberals to join the Conservative Party, where he worked to build support for Núñez.[112] Although Núñez never publicly embraced the antiblack sentiments his new lettered allies had used against him and Caribbean Liberals in the 1875 election, their budding relationship left uncertain the status of plebeian voters. Pro-Núñez opinion on the coast only exacerbated the political ambiguities. In the months before he launched his second presidential bid, Cartagena's *El Porvenir* bemoaned "the history of popular elections in Colombia," questioning whether their failure was due to "race, education, [or] poverty." Years before, *La Palestra* in Mompós had argued that "for a long time the fashionable theme was the expansion of liberties; today nothing is discussed other than peace and order and industry."[113]

These political contradictions followed Núñez to Bogotá, where his 1880–82 presidency created policies that accelerated the centralist and antidemocratic tendencies he had denounced in previous Radical administrations. New import tariffs and a national bank, which antagonized free-trade liberals, were offered in part as a reward for artisan support. He also authorized national intervention in local political, property, and labor relations, thus violating the spirit if not the letter of the Rionegro Constitution.[114] On the religious issue, Núñez pursued reconciliation with the church, tentatively begun by Liberals in the 1870s, which included restoring the legal legitimacy of church marriage, lifting the exile of bishops, and reestablishing formal relations with the Vatican after a twenty-year interruption. And in a secret agreement with the papacy in 1882, he returned the rebel parishes of Barranquilla to the diocese of Cartagena, a deal struck without any input from the parishioners themselves. Pressing for these measures were Conservatives who lauded his prochurch and procentralist measures but who ultimately objected that the administration fell short of its promised fundamental administrative regeneration.[115]

Having lost control of the national and state governments, the remaining Radical Liberals used the press and armed gangs to attack Núñez and the Independents. In their Bogotá newspapers they reverted to the antiblack and anti-*costeño* invectives of the 1875 election, and their published violations of racial etiquette garnered bitter denunciations from the president himself in unsigned editorials.[116] On the coast, militants loyal to Robles accomplished little in an undeclared rebellion against the state governments. In response to armed attacks on officials and civilians, Independents invoked a new law permitting the president to send troops into the states, a measure that struck at the heart of states' sovereignty under Rionegro. During early 1880s elections, National Guard units arrested hundreds of Caribbean workingmen, which effectively suppressed the vote in certain districts. Deposed Radicals in Magdalena found little room to maneuver, and their tactical failures against local Independents were accentuated by lettered Radicals in Bogotá still ambivalent about aligning themselves with provincial citizens who battled to bring them back to power.[117]

As pro-Robles gangs fought with little success in the coastal countryside, Independents and Conservatives insulated themselves in the cities by establishing socially exclusive clubs. Officials in Mompós had censured the plebeian "scenes of families' private life" put on "obscene" display during Carnival in 1878, yet soon afterward prominent locals resolved to withdraw altogether from the annual festivities by hosting their own separate events.[118] In 1879, lettered women in Cartagena rejected the kind of Independence Day fetes Núñez had recently hosted for working people and encouraged their families to retire to private quarters for several soirees commemorating 11 November. That same year, crowds in the city protested the arrival of a new bishop, not because he was a "white man" from Antioquia or a papal reactionary but because the celebrations organized for him by "seven gentlemen" were restricted to leading families. These actions circumvented the widespread blurring of distinctions in social interaction by imposing the lettered republic's exclusions onto local spatial relations. Along with the return of Catholic education under the Organic Decree, the creation of secluded milieus permitted prominent locals to curtail the mixing demanded by citizens in public.[119]

From the new exclusive venues for conducting lettered politics civic leaders entered the public realm with pronouncements demanding political and spiritual authority. In July 1883, Barranquilla's municipal officers entrusted Colombia's largest commemoration of the centenary of Simón Bolívar's birth to private colegios, city merchants, and the diocese, which staged three days of festivities without a semblance of popular representation. For Cartagena's own sizable celebrations, Rafael Núñez himself chose the theme "America is ungovernable," exploiting Bolívar's late-life adage to promote his own drive for a new political order.[120] Barranquilla's mayors in the same years stopped considering Carnival as a time of civic engagement and began augmenting the gendarmerie against the "bacchanals" in hopes of "eradicating the inveterate habits of the uncultured people in order [for Barranquilla] to take a seat among the number of civilized cities." Politicians still ventured into the commotion of the streets to drum up votes, but they mixed their appeals with admonishments to crowds to act with more restraint.[121]

With newfound political confidence under Núñez, commercial interests and large landholders on the coast clamored for a larger share of resources. Local Independent administrations, perhaps responding to popular suffrage or violent protests in the countryside, did perpetuate the older practices of haphazard tax breaks and price controls, especially after locusts devastated crops in the region during 1880–81.[122] Yet with the presidency and the coastal states controlled by the Núñez faction, transportation companies and politically connected merchants stopped paying even taxes that funded public works projects from which they benefited. Despite this tax resistance, in 1882 they won passage of new levies designed as "coercive measures" against champán bogas and as financial relief for steamboat operations. And in Barranquilla, businessmen joined the Bolívar Railroad and the Compañia Unida de Vapores to divide up among themselves once and for all the commons of La Loma.[123] In rural districts of the lower Magdalena Valley and around Mompós, hacendados used the locust infestations to push back against land invasions. Throughout 1882, according to one provincial governor, they armed gangs to carry out "vendettas" against fieldhands and peasant colonizers. As the violence escalated and property holders won victories over antienclosure forces, rural women and children driven off the land appeared in coastal cities begging for food, while men separated from their families and went searching for wage work in Panama.[124]

The Catholic Church and its allies pressed for the greatest gain from Núñez's political victories after 1879. They were already animated by the fight against the Organic Decree and by earlier Liberal concessions, like those from the Parra administration around the 1876 armed uprising and an 1878 law that compelled Barranquilla to relinquish its embattled cemetery to the diocese of Cartagena.[125] Once Núñez began to court the Vatican, coastal bishops discarded the rhetoric of racial harmony and began to block the promotions of priests who did not actively oppose the "spreading public concubinage" of civil marriage. In their attempt to impose discipline on the parishes, they received encouragement from newspapers that lambasted clergy for siding with the poor against the rich.[126] The response was positive among many priests, who used bishops' edicts and conservative Catholic opinion to assert their will over vecinos católicos. Some parish curates began to reject the validity of civil marriages, despite their legality, and one justified his presence in Magdalena River villages as an impediment against "abuses that workers assume to commit." In reports sent from parishes to Santa Marta's bishop in 1884, priests assailed the immorality of their own congregations and stated that they no longer accommodated dancing in the church or midnight burials, marking confidence that priest expulsions were a thing of the past.[127]

This new authoritarian ethos did not hand bishops influence over those priests who wished to ignore their mandates, nor did it offer priests power over populations accustomed to a say in local affairs. Still, since the 1850s clergy had managed to regulate access to the church when petitioners sought its validation. Anticlerical Liberals were often excluded from a role as *padrinos* at baptisms or witnesses to marriages, and legally married couples desirous of a church ceremony were forced to seek annulments, to "repent for having contracted civil marriage . . . and request pardon from the Church and its faithful for the scandal." These earlier moments of supplicant genuflection afforded the hierarchy a new imaginary for retaking control of the parishes.[128] And as the parishioners in the Magdalena River town of Tamalameque learned, ecclesiastical authority found itself increasingly able to ignore the will of the people. In early 1884, after Santa Marta's bishop removed the town's admired priest without warning, scores of illiterate women and men demanded his return in a petition that was drawn up and notarized by Candelario Obeso during a stopover on one of his journeys from the coast to Bogotá. Despite the ceremony and lettered credentials with which they conducted their dissent, grounded in their right as vecinos católicos to a voice in parish affairs, the parishioners received nothing but silence from the diocese.[129]

DEATH AND REGENERATION

The collapse of popular politics came by way of the commotions Caribbean citizens had long upheld, in a failed armed campaign that ended on the coast. In September 1884, with no clear factional majority in Congress, with Liberal leadership and the country's market economy in disarray, and with isolated groups arming themselves in Santander and throughout the central highlands, Ricardo Gaitán Obeso gathered a band of men on the savanna outside Bogotá and quickly made his way down the Magdalena River to Barranquilla.[130] The thirty-five-year-old Gaitán, an alumnus, like Candelario Obeso (no relation), of Mosquera's Colegio Militar, was a militant Liberal but a relative unknown politically until he launched his movement. His seemingly quixotic exodus from the capital, where Rafael Núñez had begun to organize his second presidential administration (which included his choice of a Conservative as director of public instruction), could be partly explained by Gaitán's political ties to the Magdalena Valley. Perhaps more important, his decision reflected deepening cleavages in his party. Aquileo Parra and the remaining lettered Radicals opposed another Núñez presidency yet also vehemently disavowed an armed movement against Bogotá. Their offer to reform the Rionegro Constitution with the Independents and Conservatives in order to avoid a repeat of the 1861 overthrow of the national government gestured to a multiparty *convivencia* of elite leaders, which earned them the enduring euphemism of Peace Liberals. As Parra and his circle stood down from violent confrontation with Núñez, Gaitán's war Liberals were left politically stranded and headed for the coast.[131]

Despite their isolation from political currents in Bogotá, Caribbean people embraced Gaitán to reinvigorate popular political traditions. As groups throughout the region joined his armed party they broke down enclosures, confiscated cattle, attacked local Conservatives, and expelled parish priests. Protestors in towns used the disruptions to stage food riots against the growing scarcity of necessities.[132] In advance of his arrival, crews of eleven steamboats anchored in Barranquilla commandeered their vessels in Gaitán's name, and coastal canal diggers exacted higher wages from the government as a condition for not following the boatmen into the armed campaign.[133] As Gaitán neared Barranquilla in January 1885, the city's National Guard battalion mutinied, precipitating the collapse of the municipal government. Unlike guard units in the rest of the republic that rushed to Núñez's defense, coastal soldiers staked their lot with his opponents and succeeded in pulling most of their commanders with them.[134] Conservative observers in the city explained the evaporation of the Independents' authority by noting "a profound dejection among the rebels against the Government of the Union," since the president's status as a native son meant little to "people of color" increasingly excluded from public life.[135]

Enthusiasm for Gaitán's campaign on the coast did not cross over to other regions, and smaller provincial uprisings steadily lost ground before dramatic shifts in national politics. As National Guard forces headed for Barranquilla, thousands of Conservative soldiers and civilian leaders instead amassed in Bogotá, ostensibly to defend the capital but also with the "uncontainable" aspirations of a minority party long locked out of national rule.[136] With Gaitán and his supporters sequestered on the coast, progovernment propagandists circulated familiar rumors of armed Liberals committing "numerous atrocities" against innocent women, and Núñez himself lashed out against the "bandit hordes" that laid siege to his native Cartagena. The uprising was also the justification Núñez used in September 1885 to declare the Rionegro Constitution void.[137]

The final blow to the war Liberals came in a series of deadly combats and postcampaign persecutions that decimated their camp. By the return of peace in November 1885, scores of field commanders were gone, and Ricardo Gaitán Obeso had been a captured, secreted to Panama, and put to death. The depletion of campaign leaders, which followed the loss of Mosquera, Nieto, and Murillo in previous years, deprived Liberals of figures committed to some degree to the popular political traditions fashioned since the 1850s.[138] For the rank and file in Gaitán's campaign, the government offered a general amnesty out of the mistaken belief that many had been coerced into fighting. The amnesty, however, did not protect Caribbean laboring men from reprisals. Steamboat crews faced mass dismissals after Gaitán's defeat ensured that repressive labor measures could not further feed the uprising. And some individuals who lacked political connections or recourse to the law—like the boga Manuel Castro Viola, unable to read or sign the affidavit declaring his guilt in the uprising—were banished from the republic.[139]

The Independents and their Conservative allies sealed the victory with a new national constitution. From May to August 1886, eighteen delegates, two representing each state, met in Bogotá to draft a political charter. Calling the convention to order, the Conservative Catholic, grammarian, and main architect of the constitution Miguel Antonio Caro proclaimed an end to "the exaggerated democracy [that] has pulverized society." With this call to limit popular governance, the convention proposed the reinstatement of the death penalty and the elimination of the freedoms of speech, the press, civil marriage, and divorce. Rescinding political rights abetted the charter's centralism, with its extension of presidential terms from two years to six, presidential authority to appoint governors, and demotion of the federal states to departments financially and politically dependent on the national state. Its centralist tendencies stopped, however, at the door of the Catholic Church, which became not only the country's moral arbiter but also the independent costeward of national citizenship. After a generation of experiments in local politics and democratic reforms, the new constitution established public authority removed from the imperatives of popular will.[140]

In debates over suffrage rights, an issue that the Rionegro Constitution had left to the states, convention delegate and former Liberal abolitionist José María Samper proposed national literacy and property qualifications as a rubric that would offer the franchise to "persons of good judgment" but would exclude "the beggars." Many of his new Conservative colleagues concurred despite their party's success in the only presidential election under rules of universal manhood suffrage in 1856. Yet with so much at stake, the proposal did not go unchallenged. One of Samper's critics was Conservative delegate José Ospina Camacho, who reminded the convention that in half the republic "universal suffrage has always existed; that in those States the masses are accustomed to approach the urns; that they consider the faculty of voting as a right." Such a political culture, Ospina insisted, could not be overturned without consequences. "If now, with a single stroke we deprive them of what they call, with or without reason, their right, we are going to produce a cause of discontent that can separate us from the goodwill of many, and convert, in tomorrow's struggle, into enemies those who today have been our greatest defenders."[141] Samper responded that universal voting was out of the question given how "in some sections of the Republic they have accepted it for reasons derived purely from interests of race, and cannot be worse the effects of that institution. . . . It is placing in the hands of ignorant masses, to a certain extent vicious and of bad instincts, the fate of the Republic." He defended the destruction of suffrage and pleaded with delegates to abolish the system of jury trials by articulating categories of active and passive citizenship, the former composed of the honorable and lettered, the latter teeming with minors, women, illiterates, laborers, and others who "lack the constitutional aptitude to elect and be elected and make up the great mass of those simply *Colombians*." Restricting suffrage in states with large populations of color was necessary given the "political tower of Babel" created by different "climates, temperaments, races, varieties, and characters." Prior to the convention, Rafael Núñez himself had been more succinct on the topic. "A written ballot in the hands of stupid peasants," he wrote in 1884, "produced only a sad farce."[142]

Lettered peace Liberals had no public response to the citizenship exclusions in the constitution of 1886, although their actions reinforced their already significant political distance from the party's popular base.

Three months after ratification of the new constitution, a party directorate voted to support pensions for the families of men killed in the 1884–85 campaign against Núñez. To receive benefits, widows were required to prove that they had been married legitimately by either the state or the church—a replay of letrado attempts to block plebeian families from the 1877 national veterans' pension law, albeit this time with more success. In refusing recognition to the armed citizens who had attempted to return the party to power, the directorate's actions mirrored the exclusions of the new constitutional order. The pension measure was a reminder that for decades Liberal supremacy had sustained contradictions of law, race, and politics, which the country's new rulers scorned by way of their own lettered contempt. "The convention doctors of Rionegro did not have very clear and correct notions of the contrariness of their own law," quipped one published 1887 obituary of the defeated party and its defunct constitution. Liberal politics and values, it continued, had been as detrimental to public life as "the black man who did not know how to read."[143]

With the repeal of formal rights for illiterate men of color in the Cauca, Panama, Antioquia, Magdalena, and Bolívar, the kinds of local political relationships sustained by El Carmen's alcalde Ignacio Mendoza and Casimir Valencia were thrown into doubt. It did not bode well that many Liberals had switched from defending the legacies of the 1850s to proclaiming a new moral and political regeneration based not on freedom but on exclusionary authority. There had been no single moment when emancipation's democratic reforms had been overturned, yet after political reversals over education, marriage, labor, and suffrage guarantees, the unlettered and impoverished found formal access to public life closed to them. In this nadir of Colombian citizenship, disenfranchised Caribbean communities began to experience and to confront the vicissitudes of a new order.

CHAPTER SIX

A Hungry People Struggles

> At the shores of the Caribbean
> a hungry people struggles,
> preferring horrors
> to a deceitful peace.
> —Rafael Núñez, National Hymn of Colombia, 1887

> Will the oppressors open their eyes and prevent the social
> cataclysm that threatens them? We doubt it.
> —*La Voz*, Barranquilla, December 1892

What did it look like to demand recognition after disenfranchisement and in the face of encroaching hunger? The destruction of formal rights and an authoritarian ethos, fundaments of the post–1885 order known as the Regeneration, altered the political position of Caribbean citizens in the rechristened Republic of Colombia. Literacy and property restrictions on suffrage took away the vote from three out of four men in all but the most trivial local elections, which were made more so by the dissolution of the federal states and the concentration of authority in the national executive. Presidential appointment of governors who in turn appointed mayors left most political and financial resources in the hands of unelected government administrators. Yet the Nationalists, as the Independent Liberal and Conservative coalition of Rafael Núñez and Miguel Antonio Caro came to be called, left little to chance. With elections still held at regular intervals and an increasingly restive Conservative opposition, the Nationalists created machine-style politics composed of tightly held leadership circles, loyal army battalions stationed in Liberal towns during elections, and ballot box manipulation. The few literate and propertied Liberals who could still vote found their party largely unable or unwilling to participate electorally for two decades.[1]

For officials who remembered the civil war of 1859–62, mass disenfranchisement evoked the specter of the government's overthrow, so Nationalist leaders turned to the restored Catholic Church to fashion a political culture based on passive citizenship. Sanctioned with authority over civil affairs, the church offered paternalistic and symbolic forms of inclusion meant in part to soften the blow of derogated rights. Reformulated religious observance predicated on public displays of obedience did produce novel practices of inclusion for groups sanctioned by the Regeneration government. Yet even with the church again in control of parishes and schools, much of the Caribbean coast remained morally and politically suspect and outside official control, which encouraged Catholic missions to its hinterlands. The largely Jesuit project to stamp out concubinage and Liberalism reinforced the divide between city and countryside, in the process overlaying new exclusions with those of the political sphere.

The impulse behind centralizing the state, extending lettered exclusions, and insulating religion from popular control reshaped economic life as well. Rafael Núñez and other Nationalists had come to believe that free trade led to "the conversion of artisans into simple proletarian workers" and "turned citizens into slaves."[2] In order to overturn economic liberalism, the constitution of 1886 replaced emancipation's legal principle of freedom of industry and labor with state prerogatives over all economic activity. National law sanctioned monopolies for the first time since the early 1850s, transformed the legal status of work, and erected new forms of labor surveillance. Yet the farthest-reaching economic change under the new constitution was the abandonment of the gold standard and the conversion of the peso to state-backed fiat money. Soon enough monetary inflation began to affect the earning power of wage laborers and local marketers alike. While the elite opposition did roundly criticize the Nationalist economic program, lettered Liberals expressed continuing ambivalence toward the party's political base, going so far as to craft new narratives that imagined their return to power without a role for plebeian citizens. As economic and fiscal monopolies eroded livelihoods, Liberal leaders downplayed the existence of laboring people, past and present.

The faltering economy soon enough revealed the unintended yet increasing costs of the Regeneration's political triumph. In the attempt to maintain exclusionary rule, Nationalists had exchanged outright control over the republic's social and physical peripheries for influence in urban life. As financial and political resources accumulated in Bogotá and the provincial cities of Cartagena, Barranquilla, and Santa Marta, national political leaders discovered that manipulating their opponents was easier than managing diverse and fractious populations. They left local control to bureaucrats and bishops, who attempted to rule through a combination of repression, accommodation, and indifference. In the inflationary and recessionary 1890s, Caribbean people began to challenge this balancing act. At the end of the decade, desultory protests against employers and political bosses gave way to the appearance of a man claiming to be sent from God to restore the church to its lost glory. This mass movement, known as El Enviado de Dios, rattled the region's status quo, as the Regeneration's disjointed projects met their first popular challenge.[3]

CATHOLICIZING CITIZENSHIP

Constitutional change alone did not demobilize the citizenry, given that Caribbean people continued to agitate in public, albeit with a diminished political voice and under intensifying repression. "Popular masses" in Mompós staged "antigovernment" demonstrations in early 1892. Three years later, men in a crowd of hundreds gathered at Cartagena's governmental palace to call for a longer independence holiday shouted "Down with the government!" and "Death to tyranny!"[4] Officials reacted with categorical severity to these small and evanescent acts, and they invoked the 1886 constitution authorizing punishment without trial for disrespect for authority, an offense recriminalized thirty years after its abolition during the reforms of the 1850s. For standing in public in the coastal town of Majagual in 1892 and "in a booming voice [saying] that the Government was a thief, as were all of its functionaries, that soon someone would come to punish their offenses," one man was banished to distant San Andrés island for a year.[5] Despite the risks, lettered Caribbean Liberals encouraged these agitations by providing free food and musical entertainment at public gatherings. Wealthy families moved to Barranquilla, whose more tolerant political climate offered some opportunities for public expression, while those of little means remained in their towns to organize furtively. For the disenfranchised, many of whom adorned their homes with pictures of slain Liberal leader Ricardo Gaitán Obeso, the Caribbean public sphere was reduced to individuals in the streets cursing the government or hurling insults at named officials.[6]

In declaring its writ over public life, the national government relied in part on repression and in part on the Catholic Church as its costeward of Colombian citizenship. The 1886 constitution guaranteed religious freedom while recognizing Catholicism as the religion of the nation and an essential element of social order. With state support for the church restored, bishops and priests gained influence over education and direct control of civil registries for births, marriages, and deaths. Divorce, still legal on the Caribbean coast under the Rionegro Constitution, was abolished by the new political charter.[7] The following year, Bogotá signed a Concordat, which brought formal reconciliation between Colombia and the Vatican, opened the country to all religious orders for the first time in forty years, and proclaimed Jesus Christ the divine authority of the people. Guiding this process from the national capital was Miguel Antonio Caro, a doctrinaire Catholic, architect of the new constitution, and acting president during Rafael Núñez's retirement to Cartagena. For Caro, literacy and property restrictions on suffrage were not sufficient assurances of order; instead, he advocated a citizenship based on positive investment in good customs and Christian morality. Other Nationalists saw the reestablishment of the church as bringing the government back in line with the majority of Colombians, which according to one member of Congress in 1890 ended the "enslavement of our compatriots" that had begun with liberal reforms in the emancipation era.[8]

As part of its new role in civil affairs, church leaders promoted ceremonies inclusive of all those willing to embrace the new order. Instead of demolishing older public cultures, they attempted to redirect them toward some combination of authoritarian, patriotic, or moralistic expression. The church hierarchy regained control of saint day celebrations and religious processions, and they rebuilt organizations in efforts to channel parishioners toward ritualized exhibitions of submission. Signs of change were seen in Barranquilla's Carnival celebrations, still the city's most visible register of public life, where local leaders retired the event's imagery of 1860s popular republicanism and propagated new messages glorifying the church and family life.[9] Santa Marta's bishop demanded more explicit and institutionalized penitence for Caribbean people's spiritual rebellion by decreeing in 1885 and 1887 that every parish in the diocese establish the Sacred Heart of Jesus.[10] Public processions and fireworks continued on a regular basis as well, although more often than before they honored fallen political leaders or the military. The continuation of religious and civic festivities was well received, as many events "were full of people," like the September 1894 funeral of Rafael Núñez, in which "the population of Cartagena, like an immense mass of water that breaks its dikes, overflowed to the point where the aggrieved followers had to gather." The funeral procession was viewed by a crush of "women and men of every society, the elderly, the poor and those not so poor." According to one account, only fishermen and bogas did not attend the ceremonies.[11]

To manifest the restoration of its authority in Colombia, the ecclesiastical hierarchy granted sainthood to Pedro Claver. Decades of work by conservative Catholics yielded success just months after the government signed the Concordat, when the Vatican canonized the "slave of the blacks" as Colombia's patron saint. Anticlerical letrados clamored that

Claver was a "Cartagenero saint invented by Núñez and his thugs in order to mislead . . . the idolatrous part of those coastal peoples." If to some sainthood was a ploy to deceive illiterate believers into supporting the Regeneration, to many others it was a tribute to the victory over plebeian Catholics in the decades-long fight for control of the parishes. At the same time, Claver's role in baptizing thousands of Africans was not lost on observers, and some promoters of sainthood status appeared to consider the selection a symbolic replacement for the formal rights Caribbean men of color lost in 1886.[12]

Yet in the cultivation of a new public faith in coastal cities, differences of gender and social class more than color shaped reinstitutionalized religious practice. Priests understood that women were the mainstay of their rebuilding efforts. In Barranquilla's San Roque parish, home of the city's population of bogas, stevedores, and market women, hundreds of male worshippers joined new Catholic cofradías established by the church. Nonetheless, the parish received an even more enthusiastic response from many more "señoritas of good conduct, faithful and observant of the prescriptions." In some religious processions and festivals women comprised nine out of ten attendees.[13] As female parishioners formed a ubiquitous presence in urban Catholicism, social differences became evident, in which religious processions known for attracting large numbers of plebeian women were avoided by their counterparts from "high society."[14] Barranquilla's Carnival continued to attract thousands of revelers to the streets, even as lettered women celebrated in the Club de Barranquilla, which opened its doors to all willing to pay its exorbitant entrance fee. In Cartagena's Santo Domingo parish, women of "elegant society" dominated religious festivities, although some complained of their "generally worldly character." Assured of their standing within private life, they stood only to lose by publicly demonstrating their religious convictions alongside domestic servants, cooks, and market women.[15]

The eagerness among many urban Catholics to join obedient public worship did not assuage the paranoia of Nationalist leaders. Expectations that a faction of the Liberals would organize an armed revolt, and the public statements of individuals to this effect, cast suspicion on otherwise peaceful festivities. During 1891 Christmas fandangos in El Carmen, one person's cry from the crowd in favor of Liberalism led to the imprisonment of dozens of spectators.[16] The attempt to establish in this political climate religious societies and clubs, part of the church effort to renew Catholic public life, often ended in governmental refusal. In April 1893, Cartagena carpenters requested approval of a new Catholic mutual aid organization, which would "tend to the general welfare of the association without becoming involved in politics," but the departmental governor ruled against their application on the grounds that only national officials could authorize it.[17] The carpenters' timing was poor, coming just three months after a riot by artisans in Bogotá stoked fears of conspiracy and led to a new round of repression of Liberals and craftsmen.[18]

A response more common than police surveillance and arrest was official repudiation of Caribbean Catholics who continued to petition for a voice in their religion. In the new church-parishioner relations, the hierarchy had at its disposal the 1887 Concordat, which extinguished the juridical concept of the vecino católico.[19] Regardless of this restored authority, coastal parishioners still disrupted collections as a protest against compulsory tithing, even when funds were used for the upkeep of their own parishes' chapels and cemeteries. Priests and bishops, however, appeared less inclined to negotiate with the faithful.[20] After refusing offerings to the diocese in June 1892, nearly forty illiterate women and men in Ciénaga wrote Santa Marta's bishop Rafael Celedón to explain their actions. In a petition that invoked and instantiated the old parishioner sovereignty, they demanded a return of dancing during the procession of Corpus Christi, a practice recently banned by Celedón. "It is impossible that this custom—already established—would disappear here," they wrote, "as it embodies a faith with which it would be hard for us to part without our spirit suffering terrible commotion." The authoritarian public Catholicism of the time allowed bishops to judge the worth of local traditions and popular participation, and per his reestablished mandate, Celedón chose not to respond to the parishioners.[21]

The bishops could not afford to ignore education in a similar fashion, given their restored authority over schools. And their imperative in instruction, which included priestly oversight of all teaching, reinforced many of the inequalities that had formed out of the struggle against the Organic Decree in the 1870s. In part as acquiescence to lettered Caribbean families that had fought for years to limit social mixing, private (and hence religious) academies created a system of three classes, the first for children who paid to matriculate, the second and third for children on scholarship. In the girls' Colegio de Presentación in Barranquilla and those run by Franciscan sisters in Cartagena, religious orders strived "to develop progress in our proletarian classes," all the while ensuring that they had limited contact with children of privilege.[22] Schools determined (social) class placement through a combination of family wealth and literacy status, as demanded by influential locals. Protestant missionaries in the region had to abide the same social prejudices, and they noted among "the rich and the poor" that the "former will not attend a school which attempts to reach the latter."[23] The goal of social separation, which was tied to a moral paradigm of preventing corruption among elite children, pursued students beyond the classroom. After complaints by parents that social mixing occurred after school hours, Cartagena police began patrolling girls' academies to discourage loitering by poor young men and took up monitoring cockfights and other leisure spectacles to keep young male colegio students away from "day laborers."[24]

The attention to urban schools entrenched geographical as well as social divides. When public funds were available, coastal governments subsidized existing private primary schools or colegios in cities and towns, a rationing of resources that ensured lettered children Catholic education and guaranteed placement to politically loyal families. The emphasis on urban schools was also in part the effect of ending the Organic Decree's attempt at compulsory attendance, a change that excused departmental officials from raising revenue beyond meager outlays for teacher salaries.[25] As a result of these measures, education spending remained flat and disparities widened across the region in the 1890s. Total student enrollment in Bolívar did not keep pace with population growth, and in 1895 the department still maintained fewer schools than during the early 1870s. Magdalena managed to expand the number of instructional institutions but witnessed a decline in student population from the Organic Decree era (see Table 4.1). The countryside remained locked out from even these scarce resources, as Magdalena ran few schools beyond Santa Marta; and in Bolívar, only 4 percent of Cartagena's school-age children matriculated, which was nonetheless more than double the rate of the rural districts.[26] When businessmen in Cartagena appealed for more educational opportunities for rural and poor urban children in the late 1890s, the department's director of public instruction denounced the idea because the "sentiment of equality would come to have barbarous application," mainly by taking away learning opportunities from girls of wealthier families. Others blamed the state of rural schools not on finances but on "the incompetence of the Teachers," who were often removed from their positions for being "anti-Catholic." With little public financing forthcoming, education remained private, secondary, Catholic, and urban, and by the turn of the century Colombia displayed some of the highest rates of illiteracy in Latin America.[27]

Even as the focus remained on educational and spiritual life in the cities, Celedón and other coastal bishops sought to exert church-and-state influence over the Caribbean countryside. The absence of an ecclesiastical presence beyond many towns was palpable, where the bishops perceived unorthodox religious practices to be the rule and where sacred and profane rites took on a ludic menace. In Magdalena River villages like Sitionuevo, pre-Lenten festivities served as scenes of fistfights, clubbings, and even shootouts between locals, steamboat travelers, and on-duty soldiers.[28] Many curates concurred with remarks by the vicar of Ocaña in 1886 that the lack of priests meant "the shores of the Magdalena are found settled in the shadows of death," which sainthood for Pedro Claver would not change. Santa Marta's vicar responded to calls for a Catholic mission to the region by insisting that its real impetus was to attack the "dispirited" feeling among the population brought on by "the damned Gaitán revolution" of 1885. Or as Colombian priest Frederico Aguilar put it, the "indolence and death" on the coast was the legacy of "the political-agitator mania of many."[29]

With a new sense of urgency, priests began missionary activities in the Caribbean countryside from the moment the new constitution went into force. They found easy support from Nationalist leader Miguel Antonio Caro, who opined that "the missionaries must be left in complete liberty to establish the civil regimen" in areas where they worked. The Jesuit order, whose members had proselytized bogas and other populations in the Magdalena Valley before their expulsion in 1850, was the first to return to the region.[30] During the two weeks the missionary priests spent in El Banco and Tamalameque in August 1886, they took more than 1,000 confessions and conducted a dozen marriages "of persons who were living in illicit union." Because the region's rates of church marriage stood well below the national average, the priests worked hard to identify and consecrate free unions. In effect, the Jesuits measured their success by the thousands of sacraments given, the hundreds of confessions taken, and the scores of marriage ceremonies conducted.[31] Partisan motives were not so apparent in the day-to-day work of baptizing newborns and conducting mass, although they had chosen to begin their efforts in districts that had joined Gaitán, in particular those parishes that had expelled their priests during the 1885 campaign. No strangers to political symbolism, the Jesuit priests held mass at the battle site on the shore of the Magdalena River near Tamalameque where Gaitán had been defeated.[32]

By all accounts, local populations welcomed the missionaries so long as they accepted prevailing customs. Even as foreign priests claimed victory over concubinage and moral laxity, they validated some aspects of legally defunct parishioner control. In Tamalameque, instead of castigating profane practices, Jesuits preached against a backdrop of drumming, song, and *mapalé* and *zangarriado* dancing. Caribbean vecinos católicos also demanded the right to board riverboats to receive blessings from traveling Spanish priests. The tolerance demonstrated by the missionaries toward these assertive acts contrasted with the behavior of the region's bishops.[33] Fearful of crowds that had once expelled priests, Celedón would only conduct parish visits when accompanied by a contingent of soldiers. Parishioners protested this armed entourage by refusing to attend mass and fleeing to outlying districts, which compelled chagrined alcaldes to decree that military recruitment would not take place and that the rights of inhabitants would be guaranteed. Although Celedón expressed concern over the popular hostility toward his display of force, he did not abandon the practice.[34]

Nor did the receptivity between parishioners and visiting priests obscure the missionaries' marking of Caribbean worshippers as possibly unassimilable others. Several priests came to Colombia directly from Africa to dedicate their lives "to the descendants of the wretched slaves evangelized by Saint Pedro Claver, on these coasts of the Caribbean," and promised to attend to "the blacks of Guinea and those of New Granada . . . with the same charity."[35] The Vatican further racialized Colombian missionary work in the 1890s by conferring on Claver costanding as "heavenly patron of the colored race," which made Colombia's patron saint the guiding spirit of the worldwide Negro Missions. This was a delicate organizational measure given the propensity among lettered Colombians to claim pure Hispanic descent.[36] While the fixation on blackness was in part attributable to foreign priests with little knowledge of local mores, native-born priest Frederico Aguilar put his own stamp on Caribbean inferiority by impugning the region's "backwardness, dirtiness, poverty, and disorder." Foreign and Colombian clerics all assumed an orthodoxy that coastal populations equally lacked, and they considered local ministers who were woven into the fabric of folk belief a nuisance to be extirpated if the missions were to succeed.[37]

This portrayal of Caribbean people as bereft of the Catholic doctrine aided the transfer of governmental resources from education to the missionaries at a moment when coastal citizens were demanding more schools. In the 1890s, a national subsidy was "applied principally to the catechizing of the riverside populations of the Magdalena," yet this money came out of funds set aside for public instruction.[38] Liberals and dissident Conservatives charged Nationalists with withholding education as some kind of tool of "political domination," so that "day after day the Government loses prestige among the popular masses," although they too blamed the poor for a supposed antagonism toward schooling.[39] On the coast, the government did lose prestige, but there was little popular antagonism toward education. In Cartagena Bay, bogas and fishermen "show themselves hostile to every public act, denying their services for the most urgent of necessities," primarily because "they lament not having a school in this place." In the same years, illiterate market women in Cartagena province sent petitions to the prefect with demands for education for their children. Protestors may have welcomed missionaries into their communities, but their priority remained schooling and literacy for their families.[40]

FORGETTING PEOPLE OF COLOR

Jesuit designs to stamp out Liberalism by missionizing the coast complemented the breakdown of Liberal Party organization. Denied access to either elective office or newspapers, with many leaders forced into exile, Liberal politics all but ceased to exist publicly in the years after 1885. Liberals' ability to regain their lost standing was hampered by Nationalist paranoia and by new legal definitions of *subversive* that discredited many of the civic traditions of the Rionegro era.[41] Not until the early 1890s did party members found new outlets of opinion and again start electioneering, often by forming alliances with anti-Nationalist Conservatives. When this new effort began, however, the party had few resources, no chance of winning majority power, and internal divisions that had persisted from the time of the Gaitán campaign. With the war faction depleted, the Liberal directorate under Aquileo Parra and Luis A. Robles conceded to the Nationalists on centralism, the church, marriage, and education—all concessions, to be sure, with origins before the party's defeat in 1885. Their stated positions did not venture much farther than advocating minority congressional representation, and even militant anti-Regeneration Liberals like former president Santiago Pérez made few overtures to a bygone popular politics. The directorate's first tentative alliances with party members outside the national capital came only after 1891, which took place under continued governmental harassment and among party members split over issues of electoral abstention and political violence.[42]

In this new political culture, lettered Liberals at home or abroad turned to their writing as a recourse, and in several works they depicted blackness to make sense of their defeat. The historical novel *Lo irreparable* (1889), by anticlerical radical and prolific author José María Vargas Vila, is set on a plantation and invokes the social death of racial slavery and the isolation of free blacks as meditations on the Liberal Party's demise. In "El rey de los espantos," Eduardo Posada's story of putrefaction and mass killing that ends with the failure of Gaitán's Caribbean campaign, the atmosphere of loss is heightened by a lone boga "singing the verses of Candelario Obeso."[43] Posada was not alone in appropriating Obeso's metaphor of sorrow as a lament for the Liberals' downfall. Santiago Pérez Triana, son of the former president, covertly fled the country in August 1893 to avoid imprisonment. In his memoir of flight, Pérez included a stanza from Obeso's "Cancion der boga ausente" as the epigraph, although Pérez's infelicitous misquoting—"Bogá, Negrito, bogá"—may have evoked black minstrelsy for Spanish readers. Black personae both fictional and real had come to stand in for the suffering of lettered men.[44]

Liberal journalist and former abolitionist Medardo Rivas found this poetic bathos an insufficient response to political circumstances and set out to conceive an alternative intellectual project to reclaim the party's history and, by extension, future prospects in Colombia. His last major work, *Trabajadores de la tierra caliente* (Laborers of the Hot Land, 1899), told the story of the young men who at midcentury had left Bogotá for the Magdalena Valley to seek their fortunes in the booming tobacco industry. The opening sections of *Trabajadores* situate the story in costumbrista style, with adumbrated depictions of black people as slaves and free mulattoes as rapists, a dissolute lowland population saved from itself by the modern Spartacus, the Liberals of 1849. Yet in freedom the people are not redeemed, becoming only "lazy blacks" among a mestizo population that is itself "like an Arab woman," until finally all are salvaged by "arrogant youth, of white color" from Bogotá. Once letrados take up their role as the true laborers of the land, people of color disappear altogether from Rivas's narrative, to be replaced by statistics on agricultural production. His fictionalized paean to industrial freedom looked simultaneously forward and back, offering a lesson to elite youth about virile entrepreneurial activity, mastery of tropical nature, and racial myth-making.[45]

Trabajadores also conformed to Regeneration political realities by situating lettered men as agents of change and expunging all others who had fought for freedom. People of African descent vanish from the narrative as it approaches the present, allowing Rivas to imagine a Liberal revival through the post-1885 system of limited suffrage. Like many of his peers, Rivas's politics had moved over a half century, and he had broadened out from his antiboga tirades in earlier decades to a lettered politics devoid of popular participation. Even his book's leitmotif of whitening, which drew from the well of his party's old nemesis, conformed to certain political expectations among party elites. Rafael Núñez, citing Herbert Spencer's theories, had quipped in 1883 that "the ethnologically inferior groups are no more than a passing cloud destined to disappear in the general irradiation of progress," and any deferral in this march exposed Colombia "to domination by another race."[46] After Miguel Antonio Caro and a resurgent Catholic orthodoxy undercut the allure of Social Darwinism in Nationalist circles, Liberal intellectuals still took comfort in its teleology in order to imagine their party as the future of the republic. Implicit in the racial progression of *Trabajadores* was an anticipated political constituency of the few amid the mass disenfranchisement of men of color. The book's claims to manly, rational expertise in business, moreover, countered Nationalist polemics against fey Liberal *doctores* and appealed directly to free-market dissidents in the Conservative camp.[47]

The return of Luis A. Robles to public life personified the kind of lettered and business-oriented Liberal politics Medardo Rivas touted on the page. Soon after the 1879 coup that toppled his government in Santa Marta, Robles had withdrawn from the coast to a life of law and letters in Bogotá. In 1892, voters sent him to Congress—the first Liberal there in eight years—not from his native Magdalena but from Antioquia, where dissident Conservatives nominated him in protest against Miguel Antonio Caro's administration. In Congress Robles advocated press freedoms and fiscal restraint while also pursuing numerous accords with Caro and the Nationalist majority. After one term in Congress, the party's "black" hero (according to racial etiquette–defying poet and Obeso eulogist Antonio José Restrepo) relinquished his seat to Antioqueño Liberal militant Rafael Uribe Uribe, joined the national directorate, taught law in private universities, and set about compiling the republic's commercial code.[48] Upon his death in 1899, ideologues condemned the country's only nationally known man of color as a subversive and anti-Catholic "agent of Hell," rhetoric that obscured his public efforts to build a *convivencia* among all political parties. Luis A. Robles's color, lettered credentials, and start in Caribbean popular politics had shaped his career, while his work late in life exemplified the possibilities of a Liberal Party without its former political base.[49]

Intellectuals of the Nationalist majority countered Liberals by offering more pessimistic views on race as part of their own ideological imperative for continued supremacy. Some writers stoked patriotic fervor against European (and perhaps specifically Jesuit) stereotypes of Latin Americans as "African hordes" and demanded international acknowledgment of the whiteness of the region's ruling class. These plaints, however, were typically dwarfed by other perspectives on racial conflict and mixing.[50] Miguel Antonio Caro, for one, blamed Social Darwinism and economic liberalism for letting "racial conflicts resolve themselves *in liberty. Laissez faire!*" José María Samper claimed for himself a scientific viewpoint in the late 1880s, when he recanted an earlier faith that liberalism would bring about a positive race mixing—that is, one beneficial to whites—and posited that incomplete amalgamation after slavery accounted for ethnic hatreds and social calamity.[51] Samper and other Conservatives in the Nationalist camp, while sometimes at odds, shared the supposition that race mixing had proceeded without whitening the population. Returning from exile, priest Federico Aguilar noted that "while in our country 20 percent are blacks, mulattoes, and zambos . . . 10 percent [are] Indians who speak Spanish, already half-absorbed by the white race." For Aguilar and Samper, indigenes were disappearing even as people of African descent presented a demographic dynamism. Such evidence in part justified Nationalists' focus on organic unity, Catholic morality, and state power as keys to a true racial amalgamation, in particular as mass European immigration failed to materialize. At the same time, portents of black fecundity positioned the Nationalists against utopian Liberal views on whitening, and given lettered families' venerable propensity for endogamy, the ruling party appeared to offer the stronger case as the republic's guardians against racial decay.[52]

REDEFINING LABOR AND COMMERCE

Pessimistic ideas of race competed with other powerful visions of technology's inexorable progress. The continuing allure of industrial power was its capacity to surpass human exertion, even to replace humans altogether, and none other than stalwart antipositivist Miguel Antonio Caro defended technology's liquidation of "many workers" as being a "general benefit."[53] Some Nationalists expressed hope for a significant expansion of the railroads, but before the turn of the century, the machine still most in evidence in the tropical garden was the steamboat. And the persistence of steam technology on the Magdalena River allowed writers to shift from blaming bogas for the country's economic failings to relegating them to the dustbin of history. These arguments resembled concurrent claims of vanishing Indians, in this case not as the result of racial mixing or the civilizing process but because the pole men had been bested by modern capital.[54] Before writing *Trabajadores*, Medardo Rivas had elegized, "with the substitution of steamboats for champanes, [the boga] is disappearing, if he has not already finished." Salvador Camacho Roldán offered terse agreement in the late 1880s: "Today, navigation with pole and oar almost eliminated."[55] Colombian biographies, geographical manuals, and travel accounts began to describe the "dictatorship" of Magdalena boatmen as a curious historical footnote. Even pessimists who warned of a rising black demographic tide told of the boga's death knell.[56]

The intellectual erasure of bogas defied observable reality even while inciting legal reform. Foreign travelers continued to meet and write about boatmen, and a military report on the 1895 Magangué trade fair counted 800 champanes, a fleet that would require a labor force of perhaps 15,000 bogas, more than were believed to have worked the entire river before the steam age.[57] Yet the apparent expansion of manual labor in transportation did not prevent letrados from redacting mention of bogas from national legislation. In public policy and law, human-powered watercraft were still taxed, and boatmen endured compulsory obligations to the customs service and additional prison time for criminal convictions. Bogas also remained implicit in commercial codes that exempted steamboats from any damages they might cause to other vessels in their operation on the river.[58] Beyond these legal encumbrances, lawmakers deleted bogas from any new or revised statutes. Salvador Camacho Roldán noted how the overall effect of bogas' diminishing legal and literary presence shaped governmentality. The Office of River Inspection, as the old boga service was renamed, regulated and kept statistics on steamboats only and excluded data on champanes and bongos. "Even the names of these last two vehicles will shortly disappear," he opined.[59]

The shift in representations of the bogas was one effect of the broader legal transformation of labor under the Regeneration. While reaffirming the abolition of slavery, the 1886 constitution replaced the emancipation era's open-ended yet intertwined concept of free industry and labor with prerogatives vested in the national state to determine licit work and economic activity. This change tied labor to citizenship in new ways, as the constitution defined full civil standing as open to "all male Colombians who have attained the age of twenty-one years and who exercise a profession, art, or employment, or who follow a lawful occupation or other legitimate and recognized means of support." This redefinition of labor was a victory for lettered culture, given the letrado penchant for identifying codified knowledge and public reputation as essential aspects of recognition. It also subordinated wage workers' legal right to freely engage in contracts to the priority of "good customs or public order." In different judicial cases during the 1890s, the Supreme Court interpreted the state's authority to define legitimate work to mean that employers could withhold pay for contracted labor "as a guarantee of the completion of the contract" and that employers could garnish wages as compensation for damages caused by employees on the job.[60] This extension, in essence, of the old boga clause to all types of work also had the effect of depriving boatmen of a legal existence as a special class of labor. And since one of the few nonpolitical deficiencies delineated in the constitution by which citizens could lose political rights was "habitual drunkenness"—part of bogas' public reputation—the newly circumscribed definitions of labor and behavior reinforced the denial of suffrage to illiterate and propertyless men.[61]

Along with the new judicial and state authority to define free labor, the constitution's establishment of "companies and corporations that are recognized in Colombia as artificial persons" opened the way for exclusive economic privileges, which were felt most dramatically on the coast. With the relegalization of monopolies, foreign and Colombian financiers accumulated control over most of the transportation and shipping industries.[62] Emblematic of the new commercial privileges was Cuban-born U.S. citizen Francisco J. Cisneros's Compañía Colombiana de Transportes (CCT). In the 1880s and 1890s, the CCT bought up private and public enterprises, eventually controlling nearly 85 percent of the Magdalena steamboat industry, one of the Caribbean railroads, the Puerto Colombia pier (opened in 1893 and used for shipping 85% of all national exports), large tracts of land, and all coastal canalization projects. The CCT's ascendance was buoyed in part by the coffee industry, whose exports rose by half in the first five years of the Regeneration, although the company's dominance had been assured by winning the national postal monopoly in 1886. With shipping in the hands of a few investors, Cisneros exerted influence over public revenues and commerce, reducing the tax burden of the CCT while making small-scale farmers and merchants in the Colombian interior pay more to move their products to market.[63]

Coffee exports and the concentration of shipping under the CCT for a time expanded employment on steamboats, railroads, and docks. In Barranquilla, the CCT hired more than 750 regular and day laborers to work as boat crews, stevedores, or diggers. The two Caribbean railroads hired close to 1,000 men, primarily for road maintenance, and port enterprises in Cartagena, Santa Marta, and Barranquilla contracted thousands more dockworkers.[64] Craft and mechanical trades in shipyards and rail maintenance grew along with the commercial monopolies, and dredging operations brought more employment. The capital-intensive CCT redistributed labor, as the extension of the railway allowed its employees to shift goods directly from steamboats in Barranquilla to rail cars and eventually onto ships at the Puerto Colombia pier. Although still minimal, the integration of infrastructure was sufficient to deprive bogas and haulers of the porterage trade through the city and along the Caribbean shore. Over protests against their displacement, the government backed Cisneros and the CCT.[65]

Men who were extended the legal status of legitimate labor by working for a monopoly enterprise were not freed from state control. On the contrary, the Office of River Inspection transferred its regulatory apparatus from champán bogas to steamboat crews. "For offenses more or less serious," wrote Barranquilla's inspector in 1890, "the writer has seen it as an urgent necessity to rule unfit many steamboat crew members, those who despite the rigidity with which they are treated by the respective authority, do not therefore stop committing their offenses of insubordination aboard the ships."[66] New rules banned women from work areas, "as they make [the crews] abandon their duties to attend to them and care for them"; prohibited "gatherings and heated discussions on the lower deck"; and outlawed alcohol consumption among boat workers. With constitutional powers to punish disrespect for authority aboard ships, inspectors fired scores of boatmen, sometimes en masse from a single crew. On shore, local police forces were instructed to patrol areas of public leisure and to arrest crew members who violated (or were suspected of violating) midnight curfews, engaged in "unlawful diversions," or were "without occupation on Mondays."[67]

For the majority of working people, the heightened regulation of labor and leisure around enterprises like the CCT was a lesser interference than the combined effects of paper money and economic recession. In 1885, the Nationalist government abandoned the convertibility of the peso and deprived merchants and private bankers of the right to a domestic trade in gold-backed bills. While the so-called fiat money bolstered administrative power in Bogotá, within three years it had lost half its value, and over the next decade it would do so again.[68] Outside Nationalist circles, the government's monetary policies were tremendously unpopular, even as critics at the outset of the reforms had little influence over public opinion. Some artisans and owners of small shops may have benefited early on from the depreciation of the value of debts, but any initial gains from inflation disappeared amid growing public expenditures and unchecked money printing. The market panics and world trade recession of the 1890s appeared locally as a post-1895 decline in coffee exports, which aggravated already dire economic conditions.[69]

Available information on wage rates speaks to the erosion of earning capacity under money inflation and at a time of declining paid employment. In August 1884, shortly before Colombia abandoned the gold standard, the U.S. consul stated that Barranquilla's railroad mechanics received at least 2.00 pesos daily; followed by masons, carpenters, and boat pilots with 1.60 or more; railroad linemen with 1.25; bogas and stevedores with 1.00; and railroad porters, haulers, cooks, washerwomen, seamstresses, and private- and public-sector manual laborers with 0.50–0.80 daily. The consul further claimed that wages were at subsistence levels and had not changed since the 1870s.[70] The erosion of earnings quickened under fiat money. Foreign merchants in Santa Marta, Barranquilla, and Cartagena who hired locals for various types of work in 1889–90, when the Colombian peso's value had already declined by half, offered wages unchanged since the consul's report more than five years earlier. "It is difficult to save anything with my family," testified one Barranquilla stonemason who earned 1.61 pesos daily before currency depreciation took hold, "and the very little that is saved is by my wife from her chickens, pigs, and goats."[71]

As the purchasing power of wages declined, employees on steamboats and railroad lines began to protest threats to their livelihoods. The two coastal railroads experienced almost weekly derailments in the mid-1890s, although any attempt to catch culprits appeared unlikely on the CCT-controlled Bolívar line, with more than 500 laborers and little police presence along the route from Barranquilla to Puerto Colombia. These actions, along with camp brawls and collective drinking, were signs that employers and the state still lacked the means to impose constitutionally mandated good customs and public order. There was even less they could do to stop sympathetic peasants who may have joined in derailing trains to protest the railroads' refusal to compensate them for homes burned down by sparks given off by passing engines.[72] Despite the dangers involved, men began wrecking steamboats as well, for much the same reasons. Crew on the *Roberto Calixto* took the perilous step of trying to blow up their ship's boiler in May 1890, after months of onboard conflict between crew, captain, and passengers. At issue were harsh onboard discipline and employment ashore in Barranquilla, which offered "better remuneration than on the steamboats themselves," according to the river inspector, who nevertheless offered as a response only "severe punishment for the delinquents."[73]

Coastal artisans reacted to deteriorating social conditions by forming the region's first labor organizations. In September 1891, Magdalena steamboat pilots created an association as part of their demand for a wage increase and control over the selection of apprentices.[74] Their impetus had been a December 1890 presidential decree requiring government-issued patents for all captains and pilots and attempts by the CCT to reduce their pay by 20 percent, "leaving us with a *hunger ration*," they protested. Perhaps years of proartisan statements by Rafael Núñez also played a role in their unprecedented move to organize collectively.[75] Some Barranquilla Conservatives backed the pilots' association as preferable to "the brutal and sterile method of force" witnessed in the wrecking of steamboats and rail lines.[76] Declining wages compelled Caribbean artisans to engage in the public sphere as well. The first to do so were Barranquilla's carpenters, who in 1891 founded a society and newspaper, *La Voz del Artesano*. They were soon followed by the city's bricklayers with their launching of the paper, *El Obrero*. While craftsmen had engaged in autonomous politics and opinion in Bogotá for decades, this tradition was largely unknown on the coast until the inflationary 1890s.[77]

Public officials did not distinguish labor organizing from political subversion and reacted to Caribbean artisans with increasing repression. The steamboat pilots had begun their association at a time when river inspectors were attempting to quash "insubordination aboard the ships," an atmosphere of repression that compelled the pilots to state that the politics of their members were heterogeneous and not antigovernment.[78] Such declarations offered little cover, since labor groups were denied official standing without state approval, and any activities on their part could be perceived as a threat to authority. The Office of River Inspection, which routinely dismissed known or suspected Liberals from steamboat crews, used the same power to remove the CCT pilots who had founded the association.[79] In October 1892, months before a riot involving Bogotá artisans led to a nationwide crackdown, Barranquilla's officials were forcibly dissolving the craft unions and using the national law curtailing press freedoms to shut down their newspapers. "The greater part of the artisans," reported a local paper, "have been warned against proposing the founding of new Societies."[80]

With inflation continuing to erode earnings, the determined actions of some laborers won wage concessions, albeit unaccompanied by an extension of legitimate public standing. In late April 1893, CCT employees of the customshouse and railroad in Barranquilla refused to work without a 25 percent wage increase. It was not the only strike of the period—the boatmen of Cartagena Bay had stopped work to protest low pay in September 1890, as did Cartagena's trash collectors in late 1894—though the Barranquilla action appeared to be the country's largest strike of the decade.[81] Instead of negotiating with striking workers, the government called up an army battalion to load rail cars and boats. Local anti-Nationalist opinion lambasted the action and endorsed "the petition of the *obreros*" as "very just, given the lack of provisions and items of great necessity and consumption." One Barranquilla newspaper blamed the strike on the government itself for its recent passage of a tax on food that hurt the working poor. Such support for the strike earned one dissident Conservative newspaper a six-month suspension.[82] Little is known about how many hundreds of employees took part or how and when the strike succeeded, but by July the governor reported that "the railroad company pays peons 15 reales [1.70 pesos, about double the prestrike wage], and it is difficult to find anyone who would serve in positions for less." Although he acknowledged the victory of the railroad men, the governor's reference to them as peons stood in contrast to other CCT employees, such as steamboat mechanics, who had won the legal status of "competent workers [*obreros competentes*]." Laborers scored a pay increase but without earning newfound legitimacy, despite forcing the largest commercial monopoly into one of the country's first wage negotiations.[83]

POLICING MARKETS AND WOMEN

Laboring men agitated for higher wages just as local markets endured pressures of their own. Money depreciation, new import tariffs, and wage demands by employees reduced returns for many private enterprises, and the collapse of all save one of the country's private banks augured a difficult path to commercial recovery.[84] In response, a free-trade Conservative bloc joined Luis A. Robles in the early 1890s Congress to challenge the political hold of Caro and the Nationalists. Disapproval of economic reforms, however, did not stop many coastal financiers and transportation monopolies from exploiting government policies as a hedge against inflation. Some merchants petitioned Bogotá to lessen their obligations to local administrations, citing an 1888 law that deprived municipalities and departments of taxation authority.[85] Many more enterprises acquired national lands and resources to stabilize their wealth. Rafael Núñez's 1885 confiscation from the federal states and municipalities of all untitled public lands, floodplains, riverbanks, and coastal salt-drying beds, "whose dominion the Nation has recovered," led to a bonanza in property concessions for investors and creditors. During the 1890s, one Italian national acquired more than 100 buildings in Cartagena to become the largest landlord of the city's "palaces turned into tenement houses."

In the same years, the Cartagena Railway refused to complete construction on a new train station until the government granted it more national lands.[86] Massive land acquisitions and other types of concessions offered generous terms to investors. In 1891, Boston-based Cartagena Terminal & Improvement Company won the contract to build city docks, which stipulated exclusive rights to the bay as well as fines or imprisonment for bogas and fishermen who used its waters without authorization. While private enterprise and public officials were sometimes at loggerheads, in general public grants in the form of land or monopolies offered ample rewards with few strings attached.[87]

Coastal businessmen attempted to exert control over local marketplaces as another hedge on the declining value of the peso. In 1886, they launched an effort to drive poor ambulatory peddlers out of Barranquilla's new market building, which had recently opened with a private event for the city's leading families. In justifying social exclusions they invoked the building's potential to "fulfill its double role of establishing order and being a financial medium." Three years later, dozens of Barranquilla merchants unsuccessfully petitioned Bogotá for authority over the old open-air marketplace in front of the San Nicolás Church. Given the centrality of waterfront markets in the urban food supply, the merchants appeared eager to replace local relations of subsistence with commercial arrangements guided by profit accumulation. Provisioning of food to cities and towns, which had taken place largely free of interference, came to be seen by some in the business community as a resource that could be monetized or auctioned off as a concession.[88]

Local governments, pressed by inflation as well as by lost taxes, turned to the same markets as a source of revenue. Municipalities levied a host of new fees on stall operators and enacted rules governing commercial venues meant to ensure that employees and customers alike maintained "composure" and "good conduct" or else suffered penalties for their "abuses and disorders."[89] Elite Caribbean opinion complained that these tactics confirmed local officials as "weak men . . . of little value" whose patronage appointments or lack of training led to an abuse of authority. There was, nevertheless, a financial logic to market regulation.[90] Having lost the right to tax yet having gained constitutional powers to impose fines for disrespect of authority, police converged on marketplaces to raise municipal funds. In the mid-1890s, patrols in Santa Marta and Cartagena made on average 85 and 160 monthly arrests, respectively, in the main from alleged incidents against authority in the waterfront markets, with the majority of arrests ending in fines paid to city coffers. Barranquilla's prefect put forward a similar plan

Caño Mercado, Barranquilla, crowded with canoes laden with corn and fruits, 1906.
Courtesy of Underwood & Underwood Glass Stereograph Collection, Archives Center,
National Museum of American History, Smithsonian Institution.

to charge fees to every person arrested, which would be beneficial "from a moralizing point of view, more than on account of the financial point of view," he claimed. Memories of rural armed resistance to tax farming in earlier decades may have led Regeneration officials to concentrate their harvesting of public revenue from the poor in the urban markets instead.[91]

Female traders led the protest against this rising public and private interference. As both provisioners and consumers who lived near subsistence levels, laboring women stood to lose from even moderate increases in levies. When Cartagena substantially (and perhaps unconstitutionally) raised the municipal tax on fish in late 1890, market women spent days in front of the municipal building, singing, chanting, and issuing death threats until the city council reversed its decision. "It has been considered by the contributors, and is in effect onerous," the council conceded, "for these poor women for the most part, to whom the Concejo must bring relief." Despite similar protests, Barranquilla's city council refused to repeal its own tax on fish, with council members lamenting the need to keep such an "inhumane tribute." Women also petitioned for new concessions to sell fish outside the market, although after the protests Cartagena's council appeared less willing to approve requests from female vendors.[92]

Market women's protests coincided with the rising visibility of independent female labor. Plebeian women were embedded in urban networks of wage earners and traders, although they often congregated in separate places from men, in part for socializing and group child-rearing but also perhaps to exert a united will before customers and competing vendors. A British traveler in the late 1880s reported that in the channel that ran from Barranquilla's waterfront to the Magdalena River "at least a hundred or a hundred and fifty half-naked women and children, laughing and talking, splashing and screaming, were engaged in washing the linen for the more wealthy people of the town." The U.S. consul similarly commented that in Barranquilla laundresses "abound[ed]."[93] Their counterparts in coastal city hostels appeared to join together when they refused to work during holiday seasons, thereby disregarding the demands of business operators and travelers. An engineer from the United States complained of the "wretched" service in 1889 Cartagena: "My washing has been out for two weeks and I can't even learn where it is," he wrote. "In response to enquiries the old lady only says mañana." Frustrated employers found they had little leverage over women who may have collectively set the pace of their labor.[94]

Regeneration concerns for moral and social order offered officials and businessmen a new rhetoric for regulating the behavior of women who worked in public. In lettered opinion, street vendors stood alongside, if not in place of, women who engaged in paid sex. Cartagena's *El Porvenir* insisted on new measures in 1892 to counter the polluting activities of "food hawkers . . . with their ridiculous mobile shops" as well as "women of bad life."[95] Although prostitution was not criminalized, Caribbean women found "wandering the streets and maliciously entertaining"—charges easily applied to street vendors—were fined and jailed for up to ten days. In Cartagena, three out of four individuals arrested for public scandals and

A Colombian washing day along the Magdalena River, near Barranquilla, 1906. Courtesy of Underwood & Underwood Glass Stereograph Collection, Archives Center, National Museum of American History, Smithsonian Institution.

disrespect for authority in the early 1890s were women.[96] New hygiene juntas, in contrast, worked not to incarcerate prostitutes but to regulate "the way in which public women must live," by monitoring their movements and intervening among the presumably infected and disorderly.[97] Hygienic authority over women in public also allowed officials to block marketing activities by illiterate vendors like Inocencia Hernández, who in January 1893 had requested by written petition the authorization to operate food stalls along Cartagena's walls. While still vital to urban populations, provisioners were recast as disruptive market elements needing public oversight and liable for new poor taxes. These actions reversed the latitude shown to market women in earlier decades, when advocates of industrial freedom had considered selling goods locally to be a sedentary and feminine occupation.[98]

The shifting gendered and racialized attitudes toward market women made clear how letrados advanced the prostitution question to reflect on economic change. On Caribbean city streets they noted "a great reunion of people of all social classes and colors . . . even the daughter of Eve who occupies the place of the *femmes communes*."[99] Perhaps deteriorating economic conditions led more women to exchange sex for money, although claims to prostitution's role in moral contamination and the "degeneration of the race" predated the hard times of the 1890s. Instead, the censure against women in the market seemed to take its cues in part from conservative views of plebeian women's unsanctioned family and sexual lives during the older religious struggle on the coast.[100] For commercial advocates, moreover, prostitution may have come to signify a more explicit relationship between women's behavior and recognizable laws of civilization and political economy. According to Salvador Camacho Roldán, the Magdalena Valley owed its "industrial lethargy" to its populations of "vagrants and prostitutes," "old champán bogas," and "black or mixed race" people unwanted in other regions. Like the legal redaction of the bogas, identifying and disciplining women who worked in public were essential prerequisites to economic development.[101]

The focus on Caribbean workingwomen intensified along with particular changes in the legal regimes of marriage and property. National law that abolished divorce and reestablished church marriage as the only official form of matrimony for Catholics also stripped married women of the right to property. In place of property, "honest women," as well as minors and priests, gained status as a newly protected class of individuals freed from excessive forms of punishment, including for the crime of disrespect for authority.[102] Plebeian women who lacked church-sanctioned marriages yet controlled the greatest share of their households' wealth were conspicuous in their noncompliance with the new legal distinctions. As changes in marriage law threw into doubt their property rights, poor women's status in the market and employment was increasingly framed as a scandal against public order. Accusations that market women practiced prostitution or worse, predatory pricing flowed from their ambiguous legal position, and as currency depreciation eroded consumer spending power, Cartagena businessmen charged female hawkers and go-betweens

with taking advantage of their positions to raise prices on food.[103] During a cholera outbreak in 1892, the mayor of Barranquilla acted on this
belief by intervening in the selling of food items at the city's marketplace
to prohibit what he considered price gouging by female vendors. In the
best of times marketers' dual role as provisioners for urban consumers
and brokers for rural producers caused tensions, yet the declining value
of paper money and the new relationship between marriage and property
after 1885 left them as prime targets of expanded regulation.[104]

Officials rarely mentioned property or marital status in their policing
duties, and in the main the regulation of food provisioning and other market relations was justified by recourse to older paternalistic and democratic rhetoric. In the 1890s, coastal municipalities set up free medical
treatment and food lotteries for the "poor class" with no means of subsistence. Given public penury, responsibility for providing for "the most unfortunate of the beggars" often fell to businessmen, women from prominent families, and prochurch artisans.[105] Wages and working conditions
also needed government protection, according to one Barranquilla newspaper in May 1893, because the "proletarian class, by its condition, it can
be said, lacks the means and knowledge" to help itself.[106] Barranquilla tied
poor relief to regulation by keeping open its old market after unveiling the
exclusive new one because the former venue satisfied "the need for food
of a respectable number of persons with scarce resources," including "the
laboring part of this pueblo and the beggars from within and outside the
city." The same ruling also provided for more police to "preserve a rea-
sonable order" and to collect taxes from "that immense influx of mobile
food sellers from neighboring pueblos."[107] Cartagena's government took a
different tack when it acknowledged "the high cost of living in this city"
by invoking a universal sense of "equity and justice" to deny individual
petitions for poor relief.[108] Governors and judges overturned local taxes
on garden plots, market stalls, huts, ejidos, and burials, sometimes in the
name of equity or justice but always with the prerogatives of the national
state clearly defined. The resulting dynamic was a perverse one in which
local governments chosen by popular manhood suffrage relied on revenue appropriated from the working poor, which the national government
could annul at will and, if it so chose, in the name of popular justice.[109]

Paternalism toward the poor also worked to the benefit of the commercial monopolies in explicit ways. Cartagena and Barranquilla banned
use of local lagoons for drinking water, which had to be purchased from
the new private aqueduct, although they did include provisions for sales to
their city's growing impoverished populations at "a reduced price."[110] And

during the money inflation and food scarcity of the late 1890s, the Compañia Fluvial de Cartagena, one of the city's largest enterprises, offered fresh water on Saturdays to "the destitute class" of the city. *El Porvenir*'s editors lavished praise on the company's charity, in part by contrasting it with price-gouging *aguadores*. According to the paper, these traditional water peddlers wielded a dangerous command over a vital substance and should either have their prices set by public authority or else be eliminated altogether. The editors also used the continued presence of street vendors to appeal for a new commercial water supply, a contract possibly to be awarded to the very same Compañia Fluvial.[111]

When paternalism proved insufficient to promote business interests, public officials summoned their constitutional powers to punish disrespect for authority. After the Barranquilla railway strike in late April 1893, the prefect for the Dique Canal (along which ran a section of the Cartagena railroad) preemptively placed his province under martial law. When crowds from the town of Soplaviento rushed to the defense of railroad workers being arrested, soldiers fired on them. Locals protested that the prefect was "prohibiting in this manner the free transit of the farmers, food sellers, fishermen, etc., that is to say, curtailing individual liberty as if public order were disturbed." They also pointed out that the prefect was an employee of the railroad. When the governor of Bolívar ordered an investigation of the incident, the prefect responded that his actions had been carried out "with the object of apprehending workers and preserving order." In response to the petitioners' "jeremiad of *curtailed guarantees*," the prefect proffered, "I have here the sentimental story of a citizen who laments usurpation of guarantees and does not know to respect authority instituted for the security of those guarantees." The governor's ambiguous resolution to the incident entailed placing troops under the command of Soplaviento's mayor and ordering further investigations of "irregularities," another instance of labor and markets falling under pressure from monopolies and authoritarian governance.[112]

The political opposition that criticized national policies and local irregularities had little to offer disenfranchised citizens during the economic crises at the turn of the century. Among government critics few went as far as Miguel Samper, a disenchanted onetime supporter of the Regeneration, who lambasted the "social oligarchy of money and dress [that] weighs over the poor classes and the subjugated races, that are far, very far, from enjoying the equality of rights that all constitutions and political parties have promised them." Perhaps the one who came closest was Rafael Uribe Uribe, the sole Liberal in Congress, who criticized inflationary paper money for destroying the livelihoods of "the common peon" and "the poor classes." Other lettered Liberals, however, drew their attention to Medardo Rivas's advocacy of the "rights of man" and "liberty of instruction," which under no circumstances were to supersede the "freedom of industry [and] property."[113] Some free-trade Conservatives joined Samper in advocating reduced tariffs on imported foodstuffs to alleviate the suffering of coastal populations, yet they also called for debt consolidation so that it would fall over "all the social classes"—not just the wealthy but, specifically, "the laboring strata" as well.[114] Such a redistribution of individuals' obligation to the public debt would have been onerous for most wage earners, given that consumer prices for basic items quintupled between 1885 and 1899. Faced with a severe loss of earning power and food scarcity, laborers threatened disruptions on the Cartagena railroad, which won them new pay and time concessions, and "peons" on a hacienda near that city declared a strike. Some in the local business community claimed not to understand the "cause" of these actions.[115]

THE MILLENNIAL STRUGGLE

The first reports arrived to distant state and church officials in October 1898. A man known as El Enviado de Dios (The One Sent from God) had appeared in Chiriguaná, Magdalena, bearing on his back an invisible crucifix and followed by disciples who hung banners depicting the image of the holy cross. People flocked "to hear his word, and to be cured of their infirmities from which they suffer" by receiving a blessed cloth on their heads or by kissing the "crucifix" he carried.[116] El Enviado and his followers moved west and south through recently expanded cattle estates to the Magdalena River, visiting villages and gathering women and men along the way. Officials in Guamal reported that he arrived "surrounded by more than 4,000 people who paid tribute to him in a cult of accentuated idolatry," and by the time he reached El Banco in early November, the crowds had grown to 7,000. Bogas spread word along the river south to Tamalameque and north to Barranquilla and Cartagena, inspiring hopes of El Enviado's appearance far beyond his actual path. One priest warned that the "obsession is great" and that the movement "has deep roots that have penetrated not only in the pueblos through which he passed but through those quite distant." By the time of his approach to Mompós days later, he had attracted perhaps 10,000 peaceful followers.[117]

Omens had portended his arrival—an earthquake shook the Magdalena Valley in July, the river flooded and yellow fever erupted that October—yet

Enviadistas were not animists reflexively bracing against the fortunes of nature.[118] Instead, the movement appeared to trace paths cut by Gaitán's protestors in 1885 and soldiers of the counterrepublic in 1860, events many locals had lived through. There had also been the more recent abortive Liberal uprising of early 1895, which had been embraced by many "mulattoes" and people "of Negro and Indian blood" of the coast, according to one foreigner.[119] By the turn of the century the longing for renewal was again in evidence, as once steadfastly progovernment coastal towns had begun to "show themselves indifferent" to official rule. For Caribbean Liberals, indifference may have come after expectations of a lopsided victory in the 1897 elections had been dashed by Nationalist fraud. Another sign of restiveness was the massive crowd in Barranquilla in July 1898 that had warmly received a speech by Rafael Uribe Uribe calling for rebellion against the government. Coastal officials, moreover, had warned Bogotá for years that individuals were "attracting the masses with promises that the day of vengeance was near."[120]

Thousands thronged to El Enviado in anticipation of jubilee, and, as in contemporaneous movements around the world, his followers came to hear him preach a remedy for dispossession. He may have been joined by some Magdalena peasants who had formed a "revolutionary junta" in 1896 to protect their holdings against confiscation, perhaps to prevent a fate similar to that of colonos who had been driven out of the countryside by hacendado violence in the 1880s.[121] By the time he arrived on the scene, years of recession had curtailed wage work and had eroded subsistence for those still able to find paid employment. And perhaps more important than the *terremoto* of 1898 was the tax increase on the government liquor monopoly that year. Much of this history could be heard through El Enviado's preaching against land enclosures and the wealthy with prophecies, as one priest summarized them, "that soon will come the day when the wage for the poor will be 1.50 pesos and [for the rest] 20 centavos—That the rich will be the poor, and they the rich."[122] For Enviadistas enduring deteriorating living standards and even real hunger, his preaching signaled justice and a coming rearrangement of the social order.

And yet his principal message about dispossession seemed to be a spiritual one, as his movement reignited the popular Caribbean religious traditions of past decades. Along with powers to heal the sick, El Enviado's followers "believe him to be anointed by God to introduce reforms to the Catholic Church."[123] As women and men retook control of parish cemeteries and chapels, he ordered them to attend mass, forbade song and dance during religious observance, and excluded them from contact with nonfollowers. They stole cattle for him, which he ordered slaughtered, "of which half goes to the poor, and the rest he leaves to the benefit of the Church without touching the money."[124] He contrasted his own methods to those of priests he judged "the exploiters of Humanity"—men who robbed the people through baptismal and burial fees—and which he countered by preaching that "each should give willingly what they can and want to give." One observer noted, "The only thing heard in the entire street is a murmur approving and commenting favorably on the pronouncements."[125] Hearing the message, Enviadistas arrived at each new parish eager to force priests into submission, and the latter either prostrated themselves or fled. As another sign of moral restoration, parishioners reasserted in public the respectability and legitimacy of their family lives, which El Enviado validated through consecrations of unions and baptisms of children without payment.[126]

Caribbean civil officials believed that spiritual protest would quickly segue into general rebellion. They comprehended the movement's earthly implications, the likelihood that "the fanaticism of these poor people could lead them to offer resistance to the police," and that followers would "disavow completely civil and ecclesiastical authorities and impede the collection of all public revenue."[127] Bolívar's governor chose not to wait for news of whether El Enviado would render unto Caesar what was Caesar's and requested intervention from the Ministry of War. A gunboat patrolling an arm of the Magdalena River in mid-November 1898 arrested the messiah, who peacefully surrendered to authorities. It became known that El Enviado was "an obscure man, of poor social condition," named Hermógenes Ramírez. This revelation only further unsettled officials, who were at a loss to understand how an unknown "lunatic" could raise a religious army in such a short time, especially one that seemed to them on the cusp of open rebellion.[128]

Their concerns were well founded: in the weeks after Ramírez's arrest, his thousands of followers scattered throughout the Magdalena Valley, arming themselves against the government. Throughout late 1898 and into 1899, Enviadistas built defenses, repelled attacks by government troops, and entered towns to assassinate officials. The prefect of Mompós reported the "revolutionary symptom" of "scandals that occurred in various villages motivated by Hermógenes Ramírez."[129] In June 1899, El Enviado's followers engaged in daily shootouts with the police in El Banco; hundreds of millenarians in Guamal walked the streets by day and burned down houses by night; and armed disciples in Mojana attempted to overthrow the provincial government. A gunboat carrying a company of soldiers patrolled the river during the early months of 1899 in a vain attempt to impose order on a world turned upside down.[130]

Elite public opinion on the coast blamed the rebellion on dissolute parish priests, eliciting protests from clergy who pleaded impotence before the chiliastic fervor. As El Banco's vicar commented in late 1898, "If all this [heresy] exists today despite the pseudo-Messiah's being captured; if they wait for him and see imaginary crosses[;] . . . if the priest can do nothing because he lacks prestige, since they do not want to listen to him; if the civil authority that has not followed along with the imposter is abandoned, because [the people] have not given it their support to diminish various scandals; if this is true, as everyone can be persuaded of, I ask, what is the remedy?"[131] The problem reached far beyond a few parishes, as rumors and sightings flourished across the coast long after El Enviado's arrest. A man in Morales claimed to be the messiah; market women in Cartagena offered food to the poor in honor of Hermógenes Ramírez; and word spread of a possible attack in the name of El Enviado "by the people against the commerce of Barranquilla."[132] And even as the vicar declared victory over "hypocrisy," he also confided, "still I do not go out into the street"; instead he issued pronouncements from the safety of his house. The solution to this state of affairs, he wrote, was an extensive missionary effort backed by the guns of government—that is, a regeneration of the Regeneration.[133]

Besides the ferocity of the fighting, what disturbed priests and civil officials most about the Enviadista rebellion, and what inspired their calls for militarized missionary work, was the absence of individuals they could identify as the uprising's legitimate leaders. Nationalist rulers on the coast and in Bogotá who were prone to call every local disturbance a Liberal conspiracy were at a loss to explain a movement by market women, bogas, peasants, and day laborers that had turned violent after the elimination of their figurehead. The region's "inhabitants, almost all of the black race," wrote one foreign Jesuit, "are very disposed to spiritual and intellectual cultivation, even if some are still tainted by the deceptions of the famous Enviado."[134] And yet his followers proved that they did not need him to carry on their protest. In Guamal, the Enviadista leader was a woman known as Doña Juana (also the name of the village where Ramírez had been captured), who led her armed group through the streets without fear of reprisal. In El Carmen as well, "the women formed tumultuous public demonstrations," and female disciples led violent attacks against the prefect. By September 1899, a widely dispersed and unorganized movement had expelled or killed dozens of priests, soldiers, and public officials.

Although, unlike the Canudos in Northeastern Brazil, they founded no permanent settlement, Enviadistas continued to live and carry out armed assaults throughout the lower Magdalena Valley. Unwilling to contemplate what conditions may have precipitated ongoing mass violence, regional officials could only consider measures to wipe out its symptoms.[135]

Enviadistas attempted to dismantle the Regeneration's authoritarian relations of state, church, and property along a periphery that possessed few material or political resources. They won some concrete concessions from local officials who had been threatened with annihilation, which was a sign less of the movement's strength than of the chronic weakness of public force in rural districts. The Enviadistas' physical distance from the centers of official power accentuated this dynamic. Civil and religious leaders in the coastal cities had limited means to counter them yet could disregard an isolated rebellion that had little chance of disrupting their rule.[136] Bogotá, distracted at the moment of El Enviado's arrival by controversies over presidential succession, hardly registered the movement threatening to engulf the Caribbean backlands. Nevertheless, even as Hermógenes Ramírez followed Ricardo Gaitán Obeso to a death in the Panamanian dungeons, both leaders kept disciples who remained willing to go to war in their names.[137]

CHAPTER SEVEN

Class War of a Thousand Days

Two lethal years had already passed when the police inspector for Pié de la Popa informed the prefect about the troubles in his district caused by the armed conflict. The inspector complained that every Sunday hundreds of men and women, "among them army deserters, convicted criminals, and other bad elements who, due to the state of war, do not pass through the public streets or live in this place, but who on the days of fiesta gather in large groups." The crowds made a mockery of his authority, since "due to the distance and the lookout position that they establish, they are confident that they will never be captured." The distance described by the inspector in his September 1901 report was not a physical one, however, since Pié de la Popa lay within sight (and cannon shot) of the walls of Cartagena and a leisurely half-hour walk from the headquarters of the region's civil, military, and religious institutions.[1] Instead, the crowds there seemed to fall into the interstices between the protective inclusion of the wartime government and a social anonymity that a monopoly of force could not surmount. In the conflict that came to be known as the Thousand Days' War (1899–1902), this distance often proved unpredictable yet ineluctable all the same.

Launched by Liberals in October 1899, the Thousand Days' War erupted into other ongoing conflicts that helped explain its terrible prolongation. Partisan motivations for the war were clear on both sides. The militant faction of the Liberal Party rebelled in attempts to regain political power and public standing after fifteen years of near total exclusion under the Nationalists. In response to the unfolding rebellion, the partisan government became increasingly intransigent, as personified by officials like Bolívar's civil-military governor, Joaquín Vélez, a Conservative from Cartagena who had fought against Juan José Nieto's popular coup in 1859. Yet within this political violence, which was not unlike earlier partisan clashes, appeared other social struggles. In addition to fast depreciating scrip, the state and insurgents funded the war by expropriating property, labor, and commodities. As the country's commercial economy verged on collapse, the military strategy of expropriation changed the nature of fighting and closed off possibilities for peace long after the exhaustion of partisan hostilities. As battlefields passed from standing armies to locally organized guerrillas and progovernment civic battalions, banditry, coercion, and theft entered the logic of sustaining combat forces. The guerrillas' survival strategies and government's policy of taking no quarter were guided by similar exigencies.

Both the Liberal insurgents and the Nationalist (after July 1900, Conservative) government forces marshaled supporters of all social ranks, yet deepening differences in geography and status shaped the war for material survival. Bogotá was rarely under imminent military threat from rural guerrillas, and while the Liberals enjoyed a wide range of movement this was only in the increasingly distant backlands. The state pooled its resources and followers in the cities, where it defended citizens deemed legitimate and honorable while policing impoverished urban working populations. The reproduction of lettered distinctions allowed legitimists to portray the war as a rebellion of nobodies, which deprived guerrillas of standing as formal combatants and made negotiations unacceptable. Denying the rebellion legality also permitted government expropriations of property and labor from a growing class of Colombians designated as enemy subversives.[2] The divide between lettered legality and unlettered subversion did not prevent the appearance of internal tensions within each camp over status and legitimacy, which hampered the war effort for the Liberals and government alike. Estimates on the war dead, which range from 40,000 to 100,000, were a grim reflection of partisan hatreds but also of the bureaucratized and mechanized violence guided by material dispossession and the mass denial of citizenship rights.[3]

In the Caribbean region, social and cultural distinctions prevailed from the start of the war. From the foothills of the coastal Sierra Nevada, Sabas Socarrás was one of the first to join the Liberal rebellion, and over the years he rose through its ranks and earned respect from fellow insurgents. With few standing armies and a vast countryside relinquished by government forces, Socarrás and members of other guerrilla bands dominated the region. Yet camaraderie among Liberals of various classes, regions, and backgrounds did not provide them with the military capacity to take on the cities. Nor did they have the means to subvert the illegitimacy imposed on them by the government and its allies, as their relegation to the same backlands that nourished the ongoing Enviadista rebellion reinforced their marginal standing. Combat at the turn of the century, along with its related antecedent rebellion in 1895, underscored preexisting antagonisms that cast Caribbean Liberals, peasants, and laborers as outsiders to and enemies of the republic.[4] Like the crowds gathered at Pié de la

Popa, other disenfranchised citizens of the coast experienced the war as both the limits of state power and the ramification of exclusions enacted after 1885 to dismantle emancipation's democratic legacy.

GUERRILLA WARFARE

On the night of 19 October 1899, men in Cartagena quietly exited the city and headed "in an unknown direction," although soon it was clear that they had joined others in revolt in the Caribbean countryside.[5] This revolt, which coincided with others across the country, inspired new multiclass and multiregional concord among Liberals. Some men from the coast and the Cauca traveled to the department of Santander, site of the formal commencement of hostilities, where they were embraced as "those noble blacks. . . . Heroes without names!" These insurgents may have been inspired by Liberal leader Rafael Uribe Uribe's aide-de-camp, Saúl Zuleta, a "mulatto" who began the war as a sergeant major and ascended to the rank of colonel.[6] Perhaps General Ramón "El Negro" Marín or Colonel José Cinecio Mina, men of color who led Liberal forces in Tolima and the Cauca, respectively, encouraged other Caribbean men to fight.[7] Social and interregional mixing took place in the opposite direction, too, when Sabas Socarrás welcomed youth from Antioquia, Boyacá, and Santander, who traveled to the coast to join guerrillas who were, according to one foreign observer, "endless gradations of mulattoes, half-breeds and mixtures of Negro and Indian blood." In the early months of the rebellion, Liberals appeared to reignite the popular enthusiasm behind Gaitán's 1885 campaign, and before that, the counterrepublic of 1860.[8]

The Liberals' standing armies met defeat, however, in Santander in May 1900, after which the incipient national movement dissolved into small-scale, localized, and autonomous guerrilla forces. In the Caribbean region, rural warfare had held sway since the war's commencement, with small units confronting much larger, albeit not necessarily better prepared, government troops.[9] Coastal insurgents severed the cities from their hinterlands but did not hold any territory for long, choosing instead to remain in forest and mountain havens, "and when they appear[ed] in some small, defenseless town they vanish[ed] immediately after" their attacks.[10] Armed Liberal forces used their knowledge of the terrain and relations with local populations to their advantage in hit-and-run operations that outmaneuvered more encumbered army battalions.[11] They also hired indigenous and peasant men as scouts or lookouts, and they relied on an ability to blend in with noncombatant populations. Guerrilla leader

Joaquín Mercado Robles and his troops operated on the outskirts of Cartagena with little fear of attack because they had personal connections to several Dique Canal villages, which provisioned them and kept them informed on government troop movements. At the height of the fighting in 1900–1901, more than a dozen separate guerrilla groups, each with a few hundred to a thousand men, wandered their own coastal territory in continuous circuits of attack and flight.[12]

Reinforcing the guerrilla nature of the Caribbean war were the Enviadistas, who by the time of the Santander declaration had been carrying out armed attacks on local authorities for nearly a year. Some men appeared to leave coastal cities to join directly with the millenarians entrenched in the Mompós region. Even as official concern shifted from the Enviadistas to Liberals in October 1899, the local rebellion began absorbing armed disciples and their tactics to fuse partisan violence with a revolutionary folk Catholicism.[13] After Liberals declared war, Caribbean parishioners began a new round of expelling priests, who were forced either to flee to the cities or join the rebellion. Enviadistas and Liberals succeeded in recruiting many of them. Unlike priests elsewhere in the country, who had "helped the Government efficaciously[,] . . . here they cause damage to it" by acting as "exaggerated propagandists" of the insurgency, conduits of information, or even guerrilla leaders in their own right.[14] Fearing harm would come their way, a few doctrinaire clergy who refused to submit in the lower Magdalena River villages, a region "obligatory for the Revolution," beseeched Santa Marta's bishop Celedón for reassignment to more sympathetic parishes in Antioquia or Tunja.[15]

Guerrilla priests alerted contemporaries to the emergence of a new class of leaders from modest backgrounds and with few ties to formal politics. While literacy encouraged some men to adopt the pompous title of general, the "Liberal authorities were constituting themselves," according to Sabas Socarrás, around men who looked much like the foot soldiers they led. Alongside Socarrás and Joaquín Mercado Robles were commanders Manuel "El Indio" Vera, Rafael Hernández Cárdenas, José María Lugo, and Plácido Camacho, men who won Rafael Uribe Uribe's appreciation and respect early in the war.[16] Others on the fringes of the conflict took charge of local units as well: a "black man" named Francisco Pereira Castro who commanded forces in 1895; José Garizábalo, an "ignorant man of the people" from Ríofrio, Magdalena; a champán patrón known to outsiders only as Meneses who in 1900 organized 250 Magdalena River bogas for the rebellion.[17] This popular mobilization was noted by Rafael Uribe Uribe who hailed the rise of "distinguished Jefes and Officials of all races, of all social classes, and of all professions," which stitched the insurgency to traditions of armed citizenship that had been practiced since the 1850s.[18]

In the Caribbean countryside, guerrillas and others quickly turned to banditry. Cattle rustling, jail breaks in exchange for money, and robberies on Cartagena's railroad were so frequent from the onset of hostilities that one official feared "the coast will be a boon for the revolution."[19] The insurgents proved adept at taking towns, in particular those on the savannas south of Cartagena, and remaining long enough to commit theft but fleeing before the arrival of military forces. As government troops were spread thin across the region, guerrilla groups began lingering in towns in order to destroy public registries of property holdings or criminal court records and to burn down the homes of wealthy progovernment inhabitants.[20] Local populations sometimes facilitated these acts, and banditry blurred traditional distinctions between combatants and noncombatants. The Liberals "were totally unprovided for with supplies of any kind," noted one observer, "depending for subsistence upon their sympathizers or forced contributions from their opponents." Guerrilla attacks against hacendados and small-town governments might have strengthened the access to land for rural laborers and peasants, although such actions also made smallholders accomplices to subversion. Some villages in the Magdalena Valley that rooted out insurgents for the military may have wanted to avoid just such an accusation. Still other communities attempted to evade either active rebellion or collusion with officials when confronted with the widening civil war.[21]

Rapidly deteriorating economic conditions soon made any political motivations secondary to basic survival. Food scarcity and wartime hyperinflation led insurgents to scavenge in order to remain self-sustaining, with small detachments working at night to pilfer animals and supplies from rural farms. When not on campaign, Sabas Socarrás dispersed his men over a considerable area for ease in provisioning through petty confiscation.[22] After subsistence moved to the fore as military strategy, Liberal forces had little motivation to hold towns for long. Early in the war, Socarrás's band had endured a precarious existence in Riohacha, wracked by yellow fever and hunger, which encouraged them to bivouac in the more bountiful countryside.[23] As in other contemporary Latin American conflicts, Colombian banditry may have communicated political or entrepreneurial intent, yet as the already debilitated formal economy broke down, much of the theft appeared to be part of a struggle for sheer existence.[24]

Regardless of their motives, banditry and guerrilla warfare were the pretext the national government used to impose a policy of war without mercy. With the outbreak of war, progovernment opinion invoked an older propaganda of plebeian Liberal rape, couched in newer rhetoric of the state's legal obligation to protect honorable women and "distinguished families" from unknown yet potentially ubiquitous assailants.[25] This rhetoric encouraged government intransigence, which hardened after the July 1900 coup toppled the Nationalists and brought to power dissident Conservatives around President José Manuel Marroquín, who within a month of taking power broke off peace negotiations with Liberal leaders.[26] Bogotá's war of no compunction delineated specific and enhanced punishments for "acts of ferocity and barbarity," with each considered its own class of political crime: rape, rape of nuns, defacing churches, attacking priests, pedophilia, stealing cattle. The list of sexual deviancy and common crime that made one "an enemy of the Government" grew longer as the war dragged on.[27] Postcoup leaders took their language from penal codes that already held prospective insurgents liable for all acts of crime and terror committed during rebellion, hence turning the forty-year-old legends of Liberal savagery into the bureaucratic sinews of war. From the commencement of hostilities military justice trumped civil guarantees, and after Marroquín took power field officers were granted the authority to summarily execute captured guerrillas.[28] The vast criminalization of behavior divided an honorable, if vulnerable, citizenry from a growing mass of disenfranchised insurgents, a dichotomy that rationalized state violence. Denied even the minimal standing necessary to restart peace negotiations, Liberal rebels were rendered outside the bounds of national life.

The recrudescent discourse of savagery, which pivoted on the essential role played by plebeian men of color, was also reshaped by changing material realities. In 1895, Nationalist propagandists described the insurgents as "African hordes" descending on the country, and the government's annual published military report violated racial etiquette by describing Liberal armies as "blacks who inhabit the dense forests of the Cauca." Yet this overtly antiblack language appears to have receded after the uprising began again in 1899.[29] A shift in tone may have resulted from Liberal attempts to form an integrated, cross-regional, and multiclass alliance after the Santander proclamation, in contrast to the localized combat of the 1895 uprising. The decline in racialized propaganda also underscored the abrupt mechanization of Colombian warfare after 1899. Men who joined the rebellion in October with machetes, the weapon of the overwhelming majority of combatants in past wars, were soon issued state-of-the-art repeating rifles. Mechanization transformed the course of fighting, and Sabas Socarrás spent much time in endless pilgrimages securing first food and water and afterward bullets for the late-model European rifles his soldiers carried.[30] Firearms wiped out visible status markers in weaponry and nearly eclipsed the racially coded image of the savage Caribbean machetero. Prestige, skill, and rank still stratified armies, but foot soldiers on both sides gained a new reputation as gun-toting troops, which appeared to submerge older distinctions.[31]

Legitimists reacted to this modernization of warfare with a new rhetoric of obscurity that denied recognition to their Liberal enemies and shored up their own legitimacy. One side of the conflict was composed of a "few notable persons" and their dependents in the cities, while on the other side was a mass of unknown "people of the worst social condition" in the countryside.[32] According to polemicists, insurgents other than Rafael Uribe Uribe were an agglomeration of no-name youth, and like Caribbean leader "El Indio Vera, of terrible memory and worse achievement," none was "notable for his political, social, or military prestige, for his knowledge or his wealth."[33] According to Nationalist and Conservative leaders, this phenomenon defined relations among insurgents themselves, in which the "hordes of obscure personages that form among the Colombian Liberal traitors" made divining their motivations next to impossible.[34] While treason was at least a recognizable and punishable crime, writers lamented that "some honorable men . . . serve as unconscious instruments in the hands of unbridled mobs," a disturbing reversal of the order of things. At the same time, Caribbean guerrillas were "wretched peasants" who were converted into "anarchist multitudes" and fed by an anomic "anti-Catholic and socialist spirit." Unlike the feared but definable macheteros led by Mosquera and Nieto in 1860, the presumed "lack of banner" among Caribbean guerrillas in 1899 was a sign that public men did not number among them. Given the banditry of disenfranchised citizens on one side and the war without mercy on the other, some observers asked whether it was even a proper political conflict.[35]

The propaganda of obscurity carried clear advantages for elite Liberals already predisposed to comply with the government. Many individuals on the coast had supported political agitation since the 1880s, yet they had given a cool reception to Rafael Uribe Uribe and his coconspirators. Once the rural and millenarian warfare spread, most Caribbean letrados sided with their party's few remaining national peace leaders.[36] Government officials rewarded this pacifist stance by maintaining cordial relations with prominent party members, and even Bolívar's governor, Joaquín Vélez, national symbol of partisan intransigence, offered two seats to Liberal leaders on Barranquilla's city council during the war. Encouraged by mass arrests, twenty-four-hour curfews for known Liberals, and the suspension of suffrage and other civil guarantees, the region's peace camp grasped the political influence offered them, in the process further isolating armed Liberal forces in the countryside.[37]

The fractures of class and region shaped the internal relations within the uprising itself. After their standing armies were defeated in May 1900, Rafael Uribe Uribe, Justo Durán of Santander, and other Liberal commanders broke for the coast. Yet after the initial surge of national organizing withered and as banditry grew, these mobile officers often proved unable to cultivate and maintain lasting connections with local forces. Sabas Socarrás watched as Justo Durán arrived in Magdalena and "improvised the subaltern officers of those troops," compelled in part by the inexperience of Caribbean rebels but also by Durán's lack of personal ties in the region.[38] The strains on these relations followed patterns set in previous years when Rafael Uribe Uribe, Luis A. Robles, and other conspirators had plotted rebellion in exile. Liberals who fraternized abroad with Cuban nationalists and anti-Porfirian radicals during the 1890s had acquired political cache and materiel but had surrendered some of their firsthand knowledge of Colombian social realities. Many Caribbean men refused to acknowledge the authority of these ex-patriot and exiled leaders, especially when they sent unknown agents and foreigners to plot uprisings on national soil in 1895 and 1899. To militant Liberals of the coast, this self-styled leadership was an unknown quantity.[39]

With relationships already fraught, the rebellion's leadership from other regions often failed to impose its will on local forces. Some coastal units refused to serve under Justo Durán and deserted the ones he assumed to lead. Rafael Uribe Uribe's personal choice to lead the coastal insurgency in 1901, Boyacá native Clodomiro F. Castillo, also discovered an unwillingness to abide by outside authority, as locals rejected the "injustice" of his forcing Caribbean men to relinquish command. During three rounds of negotiations, "all with the same negative ending," Sabas Socarrás tried to mediate between Uribe Uribe's deputies and "various subaltern jefes," who proposed an "insurrection" within the rebellion itself. After the talks collapsed, Castillo was dismissed, leaving for Venezuela "with arms and munitions but with no men," while Caribbean guerrillas fought on without outside interference. When Castillo finally established his authority within the Caribbean movement late in the war, after months of building relationships with locals, Socarrás and other commanders retained wide leeway in decision-making, which Castillo had little choice but to ratify.[40]

Much of this internal dissension might be traced to Rafael Uribe Uribe's violation of the trust of Caribbean insurgents. Soon after arriving on the coast in October 1900, Uribe Uribe issued his "Decree on Guerrillas," declaring that "with the name of guerrillas exist [on the coast] diverse armed groups that, claiming to serve the Liberal Cause, only discredit it with their predations and excesses." Caribbean insurgents were, moreover, "gangs of bandits that lack all right to carry a political name" and who "dishonor the noble profession of arms." This interpretation of coastal banditry confused the guerrillas' subsistence strategies and their political goals, in effect dismissing the validity of both. Moreover, Uribe Uribe had singled out Caribbean forces even though Liberal standing armies in other regions had disbanded and guerrilla warfare was by then widespread.[41] The decree had been in part a response to local autonomy, which limited the influence of national Liberal leadership. Uribe Uribe's inability to impose discipline over local forces was proving fatal to his party's claim to be ready to begin formal peace negotiations again—and perhaps more important, ready to govern the republic again. In reproducing the government's own rhetoric of criminalization, he also squandered some of the goodwill he had established with his July 1898 Barranquilla speech calling for war. The lettered consensus on the illegitimacy of guerrilla warfare, to which some war Liberal leaders were ready to concede, undermined any potential claims plebeian insurgents may have attempted to make from service in arms. Perhaps as a consequence of Uribe Uribe's October 1900 antibanditry decree, Caribbean forces subjected his decision-making to intense scrutiny and referendum for the remainder of the war.[42]

Even as Sabas Socarrás worked to overcome differences between local troops and national officers, the breakdown of internal unity and governmental intransigence weakened the position of the coastal guerrillas. Uribe Uribe further aggrieved the Magdalena volunteers by ordering them into neighboring Bolívar in early 1901; when they refused, the Antioqueño general demanded that they disband. As Justo Durán left for Venezuela, most of the Magdalena insurgents mutinied by fleeing into the Caribbean interior and continuing to fight "sin jefes." Unable to command the region's forces and fighting a war that appeared unwinnable, the officers around Rafael Uribe Uribe counseled that he sue for peace. Marroquín's government, however, rejected their overture. Denied legal standing as combatants by the state and spurned by their erstwhile followers, Uribe Uribe and his subordinates fled the country. Impoverished

Caribbean Liberals, however, had little choice but to continue to fight in an uprising with no end in sight and without possibility of gaining official recognition.[43]

THE PREDATORY STATE

The relegation of guerrilla forces to the countryside allowed the government's civil and military establishment to concentrate its hold over cities and towns. With representative government suspended, civil administration was turned over to regional military commands, the Jefes Civiles y Militares, like Bolívar governor Joaquín Vélez, who prosecuted the war with impunity. The militarization of civil functions offered Bogotá the pretext to bestow or divest towns of their administrative status, which determined the allocation of resources and political power, an authority the government had long been denied by the Supreme Court.[44] The increasing centralization of state power was also witnessed in the military's attempts to impose honorable conduct on its forces in the hopes of projecting legitimacy against Liberal banditry, yet this attempt at professionalizing the army stood in contrast to the government's subsequent punitive measures.[45] Militarized coastal police prohibited public gatherings of more than three individuals, set curfews in every community, arrested suspected Liberals at will, and mandated passbooks for all domestic travel not related to provisioning food.[46] Masonic lodges needed approval to remain open, public schoolteachers were fired when deemed politically suspect, and transport companies were fined up to 100,000 pesos for employing individuals accused of aiding insurgents. A U.S. military officer who observed the early stages of the war commented that Colombians "suddenly awaken to the fact that the normal modicum of civil procedure has been supplanted by martial law."[47]

Militarization of civil functions encouraged further centralization of fiscal authority, which expanded its state power while ultimately undermining the public trust. The national government commandeered steamboats and railroads for military purposes and siphoned what was left of municipal funds into national coffers.[48] Bogotá also expropriated wealth by demanding loans from the Banco de Barranquilla, the country's only bank to survive the inflationary 1890s. Although private credit was frozen and business leaders viewed the measure gravely, public officials professed the right to draw down wealth accumulated through state-backed commercial monopolies and Caribbean land grabs during previous years.[49] These confiscations did not come close to paying for the war effort, however, and national officials relied on unchecked printing of paper money, which expanded their reach over the economy while simultaneously wrecking it. During the three years of war, the average annual rate of monetary depreciation was 150 percent, twice that rate during certain months. The 5:1 exchange rate with the dollar in mid-1899 had zoomed to 260:1 three years later, which gave the Colombian peso the dubious distinction as the world's most worthless national currency. Hyperinflation not only made wartime price controls on essential consumer items impossible to sustain, but the demise of the formal economy ensured that guerrillas—and many noncombatants—would resort to banditry for their subsistence.[50]

As the government went into bankruptcy, war managers guided local officials to sustain combat through predatory tactics. By 1901, they abandoned any attempt to placate potentially insurgent populations and began to penalize with taxes and property confiscations all "authors, accomplices, aids, and sympathizers of the rebellion."[51] The policy subjected entire regions deemed Liberal to liability for the war, and the Caribbean coast stood out as a prime culprit. The area's military command understood that discriminatory expropriation was an unpleasant and even counterproductive practice but argued that it "constitute[d] the right of the occupying force in enemy territory," by which it meant the entire coast.[52] Officials declared they had little choice but to take from the "disaffected," because two years into the war "lack of sufficient resources" hindered the state's ability to carry out basic functions. Beyond the appeal of retribution or financial necessity, scorched earth confiscations redistributed the economic burden of sustaining the war effort in an attempt—only partly successful, given hyperinflation—to protect progovernment citizens from financial sacrifice.[53]

Their loose definition of state enemies offered military commands no shortage of potential targets, especially where disenfranchised Caribbean populations abounded. In the earliest stages of conflict, military corridors ran through the coast, wreaking havoc on locals subjected to repeated confiscations and other privations.[54] Sweeps throughout the corridors made explicit targets of politically suspect bogas and fishermen, as the army confiscated watercraft without compensation. Officials' inherent distrust of laborers perhaps had been learned from past conflicts in which boatmen's physical mobility had made them valuable carriers of troops, supplies, and information. In order "to remove enemy elements and augment combustibles," hundreds of boats used for fishing or truck were chopped up for steamboat fuel, so that industrial technology literally consumed independent artisanal ways of life. Although motivation is impossible to determine for any given individuals, the government's destruction of watercraft may in part account for the hundreds of bogas who joined the Liberal insurgents.[55] A system of coerced payments also fell over hacendados and cattle ranchers, who protested loudly after their herds disappeared along with passing government troops, yet the laboring poor appeared to endure a disproportionate share of property seizures.[56]

These policies designed at some level to sustain the war effort created a host of other strategic problems. Some army units interpreted financial impunity as license to carry out unlimited depredations against populations in the military corridors. Yet because the military corridors followed major communication lines along the Magdalena River, the Dique Canal, and in the Ciénaga Grande, some civilians avoided theft and coercion by moving into the cities or deeper into the hinterlands.[57] Army officers judged a failure the seizing of property against those left behind because "authority is disrespected each time that a commission . . . proceeds arbitrarily, taking cattle and beasts from friends and enemies alike" without issuing receipts for future compensation. The head tax of 3,000 pesos per person imposed on the "disloyal" population in 1901 only generated more antigovernment hostility.[58] Out of a necessity to rationalize resources, the military abandoned some Nationalist– and Conservative-leaning coastal villages that it could not permanently secure. In order to consolidate governmental control over the military corridors as well as Cartagena, Barranquilla, Santa Marta, and other strategic towns, officials neglected supporters in the countryside, some of whom may have joined the rebellion as a result.[59]

The military's relationship to Caribbean populations, that of an occupying force in enemy territory, proved counterproductive in a number of ways. Caribbean soldiers in general refused to take up arms against their neighbors, and in February 1900, soldiers of Barranquilla's Junín Battalion blocked entry to the barracks of officers who tried to deliver their marching orders. In response to such acts of resistance, regional commander General Francisco J. Palacio, a Nationalist (former Liberal) and native of Barranquilla, requested that Bogotá replace locals with "men from the interior." National officials were incredulous at Palacio's assertion that "individuals of this coast do not work as soldiers," but similar complaints came from other officers in the region.[60] Palacio eventually won over Bogotá, although instead of the discipline and morality he anticipated, the soldiers he received displayed drunkenness and "immorality" after military victories. With internal dissension in government ranks unabated after the arrival of soldiers from Antioquia, the Caribbean command in September 1901 decreed the death penalty for all "culprits of desertion, cowardice, treason, and banditry" in its ranks. The decree, however, did not resolve the issue of soldiers' hunger ration, which reduced them to the same types of marauding conducted by guerrilla forces.[61] Unable to control the troops, officers seized upon Palacio's logic and blamed Antioqueño soldiers' insubordination and banditry on their "having familiarized themselves too much with the radicalism of this population." In rationale at least, it appeared that the government's promise to protect honorable families during rebellion had morphed into a war against Caribbean political culture that it was unlikely to win.[62]

Without sufficient troops or financial resources, officials relied on volunteers to sustain the war effort. Progovernment civic battalions, which predominated in some areas as early as 1899, extended the government's military reach even as they reinforced the localistic nature of the conflict.[63] At first composed of government bureaucrats, the army command soon authorized other self-provisioning units not dependent on increasingly precarious public financing.[64] Unable to deploy forces to all the dispersed guerrilla strongholds in the countryside, officers stationed units only in communities deemed loyal or vital to the war effort. In coastal cities the volunteer units were organized at the neighborhood level, with Cartagena's half-dozen civilian companies often marching in parades and drills side-by-side with regular infantry units.[65] The occasional progovernment "guerrilla" harassed Sabas Socarrás's insurgents in rural Magdalena, although most volunteers remained in cities and towns to guarantee internal security. When military forces retook communities, their first orders were to assemble local men into units to reestablish governmental control and, it was hoped, break Liberal guerrilla links to the towns.[66]

The creation of civic battalions and other paramilitary units depended to a significant degree on the institutionalization of the Catholic Church during the Regeneration. After the Liberal proclamation of war in 1899, religious orders offered their property and resources to the state, and their members took up the running of prisons and other services to ease the burden on the national administration.[67] Public officials also received an enthusiastic response from male students of colegios—which were shuttered after the war began—often animated by the possibility of spiritual warfare. Other religious institutions created by the church provided volunteers as well, like the elite male Catholic Youth, founded in Barranquilla in the 1890s, which was converted into a reserve force at the outbreak of hostilities. Propaganda depicting atheistic Liberal violations of churches, priests, and nuns, as well as the official role granted to many curates in government forces, stoked the appeal to adolescents of religious combat.[68]

Despite this enthusiastic response from lettered youth, prochurch Caribbean artisans appeared to supply the more significant paramilitary forces. Cartagena's Bolívar Battalion became the premier artisan-composed unit, but laboring men also formed self-defense units of more diverse makeup, like the "merchants, employees, and [men from] other important social guilds" who comprised the Libres.[69] Artisan-led civic battalions conformed to and reinforced the distinctions in status at the heart of the conflict, since the primary function of these units was to police "the popular masses" and suppress potential urban rebellion.[70] Nevertheless, their military service was made ambiguous by divided loyalties, and whereas many of Cartagena's craftsmen stood with the regime Rafael Núñez helped create, their brethren in Barranquilla often formed the anti-Regeneration vanguard. The role of progovernment artisans was obscured, moreover, by propaganda that touted only "distinguished youths" defending legitimacy and honor against unknown hordes.[71]

Although volunteers who took up self-defense came from varied social backgrounds, all demanded public validation or other rewards for their sacrifice. Some of the indigenous Guajiro and Arhuaco men who repeatedly ambushed the unit led by Sabas Socarrás were long-standing clients of local Conservative bosses, whose service to the government allowed them to fulfill political obligations even as they protected their communities from armed outsiders. Some of their political patrons had been passed over in the awarding of army commands, and prominent Nationalists and Conservatives sometimes mustered volunteers to demonstrate their worth to the government. Barranquilla's few progovernment artisans used their military service to demand legal recognition of a new mutual aid society.[72] Like peace Liberals who offered their allegiance to Bogotá and the local civil-military chiefs, these volunteers sought a legitimate public role at a time of mass criminalization of antigovernment and even merely indifferent populations. These mobilizations, as more institutionalized versions of an older armed citizenship, took place in cities and towns, which further cleaved urban citizens from rural subversives.

Yet just as the Liberals experienced troubled relations between officers and the rank and file, so too did volunteers break with government officials who failed to cultivate their trust. In the early phase of the fighting, Joaquín Vélez warned Bogotá that "Barranquilla is defended by civic battalions and undisciplined people, all the population being hostile." Politics was one motivation for this hostility, but so was "maltreatment" of soldiers and civilians, which often led to desertions, sometimes en masse.[73] Mal-treatment also led to one of the most significant incidents of coastal urban unrest during the war. When a fire ravaged Mompós in 1900, the 500 men of the local civic battalion refused to muster, "impelled by the quite natural desire to attend to their families threatened with perishing in the flames." Although they returned to the barracks after the emergency, their commander had them flogged for insubordination. The reaction was im-mediate, as "hundreds of subjects of all social classes" attempted to over-throw the municipal government, leading to days of public discontent and violence. Officials readily admitted that the use of corporal punishment "completely broke the harmony between the Chiefs of the Forces and the population" and robbed paramilitary troops of honorable standing. De-spite the threat of being labeled subversives, volunteers willingly disre-spected authority, and such moments of conflict may have offered effective recruiting opportunities to the insurgency.[74]

THE LABOR WAR

Between the guerrilla-controlled countryside and the militarized towns were working people who struggled to contain the effects of rapidly dete-riorating wages, markets, and working and living conditions. Urban Co-lombians without access to provisioning grounds were subjected to the full force of hyperinflation, which soon wiped out the purchasing power of wages. As a partial index of the peso's collapse, the Cartagena day labor-ers paid six reales (seventy-five centavos) and the government-employed bogas paid one peso in 1899, when the value of paper money had already faltered, were by 1903 paid ten and fifteen pesos, respectively. Neverthe-less, wage adjustments did not keep up with the climb in housing costs or the thirtyfold increase in the price of meat over the same period.[75] Most members of the middling and laboring sectors felt the war's economic ef-fects well before its end. In January 1900, officials closed Cartagena's food lottery for the poor, which had been set up during the hunger scare of the late 1890s, after it became clear that artisans and even leading families could no longer afford to contribute to it.[76]

Despite precarious urban social conditions, the concentration of war-fare in the countryside drove a mass of rural inhabitants into the coastal cities. Documentary evidence for wartime migration is scarce, yet in the years after the declaration of peace in 1902 it was noted that Caribbean cities, along with the Cauca Valley city of Cali, were experiencing the country's fastest population growth. Some of that in-migration came from the draw of new employment in factories and transportation during the second decade of the twentieth century, yet steady arrivals to coastal cities dated from the land enclosures of the early 1880s, which appeared to have accelerated with the rural violence and wartime expropriations in the countryside after October 1899.[77]

The growth of an urban landless population of unknown political loyalties and without sure employment made Barranquilla the focus of unrest and state surveillance. The Caribbean region's urban center, commercial hub, and home to the largest concentration of wage laborers demonstrated popular disaffection early in the war. In 1895, city officials suspended Carnival celebrations out of concern that rural guerrillas and urban revelers would join forces. Working people along the waterfront ignored the ban, a sign to some observers that Barranquilla harbored a movement that was "anarchist, formed of people of the worst social condition, so many of which abound in this populous city."[78] Subsequent protests might have come in response to the Nationalist government's attempts to police labor for the transportation monopoly. Just weeks before the uprising began again in October 1899, Bogotá issued a blanket decree accusing Barranquilla's thousands of stevedores of theft of port merchandise and mandating that they carry licenses and identify themselves to all passengers and merchants.[79] Once the Liberals' Santander proclamation became known, the city's dockworkers helped steamboat crews commandeer their vessels, just as many had done for Gaitán in 1885. The government's quick consolidation of a military hold over the lower Magdalena River, however, exposed transportation workers to retribution, and ship and train crews were newly regulated by government inspectors who began measuring their workplace efficiency as an indication of political affiliation.[80] Continuing concerns that the ship and railroad crews would hand the city to the insurgents led officials to deploy artisan battalions to police them and in 1900 convinced Joaquín Vélez to move his civil-military command to Barranquilla from the more dependable Cartagena. None of this unrest surprised city officials, who by the time hundreds had gathered to hear Rafael Uribe Uribe's war speech in July 1898 were applying the "radical" epithet to both militant Liberalism and labor militancy. After the outbreak of hostilities, Vélez's subordinates began referring to local shipworkers and stevedores as "traitors."[81]

Magdalena River woodcutters in the military corridors waged their own campaign against wartime depredation. When the gunboats arrived at their stations, the owners often refused to carry wood onto the ships or even to sell it in the first place. It appeared that some cutters allowed insurgents to plant dynamite in their wood stacks to be found by unsuspecting soldiers.[82] Noncompliance with the military or outright collusion with guerrillas emerged from a chronic struggle over payments, which shaped the outcome of the war in the Magdalena Valley. The chronicler Julio H. Palacio, son of General Francisco Palacio and former secretary to Rafael Núñez, reported firsthand on this struggle. Early in the war, as the gunboat *Antioquia* loaded wood at Santa Rita (near Calamar), its purser realized he did not have sufficient funds to pay the owner. Asked to come aboard, the tall and "very moreno" man was offered an IOU redeemable in Barranquilla, yet he protested that traveling to the city would be detrimental and that "you all know better than I that not even in a time of war can anyone be deprived of their property in all or in part." Instead, the woodcutter made Palacio and the ship's officers sign a contract declaring they would return with the money. "I have not studied but I have read the laws," he told the officials, "because I am a citizen and the citizen must know his rights and duties." Even if Palacio's story is apocryphal, he did capture a real struggle along the river. As a protest against military confiscations without payment, woodcutters went on strike in mid-1901, which all but idled the army's river flotilla.[83]

Compared to the woodcutters' highly visible struggle for just payment, the conflict over military impressment was far more ubiquitous and less evident. As the peso's value faded away so too did local labor markets, and the militarized state turned to impressment to keep essential goods and services moving. General Palacio confessed in September 1901 that his recruiting efforts gave him "the reputation of being a heartless slave trader," yet his press gangs continued to search "fertile regions" of the coast, rounding up bogas by the dozens to serve as unpaid porters or deckhands on gunboats.[84] Systematic incrimination of Caribbean men eroded even the minimal guarantees offered to passbook-wielding food provisioners, who faced accusations from labor-hungry officials of being "people certainly evil" and "obviously Liberal." Unemployed boatmen, passbooks or not, were labeled threats to public order as a pretext to coerce their labor. Individuals fought back against military bondage, including the six bogas who sued the government after being kidnapped from the canoe *Australia* in 1901. Over the protests of ship captains and army officers, they won a rare legal victory in the form of financial compensation for lost possessions and rights. Most other workingmen, though, chose the old strategy of flight.[85] Woodcutters left for the forest to avoid armed patrols so that "not a single man is found" to load fuel onto ships, leaving self-defense forces to handle a job they considered fit for peons. The maritime *salinas* sat empty because salt harvesters feared becoming easy marks of conscription, and the disappearance of domestic salt production forced the government to import the mineral from Curaçao at a premium.[86]

Labor coercion as a wartime exigency underscored the paradoxes of the citizenship regime under the Regeneration. Congress had passed the country's first law of universal military conscription in 1896, with the stated intent of abolishing caste distinctions innate in forced recruitment. A universal system was impracticable, however, not least because Caribbean men still considered service in arms to be an entitlement and not a duty, which led many to resist recruitment as a cornerstone of popular rights.[87] The law was also trumped by the 1886 constitution's circumscribed definition of legitimate occupation, which facilitated state expropriation of labor from individuals deemed not to work in strategic industries or positions—in other words, bogas, peasants, day laborers, and peons. Since officials distrusted Caribbean populations politically and largely excluded them from regular military service, with even paramilitary duty limited to prescribed groups, workingmen were designated as a class that could and perhaps had to be exploited through forcible means.[88]

As political repression curtailed labor and public activities, wage workers still found ways to protest the manifold insecurities of the war. In March 1895, a contingent of Liberal guerrillas carried out a hit-and-run strike against troops stationed in Puerto Colombia. After the insurgents fled and before reinforcements could arrive from Barranquilla, hundreds of dock and railroad workers ransacked the customshouse, train station, and government offices. By causing "so much loss of profits," they signaled the intolerable nature of deteriorating wartime conditions while also demonstrating the ability to act independently of armed groups. As rumors of labor strikes circulated in Barranquilla, Governor Joaquín Vélez warned Bogotá that the railroad remained "a focal point for those disaffected from the government," and that a small event on the line could shatter public order. In Colombia's main port, labor unrest had at least momentarily replaced Liberal guerrillas as the military threat.[89]

In the wake of the Puerto Colombia riot, the CCT's Francisco Cisneros was carted before the government to defend himself against charges that he lacked sufficient control over his workforce. Cisneros explained to Vélez that he did not want "to serve as an instrument for personal vendettas" and, more dubiously, that he prohibited "employees from mixing in the political opinions of Colombia." His identification of the rioters as "peons," however, offered up more than just a rhetorical ploy to fend off charges that he harbored militants. The assertion of port workers' lowly status followed from his own position as a mere procurer of labor with little direct role in workplace management and no obvious personal influence over behavior there. Labor relations based on wages of declining value, which defined employment in the CCT, had been one reason strategic industries were militarized. The soldiers attacked by Liberal guerrillas had been stationed in Puerto Colombia in the first place to prevent labor strikes.[90]

Caribbean businessmen, vulnerable to wartime labor strife as much as to hyperinflation, advocated more discipline among the working population. Some opinion commented on the "lack of occupation" that offered the rebellion a steady pool of idle hands, while a few even publicly opposed forced conscription as a theft of labor from private enterprise. Merchants and financiers also pleaded to free capital from governmental constraints so it might serve as a political solution to a war driven by "the poor class [that] survives from unproductive farming" in the countryside.[91] Others excoriated the "popular classes" for believing that "material comfort would come without great individual effort." According to this reasoning, "the sons of the pueblo, artisans, farmers, laborers" were engaged in armed struggle "to found a paradisiacal regime."[92] Businessmen also joined Cisneros in connecting unlettered obscurity to the war's labor conflicts. On the day the uprising commenced in October 1899, *El Porvenir* complained of "individuals unknown and unaware of their duties" disrupting service on the coastal railroads. To prevent these actions, the editors opined, the transportation companies should hire a sufficient workforce with a recognizable leadership from within or outside its ranks. Arguments in favor of labor leaders were novel in Colombia, a desperate response to the war and economic decline, although businessmen imagined these leaders would serve a paternalistic and disciplinary role. While demanding social harmony, they did not contemplate how political disenfranchisement and the dispossession of rural smallholders had created increasingly restive working-class populations with qualities and backgrounds unknown to them.[93]

Government agents and employers projected this desire for deferential workplace behavior onto market women as well. Within days of the outbreak of hostilities in October 1899, fishermen and male farmers had fled ahead of the expected military impressment, and most activity at Cartagena's waterfront was left in the hands of already predominant female traders.[94] Hyperinflation soon brought a new round of charges that these women engaged in price gouging, which hurt the "humble worker, the laborer, the dependent," although propagandists insisted that "the Government is not responsible" for the situation. Instead, they blamed

Liberals and the "voracity of the exploiters of the public" who controlled local produce.[95] In response to these appeals, Bogotá partially nationalized local marketplaces in early 1900, setting prices on meat and other produce to help the "humble worker," a measure designed in part to rein in women's freedom to engage in trade.[96] While commercial interests may have anticipated this measure as part of a future profit-based market in foodstuffs, public officials focused on price controls to prevent hunger and to disrupt support for the Liberals. Other military rulings made women explicit targets of regulation as well, like the nightly curfews on cantinas, all of which were run by women during the war, a ruling meant to disrupt financial support of the guerrillas. These measures also limited women's ability to sustain themselves and their families, which was of little consequence, other than as a possibly positive one, to officials in charge of the war effort.[97]

Plebeian women fought back against regulations by occupying public places and helping the rebellion. During the war, they blocked urban thoroughfares with their wares and bodies, and they set up stalls in unauthorized locations on footbridges and streets in an effort to avoid the intensified surveillance of trading activities in designated marketplaces.[98] Women also joined bogas and priests to serve as gunrunners, informants, and organizers of rumor, like the "female phalanx" largely thought to have spread false information about the coastal uprising in the early stages of the war. Women who were less surreptitious in their collaboration with guerrillas or who dared to publicly criticize army officers, like Cartagena's Casimira Guerrero in 1902, were imprisoned in the city dungeons.[99] Some may have joined the rebellion out of partisan sentiments, whereas others harbored an old hostility toward the military. In Ciénaga, the washers and cooks had a prewar reputation for opposing the presence of troops from the Colombian interior by charging them higher rates for their labor. Women appeared to deny work to an army that presented itself as an outside occupying force.[100]

With cooking and cleaning still the primary wage employment for Caribbean women, however, few could avoid entirely the work or the dangers around the military buildup. If camp followers or the occasional female combatant received gratitude, as in Rafael Uribe Uribe's paean to one "group of women, heroines without name" in his army train, these moments proved exceptional.[101] Many female workers performed prescribed tasks for army units even though military commanders, not understanding or caring to acknowledge their indispensable role in sustaining troops, attempted to prohibit their presence on gunboats and in barracks. Along with their lack of status and their dependence on deteriorating wages, some women endured threats of sexual violence. Throughout Magdalena, women worked with Sabas Socarrás "to put [themselves] out of harm's way" of drunken Liberal guerrillas bent on rape during their brief occupations of towns.[102] Others in military employment endured exploitation and violence compounded by regional and class differences. Several soldiers from Antioquia and Boyacá stationed in Cartagena in the late 1890s admitted to treating "with cruelty" the local women who cooked and cleaned for them in exchange for meager pay. Officers justified their soldiers' beating of women by accusing the latter of "awful conduct" and "horrible insults and obscene words" while in the barracks. This sanctioning of violence against women was not official policy, although military codes since the 1880s had warned of the "bad influence" on "morality and discipline" when "numerous women" were attached to battalions, or how soldiers were "incited to desert by bad women."[103] Female Caribbean workers appeared to endure poor treatment and censure in part to help unify and discipline government troops from various regions or to reinforce the soldiers' image as legitimate troops fighting a criminal insurgency. The military's condoning of such treatment may have encouraged more women to join that insurgency, fueling a cycle of conflict in Latin America's longest and deadliest civil war.[104]

THE LIMITS OF PEACE AND *CONVIVENCIA*

In August 1902, Rafael Uribe Uribe returned to Colombia after several months abroad to take charge of the Caribbean campaign—the last significant pocket of Liberal rebellion—a move that precipitated the collapse of the region's guerrillas and brought an end to the war. His troubled relations with coastal insurgents and his decision to redirect the fighting to other parts estranged many veteran troops who refused to follow him out of the Sierra Nevada foothills and toward the government stronghold of Santa Marta. Having split the ranks of the coastal forces, which had sustained themselves in Magdalena largely on their own for three years, Uribe Uribe's diminished band was defeated by the Colombian army near Ciénaga in October 1902. Soon after the battle, he signed a peace treaty on the Neerlandia plantation in the Magdalena banana zone, not far from the Caribbean Sea. A hobbled government had outlasted a reduced and impoverished rural rebellion. "The exhaustion of its adversaries, not its own strength, enabled Marroquín's government to continue in power," averred the U.S. consul.[105]

Just days after signing the Treaty of Neerlandia, Uribe Uribe issued a proclamation to the Liberal guerrillas of the Caribbean coast that promised recognition to those willing to lay down their arms. "We must say goodbye to ourselves as soldiers and prepare to welcome ourselves as citizens," he declared. "The era of white terror will pass, and better days will come."[106] Yet the treaty he had signed in the name of those soldiers promised them only individual pardons, general amnesty, an end to forced confiscations, and an unspecified future electoral reform that would likely serve the interests of the party's lettered class. Otherwise, the treaty offered only status quo ante, which for the majority of men denoted disenfranchisement beyond the politically insignificant local level. There was also lingering uncertainty over postwar relations between the party's national leadership and local allies, in particular given that Uribe Uribe two years earlier had deemed Caribbean men unfit to be either soldiers or citizens.[107]

There was no single response among Caribbean people to the formal declaration of peace. Sabas Socarrás later commented that the "exhausted and tired" men who had fought with him returned "melancholically" to their coastal homes. Yet many impoverished veterans sustained a militant popular Liberalism and scuffled for money on the streets by selling cheap printed hagiographies of Luis A. Robles to colegio students.[108] Other guerrillas and perhaps many noncombatants, either out of economic necessity or a desire to receive some material compensation for enduring years of combat, remained on the path of banditry. The region witnessed frequent robberies, organized attacks on employers, and land invasions in the two years after the Liberal forces officially disbanded. In May 1904, government troops were sent to several haciendas belonging to Cartagena's largest landowner, whom locals called a "feudal lord," after armed *colonos* and laborers tore down enclosures and occupied the lands.[109] Throughout that year, bogas boarded and robbed steamboats, leading one Barranquilla newspaper to make the dubious assertion that "those honored patrones and crews were once prized by businessmen" but that "this retrograde transformation, has become accentuated as a result of these continuous civil wars." In response to merchant pressure, the Office of River Inspection began incarcerating steamboat crews (but not captains or pursers) for any thefts aboard the boats.[110]

Postwar social unrest on the coast played a pivotal role in the rise of President Rafael Reyes and his national bipartisan convivencia. The Cauca native, explorer, and merchant had gained fame in (Nationalist) Conservative circles for his leading role in crushing the 1895 phase of the Liberal uprising, while his absence from major combat after 1899 left him free from the taint of the scorched earth tactics attributed to officials like Joaquín Vélez. This distinction mattered once Reyes and Vélez became the two major contenders for the presidential nomination in 1904. During the fiercely contested election, amid continuing chaos on the coast, many commentators considered the manipulation of ballots by Reyes supporters in Riohacha to be the act that clinched him a slim majority of electors. Vote manipulation was not insignificant, yet neither was the popular support given to Reyes by a majority of Caribbean voters who rejected the candidacy of the intransigent Vélez. Moreover, Reyes's pledge to work with leaders of all political parties promised an end to the exclusion of Liberals from national life. For this promise, Rafael Uribe Uribe, Nicolás Esguerra, Francisco de Paula Borda, and other national leaders of the Liberals' former war faction joined coastal voters behind Reyes.[111]

In April 1908, President Reyes made an excursion to the Caribbean coast as a reward of sorts for the region's part in his election victory four years earlier. The visit also allowed the president to witness the rebuilding efforts underway just a few years after the traumas of civil war, U.S. intervention, and Panamanian secession. By the time of his trip, monetary inflation was under partial control, coastal banditry had been crushed by an enlarged standing army, and the signs of economic expansion were plain. On the coast Reyes toured the Sincerín sugar *ingenio* along the Dique Canal and the United Fruit Company banana lands on the eastern shores of the Ciénaga Grande—two new industries his regime was eager to claim as its accomplishments. The president took in as well the bipartisan convivencia he had promoted, conferring with the "distinguished gentlemen" of politics and business in Barranquilla, Santa Marta, Cartagena, and Riohacha. At one stop near the site of the 1902 battle where Rafael Uribe Uribe and the coastal Liberals had been defeated, Reyes was feted by Magdalena native José María Campo Serrano, an old deputy of Juan José Nieto and a Regeneration-era national president. In a speech honoring the president's visit, Campo Serrano urged all in attendance to "forget our past errors" of partisan conflict and to "preserve public order in a firm and permanent manner." Noting the thriving banana district where the event took place, he also proclaimed "the patriotic efforts of the Chief of the Nation in giving impulse to Commerce and development to our industries."[112]

Some of Campo Serrano's contemporaries proved less sanguine about the peace and instead dwelled on the trauma of the recent past. With their novel *Pax* (1907), Lorenzo Marroquín and José María Rivas Groot joined other letrados who at the time were fictionalizing the racial, class, and religious hatreds of the war.[113] Their novel begins with a proposal by foreign investors to dredge the Magdalena River, a dream of progress that is dashed once Liberals launch a rebellion in the country's interior, which quickly descends to the Caribbean coast to destroy public works projects and lay siege to Cartagena. In conflating Gaitán's 1885 campaign against Rafael Núñez with the three years of war, *Pax* allegorized the coast as a theater for the struggle between civilization and barbarism. "They are 2,000 black, ferocious savages, half naked, exhibiting their oddly white teeth with the gesticulations of orangoutangs, and brandishing with wild frenzy, above their yellow caps, the flashing, broad blades of their machetes." The hordes of Caribbean macheteros, followed by women and children and commanded by a mulatto who presumptuously calls himself a general, are also atheists bent on redistributing the nation's wealth. While some political leaders in the novel are effete and corrupt—Marroquín was the son of the national president installed after the July 1900 coup—they are distinct and recognizable as individuals who defend Colombia from the malevolent forces seemingly outside the nation, yet seeking entry in order to destroy it.[114]

Both the antiplebeian hysteria of *Pax* and Campo Serrano's paean to lettered convivencia and commercial progress left little room for a reckoning with the disenfranchisement of the majority of Colombians. The war that had begun as an attempt to win Liberals formal standing in politics was fought through intensifying asymmetries of legal and social status. Although some combatants managed to claim legitimacy for their service in arms, guerrillas could not overcome Regeneration-era exclusions, and unlike the Mosquera-Nieto alliance of 1860, insurgents erected no counterrepublic in 1899. Instead, combat at the turn of the century brought a quick turn to predation and diminished political prospects. Under the postwar Reyes presidency, Liberals gained minority status without any significant expansion of voting rights—an acceptable scenario for many leaders and one contemplated by Medardo Rivas in his *Trabajadores* just before the onset of the war. With no other substantive change in citizenship rights forthcoming, many of the political and social questions that had driven the conflict remained unresolved.

For illiterate Caribbean people, state coercion, disease, theft, and mass violence had followed two decades of dispossession. During the war some distinctions had been leveled in unanticipated ways, even as the government's military effort had been sustained by denying recognition to bogas,

Enviadistas, peons, and laboring women, which the Liberal guerrillas in the backlands could do nothing to change. And as Lorenzo Marroquín and José María Rivas Groot's novel made clear, this misrecognition was easily refashioned for times of peace. Still, citizens had taken action regardless of their civil status and often without acknowledged leaders, and they would continue to do so in a postwar republic defined by new boundaries, opportunities, and troubles.

Epilogue

In February 1910, more than 1,000 stevedores, steamboat crew members, and railroad workers walked off their jobs in Barranquilla after their employers cut wages by 25 percent. Canal diggers, female and male factory workers, and shop laborers soon joined them, and after a week of escalating conflict across the coastal city, the shipping consortium conceded, restoring the original wages and ending Colombia's first general strike. Three years later, employees of the same enterprises again stopped work, this time to demand a 25 percent wage increase and a reduction in hours. Fearing another shutdown of the national transportation sector and a halt to the country's coffee exports, Barranquilla's municipal officials quickly negotiated a settlement. Then in January 1918, during a time of mass unemployment, rising food prices, and other economic dislocations brought on by the First World War, men and women went on strike in Barranquilla, Cartagena, Santa Marta, the banana zone of Magdalena, and several points along the Magdalena River. This uncoordinated and, for Colombia, unprecedented wave of strikes was led by tens of thousands of working people across more than 100 miles of the coast. Although the January 1918 Caribbean strikes provoked the government to declare a month-long state of siege over the region, they succeeded in gaining new concessions from employers and won for all of Colombia's wage workers the legal right to strike.[1]

Deteriorating social conditions had triggered many of the strikes even as working people's actions had been shaped by the expectations for and limitations of political reform in the wake of the Thousand Days' War. After assuming office in 1904, President Rafael Reyes included Liberals in his cabinet and handpicked Assembly, yet he also suspended the constitution and Congress. Mass protests against his increasingly autocratic rule and, especially, his ill-timed treaty with the United States over Panama led to his government's collapse in June 1909. Constitutional reforms enacted the following year raised anticipation of democratic change through the reinstatement of press freedom, the abolition of capital punishment, limits on presidential powers, more authority for the restored and popularly elected Congress, the direct election of the president for the first time since 1856, and guaranteed minority party representation in Congress. The bipartisan lettered leadership in Bogotá that controlled the reform process, however, did not reinstitute universal manhood suffrage.[2] The continuing exclusion of illiterate and propertyless men, the ongoing influence of anti-Reyes demonstrations after the president's fall from power, and the return of partisan politics were all catalysts for the Caribbean general strikes. As older forms of disenfranchisement and dispossession persisted amid calls for change, Caribbean wage workers expressed demands for political and economic freedom as inseparable in their attempts to remake citizenship after 1909.[3]

The strikes had other immediate and unintended effects that included a more institutionalized Jesuit coastal mission. Labor militancy, Vatican dictates, and the bipartisanship that followed the Thousand Days' War transformed missionary objectives from stamping out Caribbean Liberalism, as had been the goal during the Regeneration, to confronting class conflict. Jesuits tended to the coastal region's "honorable poor," the "stevedores," and the large "floating population" searching for work in the rapidly expanding sugarcane fields, banana plantations, factories, and transportation sector.[4] In the old Enviadista hotbeds along the Magdalena River and in districts where rural warfare or vast accumulations by cattle ranching had displaced colonos from provision grounds, parishioners refused entry to the priests.[5] Yet other populations welcomed them, and in addition to their impressive statistics in marriages and baptisms performed, priests could draw personal inspiration from the story of Agustín Macías, "an old disciple of that false messiah," who renounced El Enviado to become a parish rector and a supporter of the visiting priests.[6] According to Antonio José Uribe, the Jesuits' most fervent proponent in Congress, the missions' attention to the social question made them successful "simultaneously in their arduous labor of winning citizens for the patria and souls for heaven."[7]

If the church mandate on the social question was guided by the hope of an orderly inclusion of restive working classes into national life, the official and lettered response to the strikes nonetheless marginalized Caribbean people once more. In Bogotá and Medellín, wage workers came to be incorporated into priest-run organizations guided by the papal *Rerum Novarum* encyclical urging reconciliation of labor and capital, whereas the Jesuits' coastal mission fell under the purview of a 1912 law to civilize the Indians. State and church could no longer ignore class conflict, yet they considered the urban working-class Caribbean Catholics who led the country into the era of labor strikes not yet part of the nation, a perception reinforced by the era's public opinion.[8] "What Colombian has not experienced something like the feeling of shame at disembarking in Puerto Colombia?" asked the editors of Bogotá's *Revista Moderna* in 1915. "Those shacks covered in palm leaf, those narrow streets in which swarms a population of naked *negritos* create the impression of treading upon inhospitable shores and not of a country marching on the road to progress."[9] Other intellectuals countered that "the black man is not being left behind" but was being absorbed into a triethnic amalgam, although even advocates of mestizaje did not consider race mixture an adequate solution to the economic and spiritual poverty of "inferior social classes" prone to labor agitation.[10]

The rise of a new debate over racial decline was intimately tied to the Caribbean industrial conflicts. In January 1918, amid striking workers laying siege to Cartagena, a national medical congress met in that city, where psychologist Miguel Jiménez López created a furor with his lecture, "Some Signs of Collective Degeneration in Colombia and Other Countries."[11] Using European eugenics studies, national police statistics, and his own clinical trials, Jiménez López concluded that all racial components in Colombia—Spaniard, Indian, and African—had deteriorated individually and in their admixtures with the others. Only the introduction of white Northern European blood into the national body would stem the tide of decline.[12] Few thinkers agreed with all of Jiménez López's arguments, although during the 1920s and 30s many used Caribbean people of color as a foil in staking out their positions. Liberal medical doctor and educator Luis López de Mesa argued that the Magdalena River channeled "African blood" into the Colombian interior to create deleterious mixtures with whites.[13] Enrique Naranjo Martínez, director of the Office of River Inspection during the coastal general strikes of the 1910s, agreed with López de Mesa about the racial degeneration of "our proletariat," in particular among coastal workers, who lived "almost in the condition of the primitive peoples." Naranjo argued that the Jesuit mission could raise the "oppressed races . . . the Indian, the black, the mulatto, or the mestizo," although ultimately he concurred with Miguel Jiménez López that such uplift would be incomplete without "injections of good white blood."[14]

The renovation of racial thought and cultural hierarchies against Caribbean working peoples' attempts to expand rights was a reminder of the ongoing struggle for recognition. As political heirs to the striking bogas of 1857, Caribbean men in transportation, factories, and mechanical trades demanded and eventually won the right to be considered *braceros* or *obreros*—as honorable workers who organized unions, joined in modern industrial relations, and freed themselves from the status of servile *peones*. Their success, however, did not include female factory workers, household servants, independent washerwomen, market traders, or bogas. Like the 1910 constitutional reforms that expanded civil guarantees without ending the most significant political exclusions, the language of modern class incorporated new groups into the category of worker through existing racialized, gendered, and lettered distinctions. Even this narrow opening for some men did little to prevent the violence of capitalist productive relations. When 30,000 workers demanding wage increases, shorter work days, and an end to payment in United Fruit Company scrip went on strike in the Magdalena banana zone in December 1928, a Colombian army battalion opened fire on the crowds, killing perhaps hundreds of men. The *masacre de las bananeras* reverberated across Colombia as the country's worst scandal and played a role in the return of the Liberals to national power in 1930, yet it did not spark a mass movement among workers and led to no immediate improvement in working conditions or to the sanctity of the right to strike. Amid dramatic changes and often violent setbacks, Colombians would continue to struggle over the meanings of political and economic freedom.[15]

CARIBBEAN PEOPLE HAD PRODUCED wealth, marketed the earth's resources, practiced religious faith, and fought for political causes along with or in defiance of their fellow Colombians. As actors in exceptional and quotidian events—appealing for just wages, education for their children, respectability for their families, and a voice in local affairs—they helped forge the life of the republic. Some of these actions had been witnessed long before the last slaves won their freedom, yet emancipation changed the conditions under which they translated into new forms of public validation. Colombians of African descent helped fashion a new political culture that for some time served as the basis for all citizenship. With the coming in the 1880s of the Regeneration, which was erected in part to curtail the civic role of men of color, struggles for recognition continued among the disenfranchised, albeit under increasingly adverse circumstances. Emancipation had played too significant a role in defining democratic life to be immediately defeated by the legal repeal of constitutional guarantees. Indeed, popular demands for a political voice outlasted universalist formal rights, revealing the contradictory nature of postemancipation citizenship.

Vestiges of the work of recognition are everywhere evident in the symbols of the Colombian nation. Barranquilla's Carnival celebration, today part of the country's cultural patrimony, was a modest affair before civic leaders harnessed its social creativity to win political support in the years after the abolition of slavery. The former rebel parish of San Roque still functions in the central district of that coastal metropolis. Colombia's patron saint, Pedro Claver—Cartagena's "slave of the blacks"—was in part an attempt by church and national leaders to appease Caribbean citizens disenfranchised by the 1886 constitution. And Santa Marta's former slave hacienda of San Pedro Alejandrino has become a national monument in honor of Simón Bolívar, its conversion into a heritage site requiring the expulsion of peasants who had occupied its lands since the 1870s. The country's name is itself a relic of past contestations, when Liberals in the 1860s anxiously conjured up the spirits of the past (to paraphrase Marx) in order to declare victory in their self-conscious defense of the legacy of emancipation. In each instance local struggles were converted into symbols shared by all Colombians, surviving today as artifacts of the tensions at the heart of the postemancipation experience.

Such artifacts attest to the power of freedom to define social possibilities for the formerly enslaved and the already free alike. In the postbellum United States, the hegemony of the contract in the market society was contingent on slave emancipation, even as contractual relations spread far beyond the former slave states or the lives of freed slaves. In Cuba and Haiti, abolition and national independence became intertwined once white creoles, free people of color, and slaves comprehended the mutually constitutive nature of slavery and colonial rule. And yet appeals to emancipation, market freedom, and national liberation have arisen together since the Age of Revolution without consensus over how to reconcile their often contradictory meanings.[16] As Candelario Obeso forcefully argued in his *Cantos*, the problem was how to create public life founded on yet necessarily transcending the experiences of the few, a problem as true for former societies-with-slaves as for former slave societies. The legal fiats that ended legal bondage across the Atlantic world offered no guidance on what this freedom would look like; the public celebrations of January 1852 in New Granada were no different.[17]

Still, the experiences of the Magdalena bogas and coastal market women, who were free and independent by the time of emancipation, were not the same as those of the freed slaves of 1830s Jamaica, 1860s South Carolina, or 1880s São Paulo. The case of Colombia, where the last people in bondage were liberated into populations of free majorities of color and where plantations did not define the system of production, reminds us that there was no single emancipation process. The study of societies-with-slaves offers not just new perspectives on manumission, politics, and work but also recalls how opportunities and constraints under which people fashioned lives for themselves varied across postemancipation societies. Understanding the experience of freedom, Rebecca Scott argues, requires examining the capacity of free people to act under divergent social, environmental, and political conditions. Taking into account the consequences of human agency, in other words, not only helps explain the outcomes of particular struggles but also provides new contours to historical meanings of freedom.[18]

The degrees of freedom varied as much within as across national borders. On occasion citizens in Colombia created interregional alliances with broad impact, yet national conditions were often secondary to the local circumstances that defined the prospects for public life. Intense and often racialized conflicts around plantations in the Cauca Valley, and the strength of political conservatism in that region, produced a postemancipation experience distinct from that of the Caribbean region. The particularities of the jungle extractive economy, geographical isolation, and numerical dominance of African-descended peoples in the Pacific coastal lowlands were equally unique.[19] Political leadership and partisan affinities varied across Colombia, and contemporaries who considered *Caribbean* synonymous with *Liberal* would not have made the same assumption of many other regions. Even on the coast, differences between locals and *forasteros*—exploitative outsiders, regardless of place of origin—were as real as the relations between them were fraught. In Colombia there was no single political culture and no single expression of postemancipation citizenship.

National boundaries also appear to dim from certain transnational angles. The Atlantic turn in histories of the Americas has inspired new questions about slave rebellion, African ethnicity, the circulation of revolutionary ideas, and the boundaries of postemancipation processes.[20] Colombia in the period after slavery falls in line with this trend by reflecting global tensions over ideologies of race, rights, labor, and freedom. Thomas Holt's observation about early nineteenth-century British abolitionism, that "'racism' was embedded in the very premises of a presumably nonracist liberalism," is applicable to republican Colombia, where abolitionist letrados espoused the annihilation of the Magdalena bogas and permitted the circulation of antiblack propaganda in wartime. The struggle within these social contradictions had a transnational dimension as well. Candelario Obeso was himself a "nineteenth-century Atlantic Creole," traveling to Panama, Tours, and Paris (journeys of which we know little), translating European literature and philosophy, and reflecting on the possibilities for egalitarian citizenship in Colombia by writing about the horrors of slavery in contemporary Cuba. The struggle over the meanings of freedom, then, was shot through with border-crossing ideas and individuals.[21]

Despite these caveats, the work of recognition was fundamentally national in scope, and a goal of this study has been to examine the relationship between local and translocal developments within Colombia. Citizens acted under the same national constitutions, through adjuncts of the same political parties, and in the face of similar religious and economic conditions. When they took to the public they did so with demands that transcended their immediate circumstances. Regional interests inflected national programs, and the vagaries of world markets and geopolitics shaped Colombian citizenship, all with unintended effects. Local and global dynamics constituted the possibilities for the making of constitutional guarantees. How citizens reconciled particular experiences with universalizing ideals shaped the content and expression of Colombian citizenship.

Framing narratives around citizenship—rights and standing, as well as degrees of inclusion and exclusion—can also move us beyond dichotomous models premised on domination and resistance. The outcomes of struggles over recognition, then, offer new perspectives on what is often depicted as elite-subaltern relations in modern Latin America. Civil and religious authorities in nineteenth-century Colombia discovered that their command over plebeian populations went only so far, and they often relied instead on the capacity to acknowledge, discredit, or altogether ignore those populations. Illiterate and impoverished citizens consequently found it easier to escape constraints imposed by governments, bishops, or employers than to gain a hearing from them. Caribbean market women occupied public places and demanded respect from elite travelers and priests, and some more prominent men were denied the vote when challenged by armed gangs of quasi-enfranchised youths. In their writings, letrados could deny bogas personhood and depict their existence as one of unmitigated savagery, yet in their travels on the river they had little choice but to submit to the boatmen's will. To cite such examples is not to dismiss the realities of poverty and social inequality, but these instances do paint a more complex picture of public interactions among citizens who continually marked social differences through those interactions.

Placing struggles over citizenship at the center of modern Latin American history may in fact offer new perspectives on the durability of social inequality. Within the region, Colombia today ranks in the top tier of countries for resource misdistribution, and within Colombia the Caribbean coast shows some of the highest rates of poverty and illiteracy and lowest rates of participation in the formal economy.[22] Studying the contradictions of rights and access to material goods over time can provide insight on some of these legacies of inequality. In the nineteenth century, opponents of popular democracy in Colombia invoked universal principles of rights and morality to counter local efforts to control land, taxation, and labor. Arguments that plebeian economic independence undermined unity were employed to stymie social change, and invocations of national interests only exacerbated a growing divide between formal rights and material poverty. Discrimination permeated the ideals of social inclusion and cohesion, which had the effect of reproducing inequalities in status or resources. The universalizing impulse of civil equality after 1850 and of an organic moral order after 1885 did little to change property relations or literacy rates. The postemancipation constitution of 1853 defined free labor and learning in ways that left up to private citizens the substance of their practice. Subsequent reforms from 1870 onward centralized authority and constrained legal meanings of freedom, which added new formal barriers to mobility and political participation. The goal of national unity has coexisted comfortably with discrimination and inequality for generations.[23]

The tensions between a universal sense of belonging and persistent inequality point once more to the power of race. Studies of racialization argue for the need to abandon the perception of a monolithic or unchanging racism and compel us to note instead how changes in economy and politics reshape racial ideologies.[24] Still, there was a certain continuity in Colombia's changing racial order. Early twentieth-century eugenicists shared with Conservative nationalists of the 1890s, costumbrista authors of the 1870s, and abolitionists of the 1850s a similar universalizing goal, which they expressed by denying the public legitimacy of racial differences even as they permitted antiblack racism in private and anonymous relations. Some lettered Colombians considered this public-private distinction—denying the role of race in the former while permitting racial discrimination in the latter—to be an antidemocratic practice that limited the political prospects of the citizenry. Yet just as many conceived of this ethos as a liberatory gesture of inclusion for the majority. This study has attempted to demonstrate that racialization at the pivot point of public and private was itself not unchanging but was contingent on social and political transformations. How racial ideology shaped labor struggles, political mobilizations, and representations in literature was framed by distinct understandings of gender, literacy, and social class. One consequence of race-making through distinctions of public and private life, whether intended or otherwise, was the repudiation of Candelario Obeso's black citizen.

Historicizing race after slave emancipation, moreover, only under-scores mestizaje as the dominant racial ideology of the twentieth century. The process of imagining the Colombian nation as a product of racial mix-ture falls outside the scope of this study, and the postemancipation era is defined here in part as the time before the hegemony of mestizaje. After 1920, mass politics, the restitution of adult male suffrage (1936) and in-troduction of women's suffrage (1956), the expansion of state institutions, the spread of primary education and literacy, and intensifying capitalist production encouraged intellectuals to reconsider fundamental aspects of national identity. One cultural consequence of this reexamination was the raising of the mestizo to a position of preeminence. Writing in the middle of the century, politician and scholar Otto Morales Benítez ar-gued that the Colombian mestizo was "the present type" because "eco-nomic development has propelled miscegenation." The "hybridization of the race" produced the "mestizo [who] acted with the sense of possession of the land, of 'his' land." Morales Benítez was not alone in heralding mes-tizaje.[25] This approbation of racial hybridity borrowed from nineteenth-century antecedents, in particular from positivism's telos of disappearing ethnic groups. At the same time, the workings of the ideology of mestizaje marked a shift from the postemancipation ethos, which had required the liberal disavowal of racial differences among public individuals. In terms of citizenship, however, the new racial order perpetuated the impossibility of imagining black citizens.

Indigenous and African-descended Colombians have not been posi-tioned in the same relationship to this mestizaje. As Peter Wade notes, Indians have remained a racial Other in some continuous fashion since the colonial era, while people of African descent became "ordinary citi-zens" who nevertheless could be excluded from the nation. In Colombia and elsewhere in Spanish America, moreover, the mestizo as national norm was generally perceived to be a person of European and Indian an-cestry.[26] The Caribbean case communicates regional and local variations in this ideological schema. While Orlando Fals Borda in his multivolume study of the Magdalena River depicts the population as a "cosmic" amal-gamation of the Indian, European, and African, more recent scholarship has noted the general disavowal of any indigenous presence in contem-porary Caribbean Colombia. Despite the existence of significant indig-enous populations along the coast—especially the Wayúu (Guajiros) of the Guajira Peninsula and the Kogui, Arhuaco, and Wiwa of the Sierra Nevada—Caribbean mestizaje has been defined by whether to recog-nize African descent within variations of blackness and whiteness. This *costeño* variant of mestizaje persists within a national racial order defined by an assumed indigenous-white mixture.[27]

In retrospect the primacy of mestizaje in national discourse may appear short-lived, as recent decades have brought to Colombia multiculturalism and racial pluralism. Easily the most significant moment in the multicultural turn was the passage of the 1991 constitution—replacing the century-old Regeneration one—which addresses the country's indigenous and Afro-Colombian populations in direct and unprecedented fashion. To be sure, it does not treat the two minority groups equally, as its detailed delineation of rights for indigenous groups overshadows the two brief references to black people. Moreover, commentators have noted that its definition of "comunidades negras" as certain types of rural settlements on the Pacific coast excludes both the majority of Afro-descended people and entire regions of the country, including the Caribbean coast. Nevertheless, the constitution's "Fundamental Principles" require the national state to "recognize and protect the ethnic and cultural diversity of the Colombian Nation" and to create new legislation to that effect.[28] The latter obligation has led to new laws and state policies recognizing Afro-Colombians, with the added effect of endorsing related activities by Afro-Colombian cultural organizations, scholars, educational institutions, and activists. Candelario Obeso's dual vision of black citizenship can be glimpsed in the new ideal of the plural nation. "Claims for the recognition of difference," writes Nancy Fraser on global multiculturalism, "promote both universal respect for shared humanity and esteem for cultural distinctiveness." The recuperation in recent decades of the bogas, cimarrones, Luis A. Robles, and especially Obeso himself as icons of Afro-Colombia—and in Obeso's case as an important figure in diversifying the national literary canon— has been part of this turn to multicultural citizenship.[29]

This transition from a national identity based on racial mixture to one grounded in pluralism and multiculturalism has not come close to settling the issue of Afro-Colombian visibility. As Peter Wade and Elisabeth Cunin note—echoing arguments made by Colombia's writers and activists of color since the 1940s—the shift from mestizaje to multiculturalism has produced less rupture than increased ambiguity over the marking and blurring of racial difference. This ambiguity can be spotted in cultural productions, politics, and everyday life. In the Caribbean "black slum" of *Chambacú* (1965), Afro-Colombian novelist Manuel Zapata Olivella's allegory of racist exclusion and oppression in mid-twentieth-century Colombia, there remains "the spirit of race mixing, borne in the blood." Forty years later, during the national census of 2005, nongovernmental organizations encouraged citizens to count themselves as Afro-Colombian by maintaining that the plethora of presumably still common self-ascriptions—*negro, mulato, zambo, raizal, moreno*—were categorically the same. The census tallied Afro-Colombians as just over 10 percent of the national population, far below most scholarly and activist estimates and only slightly higher than approximations from earlier times when the enumeration of people of color was systematically suppressed. Defining the terms of black representation remains a challenge in part because pluralism, while raising expectations of a visible black role in society and politics, has not fully supplanted older notions of color blindness, mestizaje, and denial.[30]

In recent decades, the country's endemic violence, armed politics of the left and right, and organized terror by state and nonstate actors have often defined the limits of a pluralistic democracy. Since the 1980s, labor organizers, teachers, politicians, and black and indigenous community leaders have been the primary targets of assassination, kidnappings, and forced displacements. The current assault on trade unionists only worsens the national labor movement's historical weakness and fragmentation, which is largely a legacy of the state's violent destruction of its militant leading sector, the transportation workers of the Magdalena River, in 1945. What has changed in recent decades, in particular with the implementation of neoliberal market reforms that coincided with the 1991 multicultural constitution, has been the rise of a "dirty war" against trade unions that allows the state to deny culpability. The possibility of organized labor serving as the foundation for a renewal of democratic citizenship appears remote.[31]

The racialized nature of political violence in contemporary Colombia has also become increasingly apparent. Even as the multicultural national constitution and, in recent years, the expansive rights regime of the Supreme Court of Justice have raised the civil standing of Afro-Colombians (as well as trade unionists; indigenous people; gays, lesbians, and transgendered persons; homeless youth; and internally displaced persons), armed conflict has preempted systematic efforts to address social exclusion and inequality. Progressive legal pluralism that ties new classes of citizens to the state has had little effect on the destruction of individual rights in daily life. The government's granting of legal land titles to individual African-descended families (often staged as political spectacle, such as during the sesquicentennial commemoration of emancipation in 2001–2), belies the mass displacement of rural black communities by armed groups and extractive industries. One consequence of public violence during the multicultural turn has been a substantial shift in perception from the nineteenth-century view of black men as barbaric perpetrators in civil wars to the present image of minority groups as the main victims of the current conflict.[32]

Despite enduring disproportionate rates of violence, exclusion, and poverty, black working people struggle to live in a Colombia that is more than just a "heralded tomb for the exotic races," as Candelario Obeso hailed it. Contemporary Afro-Colombian culture and politics abound, in part as a response to the armed conflict and its manifold dispossessions. Representations of Afro-descended people and blackness in the public sphere have flourished while also becoming more contested, and today, academics, activists, artists, NGOs, and state institutions compete to define black culture and its incorporation into the nation. Afro-Colombian struggles for rights and standing in public life since emancipation have produced significant gains but also unintended exclusions, violent reactions, and shattering reversals. The struggles themselves have often been erased from view. And yet each new generation in Colombia, like its counterparts elsewhere in Latin America, has made its history, with today's black citizens more than ever refusing to accept disavowal as a response to their demands for recognition.

Notes

Abbreviations

AAC	Archivo del Arzobispado de Cartagena
AC	Archivo del Congreso, Bogotá
ACMB	Archivo del Concejo Municipal de Barranquilla
AGN	Archivo General de la Nación, Bogotá, Sección República
AHC	Archivo Histórico de Cartagena
AHESM	Archivo Histórico Eclesiástico de Santa Marta
AHMG	Archivo Histórico del Magdalena Grande, Santa Marta
BLAA SLRM	Biblioteca Luis Ángel Arango, Bogotá, Sala de Libros Raros y Manuscritos
BN	Biblioteca Nacional, Bogotá
CB	Correspondencia (Bolívar)
EOR	Fondo Enrique Ortega Ricaurte, Serie Negros y Esclavos, Caja 182, Carpeta 666
FGMD	Fondo Guerra de los Mil Días
NARA	National Archives and Records Administration, Washington, D.C.

Introduction

1. Prescott, *Candelario Obeso y la iniciación de la poesía negra*.

2. Obeso, *Cantos populares* [1877], quoted from 27, 30. Cf. Prescott, *Candelario Obeso y la iniciación de la poesía negra*, 84–93.

3. For the demographic predominance of the free over the slave population, see Sharpe, *Slavery on the Spanish Frontier*, 198–99; and McFarlane, *Colombia before Independence*, 353.

4. Restrepo Canal, *La libertad de los esclavos en Colombia*, iii–xxix, quoted from xxii.

5. Mosquera, Pardo, and Hoffman, *Afrodescendientes en las Américas*; Sexta Catedra Anual de Historia Ernesto Restrepo Tirado, *150 años de la abolición de la esclavización en Colombia*; Archivo General de la Nación, *La esclavitud en Colombia*. For the structural nature of historical erasure, see Trouillot, *Silencing the Past*.

6. Ortega Ricaurte, *Negros, mulatos y zambos en Santafé de Bogotá*; Maya Restrepo, *Geografía humana de Colombia: Los afrocolombianos*; Helg, *Liberty and Equality in Caribbean Colombia*; Lasso, *Myths of Harmony*; Múnera, *El fracaso de la nación*; Leal, "Landscapes of Freedom"; Leal, "Recordando a Saturio"; Crawford, "Politics of Belonging on a Caribbean Borderland"; Sanders, "Contentious Republicans"; Gutiérrez Azopardo, *Historia del negro en Colombia*.

7. Pardo Rojas, Mosquera, and Ramírez, *Panorámica afrocolombiana*; Camacho and Restrepo, *De montes, ríos y ciudades*; Taussig, *The Devil and Commodity Fetishism*

in South America; Wade, *Music, Race, and Nation*; Wade, *Blackness and Race Mixture*; Cunin, *Identidades a flor de piel*; Arocha and Friedemann, *De sol a sol*.

8. The collective output of this cadre, led by Jorge Artel, Aquiles Escalante, Amir Smith Córdoba, Rogerio Velásquez, Delia Zapata Olivella, Manuel Zapata Olivella, and others, is quite large. For overviews of this literature, see Lucía Ortiz, *"Chambacú, la historia la escribes tú."*

9. Galvis Noyes, "La abolición de la esclavitud en la Nueva Granada"; Castellanos, *La abolición de la esclavitud en Popayán*; Romero Jaramillo, "La segunda liberación"; Romero Jaramillo, "Manumisión, ritualidad y fiesta liberal en la provincia de Cartagena"; Bierck, "The Struggle for Abolition in Gran Colombia"; quoted from "Manumisión," *El Ciudadano*, 15 August 1850.

10. González, "El proceso de manumisión en Colombia"; Sanders, "Contentious Republicans"; Leal, "Landscapes of Freedom"; quoted from Romero Jaramillo, "La segunda liberación."

11. Herzog, *Defining Nations*; Lomnitz, "Nationalism as a Practical System"; Guerra, "The Spanish-American Tradition of Representation and Its European Roots"; Sabato, "On Political Citizenship in Nineteenth-Century Latin America"; Guardino, *Peasants, Politics, and the Formation of Mexico's National State*; Guardino, *The Time of Liberty*.

12. Cooper, Holt, and Scott, *Beyond Slavery*, 3; Holt, *The Problem of Freedom*; Saville, *The Work of Reconstruction*; Saville, "Rites and Power"; DuBois, *A Colony of Citizens*; Butler, *Freedoms Given, Freedoms Won*; Montgomery, *Citizen Worker*.

13. Galindo, *Estudios económicos i fiscales*, 298–99.

14. Figueroa, *Sugar, Slavery, and Freedom in Nineteenth-Century Puerto Rico*; Rebecca Scott, *Slave Emancipation in Cuba*; Scott et al., *Abolition of Slavery and the Aftermath of Emancipation in Brazil*; Schmidt-Nowara, *Slavery, Freedom, and Abolition in Latin America*; Mintz, *Caribbean Transformations*; Holt, *The Problem of Freedom*.

15. For bogas, see Posada-Carbó, "Bongos, champanes y vapores en la navegación fluvial colombiana"; and Solano, "De bogas a navigantes." Scant work exists on women of color or female marketers, but see Appelbaum, *Muddied Waters*; Helg, *Liberty and Equality in Caribbean Colombia*; Sanders, "Contentious Republicans"; Leal, "Landscapes of Freedom"; and Friedemann and Espinosa Arango, "Las mujeres negras en la historia de Colombia."

16. Holt, *The Problem of Freedom*.

17. Cooper, Holt, and Scott, *Beyond Slavery*, 13; Mehta, "Liberal Strategies of Exclusion"; Wade, "Racial Identity and Nationalism." For the concept of recognition, see Fraser, "Rethinking Recognition," quoted from 107; and Taylor, *Multiculturalism*, quoted from 27, 40. For recognition in Latin American (indigenous) contexts, see Gould, *To Die in This Way*; and Caplan, *Indigenous Citizens*.

18. Rebecca Scott; *Degrees of Freedom*, 269; see also Rebecca Scott, "Public Rights and Private Commerce," 237.

19. Flórez Bolívar and Solano, *Infancia de la nación*; Aguilera Peña and Vega Cantor, *Ideal democrático y revuelta popular*; Vega Cantor, *Gente muy rebelde*; Posada-Carbó, "Elections before Democracy"; Roldán, *Blood and Fire*; Sowell, *The Early Colombian*

Labor Movement; Guardino, *Peasants, Politics, and the Formation of Mexico's National State*; Sabato, *The Many and the Few*; Mallon, *Peasant and Nation*; Walker, *Smoldering Ashes*; Chambers, *From Subjects to Citizens*; Ferrer, *Insurgent Cuba*; Rebecca Scott, *Degrees of Freedom*; Saville, "Rites and Power."

20. Barkley Brown, "To Catch the Vision of Freedom"; Appadurai et al., "Editorial Comment"; Sabato, "On Political Citizenship in Nineteenth-Century Latin America," 1299; Borges, *The Family in Bahia*; Cooper, Holt, and Scott, *Beyond Slavery*, 16.

21. Habermas, "The Public Sphere"; Fraser, "Rethinking the Public Sphere"; Eley, "Nations, Publics, and Political Cultures"; Rama, *The Lettered City*.

22. For the cultural politics of (indigenous) literacy in the Andean republics, see Aguirre, "*Tinterillos*, Indians, and the State"; and Larson, "Forging the Unlettered Indian."

23. Archila Neira, *Cultura e identidad obrera*; Vega Cantor, *Gente muy rebelde*; Solano, *Puertos, sociedad y conflictos en el Caribe colombiano*; Bergquist, *Labor in Latin America*; Farnsworth-Alvear, *Dulcinea in the Factory*; Safford, *The Ideal of the Practical*; Urrutia, *The Development of the Colombian Labor Movement*; LeGrand, *Frontier Colonization and Peasant Protest in Colombia*. For commercial transformations, see Safford, "Commerce and Enterprise in Central Colombia"; and Stanley, *From Bondage to Contract*.

24. See Sabato, *The Many and the Few*; and Sanders, "Contentious Republicans," 176–89. On the dangers of misrecognition, see Taylor, *Multiculturalism*, 25–26; and Fraser, "Rethinking Recognition."

25. For a similar dynamic in late colonial Peru, see Herzog, *Defining Nations*, 3.

26. Mintz, *Caribbean Transformations*; Holt, *The Problem of Freedom*; Saville, *The Work of Reconstruction*.

27. For the contemporary aspects of this, see Wade, *Music, Race, and Nation*, 20.

28. De la Fuente, *A Nation for All*, 9–10, 18–19.

29. For the relationship between race, gender, and nation, see Higginbotham, "African-American Women's History"; Appelbaum, Macpherson, and Rosemblatt, "Introduction: Racial Nations"; and Wade, *Race and Sex in Latin America*.

30. Ferrer, *Insurgent Cuba*.

31. On honor vis-à-vis citizenship, see Chambers, *From Subjects to Citizens*, 4–5, 189–215; Guardino, *The Time of Liberty*, 3; and Guardino, *Peasants, Politics, and the Formation of Mexico's National State*, 84–85.

32. For the racialized separation of the economic and the political spheres, see Holt, *The Problem of Freedom*; and Montgomery, *Citizen Worker*. For a periodization of Latin American racial orders, see Appelbaum, Macpherson, and Rosemblatt, "Introduction: Racial Nations," 4–8.

33. For caveats about racial terminology, see Appelbaum, *Muddied Waters*, 9–11; Helg, *Liberty and Equality in Caribbean Colombia*, 253–56; Andrews, *Afro-Latin America*, 1–10; Ferrer, *Insurgent Cuba*, 10–12; and de la Fuente, *A Nation for All*, 3–5.

34. On languages of class and labor, see Farnsworth-Alvear, *Dulcinea in the Factory*; Weinstein, *For Social Peace in Brazil*, 1–3; Joan Scott, "On Language, Gender, and

Working-Class History"; and Sewell, "Toward a Post-materialist Rhetoric for Labor History."

35. Weinstein, *For Social Peace in Brazil*, 2–3.

36. For the concept of metalanguges, see Higginbotham, "African-American Women's History." See also Stedman Jones, *Languages of Class*; and Appelbaum, Macpherson, and Rosemblatt, "Introduction: Racial Nations."

37. Turner, *From Chattel Slaves to Wage Slaves*; Rebecca Scott, *Slave Emancipation in Cuba*; Figueroa, *Sugar, Slavery, and Freedom in Nineteenth-Century Puerto Rico*. For Caribbean Colombia's lack of plantations, see Abello Vives, *Un Caribe sin plantación*.

38. Nodin Valdés, "The Decline of Slavery in Mexico"; Blanchard, *Slavery and Abolition in Early Republican Peru*; Lombardi, *The Decline and Abolition of Negro Slavery in Venezuela*; Aguirre, *Agentes de su propia libertad*; Blackburn, *The Overthrow of Colonial Slavery*, 331–79; Schmidt-Nowara, *Slavery, Freedom, and Abolition in Latin America*, 105–16, 180–81.

39. See essays by Lowell Gudmundson and Justin Wolfe in their collection *Blacks and Blackness in Central America*; Sanders, "Contentious Republicans"; and Leal, "Landscapes of Freedom." For emancipation in other societies-with-slaves, see Berlin, *Many Thousands Gone*, 228–55. Quoted from Holt, "The Essence of the Contract," 38.

40. Cooper, Holt, and Scott, *Beyond Slavery*, 3–4.

41. Aguilera Peña and Vega Cantor, *Ideal democrático y revuelta popular*; Delpar, *Red against Blue*; Bushnell, "Politics and Violence in Nineteenth-Century Colombia"; Helguera, "The Problem of Liberalism versus Conservatism in Colombia"; Posada-Carbó, "Limits of Power"; Deas, "Colombia, Ecuador and Venezuela"; Bergquist, *Coffee and Conflict in Colombia*; Henderson, *Modernization in Colombia*.

42. See, e.g., Appelbaum, *Muddied Waters*; Londoño-Vega, *Religion, Culture, and Society in Colombia*; Sowell, *The Early Colombian Labor Movement*; and LeGrand, *Frontier Colonization and Peasant Protest in Colombia*.

43. For scholarship on the region, see Posada-Carbó, *The Colombian Caribbean*; Solano, *Puertos, sociedad, y conflictos en el Caribe colombiano*; Múnera, *El fracaso de la nación*; Fals Borda, *Historia doble de la costa*; Meisel Roca, *Historia económica y social del Caribe colombiano*; Nichols, *Tres puertos de Colombia*; Helg, *Liberty and Equality in Caribbean Colombia*; and Lasso, *Myths of Harmony*.

44. Quoted from Fals Borda, *Historia doble de la costa*, 1:156B; see also Posada-Carbó, *The Colombian Caribbean*, 12–14.

45. Nichols, *Tres puertos de Colombia*; Safford, "Social Aspects of Politics in Nineteenth-Century Spanish America," 355.

46. Solano, *Puertos, sociedad y conflictos en el Caribe colombiano*; Nichols, *Tres puertos de Colombia*; Van Ausdal, "The Logic of Livestock."

47. Nichols, *Tres puertos de Colombia*; Safford, "Social Aspects of Politics in Nineteenth-Century Spanish America," 355.

48. Palacios Prediado, *La trata de negros por Cartagena*; Meisel Roca, "Esclavitud, mestizaje y haciendas"; Helg, *Liberty and Equality in Caribbean Colombia*, 47.

49. Safford, "Social Aspects of Politics in Nineteenth-Century Spanish America," 361; Posada-Carbó, *The Colombian Caribbean*, 238–39.

50. For Colombian regional histories, see Appelbaum, *Muddied Waters*; Posada-Carbó, *The Colombian Caribbean*; Rausch, *The Llanos Frontier in Colombian History*; and Londoño-Vega, *Religion, Culture, and Society in Colombia*.

51. DuBois, *A Colony of Citizens*, 28; cited by Childs, *The 1812 Aponte Rebellion*, 15.

Chapter 1

1. P. Gutiérrez to Governor, Remolino, 5 and 12 August 1849, AGN, Gobernaciones (Santa Marta), 28:571–72.

2. Aguilera Peña and Vega Cantor, *Ideal democrático y revuelta popular*, 89; Gutiérrez Sanín, *Curso y discurso en el movimiento plebeyo*; Posada-Carbó, "New Granada and the European Revolutions of 1848"; Colmenares, *Partidos políticos y clases sociales*; Gilmore, "Nueva Granada's Socialist Mirage"; Bushnell, *The Making of Modern Colombia*, 101ff.; Safford and Palacios, *Colombia*, 197ff.

3. Cf. Gilmore, "Nueva Granada's Socialist Mirage"; Colmenares, *Partidos políticos y clases sociales*, 141–53.

4. Kerr-Ritchie, *Rites of August First*, 14.

5. Sharp, *Slavery on the Spanish Frontier*, 148–50; Romero Jaramillo, *Esclavitud en la provincia de Santa Marta*, 128, 165; Sourdis Nájera, "Ruptura del Estado colonial y tránsito hacia la República," 215–16, 221; McFarlane, "*Cimarrones* and *Palenques*," 131–51; Galvis Noyes, "La abolición de la esclavitud en la Nueva Granada," 54–55; Blanchard, *Under the Flags of Freedom*, 8–9, 15, 65–66; Ospina Vásquez, *Industria y protección en Colombia*, 126; Earle, "The War of the Supremes," 132–33.

6. Felipe Pérez, *Geografía general física y política*, 1:107, 124, 156, 224; Arcila Estrada, "Poblamiento y cultura en el sur de Bolívar," 75, 77.

7. For first-person accounts, see "Notes on New Granada by an English Resident," 27; Mollien, *Viaje por la República de Colombia*, 37; Le Moyne, *Viajes y estancias en América del Sur*, 52, 53; Dessalines d' Orbigny, *Viaje pintoresco a las dos Américas*, 1:71, 73; and Ancízar, *Peregrinación de Alpha*, 515.

8. Helg, *Liberty and Equality in Caribbean Colombia*, 20–26.

9. Antonio del Real, Santa Marta, 17 January 1849, AGN, Gobernaciones (Santa Marta), 28:31; Le Moyne, *Viajes y estancias en América del Sur*, 35, 37. For free people's distinction from slaves and disinterest in abolition elsewhere in the Caribbean, see Fick, *The Making of Haiti*, 137; and Heuman, *Between Black and White*, 14–15.

10. Corrales, *Efemérides y anales*, 3:121–33, quoted from 131; see also Helg, *Liberty and Equality in Caribbean Colombia*, 206–36.

11. Sourdis Nájera, "Ruptura del estado colonial y tránsito hacia la República," 216–17; LeGrand, *Frontier Colonization and Peasant Protest in Colombia*, 19–20; quoted from Quijano, *Ensayo sobre la evolución del derecho penal en Colombia*, 52.

12. Le Moyne, *Viajes y estancias en América del Sur*, 35.

13. Moreno to Governor, Mahates, 12 March 1850, AGN, Manumisión, 1:292.

14. Gonzáles, "El proceso de manumisión en Colombia," 194–95; Sanders, "Contentious Republicans," 119–20; Castellanos, *La abolición de la esclavitud en Popayán*, 29–31, 38–39.

15. Lohse, "Reconciling Freedom with the Rights of Property"; Castellanos, *La abolición de la esclavitud en Popayán*, 38–56.

16. For the apprenticeship system (*concierto*), which did not function in the Caribbean region, see Gonzáles, "El proceso de manumisión en Colombia," 212–17; and Castellanos, *La abolición de la esclavitud en Popayán*, 72–83.

17. Gonzáles, "El proceso de manumisión en Colombia," 210; Romero Jaramillo, "Aproximación a la historia de la comunidad negra en el departamento del Atlántico," 22.

18. Herndon and Gibbon, *Exploration of the Valley of the Amazon*, 1:258; Jaramillo Uribe, *Ensayos sobre historia social colombiana*, 237–38; cited in Castillo Mathieu, *Esclavos negros en Cartagena y sus aportes léxicos*, 143; Castellanos, *La abolición de la esclavitud en Popayán*, 86; Romero Jaramillo, *Esclavitud en la provincia de Santa Marta*, 160, 167.

19. Posada-Carbó, "New Granada and the European Revolutions of 1848"; Grusin, "The Revolution of 1848 in Colombia." For the democratic societies, see Colmenares, *Partidos políticos y clases sociales*; Escobar Rodríguez, *La revolución liberal y la protesta del artesanado*; Sowell, *The Early Colombian Labor Movement*; and Aguilera Pena and Vega Cantor, *Ideal democrático y revuelta popular*.

20. Lemaitre, *Historia general de Cartagena*, 4:175; quoted from *El Artesano*, 1 February 1850; and Governor to Gobierno, 24 March 1852, AGN, Gobernaciones (Cartagena), 41:204–6.

21. *El Artesano*, 1 February 1850.

22. "El nuevo gobernador," *El Correo de la Costa*, 31 October 1849; "Variedades," ibid., 7 November 1849; "Miscelánea," ibid., 5 March 1850; Bushnell, *The Making of Modern Colombia*, 104.

23. Various oficios, Santa Marta, San Miguel, May 1851, AGN, Gobernaciones (Santa Marta), 31:541, 939–43; 32:338, 340, 344; Aguilera Pena and Vega Cantor, *Ideal democrático y revuelta popular*, 112–13; Grusin, "The Revolution of 1848 in Colombia," 37.

24. See Posada-Carbó, "Elections before Democracy."

25. "Rapida ojeada," *El Correo de la Costa*, 12 December 1849; "Variedades," ibid., 7 November 1849; ibid., 5 December 1849.

26. Calvo to Gori, Cartagena, 7 December 1849, BN, Fondo Antiguo, 164:253–54.

27. Jefe Político to Governor, Cartagena, 9 January 1851, AGN, Gobernaciones (Cartagena), 31:154–56; Decrees and reports, November–December 1850, AGN, Gobernaciones (Mompós), 29:267–69, 322–23; see also Bensusan, "Cartagena's Fandango Politics."

28. Le Moyne, *Viajes y estancias en América del Sur*, 31; José María Samper, *Viajes de un colombiano en Europa*, 32.

29. Helg, *Liberty and Equality in Caribbean Colombia*, 98–99; Castillo Mathieu, *Esclavos negros en Cartagena y sus aportes léxicos*, 147; Fals Borda, *Historia doble de la costa*, 1:157B.

30. Calvo to Gori, Cartagena, 23 November 1849, BN, 164:250; Governor to Relaciones Exteriores, 2 November 1849, AGN, Gobernaciones (Cartagena), 51:415–16; "Escuela pública de Soledad," *El Correo de la Costa*, 17 April 1850.

31. Sanders, "Contentious Republicans," 114, 132.

32. *Enciclopedia del Semanario de Cartagena*, 1 August 1850; *El Ciudadano*, 15 August 1850

33. Troncoso to Gobierno, 20 March 1850, AGN, Gobernaciones (Santa Marta), 29:381.

34. Castellanos to Relaciones Exteriores, 15 March 1850, AGN, Gobernaciones (Mompós), 28:542; Cuadro esclavos manumitidos, 30 September 1850, AGN, Manumisión, 1:354; "Manumisión," *Gaceta Oficial*, 23 April 1851; quoted from "Celebración del 7 de marzo i acto de manumisión," *Gaceta Oficial*, 23 April 1851.

35. Escobar Rodríguez, *La revolución liberal y la protesta del artesanado*, 145–47; Gutiérrez Sanín, *Curso y discurso en el movimiento plebeyo*, 131–47.

36. Troncoso to Gobierno, 20 March 1850, AGN, Gobernaciones (Santa Marta), 29:381; Restrepo Canal, *La libertad de los esclavos en Colombia*, 55–56.

37. "Informes," *Gaceta Oficial*, 19 January 1851; see also Lohse, "Reconciling Freedom with the Rights of Property," 212–13; Gilmore, "Nueva Granada's Socialist Mirage," 195.

38. Colombia, *Codificación nacional*, 14:162–66; González, "El proceso de manumisión," 229–31.

39. Restrepo Canal, *La libertad de los esclavos en Colombia*, 110, 144, 146–47; Lohse, "Reconciling Freedom with the Rights of Property," 211–16; Safford and Palacios, *Colombia*, 204–5; Gilmore, "Federalism in Colombia," 207.

40. "Mensaje constitucional al Congreso de 1851," *Gaceta Oficial*, 2 March 1851.

41. Restrepo Canal, *La libertad de los esclavos en Colombia*, 87–167; Colombia, *Codificación nacional*, 14:415–19, quoted from 416.

42. Gómez to Gobierno, Santa Marta, 9 June 1851, AGN, Gobernaciones (Santa Marta), 32:11.

43. Oficios, Mompós, 13 October 1851, AGN, Gobernaciones (Mompós), 30:142–43.

44. *El Eco de los Andes*, 5 January 1852.

45. "Sabanero," *El Orden*, 3 April 1853.

46. For the public manumission ceremonies, see McGraw, "Spectacles of Freedom"; Romero Jaramillo, "Manumisión, ritualidad y fiesta liberal en la provincia de Cartagena"; and Sanders, "Contentious Republicans," 132–35, 151, 155, 184.

47. Lasso, *Myths of Harmony*, 58–60.

48. Colombia, *Codificación nacional*, 13:20; Colombia, *Recopilación de leyes* (1845), 106–7; "Decreto ejecutivo sobre manumisión," *Gaceta Oficial*, 25 July 1850; Lohse, "Reconciling Freedom with the Rights of Property," 213; quoted from "Manumisión," *Gaceta Oficial*, 28 May 1851.

49. "Celebración del 20 de julio," *Gaceta Oficial*, 25 August 1850; "Informes," *Gaceta Oficial*, 5 January 1851; quoted from Governor to Relaciones Exteriores, Mompós, 7 June 1851, AGN, Gobernaciones (Mompós), 30:93.

50. Hernández de Alba, *Libertad de los esclavos en Colombia*, 70; "Manumisión," *Gaceta Oficial*, 11 October 1851.

51. Governor to Relaciones Exteriores, 26 November 1851, AGN, Gobernaciones (Cartagena), 52:2; Arcos, "Manumisión de siervos," 291–92.

52. Informe, Junta de Manumisión, 1 January 1852, AGN, Gobernaciones (Sabanilla), 8:880; Castellanos, *La abolición de la esclavitud en Popayán*, 119; Romero

Jaramillo, "La segunda liberación," 101–2; "Medellín," *Gaceta Oficial*, 17 January 1852.

53. Restrepo Canal, *La libertad de los esclavos en Colombia*, 110; Corrales, *Efemérides y anales*, 4:87–90; Lemaitre, *Historia general de Cartagena*, 4:178–79.

54. Informe, Miguel Vidales, Majagual, 5 January 1852, AGN, Gobernaciones (Mompós), 31:376

55. Governor to Relaciones Exteriores, Cartagena, 21 March 1851, AGN, Gobernaciones (Cartagena), 51:679–83; quoted from "Manumisión," *Gaceta Oficial*, 28 November 1850; see also García, *Himnos y símbolos de nuestra Colombia*, 50, 58–9. For liberty caps in France, see Wrigley, *The Politics of Appearances*, 135–59.

56. "Resumen jeneral," *Gaceta Oficial*, 23 February 1851; "Resumen," *Gaceta Oficial*, 4 February 1852. For gender disparaties in manumission, see Patterson, *Slavery and Social Death*, 263–65.

57. "Manumisión," *Gaceta Oficial*, 28 May 1851.

58. Memorial, Junta de Manumisión, 21 October 1850, AGN, Gobernaciones (Mompós), 28:868; quoted from "Manumision," *Gaceta Oficial*, 3 May 1851; and "Libertad de esclavos," *Gaceta Oficial*, 3 March 1852.

59. Patterson, *Slavery and Social Death*, 211ff.

60. Memorial, Junta de Manumisión, 21 October 1850, AGN, Gobernaciones (Mompós), 28:868.

61. Arcos, "Manumisión de siervos," 293; "Relación," *Gaceta Oficial*, 21 December 1850; see also Corrales, *Efemérides y anales*, 3:99–100; Sanders, "Contentious Republicans," 148.

62. Cuadro de los Esclavos Manumitidos, Cartagena, 28 November 1849, AGN, Manumisión, 1:146; Cuadro de Esclavos Manumitidos por las Juntas, Santa Marta, [1853], ibid., 3:655.

63. "La abolición de la esclavitud," *Gaceta Oficial*, 23 February 1851.

64. "Manumisión," *Gaceta Oficial*, 26 January 1851.

65. "Manumisión," *Gaceta Oficial*, 31 October 1850; "Libertad de esclavos," *Gaceta Oficial*, 5 September 1850; quoted from "Libertad de esclavos," *Gaceta Oficial*, 13 December 1851.

66. López Tagle to Relaciones Exteriores, Cartagena, 21 March 1851, AGN, Gobernaciones (Cartagena), 51:684; quoted from Corrales, *Efemérides y anales*, 4:90.

67. Etzioni, "Toward a Theory of Public Ritual."

68. Resolución del Alcalde, Cartagena, 6 June 1856, AGN, Gobernaciones (Cartagena), 40:193.

69. Lei Adicional a la de Manumisión, 12 March 1855, AGN, Congreso, 31:517; see also Castillo, *Etnicidad y nación*, 178.

70. "Celebración del 20 de julio en la ciudad de Neiva," *Gaceta Oficial*, 25 August 1850.

71. Cf. Berlin, *Slaves without Masters*, 29–50, 91–3; Bergad, *Comparative Histories of Slavery in Brazil, Cuba, and the United States*, 104, 199.

72. *Gaceta Mercantil*, 27 March 1850; *El Demócrata*, 10 June 1850. For the colonial history of race, see Gutiérrez de Pineda and Pineda Giraldo, *Miscegenación y cultura en la Colombia colonial*.

73. Schmidt-Nowara, *Slavery, Freedom, and Abolition in Latin America*, 3.

74. Colmenares, *Partidos políticos y clases sociales*, 146–47.

75. Gibson, *The Constitutions of Colombia*, 202; quoted from Murillo Toro, *Obras selectas*, 91, 90.

76. *Gaceta Oficial*, 1 September 1853, quoted in Gilmore, "Federalism in Colombia," 292. See also Gilmore, "Nueva Granada's Socialist Mirage," 201 (n. 26); Posada-Carbó, "New Granada and the European Revolutions of 1848"; Safford and Palacios, *Colombia*, 197ff.; Bushnell, *The Making of Modern Colombia*, 101–17; Sanders, "Contentious Republicans," 182, 185; and Sabato, "On Political Citizenship in Nineteenth-Century Latin America," 1297.

77. Colombia, *Leyes i decretos* (1853), 136–46, quoted from 137; Deere and León, "Liberalism and Married Women's Property Rights in Nineteenth-Century Latin America," 637.

78. The following chapters discuss these reforms.

79. Alarcón, *Compendio de historia del departamento del Magdalena*, 180.

80. Patterson, "Three Notes on Freedom," 16; Hernández de Alba, *Libertad de los esclavos en Colombia*, 74; quoted from Ancízar, *Peregrinación de Alpha*, 401.

81. Sears to Nieto, Cartagena, 16 December 1851; Resolución, Juan José Nieto, 20 December 1851, AGN, Gobernaciones (Cartagena), 52:553–59.

82. For racial ascriptions (*filiaciones*) of convicts and fugitive soldiers, see AGN, Gobernaciones (Cartagena), 51:passim.

83. Gibson, *The Constitutions of Colombia*, 202; Londoño Tamayo, "El juicio por jurados en el proceso de construcción de la justicia en Colombia," 62–63.

84. "No. 1," *La República*, 7 March 1850.

85. Araújo to Fiscal, Cartagena, 3 December 1852, AGN, Juzgados y Tribunales, 16:220; see also Cooper, Holt, and Scott, *Beyond Slavery*, 15.

86. Camacho Roldán, *Escritos varios*, 26–31, quoted from 26.

87. Araújo to Governor, Cartagena, 28 April 1852, AGN, Gobernaciones (Cartagena), 52:788; quoted from "Remitidos," *El Patriota*, 17 February 1853.

88. Quijano, *Ensayo sobre la evolución del derecho penal en Colombia*, 128.

89. Governor to Gobierno, Barranquilla, 22 July 1852, AGN, Gobernaciones (Sabanilla), 4:37; Quijano, *Ensayo sobre la evolución del derecho penal en Colombia*, quoted from 146–47.

90. *El Eco de los Andes*, 7 December 1852; *El Iris*, 7 April 1853; quoted from Governor to Jefe Político, Santa Marta, 9 July 1850, AHMG, Caja 11 (1850), 361.

91. Nieto to Relaciones Exteriores, Cartagena, 30 October 1852, AGN, Gobernaciones (Cartagena), 53:204–5.

92. Jefe Político to Governor, San Miguel, May 1851, AGN, Gobernaciones (Santa Marta), 31:939–43; Urrutia, *The Development of the Colombian Labor Movement*, 23.

93. Colombia, *Historia electoral colombiana*, 114.

94. Goenaga, *Lecturas locales*, 213; quoted from Regaile to Dávila, Santa Marta, 16 July 1849, AGN, Gobernaciones (Santa Marta), 28:533; see also Corrales, *Efemérides y anales*, 4:25–40; and Alarcón, *Compendio de historia del departamento del Magdalena*, 179–80.

95. José Eusebio Caro, *Poesías de D. José Eusebio Caro*, 65.

96. Calvo to Gori, Cartagena, 21 September 1849, BN, Fondo Antiguo, 164:231.

97. Quoted from *El Pobre*, 14 September 1851 (emphasis in original); see also *El Parapote*, 24 June 1852.

98. Governor to Gobierno, Cartagena, 2 November 1852, AGN, Gobernaciones (Cartagena), 41:644–46, quoted from 646; quoted from Araújo to Fiscal, Cartagena, 3 December 1852, AGN, Juzgados y Tribunales, 16:222.

99. Corrales, *Efemerides y anales*, 4:89–90.

100. *El Pasatiempo*, 17 January 1852.

101. For another version of the dance legend, see *El Picol*, 16 March 1852. For contemporary ideas of interracial sex, see Wade, *Blackness and Race Mixture*, 312.

102. Posada-Carbó, *The Colombian Caribbean*, 31; Meisel Roca, "Esclavitud, mestizaje y haciendas," 260–61, 276–77; Ospina Vásquez, *Industria y protección en Colombia*, 126; Alarcón, *Compendio de historia del departamento del Magdalena*, 183; quoted from Governor to Gobierno, 4 June 1849, AGN, Gobernaciones (Cartagena), 37:404.

103. For the Cauca *zurriago*, see Sanders, "Contentious Republicans," 157.

104. Solaún and Kronus, *Discrimination without Violence*; Wade, *Blackness and Race Mixture*, 20, 27–28, 85.

105. Posada-Carbó, "Popular and Labour Participation in Colombian Electoral Politics," 18. For local variants in partisanship, see Sanders, "Contentious Republicans," 150; and Gutiérrez Sanín, *Curso y discurso en el movimiento plebeyo*, 99.

106. Colombia, *Historia electoral colombiana*, 115–16.

107. Alarcón, *Compendio de historia del departamento del Magdalena*, 184; Urrutia, *The Development of the Colombian Labor Movement*, 40; quoted from Jefe Político to Governor, Ciénaga, 24 February 1852, AGN, Gobernaciones (Santa Marta), 33:33.

108. Sowell, *The Early Colombian Labor Movement*, 58, 73, 76.

109. Lemaitre, *Historia general de Cartagena*, 4:181–83.

110. Corrales, *Efemérides y anales*, 4:129–30; Alarcón, *Compendio de historia del departamento del Magdalena*, 184; quoted from Codazzi, *Resumen del diario histórico del ejército del Atlántico*, 5.

111. Informe del Gobernador, Mompós, 10 September 1854, AGN, Gobernaciones (Mompós), 33:791–93; Núñez to Hacienda, Cartagena, 25 September 1854, AGN, Gobernaciones (Cartagena), 33: 405; Governor to Gobierno, Barranquilla, 21 September 1854, AGN, Gobernaciones (Sabanilla), 3: 735; Codazzi, *Resumen del diario histórico del Ejército del Atlántico*, 4–10.

112. Alarcón, *Compendio de historia del departamento del Magdalena*, 184–87, quoted from 186; José María Samper, *Viajes de un colombiano en Europa*, 32.

113. Broadside, Cartagena, 11 August 1854, AGN, Guerra y Marina, 838:400.

114. "Remoción escandalosa," *El Correo de la Costa*, 12 December 1849; "El gobernador i el administrador jeneral de hacienda," ibid., 26 December 1849; quoted from Calvo to Gori, Cartagena, 29 June 1849, 22 November 1850 BN, 164:203, 350.

115. Jefe Político to Governor, Barranquilla, 27 January 1854, AGN, Gobernaciones (Sabanilla), 3:576; Gilmore, "Federalism in Colombia," 302; quoted from Alarcón, *Compendio de historia del departamento del Magdalena*, 184.

116. District Judge to Governor, Plato, 31 January 1854, AGN, Gobernaciones (Santa Marta), 36:176; Cudris to Governor, Plato, 28 January 1854, ibid., 36:162.

117. Gilmore, "Federalism in Colombia," 311.

118. Governor to Hacienda, Barranquilla, 5 October 1854, AGN, Gobernaciones (Sabanilla), 3:748–49; Safford and Palacios, *Colombia*, 213–14.

119. Corrales, *Efemérides y anales*, 4:149; Alarcón, *Compendio de historia del departamento del Magdalena*, 186–87.

120. Safford and Palacios, *Colombia*, 214. For Obando, see Colombia, *Causa de responsabilidad contra el ciudadano presidente de la República*.

121. Quoted from Urrutia, *The Development of the Colombian Labor Movement*, 40.

122. Gilmore, "Federalism in Colombia," 311.

123. Colombia, *Codificación nacional*, 17:24–32.

124. Quoted from José María Samper, *Derecho público interno*.

125. Gilmore, "Federalism in Colombia," 359, 366; quoted from "Las mayorias," *El Loco*, 30 September 1856.

126. Bushnell, "Voter Participation in the Colombian Election of 1856," 242; Gilmore, "Federalism in Colombia," 368–70, 262.

127. Bushnell, "Voter Participation in the Colombian Election of 1856," 241–44.

128. Ibid.

129. Ospina Rodríguez, *Antología del pensamiento de Mariano Ospina Rodríguez*, 313, 315, 386.

130. Reclus, *Viaje a la Sierra Nevada de Santa Marta*, 61; Judge to Governor, Plato, 4 January 1855, AHMG, Caja 3 (1855), n.p.

Chapter 2

1. Felipe Pérez, *Anales de la Revolución*, 47. For the war, see Bushnell, "Politics and Violence in Nineteenth-Century Colombia," 16; Park, *Rafael Núñez and the Politics of Colombian Regionalism*, 21–23; Sanders, "Contentious Republicans," 231–41; Uribe de Hincapié and López Lopera, *La guerra por las soberanías*.

2. Piñerez to Ospina, Cartagena, 6 August 1857, BN, Fondo Antiguo, 189:175; Governor to Guerra, Cartagena, 14 September 1857, AGN, Guerra y Marina, 900:459; Prefect to Governor, Mompós, October-December 1857, AHC, Gobernación, Legajo 1:87–91, 116ff., Legajo 23; Prefect to Gobierno, Mompós, 24 November 1857, AGN, Gobierno, Primera, 557:779.

3. "Mensaje del Gobernador del Estado de Bolívar," *Gaceta Oficial del Estado de Bolívar*, 1 October 1858; "Escrito del Procurador del Estado," ibid., 27 February 1859; "Mompós," *El Vapor*, 18 November 1857; quoted from "Estado de Bolívar," *El Vapor*, 4 October 1857.

4. Deputados to Ospina, Santa Marta, 17 September 1857, AGN, Gobierno, Primera, 557:616–19; Felipe Pérez, *Anales de la Revolución*; Alarcón, *Compendio de historia del departamento del Magdalena*, 189–91; quoted from Romero to Ospina, Santa Marta, 1 October 1857, BN, Fondo Antiguo, 211:161–63.

5. "Mensaje del Gobernador del Estado de Bolívar," *Gaceta Oficial del Estado de Bolívar*, 1 October 1858; Miramón to Ospina, Santa Marta, 3 September 1857, BN, Fondo Antiguo, 211:79

6. Corrales, *Efemérides y anales*, 4:197–209; Alarcón, *Compendio de historia del departamento del Magdalena*, 192; Gilmore, "Federalism in Colombia," 399–401; Gibson, *The Constitutions of Colombia*, 221–23.

7. Alarcón, *Compendio de historia del departamento del Magdalena*, 184–87, 190–91.

8. "La situación," *El Vapor*, 9 May 1858; Harrison, "The Evolution of the Colombian Tobacco Trade," 163; Ospina Vásquez, *Industria y protección en Colombia*, 215; quoted from José Manuel Restrepo, *Diario político y militar*, 4:738.

9. Safford, "Commerce and Enterprise in Central Colombia," 17, 28, 107–8; quoted from "Editorial," *El Vapor*, 10 February 1858.

10. "A las Asembleas constituyentes," *El Vapor*, 18 October 1857; Eyzaguirre, *Los intereses católicos en América*, 235–38, quoted from 236.

11. "Circular sobre prisión por deuda," *Gaceta Oficial del Estado de Bolívar*, 28 February 1858; see also ibid., 28 March 1858.

12. José Manuel Restrepo, *Diario político y militar*, 4:737.

13. Felipe Pérez, *Anales de la Revolución*, 140; Pombo and Guerra, *Constituciones de Colombia*, 83.

14. Uribe de Hincapié and López Lopera, *La guerra por las soberanías*, 106; Gibson, *The Constitutions of Colombia*, 247–48.

15. Alarcón, *Compendio de historia del departamento del Magdalena*, 193.

16. Azuero to Gobierno, Santa Marta, 2 February 1859, AGN, Gobierno, Primera Antigua, 1:675.

17. Visto, Juzgado Primero Suplente, Cartagena, 13 June 1859, AGN, Correspondencia (Bolívar), 2:291–94; see also Borda, *Conversaciones con mis hijos*, 1:211.

18. Calvo to Hacienda, Mompós, 26 August 1859, AGN, Correspondencia (Bolívar), 2:304–41; Valiento to Ospina, Cartagena, 6 August 1859; Gutiérrez to Ospina, Cartagena, 6 July 1859, BN, Fondo Antiguo, 189:398, 188–90; Romero to Ospina, Santa Marta, 24 December 1859, BN, Fondo Antiguo, 211:213–14; Bernal to Calvo, Cartagena, 10 January 1859, AGN, Gobernaciones Varias, 21:504; *La Reforma*, 21 July 1859; Alarcón, *Compendio de historia del departamento del Magdalena*, 196.

19. Juan José Nieto, "Bosquejo histórico," 60; Lemaitre, *Historia general de Cartagena*, 4:193ff.

20. Calvo to Hacienda, Mompós, 26 August 1859, AGN, Correspondencia (Bolívar), 2:291; Juan José Nieto, "Bosquejo histórico," 53, Lemaitre, *Historia general de Cartagena*, 4:196; Uribe de Hincapié and López Lopera, *La guerra por las soberanías*, 107.

21. Alcalde to Gobierno, Calamar, 27 July 1859, AGN, Guerra y Marina, 905:132; Uribe de Hincapié and López Lopera, *La guerra por las soberanías*, 106.

22. Calvo to Hacienda, Mompós, 26 August 1859, AGN, Correspondencia (Bolívar), 2:304–41; quoted from Corrales, *Efemérides y anales*, 4:320.

23. Lemaitre, *Historia general de Cartagena*, 4:196; quoted from Juan José Nieto, "Bosquejo histórico," 69–70.

24. Corrales, *Efemérides y anales*, 4:220.

25. Calvo to Ospina, Mompós, 11 September 1859; Barranquilla, 25 November 1859, BN, Fondo Antiguo, 211:66, [70?]; Prefect to Gobernador Provisorio, 4 October 1859, AHC, Legajo 13.

26. Letters to Ospina from Miramón and Romero, Santa Marta, various dates, August-December 1859, BN, Fondo Antiguo, 211:60–61, 135–36, 202, 150–52, 154; quoted from Miramón to Ospina, Santa Marta, 23 October 1850, 211:147–48; see also *La Reforma*, 21 December 1859; Nichols, *Tres puertos de Colombia*, 161–62, 166.

27. Corrales, *Efemérides y anales*, 4:387–88, 395–400.

28. Guardino, *Peasants, Politics, and the Formation of Mexico's National State*, 159.

29. Felipe Pérez, *Anales de la Revolución*, 222; quoted from Corrales, *Efemérides y anales*, 4:217, 218.

30. Corrales, *Efemérides y anales*, 4:220, 221–36; cf. Uribe de Hincapié and López Lopera, *La guerra por las soberanías*, 53, 57–59; Tirado Mejía, *Aspectos sociales de las guerras civiles en Colombia*, 32; quoted from "Ofrecimiento patriotico," *Gaceta Oficial*, 19 July 1851.

31. Codazzi, *Resumen del diario histórico del Ejército del Atlántico*, 5–10.

32. Corrales, *Efemérides y anales*, 4:313, 284–97.

33. Uribe de Hincapié and López Lopera, *La guerra por las soberanías*, 129; Cuervo, *Cómo se evapora un ejército*, 19–20.

34. Gibson, *The Constitutions of Colombia*, 249–59; Uribe de Hincapié and López Lopera, *La guerra por las soberanías*, 129.

35. Mosquera, *Discurso del presidente provisorio de los Estados Unidos de Colombia*, 57–79; Colombia, *Actos oficiales del Gobierno Provisorio de los Estados Unidos de Colombia*; Uribe de Hincapié and López Lopera, *La guerra por las soberanías*, 193–94.

36. Tirado Mejía, *Aspectos sociales de las guerras civiles en Colombia*, 37–40; Sanders, "Contentious Republicans," 237–40.

37. Arboleda to Guerra, Santa Marta, 8 September 1860, BLAA SLRM, Archivo Julio Arboleda, Caja 2, Carpeta 2, 1123/1; Alarcón, *Compendio de historia del departamento del Magdalena*, 199, quoted from 201. This point is made in the case of Mexico in Guardino, *Peasants, Politics, and the Formation of Mexico's National State*.

38. "Las bóvedas de Bocachica," *El Repertorio Colombiano*, October 1878, 315.

39. Governor to Comandante General, 28 July 1862, AHC, Gobernación, Legajo 28; quoted from Corrales, *Efemérides y anales*, 4:264, 271. The phrase "armed citizens" continued to hold currency in the postwar years. See Colombia, *Ordenanzas para el réjimen, disciplina, subordinación i servicio de la Guardia Colombiana*, 161.

40. Corrales, *Efemérides y anales*, 4:403.

41. Juan José Nieto, "Bosquejo histórico," 69, 53.

42. Valencia Llano, "De los bandidos y políticos caucanos," 8; Sanders, "Contentious Republicans," 234.

43. Borda, *Conversaciones con mis hijos*, 1:277–78; Corrales, *Efemérides y anales*, 4:271; see also José María Samper, *Historia de una alma*, 310; quoted from "Las bóvedas de Bocachica," *El Repertorio Colombiano*, October 1878.

44. Juan José Nieto, "Bosquejo histórico," 110; see also Hunt, *Politics, Culture, and Class in the French Revolution*, 52–60.

45. García, *Himnos y símbolos de nuestra Colombia*, 41.

46. Guzmán, *Datos históricos suramericanos*, 1:364–65.

47. Chernak, "Participation of Women in the Independence Struggle in Gran Colombia"; quoted from Borda, *Conversaciones con mis hijos*, 1:219.

48. Colombia, *Actos oficiales del Gobierno Provisorio de los Estados Unidos de Colombia*, 326–27; Cuervo, *Cómo se evapora un ejército*, 104, quoted from 156.

49. Bolívar, *Código civil del Estado Soberano de Bolívar* (1862), 5–6.

50. Corrales, *Efemérides y anales*, 4:238, 379; Calvo to Ospina, Mompós, 11 September 1859, BN, Fondo Antiguo, 211:66; Prefect to Provisional Governor, 4 October 1859, AHC, Gobernación, Legajo 13.

51. Governor to Secretario General, 12 September 1860, AHC, Legajo 2, Carpeta 1842–62, 83–84; Bossa to Secretario General, Repelón, Mahátes, 30 August 1860, 29 September 1860, AHC, Gobernación, Legajo 28.

52. "Dando un informe pedido por la Asamblea acerca del estado de la obra del dique," *Gaceta Oficial del Estado de Bolívar*, 3 February 1861; Comandante de Batallón Glorioso to Jefe Estado Mayor, Cartagena, 22 March 1862, AHC, Gobernación, Legajo 28; quoted from Governor to Comandante General, 28 July 1862, ibid.

53. See, e.g., Valiente to Ospina, Cartagena, 21 September 1859, BN, Fondo Antiguo, 189:404–5.

54. Calvo to Ospina, Mompós, 27 September 1859, BN, Fondo Antiguo, 211:60–61, 67–68. See also Deas, "Venezuela, Colombia and Ecuador," 228–29; Tirado Mejía, *Aspectos sociales de las guerras civiles en Colombia*, 56. For Cuba, see Rebecca Scott, *Degrees of Freedom*, 134.

55. *La Reforma*, 1 December 1859; quoted from Gutiérrez to Ospina, Cartagena, 9 October 1859, BN, Fondo Antiguo, 189:213–18.

56. Gutiérrez to Ospina, Cartagena, 5 November 1859, BN, Fondo Antiguo, 189:230, quoted from 260–62; see also Lemaitre, *Historia general de Cartagena*, 4:236 (n. 13).

57. Solaún and Kronus, *Discrimination without Violence*. This argument has been made in the case of Mexico; see Van Young, *The Other Rebellion*, 449–51.

58. Mallon, *Peasant and Nation*, 229–30; Ferrer, *Insurgent Cuba*, 48–50, 57; Helg, *Liberty and Equality in Caribbean Colombia*, 14–16, 249–52.

59. Cuervo, *Cómo se evapora un ejército*, 151, 157.

60. *La Reforma*, 1 September 1859; but cf. Conservative leader Sergio Arboleda's 1865 advocacy of federalism to preserve the separation of the races: Arboleda, *La constitución política*, 83.

61. Fernández to Ospina, Honda, 21 November 1859, BN, Fondo Antiguo, 211:3–10; *La Reforma*, 11 November 1859. See also *Boletín oficial*, no. 2, Juan S. de Naváez, Mompós, 26 August 1859, AGN, Gobernaciones Varias, 21:715; Gutiérrez to Ospina, Cartagena, 8 November 1859, BN, Fondo Antiguo, 189:230; Lemaitre, *Historia general de Cartagena*, 4:196.

62. Fernández to Ospina, Honda, 10 December 1859, BN, Fondo Antiguo, 211:17–18; Alcalde to Gobierno, Calamar, 27 July 1859, AGN, Guerra y Marina, 905:132; *La Reforma* issues for December 1859 and 21 January 1860; Alarcón, *Compendio de historia del departamento del Magdalena*, 197, 208, 218; quoted from "Calumnias desmentidas," Barranquilla, 19 November 1859, AGN, Gobernaciones Varias, 21:747; and Romero to Ospina, Santa Marta, 1 October 1857, BN, Fondo Antiguo, 211:161–63.

63. Corrales, *Efemérides y anales*, 4:406; Cuervo, *Cómo se evapora un ejército*, 36.

64. Gutiérrez to Ospina, Cartagena, 9 September, 20 October 1859, BN, Fondo Antiguo, 189:200, 203–4, 209–10; *La Reforma*, 1 December 1859.

65. Corrales, *Efemérides y anales*, 4:420; Uribe de Hincapié and López Lopera, *La guerra por las soberanías*, 200–201.

66. Uribe de Hincapié and López Lopera, *La guerra por las soberanías*, 166; Deas, "La presencia de la política nacíonal en la vida provinciana," 166 (n. 47); quoted from Felipe Pérez, *Anales de la Revolución*, 473; and *El Bogotano*, 29 July 1864.

67. Felipe Pérez, *Anales de la Revolución*, 337; quoted from 742, 617.

68. For similar process in Cuba and the United States, see Ferrer, *Insurgent Cuba*, 121; Rebecca Scott, *Degrees of Freedom*, 246; and Higginbotham, "African-American Women's History."

69. Quijano Otero, *Diario de la guerra civil de 1860 y otros sucesos políticos*, 59. For racist rhetoric in Central America, see Gould, *To Die in This Way*, 153, 164–65; and Wolfe, "'The Cruel Whip.'"

70. Anonymous to Mosquera, Barranquilla, 1 October 1861, AGN, Gobernaciones Varias, 22:429

71. Corrales, *Efemérides y anales*, 4:395–400, quoted from 417; and from Juan José Nieto, "Bosquejo histórico," 107.

72. Baraya, *Recuerdos de un viaje, campaña de Santa Marta*, n.p.; see also Felipe Pérez, *Anales de la Revolución*, 496.

73. "Los recuerdos del año de 60," *El Bogotano*, 29 July 1864; quoted from "Los gólgotas," *Los Locos*, 15 April 1869.

74. "Documentos para la biografía del Dr. José Romero," n.d. [1870s?], AHESM, Tomo 90; "20 de julio," *El Bogotano*, 19 July 1864; see also "La suerte de Colombia," *Los Locos*, 15 July 1869; and "El pueblo," *El Granadino*, 27 July 1864.

75. Vecinos de Cerete to Presidente de Convención, 24 January 1865, AHC, Gobernación, Legajo 7.

76. Corrales, *Efemérides y anales*, 4:419; quoted from 4:478, 479.

77. "La válvula inglesa," *El Nuevo Mundo*, 2 January 1862; "Caracter i tendencias de la áctual revolución norteamericana," ibid., 9 January 1862; see also Camacho Roldán, *Escritos varios*, 1:247–72.

78. Correa, *La convención de Ríonegro*, 48; Gibson, *The Constitutions of Colombia*, 263–70.

79. Bushnell, "Voter Participation in the Colombian Election of 1856," 249; Gibson, *The Constitutions of Colombia*, 265; Correa, *La convención de Ríonegro*, 63, 197.

80. Gibson, *The Constitutions of Colombia*, 269; Maingot, "Social Structure, Social Status, and Civil-Military Conflict in Urban Colombia," 339–40.

81. Jefe Municipal to Secretary General, Sitionuevo, 28 June 1876, AHMG, Caja 5 (1876), Legajo sin número; Prefect to Secretary General, Tenerife, 22 November 1865, AHMG, Caja 6 (1865), Legajo 25; Posada-Carbó, "Elections and Civil Wars in Nineteenth-Century Colombia," 633–34; Sanders, "Contentious Republicans," 246–50, 252; quoted from "Informe," *Gaceta de Bolívar*, 22 August 1868.

82. Prefect to Secretary General, Cerro de San Antonio, 3 July 1875, AHMG, Caja 4 (1875), n.f.; Posada-Carbó, "Electoral Juggling," 618, 635–37; Delpar, *Red against Blue*, 105; Park, *Rafael Núñez and the Politics of Colombian Regionalism*, 43–44.

83. Murillo Toro, *Obras selectas*, 913–14; José María Samper, *Filosofía en cartera*, 323, italics in original. Murillo's comments referred specifically to the 1863 war with Ecuador.

84. Cordova to Parra, Barranquilla, 9 October 1876, BLAA SLRM, Archivo de la Guerra Civil de 1876, 95; see also 102, 110, 155.

85. Palacio, *La guerra de 85*, 111, 59; Colombia, *Código militar* (1883), 1:7, 8, 12, 31; quoted from Alarcón, *Compendio de historia del departamento del Magdalena*, 224–25.

86. Corrales, *Efemérides y anales*, 4:495–97, quoted from 497; see also Flórez Bolívar, "La borrosa línea de lo público y lo privado en el Estado Soberano de Bolívar," 77–78; Solano, "Protesta social y cultura política popular en el Caribe colombiano," 21.

87. Pinzón de Lewin, *El ejército y las elecciones*, 33–34; quoted from Colombia, *Causa contra el presidente de los Estados Unidos de Colombia*, 1:675.

Chapter 3

1. Parra, *Memorias*, 62–64.

2. Palacios, *Coffee in Colombia*; McGreevey, *An Economic History of Colombia*; Ospina Vásquez, *Industria y protección en Colombia*.

3. Kastos, *Artículos escogidos*, 67.

4. Harrison, "The Evolution of the Colombian Tobacco Trade."

5. Rafael Gómez Picón, *Magdalena, río de Colombia*.

6. Colombia, *Codificación nacional*, 17:51–52; "Ley 39," *Diario Oficial*, 25 May 1864.

7. Cochrane, *Journal of a Residence and Travels in Colombia*, 1:108; cited in Posada-Carbó, *The Colombian Caribbean*, 20. For the colonial bogas, see Friede, *Fuentes documentales para la historia del Nuevo Reino de Granada*, 8:155–57.

8. José María Samper, *Viajes de un colombiano en Europa*, 11; Poveda Ramos, *Vapores fluviales en Colombia*, 10–13; Rafael Gómez Picón, *Magdalena, río de Colombia*, 345.

9. Le Moyne, *Viajes y estancias en América del Sur*, 47.

10. Parra, *Memorias*, 63–64; see also "Informe," *El Vapor*, 13 September 1857; Holton, *New Granada*, 39.

11. Le Moyne, *Viajes y estancias en América del Sur*, 47; Mollien, *Viaje por la República de Colombia*, 35; Hamilton, *Travels through the Interior Provinces of Columbia*, 81.

12. Cuenta de suplementos al champán *Eliza*, Mompós, 24 September 1851, AGN, EOR, 489; José Manuel Restrepo, *Diario político y militar*, 4:740.

13. Ancízar, *Peregrinación de Alpha*, 515; Cané, *Notas de viaje*, 47.

14. Kastos, *Artículos escogidos*, 66–67; Parra, *Memorias*, 67–68; Posada-Carbó, "Bongos, champanes y vapores en la navegación fluvial colombiana," 5; "El boga del Magdalena," *El Mosaico*, 13 August 1859; Bennett, "My First Trip up the Magdalena," 134; quoted from Hamilton, *Travels through the Interior Provinces of Columbia*, 80.

15. Administrador de Correos to Governor; Payment sheet, 31 March 1855, AGN, Gobernaciones (Cartagena), 34:158, 161; Parra, *Memorias*, 63–64; Le Moyne, *Viajes y estancias en América del Sur*, 49; Helg, *Liberty and Equality in Caribbean Colombia*,

68; Rafael Gómez Picón, *Magdalena, río de Colombia*, 346; Hamilton, *Travels through the Interior Provinces of Columbia*, 82.

16. Bonney, *Legacy of Historical Gleanings*, 1:474, 477–78; Holton, *New Granada*, 97; Posada-Carbó, "Bongos, champanes y vapores en la navegación fluvial colombiana," 4; Rafael Gómez Picón, *Magdalena, río de Colombia*, 346; Steuart, *Bogotá in 1836-7*, 45, quoted from 55.

17. Soborde de las Cargas, *Cuatro Hermanos*, Santa Marta, 14 February 1852, AGN, EOR, 434; quoted from Comandancia to Governor, 4 August 1856, AGN, Gobernaciones (Cartagena), 40:477–78.

18. Parra, *Memorias*, 72; Steuart, *Bogotá in 1836-7*, 60; Codazzi, *Resumen del diario histórico del Ejército del Atlántico*, 10, 11, 15; quoted from Holton, *New Granada*, 68, 78; quoted from Affadavits, Juez 20 and Jefe Político, Simití, 3 and 10 March 1850, AHESM, 73:108–9.

19. Mollien, *Viaje por la República de Colombia*, 35; Röthlisberger, *El Dorado*, 51–52.

20. Carnegie-Williams, *A Year in the Andes*, 43, 240; Steuart, *Bogotá in 1836-7*, 42, 43; Acosta de Samper, *Biografía del General Joaquín Acosta*, 325; Battersby, "New Granada," 290.

21. Adelaide L. S. Dimitry letter, Barranquilla, 26 March 1874, John Bull Smith Dimitry Papers, Box 1, Folder "Correspondence/Papers, 1868–1887"; quoted from Leay, *New Granada*, 15; quoted from Colombia, *Compilación de las disposiciones ejecutivas vigentes* (1881), 35.

22. Holton, *New Granada*, 39, 81; Acosta de Samper, *Biografía del General Joaquín Acosta*, 98.

23. Dessalines d'Orbigny, *Viaje pintoresco a las dos Américas*, 69; Steuart, *Bogotá in 1836-7*, 56–57; quoted from Balmaseda, *Obras*, 363; and Felipe Pérez, *Imina*, 40.

24. Receipt, Ensermo Miranda for Juan Miranda, Honda, 7 May 1852, AGN, EOR, 439; see also 434, 444. For children on champanes, see also Holton, *New Granada*, 39; and Balmaseda, *Obras*, 363–64.

25. "Viajes," *El Mosaico*, 1 October 1864; "La fe del indio," *El Pasatiempo*, 13 November 1877; quoted from Felipe Pérez, *Episodios de un viaje*, 38, 58; cited in Posada-Carbó, "Bongos, champanes y vapores en la navegación fluvial colombiana," 5.

26. Kastos, *Artículos escogidos*, 66; Vergara y Vergara, *Museo de cuadros*, 1:286. For colonial-era depictions, see Noguera Mendoza, *Crónica grande del Río Magdalena*.

27. José María Samper, *Viajes de un colombiano en Europa*, 27; see also Safford, "Race, Integration, and Progress," 23.

28. Ancízar, *Peregrinación de Alpha*, 501, 508, 514–15; cf. Smith Córdoba, *Visión sociocultural del negro*, 103–4.

29. Holt, "The Essence of the Contract"; Safford, "Commerce and Enterprise in Central Colombia," 37, 65; Powles, *New Granada*, 45; quoted from "No más mostrador," *El Porvenir*, 12 January 1879.

30. "Editorial," *El Vapor*, 10 February 1858.

31. Gibson, *The Constitutions of Colombia*, 202; Modificaciones a la Reforma de Constitución, AC, Antecedentes de Leyes 1853 (Senado), I:1.

32. Corrales, *Efemérides y anales*, 4:522.

33. Nichols, *Tres puertos de Colombia*, 89, 179–80; quoted from Acosta to Relaciones Exteriores, Santa Marta, 15 January 1850, AGN, Gobernaciones (Santa Marta), 29:73–77.

34. "Sr. Editor de 'El Vapor,'" *El Vapor*, 6 September 1857; Decreto de 7 de junio, Leyes del Congreso 1848.

35. Colombia, *Recopilación de leyes* (1845), 93–95.

36. Passport; liquidation sheet, Mompós, 5 December 1849, AGN, Gobernaciones (Mompós), 28:886; Colombia, *Codificación nacional*, 13:283; Duane, *Visit to Colombia*, 540.

37. Ynspección de bogas de Mompós, 19 June 1852, AGN, EOR, 470; Gastos en la balija, 30 August [1852?], ibid., 473; Rol del champán *Eliza*, Honda, 14 November 1851, ibid., 496; Preprinted receipt, Honda, 15 December 1852, ibid., 508.

38. Riascos, "Two Hundred Years of Colombian Economic Growth," 188; Ospina Vásquez, *Industria y protección en Colombia*, 428; Hernández Gamarra, *A Monetary History of Colombia*, 36; McGreevey, *An Economic History of Colombia*, 132–33.

39. Cf. *Joaquin de Mier* crew wages to public employees in Urrutia and Arrubla, *Compendio de estadísticas históricas de Colombia*, Cuadro 7A, 55.

40. Governor to Relaciones Exteriores, Santa Marta, 9 August 1850, AGN, Gobernaciones (Santa Marta), 30:8.

41. "Correo del Magdalena," *El Vapor*, 13 September 1857; Rol, Ynspección de bogas, Mompós, 30 June 1852, AGN, EOR, 475.

42. Ynspección de bogas, Mompós, 19 June 1852, AGN, EOR, 470; Rol del champán *Susana*, Mompós, 25 November 1852, ibid., 540.

43. Parra, *Memorias*, 63.

44. Passports, Gobernación de Mompós, 22 May 1848, AGN, Gobernaciones (Cartagena), 51:74; L. Blanco to Governor, Mompós, 16 August 1849, AGN, Gobernaciones (Mompós), 27:690.

45. Díaz Castro, *Manuela*, 1:10; Madiedo, *Nuestro siglo XIX*, 263.

46. Colombia, *Codificación nacional*, 14:421; Quijano, *Ensayo sobre la evolución del derecho penal en Colombia*, 128.

47. Decreto, Cabildo de Puebloviejo, 26 January 1858, AHMG, Caja 4 (1858), Legajo 40.

48. Governor to Secretario del Estado, Mompós, 27 December 1851, AGN, Gobernaciones (Mompós), 30:167; Magdalena, *Código penal del Estado Soberano del Magdalena*, 76.

49. Governor to Relaciones Exteriores, Santa Marta, n.d., AGN, Manumisión, 1:408; Paysheet, Ynspección de bogas, Mompós, 30 June 1852, AGN, EOR, 476; Resumen de los gastos del champan *Eliza*, [Honda?], 14 November 1851, AGN, EOR, 494; "Deuda interior," *El Repertorio Colombiano*, April 1880; Fernando Vélez, *Datos para la historia del derecho nacional*, 162–63 (n. 1).

50. "Correos," *El Correo de la Costa*, 3 April 1850; quoted from "Correo del Magdalena," *Gaceta Oficial*, 21 January 1852.

51. Governor to Hacienda, Cartagena, 13 August 1856, AGN, Gobernaciones (Cartagena), 40:482; Núñez to Administrador Principal, Calamar, 5 February 1854, ibid., 33:92; Proposal for contract, Administrador de Correos and Ballestas, Honda, 9 February 1857, ibid., 39:149–55.

52. Pedro Fifa, Rudecindo Marco, and D. G. Hernández to Administrado de Correos, Barrancanueva, 14 February 1857, AGN, Gobernaciones (Cartagena), 39:118-21. For Calamar, see Rafael Gómez Picón, *Magdalena, río de Colombia*, 441.

53. Administrador de Correos to Administrador Principal, Calamar, 16 February 1857, AGN, Gobernaciones (Cartagena), 39:117.

54. Contract between Gobernación and Rafael Jiraldo, 25 January 1855, AGN, Gobernaciones (Sabanilla), 6:528; Harrison, "The Evolution of the Colombian Tobacco Trade," 163-74; but cf. "La situación," *El Vapor*, 9 May 1858.

55. Parra, *Memorias*, 62.

56. Calvo to Hacienda, Cartagena, 13 June 1857, AGN, Gobernaciones (Cartagena), 39:324-26; Calvo to Ospina, Cartagena, 3 September 1857, BN, Fondo Antiguo, 211:28-29; see also "Informe, Leonardo Fernández," *El Vapor*, 13 September 1857.

57. Safford, "Commerce and Enterprise in Central Colombia," 248-54. For just price among transport workers, see Solano, *Puertos, sociedad y conflictos en el Caribe colombiano*, xiv.

58. Cf. Helg, *Liberty and Equality in Caribbean Colombia*, 69. For petitions, see LeGrand, *Frontier Colonization and Peasant Protest in Colombia*, 64, 66, 121; and Sanders, "Contentious Republicans," 47, 62-63.

59. Governor to Hacienda, Cartagena, 31 December 1858, AGN, CB, 2:131-33.

60. Decreto, Juan José Nieto, Cartagena, 8 March 1863, AGN, CB, 3:719; Jefe del Resguardo to Aduana, Cartagena, 23 June 1868, AGN, CB, 4:583; Oficio, Administrado de Aduana, Sabanilla, October 1870, AGN, CB, 5:8; quoted from Secretary General to Hacienda i Fomento, Cartagena, 14 April 1868, AGN, CB, 3:369; Informe, Governor to Hacienda i Fomento, 18 January 1876, AGN, CB, 5:845; quoted from "Lei 44," *Gaceta Oficial del Estado de Bolívar*, 31 December 1873.

61. Secretary General to Hacienda i Fomento, Cartagena, 19 November 1866, AGN, CB, 4:207; quoted from Colombia, *Constitución i leyes* (1875), 1:184.

62. Colombia, *Actos oficiales del Gobierno Provisorio de los Estados Unidos de Colombia*, 521; Colombia, *Código militar* (1883), 1:313; quoted from Juan José Nieto, "Bosquejo histórico," 110.

63. "Editorial," *El Vapor*, 10 February 1858; José María Samper, *Viajes de un colombiano en Europa*, 36.

64. Corrales, *Efemérides y anales*, 4:250-51, 323; see also Posada Gutiérrez, *Memorias histórico-políticas*, 2:179, 181, 198.

65. Colombia, *Constitución i leyes* (1875), 2:801-11; Nichols, "The Rise of Barranquilla," 168-69 (n. 53); Safford, "Commerce and Enterprise in Central Colombia," 8.

66. A. Gonzáles to Secretario del Estado, Cartagena, 8 June 1865, AGN, CB, 3:839; Jefe Resguardo to Tesorería, Cartagena, 28 October 1867, ibid., 4:328.

67. "Gran robo," *La Palestra*, 5 April 1871; quoted from "El robo," *La Palestra*, 5 May 1871.

68. Deas, "The Fiscal Problems of Nineteenth-Century Colombia," 288-91.

69. Secretario General to Hacienda i Fomento, Santa Marta, 15 January 1869, AGN, Correspondencia (Magdalena), 2:312-14; "Dique," *Diario de Bolívar*, 8 April 1880.

70. "Vapores de la Compañía Unida," *El Vapor*, 20 September 1857; Ospina Vásquez, *Industria y protección en Colombia*, 216; Harrison, "The Evolution of the Colombian

Tobacco Trade," 170; McGreevey, *An Economic History of Colombia*, 162–63; but cf. Safford, "Commerce and Enterprise in Central Colombia," 275, for shipping rates.

71. *Diario de Avisos*, 5 May 1855.

72. Holton, *New Granada*, 78; "Viajes i aventuras de dos cigarros," *El Mosaico*, 26 November 1864; see also McGreevey, *An Economic History of Colombia*, 250–51.

73. Noguera Mendoza, *Crónica grande del Río Magdalena*, 1:452; Holton, *New Granada*, 41; Poveda Ramos, *Vapores fluviales en Colombia*, 69, 369; Posada-Carbó, *The Colombian Caribbean*, 155; Colombia, *Constitución i leyes* (1875), 1:567.

74. Quoted from Noguera Mendoza, *Crónica grande del Río Magdalena*, 2:150; quoted from Reclus, *Viaje a la Sierra Nevada de Santa Marta*, 38. See also Carnegie-Williams, *A Year in the Andes*, 43–45, 240–42.

75. José María Samper, *Viajes de un colombiano en Europa*, 23.

76. Cané, *Notas de viaje*, 52–53; Posada-Carbó, "Bongos, champanes y vapores en la navegación fluvial colombiana," 11–12; Röthlisberger, *El Dorado*, 51; Poveda Ramos, *Vapores fluviales en Colombia*, 53–56, 68; Solano, *Puertos, sociedad y conflictos en el Caribe colombiano*, 3–6.

77. Kastos, *Artículos escogidos*, 65; José María Samper, *Viajes de un colombiano en Europa*, 12, 11, 27; "Progreso de Barranquilla," *La Palestra*, 23 June 1874. For global and imperialist dimensions of technology, see Adas, *Machines as the Measure of Men*.

78. "Vamos adelante," *El Porvenir*, 4 May 1879; "Revista local," *La Palestra*, 30 August 1869; Safford, "Commerce and Enterprise in Central Colombia," 8–9, 399; quoted from Murillo Toro, *Obras selectas*, 76.

79. "Vapores sobre el Magdalena," *El Vapor*, 27 August 1857.

80. Marginal note, Secretario de Hacienda, 5 July 1858, AGN, Gobernaciones (Cartagena), 39:116; Colombia, *Esposición sobre la hacienda nacional de la Confederación Granadina* (1860), 41; José Manuel Restrepo, *Diario político y militar*, 4:713.

81. Le Moyne, *Viajes y estancias en América del Sur*, 45; Duane, *Visit to Colombia*, 593; Steuart, *Bogotá in 1836-7*, 74; quoted from Robinson, *A Flying Trip to the Tropics*, 53–54; Colombia, *Constitución i leyes* (1875), 2:809.

82. Quoted from José María Samper, *Viajes de un colombiano en Europa*, 24; Holton, *New Granada*, 55; Noguera Mendoza, *Crónica grande del Río Magdalena*, 2:152. Poveda Ramos, *Vapores fluviales en Colombia*, 69, 369; Cané, *Notas de viaje*, 51, 52, 273; Hettner, *Viajes por los Andes colombianos*, 33–34; Röthlisberger, *El Dorado*, 47.

83. Colombia, *Constitución i leyes* (1875), 2:803–10; "Policía fluvial," *El Relator*, 31 July 1877.

84. Poveda Ramos, *Vapores fluviales en Colombia*, 68. For the boga inspection's militarization, see "Decreto 7 de julio," *Gaceta Oficial del Estado de Bolívar*, 28 September 1862.

85. Holton, *New Granada*, 55; Poveda Ramos, *Vapores fluviales en Colombia*, 69, 369; Cané, *Notas de viaje*, 51, 52, 273; Hettner, *Viajes por los Andes colombianos*, 33–34; Röthlisberger, *El Dorado*, 47.

86. José María Samper, *Viajes de un colombiano en Europa*, 16–17, 19, 31; Noguera Mendoza, *Crónica grande del Río Magdalena*, 2:152, 149–50; Hettner, *Viajes por los Andes colombianos*, 32–33; Cané, *Notas de viaje*, 273.

87. Noguera Mendoza, *Crónica grande del Río Magdalena*, 2:152, 149–50; see also Rafael Gómez Picón, *Magdalena, río de Colombia*, 346. For the Atlantic baptism of the line, see Rediker, *Between the Devil and the Deep Blue Sea*, 186.

88. "A propos de las monjas," *El Bogotano*, 25 August 1863.

89. Hettner, *Viajes por los Andes colombianos*, 35; Holton, *New Granada*, 82, 58; quoted from Noguera Mendoza, *Crónica grande del Río Magdalena*, 2:150.

90. "Navegación del Magdalena," *El Porvenir*, 16 March 1879; quoted from Rivas, *Obras*, 40, 53.

91. "Informe sobre el dique," *Diario de Bolívar*, 11 April 1879; quoted from Colombia, *Memoria del Secretario de Hacienda* (1867), 100.

92. Cané, *Notas de viaje*, 52–53, 45; Röthlisberger, *El Dorado*, 51–52.

93. Cané, *Notas de viaje*, 58, 59; Carnegie-Williams, *A Year in the Andes*, 44–45, 240; Röthlisberger, *El Dorado*, 51–52; quoted from 57.

94. Holton, *New Granada*, 72; Poveda Ramos, *Vapores fluviales en Colombia*, 67; quoted from Pizano, "Primeros vapores en el Magdalena," 327.

95. Helguera, "First Mosquera Administration in New Granada," 500; Acosta H., *Manual del navegante*, 12–13, 15, 82; "Policía fluvial," *El Relator*, 26 October 1877.

96. "Six Hundred Miles up the Magdalena," Leslie O. Arbouin Diary, Rare Book, Manuscript, and Special Collections Library, Duke University; quoted from "Informe sobre el Canal del Dique," *Diario de Bolívar*, 3 April 1879.

97. Cané, *Notas de viaje*, 55, 68–70; Posada-Carbó, "Bongos, champanes y vapores en la navegación fluvial colombiana," 11–12; Röthlisberger, *El Dorado*, 51; Poveda Ramos, *Vapores fluviales en Colombia*, 68; Nicolás Ortiz, *Guía de la navegación del Bajo Magdalena*, 6; Carnegie-Williams, *A Year in the Andes*, 235–36; Mozans, *Up the Orinoco and down the Magdalena*, 351; quoted from Robinson, *A Flying Trip to the Tropics*, 55. For a steamboat leisure strike, see "Six Hundred Miles up the Magdalena," Leslie O. Arbouin Diary, Rare Book, Manuscript, and Special Collections Library, Duke University.

98. Röthlisberger, *El Dorado*, 47; Palacio, *La guerra de 85*, 223.

99. Gómez, *Apuntes de viaje*, 22–23.

Chapter 4

1. Cf. Rojas, *Civilization and Violence*; Serje, *El revés de la nación*; Arias Vanegas, *Nación y diferencia en el siglo XIX colombiano*; Steiner, *Imaginación y poder*.

2. Rama, *The Lettered City*; Brown, "The Genteel Tradition of Nineteenth-Century Colombian Culture"; Deas, "Miguel Antonio Caro and Friends."

3. Martínez, *El nacionalismo cosmopólitano*; quoted from José María Samper, *Ensayo sobre las revoluciones políticas*, 339. For a similar dynamic in the United States, see Lawrence W. Levine, *Highbrow/Lowbrow*, 215–18.

4. This was not unique to Colombia. See Pocock, *The Machiavellian Moment*, 59–60.

5. For education, see Jaramillo Uribe, "El proceso de la educación del virreinato a la época ontemporánea"; González Rojas, *Legitimidad y cultura*; and Loy, "Modernization and Educational Reform in Colombia." For the public sphere, see Loaiza Cano, "*El*

neogranadino y la organización de las hegemonías"; Bushnell, "The Development of the Press in Great Colombia"; and Posada-Carbó, "¿Libertad, libertinaje, tiranía?" For "tensions between the didactic and the ideal" in the nineteenth-century United States, see Lawrence W. Levine, *Highbrow/Lowbrow*, quoted from 158.

6. Bóhorquez Casallas, *La evolución educativa en Colombia*, 348–49; Posada-Carbó, "New Granada and the European Revolutions of 1848," 229; Colombia, *Codificación nacional*, 14:52–55.

7. Molina, *Las ideas liberales en Colombia*, 28–29; Ramírez and Salazar, "The Emergence of Education in the Republic of Colombia," 14; Helg, *La educación en Colombia*, 23; quoted from Montejo, *Nuestro estado social*, 208.

8. Corrales, *Efemérides y anales*, 4:585; Nichols, "The Rise of Barranquilla," 169.

9. Ramírez and Salazar, "The Emergence of Education in the Republic of Colombia," 28; Holton, *New Granada*, 32; Wong Hiu, "Sociedad y política en Barranquilla," 144–45; Loy, "Modernization and Educational Reform in Colombia," 56–59; quoted from José Manuel Restrepo, *Diario político y militar*, 4:214.

10. García y García, *Código de instrucción pública*, v, vii; see also Camacho Roldán, *Escritos varios*, 3:586.

11. Carrasquilla, *Tipos de Bogotá*, 9, 10; see also "Las sociedades," *El Porvenir*, 24 June 1877; Deas, "Algunas notas sobre la historia del caciquismo en Colombia," 121–22.

12. Caraballo, *El negro Obeso*, 14; Corrales, *Efemérides y anales*, 4:264.

13. Valdelamar Sarabia and Ortiz Cassiani, prologue, 10; Goenaga, *Lecturas locales*, 181, 233; "Sociedades democráticas," *Gaceta Oficial*, 4 April 1850; quoted from "Light in Spanish America," *Evangelical Christendom*, May 1859.

14. Rodríguez Pimienta, *El negro Robles*, 25–26; Prescott, *Candelario Obeso y la iniciación de la poesía negra*, 61.

15. Burgos Cantor, prologue, 11–12; Prescott, *Candelario Obeso y la iniciación de la poesía negra*, 62.

16. Torres Almeida, *Manuel Murillo Toro*, 253, 297; Pinzón, *Catecismo republicano para instrucción popular*; quoted from Uribe and Restrepo, *Candelario Obeso*, 24.

17. "Decreto orgánico," *La Escuela Normal*, 7 January 1871, 4; see also Bóhorquez Casallas, *La evolución educativa en Colombia*, 354; Molina, *Las ideas liberales en Colombia*, 112.

18. Felipe Pérez, *Geografía general física y política*, 285–86; González, *Legitimidad y cultura*, 21–40; Jaramillo Uribe, "El proceso de la educación del virreinato a la época contemporánea," 227–28. By 1875, education spending absorbed more than 5 percent of the national budget and made up its fifth-largest expenditure. See Colombia, *Memoria del Secretario del Tesoro* (1876), ccii.

19. Goenaga, *Lecturas locales*, 181; Jaramillo Uribe, "El proceso de la educación del virreinato a la época contemporánea," 228.

20. Ramírez and Salazar, "The Emergence of Education in the Republic of Colombia," 16, 18; Helg, *La educación en Colombia*, 26–27.

21. "Decreto orgánico," *La Escuela Normal*, 7 January 1871; ibid., 14 January 1871.

22. Loy, "Modernization and Educational Reform in Colombia," 116.

23. See Mehta, "Liberal Strategies of Exclusion"; quoted from "Decreto orgánico," *La Escuela Normal*, 7 January 1871.

24. Obeso, *Proyecto de lei sobre orden público*, 5; Caraballo, *El negro Obeso*, 21–22; Torres Almeida, *Manuel Murillo Toro*, 2–3, 5, 294, 300; Rodríguez Piñeres, *El Olimpo radical*, 201, 205–7; quoted from Marroquín, *Obras escogidas en prosa y en verso*, 51.

25. Wilson, *A Ramble in New Granada*, 69; Bóhorquez Casallas, *La evolución educativa en Colombia*, 366–82.

26. Ramírez and Salazar, "The Emergence of Education in the Republic of Colombia," 20; Colombia, *Informe del Director General de Instrucción Primaria* (1876), 6; Santos, "Formación de maestros, escuelas normales y misiones pedagógicas," 284–87; quoted from "Decreto orgánico," *La Escuela Normal*, 14 January 1871.

27. Santos, "Formación de maestros, escuelas normales y misiones pedagógicas," 281–303; Loaiza Cano, "El maestro de escuela o el ideal liberal del ciudadano en la reforma educativa de 1870," 62–91; Molina, *Las ideas liberales en Colombia*, 109; quoted from "Decreto orgánico," *La Escuela Normal*, 7 January 1871.

28. United States, *Commissioner of Education* (1876), clxi; Colombia, *Informe del Director General de Instrucción Primaria* (1876), 142; Ramírez and Salazar, "The Emergence of Education in the Republic of Colombia," 41–42; Pérez Escobar, *El negro Robles*, 46; Rodríguez Pimienta, *El negro Robles*, 32–33.

29. Pérez Escobar, *El negro Robles*, 46, 204.

30. Fals Borda, *Historia doble de la costa*, 1:57B; quoted from Obeso, *Proyecto de lei sobre orden público*, 2,7.

31. Silva to Parra, Remolino, 23 August 1876, BLAA SLRM, Archivo de la Guerra Civil de 1876, 50.

32. Loaiza Cano, "El maestro de escuela o el ideal liberal del ciudadano en la reforma educativa de 1870," 83; Becerra Jiménez, *Historia de la diócesis de Barranquilla*, 51; Loy, "Primary Education during the Colombian Federation," 286.

33. Loy, "Modernization and Educational Reform in Colombia," 253; Máximo A. Nieto, *Recuerdos de la regneración*, 294; quoted from "Sobre la reforma en los estudios," *El Repertorio Colombiano*, November 1879; quoted from "Las selvas i la ciudad," *El Chino de Bogotá*, 25 June 1874 (emphasis in original).

34. Colombia, *Memoria del Ministro de Instrucción Pública al Congreso* (1881), 5; Briceño, *La Revolución, 1876-1877*, 139; quoted from MacDouall, *El joven Arturo*, 23.

35. Restrepo Arteaga, "Educación y desarrollo en Barranquilla," 172, 174–75; Colombia, *Memoria del Ministro de Instrucción Pública al Congreso* (1881), 52; Goenaga, *Lecturas locales*, 233, 262.

36. Montejo, *Nuestro estado social*, 182–84; Miranda Salcedo, "Familia, matrimonio y mujer," 34–35; "Estado de la diócesis de Santa Marta," *La Cruz*, 1876; Ramírez and Salazar, "The Emergence of Education in the Republic of Colombia," 16, 30; quoted from "Instrucción pública," *El Porvenir*, 10 February 1878.

37. Montejo, *Nuestro estado social*, 68.

38. Brown, "The Genteel Tradition of Nineteenth-Century Colombian Culture," 446; Ramírez and Salazar, "The Emergence of Education in the Republic of Colombia," 14; Santos, "Formación de maestros, escuelas normales y misiones pedagógicas," 291–92. For education spending, compare Colombia, *Memoria del Secretario del Tesoro* (1875), 169; with Colombia, *Memoria del Secretario del Tesoro* (1877), cii.

39. Pineda Camacho, *El derecho a la lengua*, 105–11; Rama, *The Lettered City*, 31; Fraser, "Rethinking the Public Sphere."

40. Colombia, *Leyes i decretos* (1851), 62; Deas, "La presencia de la política nacíonal en la vida provinciana," 162–64; Posada-Carbó, "¿Libertad, libertinaje, tiranía?"

41. "Decreto orgánico," *La Escuela Normal*, 7 January 1871.

42. Brown, "The Genteel Tradition of Nineteenth-Century Colombian Culture," 453–54; Posada-Carbó, "¿Libertad, libertinaje, tiranía?," 187–88.

43. Ancízar, *Peregrinación de Alpha*, 501.

44. José María Samper, *Ensayo sobre las revoluciones políticas*, 68, 90, 91; Madiedo, *Tratado de crítica*, 22–24, 222; see also Safford, "Race, Integration, and Progress," 29–32.

45. Araújo, *Tratado de geografía física i política del Estado de Bolívar*, 24–25; see also Felipe Pérez, *Geografía general física y política*, 168–73; Esguerra Ortiz, *Diccionario jeográfico*, 29, 65.

46. Arosemena, *Estudios constitucionales sobre los gobiernos de la América Latina*; quoted from "Las aristocracias," *La Alianza*, 30 May 1866; see also Sowell, *The Early Colombian Labor Movement*, 86.

47. Wade, *Blackness and Race Mixture*, 54–59, 82–92; quoted from "Comunicación sobre inmigración," *Gaceta Oficial de Bolívar*, 9 November 1862; see also Camacho Roldán, *Notas de viaje*, 114.

48. "La mujer," *El Mosaico*, February 1865, reprinted in Alzate and Ordóñez, *Soledad Acosta de Samper*, 55.

49. Acosta de Samper, *Novelas y cuadros de la vida sur-americana*, 288–301, quoted from 297.

50. Ibid., 327, 392–93; Acosta de Samper, *Una holandesa en América*, 75–77; Acosta de Samper, *Los piratas de Cartagena*, 48–49, 58; quoted from "Una familia patriota," *La Familia*, July 1884, 186.

51. See issues of *El Relator*, December 1877 to January 1879; and especially "Los diamantes," *El Relator*, 30 August 1877; see also issues of *El Elector Popular* for July and August 1877.

52. Valdelamar Sarabia and Ortiz Cassiani, prologue, 16; Rodríguez-Arenas, *Bibliografía de la literatura*, 2:89–95; quoted from Ali-Kelim, *El Elector Popular*, 10 August 1877.

53. González Echevarría and Pupo-Walker, *The Cambridge History of Latin American Literature*, 492–93; Duffey, *The Early "Cuadro de Costumbres" in Colombia*; Deas, "Miguel Antonio Caro and Friends," 65.

54. "El boga del Magdalena [1840]," *El Mosaico*, 13 August 1859.

55. Duffey, *The Early "Cuadro de Costumbres" in Colombia*, 46–107.

56. Wheat, "Nineteenth Century Black Dialect Poetry and Racial Pride," 28.

57. Isaacs, *María*; Díaz Castro, *Manuela*; Silva, *Artículos de costumbres*, 75.

58. Avelar, *The Letter of Violence*, 146. For boga speech, see Lázaro María Pérez, *Obras poéticas y dramáticas*, 294–95; Madiedo, *Nuestro siglo XIX*, 199, 244, 263.

59. Scarano, "The *Jíbaro* Masquerade and the Subaltern Politics of Creole Identity," 1430–31.

60. Díaz Castro, *Manuela*, 1:171–72, 262–65, quoted from 220.

61. Lázaro María Pérez, *Obras poéticas y dramáticas*, 294–95; Groot, *Cuadros de costumbres*, 99–134; Borda, *Cuadros de costumbres y descripciones locales de Colombia*, 12; Duffey, *The Early "Cuadro de Costumbres" in Colombia*, 18; Loy, "Modernization and Educational Reform in Colombia," 113; "El alcalde discreto," *El Fisgón*, 8 January 1874.

62. Rama, *The Lettered City*, 31; Avelar, *The Letter of Violence*, 130; Rodríguez García, "Regime of Translation," 151; quoted from Briceño, *La Revolución, 1876-1877*, 62.

63. Obeso, *Cantos*, 4.

64. Isaacs, *María*, 291; Valdelamar Sarabia and Ortiz Cassiani, prologue, 20. The Spanish here follows Obeso's orthography.

65. Obeso, *Cantos*, 11; see also 35–37; Bermúdez, *El bello sexo*, 130–31.

66. Obeso, *Cantos*, 45. For white male images of women of color, see José María Samper, *Historia de una alma*, 231; Vergara y Vergara, *Artículos literarios*, 9, 228; Felipe Pérez, *Imina*, 40; and "Vida del solterón," *El Porvenir*, 7 October 1877.

67. See Obeso, *Cantos*, 16, 35–37, 39–41; Young, *The Image of Black Women in Twentieth-Century South American Poetry*, 20; and Prescott, *Candelario Obeso y la iniciación de la poesía negra*, 107–8.

68. "Policía fluvial," *El Relator*, 31 July 1877; quoted from Cortés, *Escritos varios*, 305.

69. Lomnitz, "Nationalism as a Practical System," 335–38; cf. Prescott, *Candelario Obeso y la iniciación de la poesía negra*, 98.

70. Obeso, *Cantos*, 26–27; Avelar, *The Letter of Violence*, 113.

71. Colombia, *Memoria del Secretario de Guerra i Marina* (1878), 61; Camargo Pérez, *Sergio Camargo*, 173; Rodríguez Pimienta, *El negro Robles*, 75–78.

72. Sagher, *Nociones de táctica, de infantería, de caballería y de artillería*, n.p.; Obeso, *Cantos*, 40. See also Obeso, *Lecturas*, 83–86; and Obeso, *Lucha*, 52.

73. Franco V., *Apuntamientos para la historia*, 56; quoted from "Despuès del 5 de abril," *El Repertorio Colombiano*, February 1880.

74. Obeso, *Cantos*, 35.

75. Obeso, *Cantos*, 17; Prescott, *Candelario Obeso y la iniciación de la poesía negra*, 88–89; Jáuregui, "Candelario Obeso, la literatura 'afronacional,'" 572; "Garantías individuales," *El Porvenir*, 7 July 1878.

76. Obeso, *Cantos*, 33–34; Valdelamar Sarabia and Ortiz Cassiani, prologue, 14–15; Higginbotham, "African-American Women's History."

77. McClintock, "'No Longer in a Future Heaven,'" 105–6; Obeso, *Cantos*, 33; see also 31, 34, 35, 42–44.

78. Sommer, *Foundational Fictions*, 24.

79. Briceño, *La Revolución, 1876-1877*, 62; quoted from Obeso, *Cantos*, 33.

80. Obeso, *Cantos*, 21; cf. José María Samper, *Ensayo sobre las revoluciones políticas*, 267.

81. Obeso, *Cantos*, 22; cf. Prescott, *Candelario Obeso y la iniciación de la poesía negra*, 91–92; Jáuregui, "Candelario Obeso, la literatura 'afronacional,'" 578.

82. Obeso, *Cantos*, 23.

83. It is uncertain whether the (mis)spelling of the title was intended on Obeso's part, given that *castiza* appears correctly in the collection's table of contents.

84. José María Samper, *Ensayo sobre las revoluciones políticas*, 337.

85. Obeso, *Cantos*, 24–25.

86. Obeso, *Cantos*, 8; Prescott, "'*Negro Nací*,'" 7–8; Valdelamar Sarabia and Ortiz Cassiani, prologue, 37.

87. Brown, "The Genteel Tradition of Nineteenth-Century Colombian Culture," 446, 448.

88. Páez, *La patria*, 46; Añez, *Parnaso colombiano*, 2:213; Obeso, *Lecturas*, 88.

89. Obeso, *Lecturas*, 51, 55; Prescott, *Without Hatred or Fears*, 44.

90. Cf. Pérez Triana, *Down the Orinoco in a Canoe*, iii; see also viii.

91. Capella Toledo, *Leyendas históricas*, 189–93; Obeso, *Lecturas*, 56, quoted from 58; cf. Caraballo, *El negro Obeso*, 24–26, 28–29; Prescott, "'*Negro Nací*,'" 3, 11 (n. 6).

92. Obeso, *Secundino*, 131; Park, *Rafael Núñez and the Politics of Colombian Regionalism*, 198.

93. Obeso, *Secundino*, 182; cf. Vergara y Vergara, *Artículos literarios*, 228.

94. Obeso, *Secundino*, 149, 176–77, Duffey, *The Early "Cuadro de Costumbres" in Colombia*, 33–34. The surname Tapia (meaning mud or adobe wall) was perhaps intended to indicate that Félix was a bricklayer.

95. Obeso, *Secundino*, 143–45, 149, 173, 183–84, 186; see also Obeso, *Cantos*, 11; Rojas, *Civilization and Violence*, 76; and Duffey, *The Early "Cuadro de Costumbres" Colombia*, 39–40.

96. Arosemena, *Estudios constitucionales sobre los gobiernos de la América Latina*, 2:91; quoted from "Las letras, las ciencias, y las bellas artes en Colombia," *El Repertorio Colombiano*, July 1880.

97. Galindo, *Estudios económicos i fiscales*, 298; quoted from United States, *Report upon the Commercial Relations of the United States with Foreign Countries* (1876), 342.

98. "La doctrina radical," *El Repertorio Colombiano*, July 1878.

99. Briceño, *La Revolución, 1876–1877*, 62, 63.

100. Colombia, *Leyes* (1879), 36, 136; "Sesión del día 2 de Febrero de 1883," *Anales del Senado*, 13 February 1883; Uribe and Restrepo, *Candelario Obeso*, 15, 17–19; Prescott, *Candelario Obeso y la iniciación de la poesía negra*, 68.

101. Obeso, *Lucha*, 37–38, 70, 145.

102. Ibid., 39–40; quoted from 32; see also Núñez, *La reforma política*, 200.

103. Laverde Amaya, *Apuntes sobre bibliografía colombiana*, 149, 158–59; quoted from "Un libro de Cané," *Nueva Revista de Buenos Aires*, May 1884.

104. Silva, *Artículos de costumbres*, 189; see also Marroquín, *Obras escogidas en prosa y en verso*, 46; Caro, *Poesías de Julio Arboleda*, liii.

105. Añez, *Parnaso colombiano*, 1:168; Uribe and Restrepo, *Candelario Obeso*, 6; Caraballo, *El negro Obeso*, 35; quoted from Capella Toledo, *Leyendas históricas*, 191.

106. Prescott, "'*Negro Nací*,'" 3.

107. Groot, *Lira nueva*, xiv; quoted from Carrasquilla, *Tipos de Bogotá*, xxxiii; Capella Toledo, *Leyendas históricas*, 191; "Candelario Obeso," *Papel Periódico Ilustrado*, September 1884.

108. Uribe and Restrepo, *Candelario Obeso*, 8, 19, 24; see also Prescott, *Without Hatred or Fears*, 44; Wade, *Blackness and Race Mixture*, 243–45.

109. Uribe and Restrepo, *Candelario Obeso*, 8; Groot, *Lira nueva*, xiii.

110. Groot, *Lira nueva*, 341.

Chapter 5

1. Dispatches from Alcalde, San Juan Nepomuceno, various dates, October 1874, AGN, Gobernaciones Varias, 24:56–77; quoted from 76–77.

2. For perspectives on Caribbean politics, see Flórez Bolívar, "La borrosa línea de lo público y lo privado en el Estado Soberano de Bolívar"; Solano, "Protesta social y cultura política popular en el Caribe colombiano"; Posada-Carbó, *The Colombian Caribbean*, 28–30, 214; and Deas, "Poverty, Civil War and Politics." For the Cauca of the same era, see Sanders, "Contentious Republicans."

3. Delpar, *Red against Blue*, 104; "Un paso hacia el progreso," *El Porvenir*, 28 September 1879; quoted from "Un día de elecciones," *El Porvenir*, 23 December 1877; quoted from Magdalena, *Mensaje que el presidente del Estado S. de Magdalena dirije a la Asemblea lejislativa* (1872), 74.

4. Palacio, *La historia de mi vida: Crónicas inéditas*, 117; cited in Barón Rivera, "Perfil socioeconómico de Tubará," 7–9; see also Posada-Carbó, "Electoral Juggling," 619, 625.

5. Goenaga, *Lecturas locales*, 98–99; Corrales, *Efemérides y anales*, 4:585; Delpar, *Red against Blue*, 101.

6. Guzmán, *Datos históricos suramericanos*, 2:68; Posada-Carbó, "Elections before Democracy"; Delpar, *Red against Blue*, 97–98.

7. Park, *Rafael Núñez and the Politics of Colombian Regionalism*, 71, 89, 104, 164–65; Posada-Carbó, *The Colombian Caribbean*, 230; "Revista del estado," *La Palestra*, 30 July 1869; quoted from ibid., 15 July 1869.

8. Delpar, *Red against Blue*, 101; Park, *Rafael Núñez and the Politics of Colombian Regionalism*, 71–72; quoted from "Revista local," *La Palestra*, 5 March 1871.

9. Park, *Rafael Núñez and the Politics of Colombian Regionalism*, 76–86.

10. Adelaide Dimitry, Barranquilla, 16 November 1874, John Bull Smith Dimitry Papers, Box 1, "Correspondence/Papers 1868–1887," Duke University Rare Book, Manuscript, and Special Collections Library, Durham; Corrales, *Efemérides y anales*, 4:480; "Las fiestas," *El Porvenir*, 17 November 1878; "Elecciones," *El Porvenir*, 14 September 1879. For demonstrative partisanship, see McGerr, *Decline of Popular Politics*.

11. Corrales, *Efemérides y anales*, 4:588; *Corona funebre que la agradecida y heroica ciudad de Cartagena consagra*, 6; quoted from Goenaga, *Lecturas locales*, 186; Alarcón, *Compendio de historia del departamento del Magdalena*, 269.

12. Governor to Secretary General, Lórica, 1 March 1863, AHC, Gobernación, Legajo 23; "Santa Marta," *El Mensajero*, 5 November 1866; "Sociedad democrática," *Diario de Bolívar*, 28 December 1868; "Celebración de las fiestas," *El Porvenir*, 18 November 1877; Goenaga, *Lecturas locales*, 288; Romero Jaramillo, "La discriminación racial en Barranquilla," 276–77.

13. Flórez Bolívar, "Borrosa línea de lo público y lo privado en el Estado Soberano de Bolívar," 76; Park, *Rafael Núñez and the Politics of Colombian Regionalism*, 125; Gibson, *The Constitutions of Colombia*, 271; Delpar, *Red against Blue*, 105; Posada-Carbó, "Limits of Power," 261–62.

14. Alarcón, *Compendio de historia del departamento del Magdalena*, 219, 223–27; quoted from "Decreto sobre servicio de rondas nocturnas," *Gaceta Oficial del Estado Soberano de Bolívar*, 17 May 1863.

15. For male bravado in citizens' militias, see Montgomery, *Citizen Worker*, 68.

16. "Himno," *La Palestra*, 15 August 1869; "Discurso," *El Porvenir*, 1 December 1878.

17. "Asesinato de Abraham Lincoln," *Gaceta Oficial del Estado Soberano de Bolívar*, 14 May 1865; "Revista local," *La Palestra*, 23 July 1874.

18. "Revista local," *La Palestra*, 5 March 1871.

19. *El Elector*, 8 June 1864; Comisión del Concejo, 14 January 1880, ACMB, Libro 1880 Tesorero; see also Rey Sinning, "El eterno retorno del Carnaval de Barranquilla," 103; Wong Hiu, "Sociedad y política en Barranquilla," 146; Buelvas, "Barranquilla, la migración y Joselito Carnaval," 116–17.

20. Park, *Rafael Núñez and the Politics of Colombian Regionalism*, 166–67, 180; Posada-Carbó, *The Colombian Caribbean*, 214–15; Safford, "Social Aspects of Politics in Nineteenth-Century Spanish America," 363–64; quoted from Scruggs, *The Colombian and Venezuelan Republics*, 109.

21. Máximo A. Nieto, *Recuerdos de la Regeneración*, 262; Sanders, "Contentious Republicans," 265–66; Corrales, *Efemérides y anales*, 4:500–501; quoted from "United States of Colombia," *Foreign Relations of the United States*, 1867, 518; quoted from Röthlisberger, *El Dorado*, 253.

22. Mantilla, *Artículos escogidos de Abel-Karl*, 51; "Las aristocracias," *La Alianza*, 30 May 1868; Humphreys, "Race, Caste, and Class in Colombia," 164–65; Goenaga, *Lecturas locales*, 188–89, quoted from 189.

23. Delpar, *Red against Blue*, 46–47; quoted from "Las aristocracias," *La Alianza*, 30 May 1866 (emphasis in original); quoted from Romero Jaramillo, "Aproximación a la historia de la comunidad negra en el departamento del Atlántico," 61–62.

24. Pérez Escobar, *El negro Robles*, 46.

25. Rodríguez Pimienta, *El negro Robles*, 75–78

26. Ibid., 33–35; Pérez Escobar, *El negro Robles*; Park, *Rafael Núñez and the Politics of Colombian Regionalism*, 143; Safford, "Social Aspects of Politics in Nineteenth-Century Spanish America," 363–64.

27. "Inserciones," *La Palestra*, 7 September 1875; quoted from *El Combate*, 8 May 1875; and "Sociedad Democrática de Bogotá," *La Palestra*, 5 June 1875.

28. "La osadía de los desesperados," *El Palo de Ciego*, 15 June 1875; "Así va el mundo," *El Palo de Ciego*, 11 August 1875; see also Delpar, *Red against Blue*, 115.

29. Núñez, *La reforma política en Colombia*, 85; quoted from "Sueltos," *El Palo de Ciego*, 15 June 1875; see also Posada-Carbó, "Elections and Civil Wars in Nineteenth-Century Colombia."

30. "Combate de San Juan," *La Palestra*, 7 September 1875; *El Combate*, 17 April 1875; *El Palo de Ciego*, 1 June 1875; Alarcón, *Compendio de historia del departamento del Magdalena*, 273–91; Pérez Escobar, *El negro Robles*, 52–62; quoted from *La Palestra*, 23 December 1875.

31. Colombia, *Codificación nacional*, 20:217; Colombia, *Constitución i leyes* (1875), 1:57; Informe de Concejo, March (?) 1858, ACMB, Libro 1858, n.p.; "Lei sobre impuesto

sobre la renta," *Alcance de la Gaceta de Bolívar*, 15 November 1868; "Lei 10 de 1878," *El Porvenir*, 13 October 1878.

32. Colombia, *Constitución i leyes* (1875), 1:696–700; Governor to Secretary General, Mompós, 4 January 1862, AHC, Legajo 2, Carpeta 1862 (January-May), 6; Safford, "Commerce and Enterprise in Central Colombia," 135–36.

33. Pérez Escobar, *El negro Robles*, 47–48; Magdalena, *Leyes adicionales i reformatorias del Código judicial* (1878), 2–3, 8.

34. For elite tax resistance, see Various Documents, April 1864, AGN, Correspondencia (Magdalena), 1:501–2, 523–26; "Secretaria Jeneral del Estado," *Gaceta de Bolívar*, 3 December 1865; "Tercera carta," *El Porvenir*, 24 June 1877.

35. Decreto 12, ACMB, Libro 1878 Varios, n.f.; Decretos 24 and 29, ACMB, Libro 1879 Varios, n.p.

36. "Informe del Administrador de Hacienda," *Gaceta Oficial del Estado de Bolívar*, 20 November 1864; "Apreciaciones," *El Porvenir*, 16 December 1877; quoted from Governor to Secretary General, Magangué, 26 May 1861, ACH, Gobernación, Legajo 2, Carpeta 1842–62, 18–19.

37. Acuerdo, Cabildo Parroquial Pueblo Viejo, 24 February 1852, AHMG, Caja 4 (1852), Legajo 195; Acuerdo, Cabildo Heredia, 18 January 1855, AHMG, Caja 3 (1855), Legajo 31.

38. Safford, "Commerce and Enterprise in Central Colombia," 139; quoted from "Informe Gobernador de Magangué," *Diario de Bolívar*, 6 October 1875.

39. Colombia, *Actos lejislativos* (1860), 92; Colombia, *Constitución i leyes* (1875), 1:306; Antioquia, *Código judicial*, 206–7; Bolívar, *Procedimiento civil del Estado Soberano de Bolívar* (1882), 153–54, 106; Cauca, *Código de enjuiciamiento civil*, 207.

40. Grusin, "The Revolution of 1848 in Colombia," 137, 138; *El Eco de los Andes*, 26 January 1852; quoted from "Impuesto sobre la renta," *El Porvenir*, 28 July 1878.

41. Decreto No. 1, Concejo Municipal de Retiro, 18 December 1878, AHC, Gobernación, Legajo 15; quoted from Procurador General to Corte Suprema, Cartagena, 22 February 1879, AHC, Gobernación, Legajo 15; and "Acuerdos," *Diario de Bolívar*, 4 December 1879.

42. Gómez to Jefe Político, Ciénaga, 4 February 1854, AHMG, Caja 2 (1854), Legajo 34.

43. Pescadores to Concejo Municipal, 17 December 1883; Informe de Comisión, 3 January 1884, ACMB, Libro 1884 Informes, Proyectos de Decretos.

44. "Informe," *Diario de Bolívar*, 4 August 1875; quoted from "Administraciones de Hacienda," *Gaceta de Bolívar*, 11 March 1866; quoted from "Secretario del Estado," *Gaceta de Bolívar*, 5 September 1869.

45. Prefect to Secretary General, Santa Marta, 4 January 1876, AHMG, Caja 5 (1876); Moscarella and Barragán, "Hacia una historia ambiental de la subregión Ciénaga Grande de Santa Marta," 29.

46. "No queremos explotadores," *El Porvenir*, 26 January 1879; Domingo Jiménez, *Geografía física i política de la ciudad de Corozal*, 37.

47. Colombia, *Recopilación de las leyes y disposiciones vigentes sobre tierras baldías*, 86, 112; Colombia, *Constitución i leyes* (1875) 1:519–20; Vergara and Baena, *Barranquilla*, 81, 95, 96, quoted from 98.

48. Alarcón, *Compendio de historia del departamento del Magdalena*, 222; Powles, *New Granada*, 108–9; Viloria de la Hoz, "Empresarios de Santa Marta," 29; Romero Jaramillo, *Esclavitud en la provincia de Santa Marta*, 102.

49. Lafaurie to Robles, Santa Marta, 15 March 1878, AHMG, Caja 10 (1878), Legajo Archivo de la Presidencia, August.

50. Ballestas to Prefect, Piñón, 22 October 1878, AHMG, Caja 8 (1878), Legajo 10.

51. McGreevey, *An Economic History of Colombia*, 112–15.

52. Alarcón, *Compendio de historia del departamento del Magdalena*, 195; Colombia, *Leyes* (1879), 23; Rodríguez Pimienta, *El negro Robles*, 87; Bolívar, *Leyes de 1870*; "Lei de 3 de enero de 1863," *Gaceta Oficial del Estado Soberano de Bolívar*, 11 January 1863; see also Sanders, "Contentious Republicans," 315–21.

53. Colombia, *Memoria del Secretario de Hacienda* (1871), lxxxi; LeGrand, *Frontier Colonization and Peasant Protest in Colombia*, 56–57, 64; McGreevey, *An Economic History of Colombia*, 131.

54. Vicario to Provisor, Plato, 28 March 1857, AHESM, 81:224–25; "South America," *The Home and Foreign Record*, July 1856; Posada-Carbó, *The Colombian Caribbean*, 30; Safford and Palacios, *Colombia*, 205; Fernando Díaz Díaz, "Estado, Iglesia y desamortización," 208; cf. Abel, *Política, Iglesia y partidos en Colombia*, 27.

55. Domingo Jiménez, *Geografía física i política de la ciudad de Corozal*, 60; Alarcón, *Compendio de historia del departamento del Magdalena*, 197; Juan Pablo Restrepo, *La iglesia y el estado en Colombia*, 611; Corrales, *Efemérides y anales*, 4:544–45; Goenaga, *Lecturas locales*, 386–87.

56. Vicario to Provisor, Plato, 28 March 1857, AHESM, 81:224–25; Adelaide Dimitry letter, Barranquilla, 18 March 1874, John Bull Smith Dimitry Papers, Box 1, Folder "Correspondence/Papers 1868–1887," Duke University Rare Book, Manuscript, and Special Collections Library, Durham; "Las fiestas," *El Chino de Bogotá*, 2 July 1874; "Feria de Magangué," *La Palestra*, 23 June 1874, 15 March 1878; cf. Delpar, "Colombian Liberalism and the Roman Catholic Church," 273.

57. Becerra Jiménez, *Historia de la diócesis de Barranquilla*, 42; "Mui bien," *El Porvenir*, 8 July 1877; "A la caja," *El Porvenir*, 15 June 1879; "Fiestas i fuegos," *El Porvenir*, 3 June 1877. For La Candelaria in the colonial era, see Helg, *Liberty and Equality in Caribbean Colombia*, 98.

58. "Conspiración i fiestas," *El Porvenir*, 2 March 1879; "Fiestas de la Popa," *El Porvenir*, 10 February 1878; "Celebración de las fiestas," *El Porvenir*, 18 November 1877; quoted from "Noticias varias," *El Porvenir*, 23 June 1878; and "Fiestas," *El Porvenir*, 15 January 1882.

59. Capella Toledo, *Leyendas históricas*, 235; Romero Jaramillo, *Esclavitud en la provincia de Santa Marta*, 164; see also Taussig, *The Devil and Commodity Fetishism in South America*, 52.

60. Becerra Jiménez, *Historia de la diócesis de Barranquilla*, 42; Goenaga, *Lecturas locales*, 246; quoted from "Recepción," *El Porvenir*, 2 November 1879.

61. Along with individual petitions cited in this chapter, see those in Bernadino, *Reverendo Obispo de Cartajena*.

62. For the concept of *vecino católico*, see Colombia, *Leyes i decretos* (1853), 64; "Desafuero eclesiástico," *Gaceta Oficial*, 26 June 1851; Juan Pablo Restrepo, *La iglesia y*

el estado en Colombia, 376. For the relationship between *vecino* and citizen, see Sabato, "On Political Citizenship in Nineteenth-Century Latin America," 1292.

63. Acuerdo, Parroquía de Piñón, 18 September 1875, AHESM, 108:128; Domingo Jiménez, *Geografía física i política de la ciudad de Corozal*, 55, 59–60.

64. J. M. P. to Bishop, 14 June 1882, AAC, Copiador de Oficios, Segundo Libro, 179–84; Becerra Jiménez, *Historia de la diócesis de Barranquilla*, 211–12; quoted from Lista de los Católicos de Camarones, 18 January 1875, AHESM, 108:9.

65. Colombia, *Resoluciones del Senado* (1878), 1:426–30; Smith Córdoba, *Visión sociocultural del negro*, 275; Gutiérrez de Pineda, *Familia y cultura*, 105; Zapata Olivella, *El hombre colombiano*, 151, 153.

66. "Estado de la diócesis de Santa Marta," *La Cruz* (1876), 2:185; Juan Pablo Restrepo, *La iglesia y el estado en Colombia*, 420–68; Becerra Jiménez, *Historia de la diócesis de Barranquilla*, 213; Cura de Remolina to Bishop, 5 October 1884, AHESM, 71A:42bis; Abel, *Política, Iglesia y partidos en Colombia*, 26; "Fiesta masónica," *El Porvenir*, 6 July 1879.

67. "Light in Spanish America," *Evangelical Christendom*, May 1859, 178–79; Goenaga, *Lecturas locales*, 386.

68. "Justicia," *El Porvenir*, 25 May 1879; Curate to Bishop, Chiriguaná, 29 February 1884, AHESM, 122:154; Goenaga, *Lecturas locales*, 386.

69. Circular de Obispo Bernardino, 21 May 1870, AAC, Copiador de Providencias y Cartas, 1870–80, Parroquía de la Stma. Trinidad, 4–5; José Romero, "Estado de la diócesis de Santa Marta," *La Cruz* (1876), 2:185; Becerra Jiménez, *Historia de la diócesis de Barranquilla*, 213–14.

70. Curate to Bishop, Remolino, 5 October 1884, AHESM 71A:42bis; "Fiesta masónica," *El Porvenir*, 6 July 1879; "Light in Spanish America," *Evangelical Christendom*, May 1859, 177; Goenaga, *Lecturas locales*, 386; quoted from Presbitero to Provisor Vicario del Diócesis, Ocaña, 22 December 1863, AHESM, 88:258; quoted from Bernardino to Herrán, Havana, 28 October 1863, BLAA SLRM, Cartas al Ilustrimo Arzobispo de Bogotá Antonio Herrán, 354:15.

71. Abel, *Política, Iglesia y partidos en Colombia*, 37; Helg, *Liberty and Equality in Caribbean Colombia*, 190; quoted from "New Granada," *Christian World*, May 1862.

72. "11 de noviembre de 1811," *El Porvenir*, 30 November 1879; quoted from Guzmán, *Datos históricos suramericanos*, 2:70

73. "Informe Gobernador de Mompós," *Gaceta de Bolívar*, 31 August 1867; Circular de Obispo Bernardino, 3 September 1866, ACC (Trinidad), Libro de Circulares, 1844–66 (Barú), 26–27.

74. "Informe," *Gaceta de Bolívar*, 22 August 1868; see also Flórez Bolívar, "La borrosa línea de lo público y lo privado en el Estado Soberano de Bolívar," 93–95.

75. Ponce to Núñez, Barranquilla, 19 March 1877, AHC, Gobernación, Legajo 29; Note, Jefe de Expedición del Magdalena, Zambrano, 17 February, 1877, ibid., Legajo 36; Decreto No. 7, Alcalde, Campo de la Cruz, 22 February 1877, ibid., Legajo 14; Alarcón, *Compendio de historia del departamento del Magdalena*, 190,197; Corrales, *Efemérides y anales*, 4:544–45; Becerra Jiménez, *Historia de la diócesis de Barranquilla*, 43–44, 92; Curate to Bishop, Sitionuevo, 16 October 1877, AHESM, 110:245; Curate to Bishop, Santa Rita, 1 June 1877, AHESM, 110:73.

76. Guzmán, *Datos históricos suramericanos*, 2:69–70; "Carthagena; New Granada," *Christian World*, March 1868.

77. "Missionary Matters," *Evangelical Christendom*, April 1863, 192; Vergara and Baena, *Barranquilla*, 436, quoted from 465.

78. Becerra Jiménez, *Historia de la diócesis de Barranquilla*, 237–38; Bernardino to A. Herrán, Cartagena, 3 February 1858, BLAA SLRM, Cartas al Ilustrimo Arzobispo de Bogotá Antonio Herrán, 354:9; Corrales, *Efemérides y anales*, 4:590–91; José Eusebio Caro, *Obras escogidas*, iii; "Informe," *Gaceta de Bolívar*, 22 August 1868.

79. For other regions, see Londoño-Vega, *Religion, Culture, and Society in Colombia*; Taussig, *The Devil and Commodity Fetishism in South America*, 60–67.

80. See Posada Gutiérrez, *Memorias histórico-políticas*, 1:402; quoted from "South America," *Home and Foreign Record*, July 1856.

81. Marín Tamayo, "La convocatoria del Primer Concilio Neogranadino," 185.

82. Colombia, *Código civil* (1873), 24–25; Goenaga, *Lecturas locales*, 242; Bermúdez, *El bello sexo*, 12.

83. Goenaga, *Lecturas locales*, 85; Miranda Salcedo, "Familia, matrimonio y mujer," 25, 28 (n. 19). For the colonial origins of this sexual "counterculture," see Helg, *Liberty and Equality in Caribbean Colombia*, 93, 189–90.

84. Miranda Salcedo, "Familia, matrimonio y mujer," 25.

85. Obeso, *Cantos*, 11–12; see also Helg, *Liberty and Equality in Caribbean Colombia*, 78. For sexuality in (black) public spheres, see Appadurai et al., "Editorial Comment," xiii.

86. See Miranda Salcedo, "Familia, matrimonio y mujer," 25.

87. Bolívar, *Código civil del Estado Soberano de Bolívar* (1862), 14–19, 22, 37; quoted from 21.

88. "New Granada," *Christian World*, June 1863, 170; "Light in Spanish America," *Evangelical Christendom*, May 1859.

89. Parish data are from Libros de Bautismos spanning 1818 to 1882, located in AAC (Parroquía). I am indebted to Aline Helg for granting me access to her research notes and for inspiring this line of analysis. Any errors are my own.

90. Juan Pablo Restrepo, *La iglesia y el estado en Colombia*, 522, quoted from 521; quoted from Vallet y Piquer, *Ensayo sobre el matrimonio cristiano y el matrimonio civil*, 74.

91. Safford, "Commerce and Enterprise in Central Colombia," 257.

92. "Las fiestas," *El Chino de Bogotá*, 2 July 1874; "Feria de Magangué," *La Palestra*, 23 June 1874; "La doctrina radical," *El Repertorio Colombiano*, July 1878; Arboleda, *Poesías de Julio Arboleda*, liii; Miranda Salcedo, "Familia, matrimonio y mujer," 26, 28.

93. J. M. Pompeyo et al., Segundo Libro Copiador de Oficios (1861–), Cartagena, various dates, AAC (Trinidad), 84, 139, quoted from 142.

94. "El Matrimonio," *El Porvenir*, 8 June 1879.

95. "Estado de la diócesis de Santa Marta," *La Cruz* (1876), 2:185; "Carthagena; New Granada," *Christian World*, March 1863. For elite women in the Cauca, see Sanders, "Contentious Republicans," 181.

96. "La Hermana de Caridad," *El Porvenir*, 6 October 1878; "Las letras, las ciencias y las bellas artes en Colombia," *El Repertorio Colombiano*, July 1880.

97. Juan Pablo Restrepo, *La iglesia y el estado en Colombia*, 90. For other pronouncements on Catholic antiracism, see Torres Caicedo, *Mis ideas y mis principios*, 1:168–69; and Borda and Vergara y Vergara, *Lira granadina*, 150–51. See also Arias Vanegas, *Nación y diferencia en el siglo XIX colombiano*, 17; Jaramillo Uribe, *El pensamiento colombiano en el siglo XIX*, 282, 283.

98. Ancízar, *Peregrinación de Alpha*, 452–53; "Movimiento de población," *El Relator*, 22 June 1877; José María Samper, *Ensayo sobre las revoluciones políticas*, 271.

99. Colombia, *Leyes i decretos* (1856), 10–11; quoted from Colombia, *Código civil* (1873), 22; see also Colombia, *Resoluciones del Senado* (1878), 2:221.

100. Colombia, *Leyes* (1877), 54.

101. Colombia, *Memoria del Secretario del Tesoro i Crédito Nacional* (1878), 32–34, quoted from 34.

102. See Colombia, *Leyes* (1880), lviii–lxvi, quoted from lviii, lxv.

103. Colombia, *Resoluciones del Senado* (1878), 1:213.

104. Becerra Jiménez, *Historia de la diócesis de Barranquilla*, 40; Delpar, *Red against Blue*, 111; Sanders, "Contentious Republicans," 335; Park, *Rafael Núñez and the Politics of Colombian Regionalism*, 85–87.

105. Núñez, *La reforma política en Colombia*, 639; Sowell, *The Early Colombian Labor Movement*, 117–18; Melo, "La república conservadora," 64; Posada-Carbó, "Popular and Labour Participation in Colombian Electoral Politics," 19; Park, *Rafael Núñez and the Politics of Colombian Regionalism*, 221–22; quoted from Liévano Aguirre, *Rafael Núñez*, 432.

106. "Celebración de las fiestas," *El Porvenir*, 18 November 1877; "Las fiestas," *El Porvenir*, 17 November 1878; Colombia, *Leyes* (1880), xiv–xvii.

107. Comandante Batallón 40 to Secretary General, Ciénaga, 10 September 1878, AHMG, Caja 8 (1878), Legajo 5; "Noticias varias," *El Porvenir*, 28 July 1878; Park, *Rafael Núñez and the Politics of Colombian Regionalism*, 99–100.

108. Prefect to Secretary General, Piñón, 22 October 1878, AHMG, Caja 8 (1878), Legajo 10; Rodríguez Pimienta, *El negro Robles*, 92–93; Nichols, *Tres puertos de Colombia*, 161–62.

109. Rudas, *La insurrección en el Magdalena en 1879*.

110. "Rectificación," *El Porvenir*, 11 May 1879; Goenaga, *Lecturas locales*, 267; Melo, "Del federalismo a la constitución de 1886," 32, 35–36; cf. Delpar, *Red against Blue*, 96–97.

111. Park, *Rafael Núñez and the Politics of Colombian Regionalism*, 180–81; "Elecciones," *El Porvenir*, 14 September 1879.

112. Park, *Rafael Núñez and the Politics of Colombian Regionalism*, 184; quoted from "Revista del mes," *El reportorio colombiano*, July 1879; quoted from Miguel Samper, *Escritos políticos-económicos*, 1:305.

113. "Elecciones," *El Porvenir*, 18 May 1879; "La enseñanza primera," *La Palestra*, 20 April 1871.

114. "El Banco Nacional," *El Repertorio Colombiano*, March 1880; Felipe Pérez, *Geografía general física y política* (1883), 1:102; Park, *Rafael Núñez and the Politics of Colombian Regionalism*, 189–220.

115. Colombia, *Leyes* (1880), 70; Vergara y Baena, *Barranquilla*, 478; Goenaga, *Lecturas locales*, 387; "Revista política," *El Repertorio Colombiano*, August 1880.

116. Delpar, *Red against Blue*, 123–24; Núñez, *La reforma política en Colombia*, 85–86.

117. Governor to Secretary General, Magangué, 10 November 1880, AHC, Legajo 4, Carpeta Única; Pedro Lara to President, Santa Marta, 9 August 1882, AGN, Gobierno, Primera, 528:419–23; Oficio, Comandante de 2a División, Barranquilla, 28 November 1882, ibid., 447; see also Delpar, *Red against Blue*, 107.

118. "El Carnaval," *La Palestra*, 15 March 1878.

119. "El nuevo obispo," *El Porvenir*, 14 September 1879; "Recibimiento," *El Porvenir*, 14 September 1879. See also Lawrence W. Levine, *Highbrow/Lowbrow*, 60.

120. Corrales, *Homenaje de Colombia*, 155–58, quoted from 116; Goenaga, *Lecturas locales*, 102–10. For similar dynamics in the United States, see Lawrence W. Levine, *Highbrow/Lowbrow*, 177.

121. "Las fiestas," *El Porvenir*, 10 November 1878; "Policía," *El Porvenir*, 2 March 1879; "11 de noviembre de 1811," *El Porvenir*, 16 November 1879; "Reforma proteccionista," *El Repertorio Colombiano*, April 1880; quoted from "Nota Jefe Jendarmería," *Diario de Bolívar*, 9 September 1879; quoted from Governor to Concejo, 9 February 1882, ACMB, Libro Varios 1882, n.f.

122. "Informe Gobernador Sabanalarga," *Diario de Bolívar*, 24 August 1882; "Diligencia de visita," *Diario de Bolívar*, 13 January 1883; Goenaga, *Lecturas locales*, 83; Posada-Carbó, *The Colombian Caribbean*, 21; Nichols, *Tres puertos de Colombia*, 163.

123. "Informe sobre el Caño," *Anales de la Canalización del Magdalena*, 20 July 1881; Colombia, *Anales del Senado* (1883), 22; Personero Municipal to Concejo, Barranquilla, 26 April 1882, ACMB, Informes 1882 (1); quoted from A. Ramírez to Gobierno, Barranquilla, 18 March 1882, AGN, Gobierno, Primera Antigua, 16:524.

124. "La tram-via," *El Porvenir*, 1 January 1882; "Trabajadores," *El Porvenir*, 22 January 1882; "The Panama Canal," *Scientific American Supplement*, 12 August 1882; Zambrano, *Colombia: País de regiones*, 1:214; quoted from "Informe Gobernador Mompós," *Diario de Bolívar*, 7 August 1882.

125. Colombia, *Resoluciones del Senado* (1878), 1:448; Juan Pablo Restrepo, *La iglesia y el estado en Colombia*, 464–68.

126. "Conversaciones familiares," *El Repertorio Colombiano*, August 1878; "Matrimonio," *El Porvenir*, 5 January 1879; Delpar, "Colombian Liberalism and the Roman Catholic Church," 281–83; quoted from Curate to Bishop, Remolino, 5 October 1884, AHESM, 71A:42bis.

127. Curate to Bishop, Plato, 29 April 1882, AHESM, 118:151–52. See also various *informes* from priests to Santa Marta's bishop in 1884, AHESM, 71A:27, 41, 42bis, 43.

128. Miranda Salcedo, "Familia, matrimonio y mujer," 24; Diligencias, Promotor Fiscal del Diócesis, 21 February 1859, AHESM, 82:154–60; Bishop to Vicarate of San José, 30 November 1871, AAC (Trinidad), Copiador de Oficios, 2:60; quoted from Alcazar to Pompeyo, [December?] 1872, ibid., 2:64.

129. Vecinos to Bishop, Tamalameque, 6 February 1884, AHESM, 122:105–8.

130. Máximo A. Nieto, *Recuerdos de la Regeneración*, 122–24; Deas, "Poverty, Civil War and Politics"; España, *La guerra civil de 1885*, 83–95.

131. España, *La guerra civil de 1885*, 96; Park, *Rafael Núñez and the Politics of Colombian Regionalism*, 259–61; Sanders, "Contentious Republicans," 369; Joaquín Ospina, *Diccionario biográfico y bibliográfico de Colombia*, 22–23.

132. Curate to Bishop, San José de Buenavista, 2 November 1885, AHESM, 123:159–63; Informe, Junta Canalización, Barranquilla, [March 1887], AGN, Obras Públicas, 2220:3–17; "Navy Intelligence Report on the Siege of Cartagena," 1885, NARA, RG 45, Navy Records, Subject File, 1775–1910, 8; Lemaitre, *Historia general de Cartagena*, 4:288; Domínguez to Comandante General, Turbaco, 4 June 1885; Comandante del Escuadrón to Domínguez, Santa Rosa, 5 June 1885, AHC, Gobernación, Legajo 29.

133. "Dique," *Registro de Bolívar*, 30 July 1885; Sáenz to Gobierno, Bogotá, n.d. [1885], AGN, Gobierno, Primera Antigua, 70:591; José María Samper, *El sitio de Cartagena*, 100, 104.

134. José María Samper, *El sitio de Cartagena*, 101–2; "Navy Intelligence Report on the Siege of Cartagena," 1885, NARA, RG 45, Navy Records, Subject File, 1775–1910, 9; Eduardo Posada, *Viajes y cuentos*, 242; cf. Palacio, *La guerra de 85*, 111, 312; Alarcón, *Compendio de historia del departamento del Magdalena*, 307; Deas, "Poverty, Civil War and Politics," 275, 279.

135. Alarcón, *Compendio de historia del departamento del Magdalena*, 307–8; Park, *Rafael Núñez and the Politics of Colombian Regionalism*, 262–63; quoted from Colombia, *Noticias de la guerra*, 158; José María Samper, *El sitio de Cartagena*, 167, quotations in original.

136. Palacio, *La guerra de 1885*, 56–57, quoted from 58.

137. Máximo A. Nieto, *Recuerdos de la Regeneración*, 129; Deas, "Poverty, Civil War and Politics," 287–88; Colombia, *Noticias de la guerra*, 156, 166, 168, 174; Máximo A. Nieto, *Recuerdos de la Regeneración*, 130–31; Palacio, *La guerra de 1885*, 315; quoted from "Navy Intelligence Report on the Siege of Cartagena," 1885, NARA, RG 45, Navy Records, Subject File, 1775–1910, 9; quoted from Cartagena, *Corona fúnebre que la agradecida y heroica ciudad de Cartagena consagra*, 16.

138. Nicolás Ortiz, *Guía de la navegación del Bajo Magdalena*, 54; Posada, *Viajes y cuentos*, 246.

139. See documents of the Inspección de Navegación Fluvial, October-November 1885, AGN, Gobierno, Primera Antigua, 16:546–47, 557–68; Secretario del Estado to Gobierno, Barranquilla, 16 September 1885, AGN, ibid., 69:609; Affadvit, Manuel Castro Viola, Barranquilla, 4 September 1885, ibid., 69:603–4.

140. Melo, "La República conservadora," 63–65; Gibson, *The Constitutions of Colombia*, 306–13; quoted from Academia Colombiana de Historia, *Antecedentes de la Constitución de Colombia*, 191.

141. Gibson, *The Constitutions of Colombia*, 312; Banco de la República, *Biografía de los Constituyentes*, 4:77–85; quoted from Academia Colombiana de Historia, *Antecedentes de la Constitución de Colombia*, 263, 267.

142. Academia Colombiana de Historia, *Antecedentes de la Constitución de Colombia*, 263; quoted from José María Samper, *Derecho público interno*, 22, 23, 405; quoted from Núñez, *La reforma política en Colombia*, 800. For different perspectives on Núñez's changing politics, see Melo, "La República conservadora," 57; Delpar, "Renegade or Regenerator?"

143. Dirección Nacional Liberal, Bogotá, 10 November 1886, BLAA SLRM, MSS. 378; Molina, *Las ideas liberales en Colombia*, 91, 97; quoted from Pérez i Soto, *Vértice del ángulo*, 76.

Chapter 6

1. For political dynamics of the Regeneration, see Melo, "La constitución de 1886" and "La República conservadora"; Molina, *Las ideas liberales en Colombia*, 141–89; Posada-Carbó, "Limits of Power"; Deas, "The Role of the Church, the Army and the Police in Colombian Elections"; Delpar, *Red against Blue*, 133–83; Bergquist, *Coffee and Conflict in Colombia*, 21–99; and Appelbaum, *Muddied Waters*, 107–41.

2. Núñez, *La reforma política en Colombia*, 720–21.

3. For Caribbean resistance to the Regeneration, see Palacios, *Estado y clases sociales en Colombia*, 81.

4. "Secretaria de Gobierno," *Registro de Bolívar*, 14 January 1892; Informe, Comandancia de Policía, Cartagena, 25 November 1895, AGN, Gobernaciones (Bolívar), 3:620–22; quoted from Governor to Gobierno, Cartagena, 7 April 1892, AGN, Gobierno, Primera Antigua, 45:330–32.

5. Gibson, *The Constitutions of Colombia*, 318; Bravo Páez, *Comportamientos ilícitos y mecanismos de control social en el Bolívar grande*, 71; quoted from Román to Gobierno, Cartagena, 5 July 1892, AGN, Gobierno, Primera Antigua, 45:28–33.

6. Restrepo Arteaga, "Educación y desarrollo en Barranquilla," 167; Palacio, *La guerra de 1885*, 299. For the national perspective, see Jaramillo, "Antecedentes generales de la Guerra de los Mil Días," 68.

7. Gibson, *The Constitutions of Colombia*, 310–11, 321–22; Daniel H. Levine, "Church Elites in Venezuela and Colombia"; Appelbaum, *Muddied Waters*, 109, 246 (n. 7).

8. Jaramillo Uribe, *El pensamiento colombiano en el siglo XIX*, 285–315; quoted from Guerrero to Congress, 20 September 1890, AC, Leyes Autógrafas, 1892, 5:85–86.

9. Conde Calderón, "Carnaval, sociedad y cultura," 84–85; Becerra Jiménez, *Historia de la diócesis de Barranquilla*, 116. For similar messages in Medellín's Carnival, see Farnsworth-Alvear, *Dulcinea in the Factory*, 78.

10. García Benítez, *Reseña histórica de los obispos que han regentado la diócesis de Santa Marta*, 621.

11. "Veinte de julio," *El Porvenir*, 21 July 1898; "Para Rafael Núñez," *El Porvenir*, 27 September 1894.

12. Brioschi, *Vida de San Pedro Claver*, 138; Juan Pablo Restrepo, *La iglesia y el estado en Colombia*, 87, 88, quoted from 91; quoted from Antonio José Restrepo, *Poesías originales y traducciones poéticas*, cxxvi.

13. Sarmiento to Bishop, Iglesia de San Roque, Barranquilla, 29 August 1898, AAC, Documentos de Parroquías, Permisos para Erección de Cofradías, 1898–1902. For western Colombia, see Appelbaum, *Muddied Waters*, 109–10.

14. "Arjona y su fiesta religiosa," *El Porvenir*, 17 March 1899; quoted from "La procesión del Viernes Santo," *El Porvenir*, 6 April 1890.

15. Palacio, *La historia de mi vida: Crónicas inéditas*, 13; quoted from "Bazar," *El Porvenir*, 24 January 1895.

16. Varios Ciudadanos to Governor, Carmen, 9 January 1892, AGN, Gobierno, Primera Antigua, 45: 202–5, 207–8.

17. Salavarria and Martínez to Governor, Cartagena, 22 April 1893, AGN, Gobernaciones (Bolívar), 2:327.

18. Sowell, *The Early Colombian Labor Movement*, 106.

19. Juan Pablo Restrepo, *La iglesia y el estado en Colombia*, 376–77.

20. Mayordomo de Fábrica to Bishop, Ciénaga, 16 May 1888, AHESM, 130:262; "Iglesia de Since," *El Porvenir*, 7 July 1898; see also Bravo Páez, *Comportamientos ilícitos y mecanismos de control social en el Bolívar grande*, 53.

21. Vecinos to Celedón, Ciénega 6 June 1892, AHESM, 145:9–10.

22. Goenaga, *Lecturas locales*, 390; quoted from *El Porvenir*, 27 November 1898, 3.

23. Presbyterian Church in the U.S.A., *Fifty-fifth Annual Report of the Board of Foreign Missions*, 247.

24. "Desagradable incidente," *El Porvenir*, 11 June 1899; "Ya no hay niños," *El Porvenir*, 16 June 1899; "Acuerdo," *Gaceta Municipal* (Cartagena), 31 December 1892; quoted from "Acuerdo No. 1," ibid., 10 January 1896.

25. Colombia, *Informe que el Ministro de Instrucción Pública presenta al Congreso de Colombia* (1894), 64–65; Becerra Jiménez, *Historia de la diócesis de Barranquilla*, 50; "Instrucción pública," *El Porvenir*, 4 December 1898.

26. "Inspección de instrucción pública de la provincia," *El Vigilante*, 5 June 1891; Colombia, *Informe que el Ministro de Instrucción Pública presenta al Congreso de Colombia* (1898), 129–47.

27. Ramírez and Salazar, "The Emergence of Education in the Republic of Colombia," 3, 5; quoted from "Instrucción pública," *El Porvenir*, 19 April 1899; Bolívar, *Leyes expedidas por la Asamblea Lejislativa del Estado s. de Bolívar* (1895), 299; Colombia, *Informe que el Ministro de Instrucción Pública presenta al Congreso de Colombia* (1894), 115–6.

28. See Dilgencias Sumarias, Barranquilla, March-April 1892, AGN, Gobierno, Primera Antigua, 17:168, 171–72.

29. Vicar to Bishop, Ocaña, Santa Marta, 24 June 1886, 5 August 1886, AHESM, 125:267, 341; Aguilar, *Último año de residencia en México*, 247, 249; see also Safford and Palacios, *Colombia*, 247.

30. Rafael Pérez, *Compañia de Jesús en Colombia*, 1:40–42, 46–48, 66–67; quoted from "El darwinismo y las misiones," *El Reportorio Colombiano*, March 1887.

31. Anayes to Bishop, Guamal, 21 August 1886; Banco, 17 August 1886, AHESM, 125:364–65.

32. Becerra Jiménez, *Historia de la diócesis de Barranquilla*, 118; Anayes to Bishop, Guamal, 21 August 1886; Banco, 17 August 1886, AHESM, 125:364–65.

33. Anayes to Bishop, 17 August 1886, AHESM, 125:365; Matute, *Los padres candelarios en Colombia*, 1:49.

34. Alcalde to Bishop, 5 October 1893; Decreto No. 19, Alcalde Tamalameque, 5 October 1893, AHESM, 147:75–76.

35. Catholic Church, *Las misiones católicas en Colombia* (1919), 190; Vida y Muerte del Rdo. Padre Nicolas Rodríguez, S.J., AAC, Libro de Visitas Pastorales 1901, 38–42, quoted from 38.

36. Appelbaum, *Muddied Waters*, 108; quoted from "Apostolic Works," *Messenger of the Sacred Heart*, November 1896.

37. Matute, *Los padres candelarios en Colombia*, 1:30; Becerra Jiménez, *Historia de la diócesis de Barranquilla*, 115; quoted from Aguilar, *Último año de residencia en México*, 247.

38. Colombia, *Informe que el Ministro de Instrucción Pública Presenta al Congreso de Colombia* (1898), 64.

39. "Estado actual de la instrucción pública en Colombia," *El Repertorio Colombiano*, October 1896.

40. "Memoriales," *Gaceta Municipal* (Cartagena), 22 July 1895; quoted from Visita, Alcalde Bocachica, 22 December 1887, AHC, Gobernación, Legajo 16.

41. For definitions of *subversive*, see Gibson, *The Constitutions of Colombia*, 320; Núñez, *La reforma política en Colombia*, 518; José María Samper, *Derecho público interno de Colombia*, 78.

42. Molina, *Las ideas liberales en Colombia*, 174–75, 197; Delpar, *Red against Blue*, 133ff.; Bergquist, *Coffee and Conflict in Colombia*, 37–38.

43. Vargas Vila, *Aura ó Las violetas; Emma; Lo irreparable*; Eduardo Posada, *Viajes y cuentos*, 203–4; Avelar, *The Letter of Violence*, esp. 107.

44. Pérez Triana, *Down the Orinoco in a Canoe*, iii. Translating *negrito* is problematic, although it always carries racist connotations. Regardless, it does not appear in Obeso's poem. See Wade, *Blackness and Race Mixture*, 242, 264–65, 320; Buscaglia-Salgado, *Undoing Empire*, 309 (n. 49).

45. Rivas, Los *trabajadores de la tierra caliente*, esp. 12–58; quoted from 33, 45, 58; Safford, *The Ideal of the Practical*, 79; cf. Rojas, *Civilization and Violence*, 69–71.

46. Núñez, *La reforma política en Colombia*, 401.

47. Safford and Palacios, *Colombia*, 249; Máximo A. Nieto, *Recuerdos de la Regeneración*, 296–97.

48. Rodríguez Pimienta, *El negro Robles*, 33–35; Pérez Escobar, *El negro Robles*; Delpar, *Red against Blue*, 142; quoted from Antonio José Restrepo, *Poesías originales y traducciones poéticas*, 76.

49. Pérez Escobar, *El negro Robles*, Ch. XIII; Delpar, *Red against Blue*, 153–55; Deas, "Miguel Antonio Caro and Friends," 11; quoted from Matute, *Los padres candelarios en Colombia*, 5:189.

50. Cuervo, *Curiosidades de la vida americana en París*, vi–viii; Pérez i Soto, *La curarina, antidoto contra el montalvismo*, 50, 89; quoted from "Psicología del socialismo," *El Porvenir*, 5 March 1899.

51. "El darwinismo y las misiones," *El Reportorio Colombiano*, March 1887 (emphasis in original); José María Samper, *Filosofía en cartera*, 57–58, 114, 192.

52. Vergara y Velasco, *Nueva geografía de Colombia*, dcxlvi, dcliv; Safford, "Race, Integration, and Progress," 29–30; Appelbaum, *Muddied Waters*, 107; quoted from Aguilar, *Colombia en presencia de las repúblicas hispano-americanas*, 192.

53. Miguel Antonio Caro, *Apuntes sobre credito, deuda pública y papel-moneda*, 13.

54. For the myth of the vanishing Indian, see Gould, *To Die in This Way*.

55. Rivas, *Obras*, 64; Camacho Roldán, *Notas de viaje*, 176.

56. Quoted from "Primeros vapores en el Magdalena," *El Repertorio Colombiano*, July 1884, 321; see also Nicolás Ortiz, *Guía de la navegación del Bajo Magdalena*, 11–12; Vergara y Velasco, *Nueva geografía de Colombia*, dclvi.

57. "Feria de Magangué," *Registro de Bolívar*, 7 July 1895; Millican, *Travels and Adventures of an Orchid Hunter*, 58; "Colombia: Region of the Magdalena," *Monthly Consular and Trade Reports*, July 1896, 378.

58. "Circular," *Registro de Bolívar*, 16 March 1886; Arboleda C., *Código de aduanas*, 138, 143, 179; Colombia, *Código penal*, 119–20; Angarita, *Códigos de organización*, 29.

59. Inspector General de Bogas to Ministerio, Cartagena, 2 December 1890, AHC, Gobernación, Legajo 37; quoted from Camacho Roldán, *Notas de viaje*, 82.

60. *Gaceta Judicial*, 16 August 1899; quoted from González-Jácome, "The Assault on Classical Legal Thought in Colombia," 61; Colombia, *Jurisprudencia colombiana extractada y concordada*, 260.

61. José María Samper, *Derecho público interno de Colombia*, 31; quoted from Gibson, *The Constitutions of Colombia*, 316, 317.

62. Palacios, *Coffee in Colombia*, 17; quoted from Gibson, *The Constitutions of Colombia*, 316.

63. Horna, *Transport Modernization and Entrepreneurship in Nineteenth-Century Colombia*, 110–11, 144–51; Nichols, *Tres puertos de Colombia*, 65, 224, 130; Posada-Carbó, *The Colombian Caribbean*, 152; Palacios, *Coffee in Colombia*, 18–19.

64. Posada-Carbó, "Bongos, champanes y vapores en la navegación fluvial colombiana," 9.

65. Horna, *Transport Modernization and Entrepreneurship in Nineteenth Century Colombia*, 148.

66. Castro to Ministerio, Barranquilla, 14 May 1890, AGN, Gobierno, Primera Antigua, 16:715–39.

67. "Circular de la inspección fluvial de Barranquilla," *Registro de Bolívar*, 5 March 1886; Inspector to Alcalde, Gaira, 7 October 1896; Resolución No. 22, Concejo Gaira, 8 June 1896, AHMG, Caja 10 (1896), Legajo 3; see also Solano, "Trabajo y ocio el en Caribe colombiano."

68. Hernández Gamarra, *A Monetary History of Colombia*, 65–67; Bustamante Roldán, *Efectos económicos del papel moneda durante la Regeneración*, 27, 117.

69. Safford, "Commerce and Enterprise in Central Colombia"; Palacios, *Coffee in Colombia*, 124; Deas, "Fiscal Problems in Nineteenth-Century Colombia," 324–25; Bergquist, *Coffee and Conflict in Colombia*, 36; Safford and Palacios, *Colombia*, 257.

70. Data taken from United States Bureau of Foreign Commerce, *Labor in America, Asia, Africa, Australasia, and Polynesia*, 169–73.

71. Robert Crooke Wood letter, Cartagena, 11 September 1889, Trist Wood Papers, Southern Historical Collection, University of North Carolina at Chapel Hill; Note,

M. Carr, Santa Marta, n.d. [c.1890], Samuel Henry Lockett Papers, Series B, Box 9, Folder 139, ibid.; quoted from United States Bureau of Foreign Commerce, *Labor in America, Asia, Africa, Australasia, and Polynesia*, 175.

72. Carbonell to Governor, Barranquilla, 16 September 1889, AGN, Gobernaciones (Bolívar), 1:321–26; "Sobres casas incendiadas," *Registro de Bolívar*, 6 July 1895; Millican, *Travels and Adventures of an Orchid Hunter*, 40; Prefect to Concejo, Barranquilla, 8 August 1889, ACMB, Decretos 1889.

73. Castro to Gobierno, Barranquilla, 14 May 1890, AGN, Gobierno, Primera Antigua, 16:715–39, quoted from 739; see a similar incident reported in *El Porvenir*, 10 January 1895.

74. Contrato, Asociación de los Prácticos del Río Magdalena y sus Afluentes, Barranquilla, 4 September 1891, AGN, Gobierno, Primera Antigua, 16:893–99.

75. "Decreto No. 1111," *Diario Oficial*, 7 December 1890; Inspector de Navegación Fluvial to Gobierno, 13 January 1892, AGN, Gobierno, Primera Antigua, 45:218; quoted from "Al comercio," Asociación de Prácticos, Barranquilla, 31 October 1891, AGN, Gobierno, Primera Antigua, 16:900 (emphasis in original).

76. "La cuestión social," *La Voz*, 21 March 1892.

77. Gómez Olaciregui, *Prensa y periodismo en Barranquilla*, 219.

78. Castro to Gobierno, Barranquilla, 14 May 1890, AGN, Gobierno, Primera Antigua, 16:715–39; quoted from "A 'El Correo Nacional' (Contestación)," Barranquilla, 14 November 1891, ibid., 16:900.

79. Palacio, *La historia de mi vida: Crónicas ineditas*, 39–40; Circular, Secretario de Gobierno, Cartagena, 1 May 1893; Carbonell to Governor, Barranquilla, 16 September 1889, AGN, Gobernaciones (Bolívar), 2:373, 1:321–26.

80. "Sociedades," *La Voz*, 27 October 1892.

81. Celador to Presidente Junta Administrativo Lazareto, Caño de Loro, 30 September 1890, AHC, Gobernación, Legajo 5, Carpeta Única; "Informe," *Gaceta Municipal* (Cartagena), 21 December 1894.

82. Circular, Secretario de Gobierno, Cartagena, 1 May 1893, AGN, Gobernaciones (Bolívar), 2:373; quoted from "Huelgas," *La Voz*, 29 April 1893.

83. *Gaceta Judicial*, May 1895, 306; Governor to Ruiz Barreto, Cartagena, 3 July 1893, AGN, Gobernaciones (Bolívar), 2:461.

84. Bergquist, *Coffee and Conflict in Colombia*, 45–48. For the effects of tariffs on the coast see Vergara y Velasco, *Nueva geografía de Colombia*, 1:dcxcvi; "Flour in Colombia," *American Mail and Export Journal*, November 1887.

85. "Memoriales," *Gaceta Municipal* (Cartagena), 4 July 1895; "Acuerdo No. 2," ibid., 2 August 1895; *Gaceta Judicial*, 19 February 1900.

86. Casas Orrego, "Expansión y modernidad en Cartagena de Indias," 51; Bustamante Roldán, *Efectos económicos del papel moneda durante la Regeneración*, 41, 46, 58, 126; Gibson, *The Constitutions of Colombia*, 345; Flórez and Llanos, *Barranquilla y Sabanilla durante el siglo XIX*, 83–84, 110; "Remitidos," *Registro de Bolívar*, 20 June 1895; Fernando Vélez, *Datos para la historia del derecho nacional*, 184, quoted from xvii; quoted from Dunton, *The World and Its People*, 309.

87. McConnico to Congress, 15 December 1891, AC, Leyes Autógrafas 1892, 8:251–52; *Gaceta Judicial*, May 1895, 306–9; "Compañía Colombiana de Transportes," *La*

Tribuna, 2 April 1891; Pachón and Ramírez, *Infraestructura de transporte en Colombia durante el siglo XX*, 13.

88. Goenaga, *Lecturas locales*, 256; Denuncia, Barranquilla, 12 February 1889, AGN, Gobernaciones (Bolívar), 1:77–82; quoted from Various merchants to Concejo, 28 October 1886, ACMB, Comisiones 1886.

89. Acuerdo No. 15, 9 August 1889, AHC, Alcaldía-Acuerdos, 1889; quoted from "Acuerdo No. 9," *Gaceta Municipal* (Cartagena), 10 June 1893.

90. Quoted from "Policía," *El Porvenir*, 12 April 1899. See also Bravo Páez, *Comportamientos ilícitos y mecanismos de control social en el Bolívar grande*, 55–56; cf. Solano, "Trabajo y ocio en el Caribe colombiano."

91. For arrest statistics, see the 1894 issues of *Gaceta Municipal* (Santa Marta); "Lista de multas e impuestos," *Registro de Bolívar*, 10 April 1893; quoted from Prefect to Concejo, 1 March 1889, ACMB, Varios 1889.

92. Informe de Comisión, 2 November 1888, ACMB, Correspondencia 1888; Inocencia Hernández, *Gaceta Municipal* (Cartagena), 25 January 1892; quoted from Acuerdo No. 3, 6 April 1891, AHC, Alcaldía-Acuerdos, Tomo 3 (1891).

93. Vincent, *Around and about in South America*, 433; Solano, *Puertos, sociedad y conflictos en el Caribe colombiano*, 7; quoted from Millican, *Travels and Adventures of an Orchid Hunter*, 50; quoted from United States Bureau of Foreign Commerce, *Labor in America, Asia, Africa, Australasia, and Polynesia* (1885), 176.

94. Matute, *Los padres candelarios en Colombia*, 1:45; quoted from Robert Crooke Wood letter, Cartagena, 3 September 1889, Trist Wood Papers, Southern Historical Collection, University of North Carolina at Chapel Hill.

95. *El Porvenir*, 24 January 1892; "Policia," *El Porvenir*, 1 May 1892.

96. Bravo Páez, *Comportamientos ilícitos y mecanismos de control social en el Bolívar grande*, 58; Colombia, *Código penal* (1899), 63; quoted from police report, *Gaceta Municipal* (Santa Marta), 20 June 1894.

97. For the hygienic policing of Caribbean ports, see Médico Inspector to Hacienda, Cartagena, 26 June 1894, AGN, Gobernaciones (Bolívar), 2:802, 807–14; Governor to Gobierno, Cartagena, 31 October 1895, ibid., 3:500–503; quoted from "Proyecto de Acuerdo," *Gaceta Municipal* (Cartagena), 20 September 1895.

98. Concejo to Inocencia Hernández, *Gaceta Municipal* (Cartagena), 25 January 1893; see also Bravo Páez, *Comportamientos ilícitos y mecanismos de control social en el Bolívar grande*, 52.

99. "Tipos diversos," *La Voz*, 22 August 1893.

100. Rivas, *Obras*, 568; Matute, *Los padres candelarios en Colombia*, 2:245; quoted from Paul et al. to Congress, 6 October 1886, AC, Leyes de noviembre de 1886, 2:279–80.

101. Camacho Roldán, *Notas de viaje*, 198, 199.

102. Quintero and Espinosa, *Jurisprudencia de la Corte Suprema de Justicia*, 63; Colombia, *Código penal*, 11–12, quoted from 12.

103. "Víveres," *El Porvenir*, 12 April 1899.

104. Decreto No. 82, Alcalde Barranquilla, 14 September 1892, ACMB, Correspondencia 1892, 166; Acuerdo No. 3, 6 April 1891, AHC, Alcaldía (Acuerdos), Tomo 3 (1891). For the ambiguous position of Parisian food brokers, see Kaplan, *Provisioning Paris*.

105. "Síndico del hospital," *Gaceta Municipal* (Cartagena), 17 May 1892; "Horrible cuadro," *El Porvenir*, 14 April 1899; see also Flórez and Llanos, *Barranquilla y Sabanilla durante el siglo XIX*, 46; quoted from "Lotería para los pobres," *El Porvenir*, 22 January 1899.

106. "Ley de domésticos," *La Voz*, 8 May 1893.

107. Informe de Comisión, 27 July 1888, ACMB, Varios 1888.

108. *Gaceta Municipal* (Cartagena), 28 September 1893. For the state of housing, see Casas Orrego, "Expansión y modernidad en Cartagena de Indias," 48–50.

109. "Tribunal Superior," *Registro de Bolívar*, 26 June 1893; "Tribunal Superior," ibid., 13 July 1893; "Suspensión de acuerdos municipales," ibid., 4 August 1896; "Se suspende parte de Acuerdo No. 5," ibid., 22 August 1896; Acuerdo No. 12 de Arjona, ibid., 24 March 1897; Informe de Comisión, 2 November 1888, ACMB, Correspondencia 1888; Entry No. 130, 13 September 1887, ACMB, Proposiciones 1887. See also Escobar Ramírez, "Impuestos y reglamentos para el Carnaval de Barranquilla," 129; Bravo Páez, *Comportamientos ilícitos y mecanismos de control social de control social en el Bolívar grande*, 42–43.

110. Decreto No. 15, Concejo Municipal de Barranquilla, *Registro de Bolívar*, 13 August 1888; quoted from *Gaceta Municipal* (Cartagena), 31 August 1892.

111. "Caridad," *El Porvenir*, 17 May 1899; quoted from "Agua," ibid.; see also "Por los pobres," ibid., 22 January 1899.

112. "Documentos que se relacionan con un denuncio de los vecinos de Soplaviento," *Registro de Bolívar*, 1 May 1893 (emphasis in original).

113. "La libertad de industria," *La Crónica*, 17 July 1898; quoted from Miguel Samper, *Escritos político-económicos*, 3:212; Bustamante Roldán, *Efectos económicos del papel moneda durante la Regeneración*, 142–43; Molina, *Las ideas liberales en Colombia*, 175–76.

114. "La crisis fiscal y económica," *El Repertorio Colombiano*, August 1899.

115. "Lo de la máchina," *El Porvenir*, 10 February 1899; "Huelga," *El Porvenir*, 26 May 1899. For data on prices, see Urrutia and Arrubla, *Compendio de estadísticas históricas de Colombia*, 94–96; Ospina Vásquez, *Industria y protección en Colombia*, 453–54.

116. Curate to Bishop, Chiriguaná, 30 October 1898, AHESM, 154:368–69.

117. See telegrams reprinted in *El Porvenir*, 5 May 1899; De la Vega to Bishop, Guamal, 4 November 1898, AHESM, 154, n.f.; Gerlein to Ministerio, Cartagena, 4 November 1898, AGN, Gobernaciones (Bolívar), 5:322–23; Buendía Díaz, *Síntesis histórica del Municipio de Arjona*, 46; quoted from N. Cañizares to Bishop, El Banco, [November 1898], AHESM, Tomo 154.

118. "Magangué," *La Crónica*, 19 July 1898; "Crónica menuda," *El Correo Nacional*, 24 November 1898; "Vapores," *El Correo Nacional*, 10 November 1898.

119. Massey, "The Late Revolution in Colombia," 306.

120. For the 1897 election, see telegrams, October-November 1897, AGN, Gobierno, Primera Antigua, 57:825, 827. For Uribe Uribe's speech, see "Magangué," *La Crónica*, 15 July 1898; quoted from Sabogal to Governor, Banco, 10 February 1895, AGN, FGMD, 1:470; quoted from Prefect to Gobierno, 8 May 1888, AGN, Gobierno, Primera Antigua, 71:349–50.

121. Bergquist, *Coffee and Conflict in Colombia*, 36. For class dimensions of millenarianism, see Taussig, *The Devil and Commodity Fetishism in South America*, 60–67.

122. Curate to Bishop, Chiriguaná, 30 October 1898, AHESM, 154:368–69.

123. Ibid.

124. Ibid.

125. De la Vega to Bishop, Guamal, 4 November 1898, AHESM, 154, n.f.

126. Noe Cañizares to Bishop, El Banco, [November 1898], AHESM, Tomo 154.

127. Prefect to Gobierno, Río de Oro, 8 November 1898, AGN, Gobierno, Primera Antigua, 46:471; Gerlein to Gobierno, 18 November 1898, AGN, ibid., 5:326.

128. Prefect to Gobierno, Río de Oro, 8 November 1898, AGN, Gobierno, Primera Antigua, 46:471; Cañizares to Bishop, El Banco, [November 1898], AHESM, Tomo 154; quoted from Palacio, *Historia de mi vida* (1980), 133; quoted from Gerlein to Gobierno, 18 November 1898, AGN, Gobierno, Primera Antigua, 5:326.

129. Governor to Gobierno, Cartagena, 28 April 1899, AGN, Gobernaciones (Bolívar), 5:413–14.

130. Alcalde to Gobierno, El Banco, June 30, 1899, AGN, Gobierno, Primera Antigua, 14:145–46; Alcalde to Gobierno, Guamal, 28 June 1899, ibid., 14:144, also 404–5; Núñez to Gobierno, Cartagena, 13 May 1899, 14:234; "Negra cosecha," *El Porvenir*, 25 June 1899; "Los enviadistas," *El Porvenir*, 2 July 1899 and 6 September 1899.

131. Noe Cañizares to Bishop, El Banco, [November 1898], AHESM, Tomo 154.

132. "Otro enviado," *El Porvenir*, 12 April 1899; "Lotería de los pobres," *El Porvenir*, 27 January 1899; quoted from Núñez to Gobierno, Cartagena, 21 August 1899, AGN, Gobierno, Primera Antigua, 14:362.

133. "Por el mundo," *El Porvenir*, 30 April 1899; quoted from Noe Cañizares to Bishop, El Banco, [November 1898], AHESM, Tomo 154.

134. Telegram, Pedro Leopoldo Méndez, reprinted in *El Porvenir*, 2 July 1899; quoted from Catholic Church, *Las Misiones católicas en Colombia*, 198.

135. Telegram, Méndez to Governor, Mompox, *El Porvenir*, 7 July 1899; quoted from "Del Carmen," ibid., 3 May 1899. For Canudos and Brazilian millenarianism, see Robert M. Levine, "'Mud-Hut Jerusalem'"; Diacon, *Millenarian Vision, Capitalist Reality*.

136. "En El Carmen," *El Porvenir*, 30 April 1899; Telegrams, *El Porvenir*, 5 May 1899.

137. "Crónica menuda," *El Correo Nacional*, 5 November 1898; "Los sucesos del día 3," *El Espectador*, 26 November 1898; "Enviadistas," *El Porvenir*, 30 July 1899.

Chapter 7

1. Inspector to Prefect, Pié de la Popa, 4 September 1901, AHC, Gobernación, Legajo 34.

2. "La situación de la República," *Diario Comercial*, 28 March 1900.

3. Sánchez and Aguilera Peña, *Memoria de un país en guerra*; Martínez Carreño, *La Guerra de los Mil Días*; Plazas Olarte, *La Guerra Civil de los Mil Días*. For works that analyze social dimensions of the war, see Jaramillo, *Los guerrilleros del novecientos*; and Bergquist, *Coffee and Conflict in Colombia*.

4. Carrero Becerra, *Guerra de los Mil Días*, 39. For the relationship of peripherality to violence, see Roldán, *Blood and Fire*, 35–40.

5. "Orden público," *El Porvenir*, 22 October 1899.

6. Uribe Uribe, *Documentos militares*, 21, 33, 62; quoted from Grillo, *Emociones de la guerra*, 200, 123.

7. Deas, *Del poder y la gramática*, 307; Plazas Olarte, *La Guerra Civil de los Mil Días*, 147–48; Taussig, *The Devil and Commodity Fetishism in South America*, 65, 75–77; Arocha and Friedemann, *De sol a sol*, 198.

8. Socarrás, *Recuerdos*, 22; quoted from Massey, "The Late Revolution in Colombia," 306.

9. Socarrás, *Recuerdos*, 40; Martínez Carreño, *La Guerra de los Mil Días*, 80–81; Bergquist, *Coffee and Conflict in Colombia*, 163–64.

10. "Correos," *El Porvenir*, 10 January 1900; quoted from Jefetura Civil y Militar to Ministerio, Barranquilla, 21 November 1899, AGN, Gobernaciones (Bolívar), 5:452–62.

11. Chávez to Governor, Magangué, 9 February 1895, AGN, FGMD, 1:494; C. Jiménez to Jefe Civil y Militar, Sabanalarga, n.d. [December 1899], AGN, FGMD, 16:57–60; Socarrás, *Recuerdos*, 40.

12. Orden General del Ejército del Atlántico, Barranquilla [hereafter cited as Orden General, Barranquilla], 16 August 1901, AGN, FGMD, 298:55; Socarrás, *Recuerdos*, 51; Aguilera, *Lácides Segovia, un carácter*, 36–38; Jaramillo, *Los guerrilleros del novecientos*, 106–7, 114.

13. "Encapotados," *El Porvenir*, 14 April 1899; Telegram, Lara to Governor, reprinted in *El Porvenir*, 13 October 1899.

14. Jefe Civil y Militar to Celedón, Barranquilla, 2 February 1902, AHESM, 158:27–28; Brioschi to Bishop, Cartagena, 2 May 1903, AHESM, 158:44; quoted from Governor to Brioschi, Barranquilla, 13 May 1902, AHESM, 158:24–26; Tirado Mejía, *Aspectos sociales de las guerras civiles en Colombia*, 58.

15. Barbosa to Celedón, [March?] 1901, AHESM, 159:45.

16. Socarrás, *Recuerdos*, 25; Uribe Uribe, *Documentos militares*, 206–7, 469–70. "El jefe por aclamación" is noted in Jaramillo, *Los guerrilleros del novecientos*, 55–59.

17. Palacio, *Historia de mi vida* (1980), 59; Alarcón, *Compendio de historia del departamento del Magdalena*, 319; "La rebelión," *El Porvenir*, 16 February 1900.

18. Uribe Uribe, *Documentos militares*, 469.

19. Prefect to General Jefe del Ejército, Sabanalarga, 1 September 1901, AGN, FGMD, 78:147; Tinoco to Magistrates, Cartagena, 8 July 1902, AGN, Gobierno, Cuarta, 23:153; quoted from Comandante Jefe Militar to Jefe Civil y Militar, Magangué, 24 January 1900, AHC, Legajo 29.

20. Estasita to Governor, Cartagena, [September?] 1901, AHC, Gobernación, Legajo 30; Tovar to Gobierno, 11 January 1903, AGN, Gobernaciones (Bolívar), 5:726–27; "Sección oficial," *Diario Comerical*, 3 April 1900; "La rebelión," *El Porvenir*, 16 February 1900.

21. "La Revolución," *El Porvenir*, 4 April 1895; Sabogal to Governor, Banco, 10 February 1895, AGN, FGMD, 1:470; Alarcón, *Compendio de historia del departamento del Magdalena*, 320; quoted from Massey, "The Late Revolution in Colombia," 295.

22. "La situación y las noticias falsas," *El Porvenir*, 15 December 1899; Socarrás, *Recuerdos*, 57; see also Joseph, "On the Trail of Latin American Bandits." For economic conditions, see Bergquist, *Coffee and Conflict in Colombia*, 158.

23. Socarrás, *Recuerdos*, 27–28; see also Tamayo, *Revolución de 1899*, 61; Posada-Carbó, *The Colombian Caribbean*, 21.

24. For debates over banditry, see Joseph, "On the Trail of Latin American Bandits," 16–18.

25. "Historia de siempre," *El Porvenir*, 17 February 1895; "La rebelión," *El Porvenir*, 29 October 1899; quoted from "Familias distinguidas," *El Porvenir*, 4 March 1900; see also Vos Obeso, *Mujer, cultura y sociedad*, 2.

26. Bergquist, *Coffee and Conflict in Colombia*, 151–54, 156.

27. Orden General, Barranquilla, 26 April 1902, AGN, FGMD, 212:175, quoted from 174; quoted from "Decreto numero 4," *Diario Comercial*, 17 February 1900. For Liberal guerrilleros as rapists, see "La rebelión," *El Porvenir*, 10 November 1899; "La mano negra," *El Porvenir*, 9 February 1900.

28. Colombia, *Jurisprudencia colombiana extractada y concordada*, 489; Colombia, *Código penal*, 33; Socarrás, *Recuerdos*, 35–36.

29. "La Revolución," *El Porvenir*, 3 February 1895; Colombia, *Informe del Ministerio de Guerra al Congreso*, 22.

30. Socarrás, *Recuerdos*, 34–35, 38–39, 53, 63; see also Tamayo, *Revolución de 1899*, 64; Massey, "The Late Revolution in Colombia," 295.

31. Colombia, *Anales diplomáticos y consulares de Colombia*, 1:419; "El armamento," *El Porvenir*, 26 April 1899; Plazas Olarte, *La Guerra Civil de los Mil Días*, 258; Pardo Rueda, *Historia de las guerras*, 344–46, 364–65. For continued use of the term *machetero*, see "La mano negra," *El Porvenir*, 9 February 1900; and "Sección oficial," *Diario Comercial*, 4 April 1900.

32. "La nueva conspiración," *El Porvenir*, 2 June 1895.

33. "La situación," *Diario Comercial*, 9 April 1900; "La situación de la República," *Diario Comercial*, 28 March 1900.

34. Orden General, Barranquilla, 22 September 1901, AGN, FGMD, 212:38.

35. "Historia de siempre," *El Porvenir*, 17 February 1895; "La rebelión," *El Porvenir*, 7 January 1900.

36. Gómez Olaciregui, *Prensa y periodismo en Barranquilla*, 187, 197–99, 204, 213–14, 218; Palacio, *Historia de mi vida* (1980), 46–47; Delpar, *Red against Blue*, 172; Arango Loboguerrero, "Catarino Garza, un mexicano en la guerra civil colombiana," 267; Bergquist, *Coffee and Conflict in Colombia*, 151.

37. Goenaga, *Lecturas locales*, 335–36; Palacio, *Historia de mi vida* (1980), 63; Román to Governor, Cartagena, 3 February 1895, AGN, FGMD, 1:12.

38. Socarrás, *Recuerdos*, 26.

39. For the "Internacional liberal," see Jaramillo, *Los guerrilleros del novecientos*, 280; cited in Arango Loboguerrero, "Catarino Garza, un mexicano en la guerra civil colombiana," 267–68, 275. For the Black Atlantic significance of these same transnational networks, see Rebecca Scott, *Degrees of Freedom*.

40. Socarrás, *Recuerdos*, 58, 76, 78, quoted from 45, 39.

41. Uribe Uribe, *Documentos militares*, 151–52.

42. Cf. Jaramillo, "Antecedentes generales de la Guerra de los Mil Días," 106.

43. Socarrás, *Recuerdos*, 30–31, quoted from 32.

44. Decreto 224, Ministerio de Gobierno y Guerra, Cartagena, 20 May 1901, AGN, Gobierno, Cuarta, 21:86; Colombia, *Jurisprudencia colombiana extractada y concordada*, 373, 489.

45. Orden General, Barranquilla, 18 November 1899, AGN, FGMD, 341: 9.

46. "Decreto No. 259," *Registro de Bolívar*, 29 June 1895; Boletín Oficial No. 14, Barranquilla, 26 December 1899, AGN, Gobernaciones (Bolívar), 5:520.

47. Governor to Ministerio, 22 June 1895; and Governor to Brun, Cartagena, 1 November 1895, AGN, Gobernaciones (Bolívar), 3:214–15, 514; Decreto No. 1, Barranquilla, 19 February 1895, AGN, Gobierno, Primera Antigua, 57:194; Declaraciones, Alcalde de Santa Rosa, 4 March 1895, AHC, Gobernación, Legajo 16; quoted from Massey, "The Late Revolution in Colombia," 292.

48. "Report on the Condition and Trade in the Republic of Colombia," *Diplomatic and Consular Reports*, March 1902, 3; Laborda to Ministerio, [Santa Marta], 27 February 1902, AGN, Gobierno, Cuarta, 24:348; Colombia, *Decretos legislativos expedidos durante la guerra*, 192.

49. Colombia, *Memoria que el Ministro del Tesoro presenta al Congreso* (1904), 110–11; Colombia, *Decretos legislativos expedidos durante la guerra*, 467; "Barranquilla," *El Porvenir*, 15 December 1898; Díaz Lemos, *Compendio de geografía*, 100.

50. Carrero Becerra, *Guerra de los Mil Días*, 40; Hernández Gamarra, *A Monetary History of Colombia*, 84; Colombia, *Decretos legislativos expedidos durante la guerra*, 104, 122, 136–37.

51. Colombia, *Decretos legislativos expedidos durante la guerra*, 213.

52. Orden General, Barranquilla, 21 October 1901, AGN, FGMD, 212:57.

53. Máximo A. Nieto, *Recuerdos de la Regeneración*, 162; "Venezuela and Colombia," *The Independent*, 26 October 1901; quoted from Orden General, Barranquilla, 6 August 1901, AGN, FGMD, 212:11.

54. Colombia, *Informe del Ministerio de Guerra al Congreso*, 14.

55. Ramírez to Ortiz, Calamar, 16 September 1901, AGN, FGMD, 80:48–49; quoted from ibid., Arenal, 9 September 1901, 78:287; Socarrás, *Recuerdos*, 69, 74; Grillo, *Emociones de la guerra*, 274.

56. Orden General, Comandancia General, Flotilla de Guerra, Río Magdalena, 5 February 1895, AGN, FGMD, 300:39.

57. Dávila to General Jefe del Ejército, Cartagena, 7 September 1901, AGN, FGMD, 79:51–52.

58. Ripoll, "El Ingenio Central Colombiano," 13; quoted from Jefe Civil y Militar to Governor, Suan, 5 September 1901, AHC, Gobernación, Legajo 5, Capeta Única; quoted from Prefect to Ministerio, Cartagena, 22 July 1901, AHC, Gobernación, Legajo 30.

59. "Correos," *El Porvenir*, 10 January 1900.

60. Orden General, Barranquilla, 15 February 1900, AGN, FGMD, 341:43; quoted from Palacio to Guerra, Barranquilla, 28 January 1899, AGN, FGMD, 9:366.

61. Comandante en Jefe, Barranquilla, Calamar, 7 September 1901, AGN, FGMD, 79:47; quoted from Orden General, Barranquilla, 15 November 1899, ibid., 341:7;

quoted from Orden General, Barranquilla, 1 December 1901, ibid., 212:87. For commonalities in soldier behavior across countries, see Neiberg, *The Nineteenth Century*, 64.

62. Vélez to Amaya, Cartagena, 6 September 1901, AGN, FGMD, 78:953–54.

63. Goenega to Ministerio, Barranquilla, November 1899, AGN, Gobernaciones (Bolívar), 5:464, 452–62; Martínez Carreño, *La Guerra de los Mil Días*, 134.

64. "Frutos de la guerra," *El Porvenir*, 10 January 1900.

65. "División 'Cartagena,'" *El Porvenir*, 16 February 1900.

66. Castro to Palacio and Goenaga, Magangué, 17 February 1900, AGN, FGMD, 30:123–25; Diario Histórico de las Operaciones de Ejército de Bolívar, Barranquilla, 19 February 1895, ibid., 388:2; see also *Diario Comercial*, 2 December 1899.

67. Colombia, *Decretos legislativos expedidos durante la guerra*, 295–96.

68. "Libres de Cartagena," *El Porvenir*, 21 February 1895; "Sección oficial," *Diario Comercial*, 26 March 1900; Becerra Jiménez, *Historia de la diócesis de Barranquilla*, 117, 121; Goenaga, *Lecturas locales*, 246–47; Bergquist, *Coffee and Conflict in Colombia*, 131.

69. Dávila to Amaya, Cartagena, 5 September 1901, AGN, FGMD, 78:741; Jefe Civil y Militar to Gobierno, Zambrano, 2 March 1901, AHC, Gobernación, Legajo 30; "La Revolución," *El Porvenir*, 31 January 1895; quoted from "Libres de Cartagena," *El Porvenir*, 21 February 1895.

70. "Notas políticas," *Diario Comercial*, 13 August 1900; "Combate en Piojo," *El Porvenir*, 7 February 1900.

71. Solano, "Trabajo y ocio en el Caribe colombiano," 71; Torres Giraldo, *Los inconformes*, 3:67; Sowell, *The Early Colombian Labor Movement*, 126; quoted from "Miscelánea," *Diario Comerical*, 10 March 1900.

72. Socarrás, *Recuerdos*, 54, 57; "Sociedad Mutuo Auxilio," *Diario Comercial*, 15 March 1900.

73. Colombia, *Informe del Ministerio de Guerra al Congreso*, 45; Comandante to Jefe Civil y Militar, Magangué, AHC, 24 January 1900, AHC, Gobernación, Legajo 29.

74. Inspector Militar to Jefe Civil y Militar, [Magangué?], n.d. [1900], AHC, Legajo 29.

75. Tinoco to Magistrates, Cartagena, 8 July 1902, AGN, Gobierno, Cuarta, 23:152–53; Tribunal Superior to Vice President, Cartagena, 10 October 1902, AGN, Archivo de la Presidencia, Caja 4, Carpeta 2 (Departamentos), 3–12; Bolívar, *Leyes expedidas por la Asamblea Lejislativa del Estado* (1903), 311, 504.

76. "Lotería de los pobres," *El Porvenir*, 10 January 1900.

77. Serret, *Viaje a Colombia*, 204; Posada-Carbó, *The Colombian Caribbean*, 112; Castro Carvajal, "Aspectos de la vida diaria en las ciudades republicanas," 8.

78. Conde Calderón, "Carnaval, sociedad y cultura," 84; quoted from "Nueva conspiración," *El Porvenir*, 2 June 1895.

79. "Descargadores," *El Porvenir*, 15 September 1899.

80. Governor to Gobierno, 18 December 1899, AGN, Gobernaciones (Bolívar), 5:484–86; see also Palacio, *Historia de mi vida* (1980), 73, 81, 149–51.

81. Gerlein to Gobierno, Guerra, [Cartagena?], 29 July 1898, AGN, Gobernaciones (Bolívar), 5:307–8; Aguilera, *Lácides Segovia, un carácter*, 34.

82. Comandante "Cauca" to Comandante General, Calamar, 15 September 1901, AGN, FGMD, 79:1282–84; "Guerra de salvajes," *El Porvenir*, 3 December 1899.

83. Orden General, Barranquilla, 26 December 1899, AGN, FGMD, 341:23; del Busto to Ortiz, Calamar, 13 September 1901, AGN, FGMD, 79:1071; quoted from Palacio, *Historia de mi vida* (1980), 155–56.

84. Palacio to Jefe del Ejército, Calamar, 16 September 1901, AGN, FGMD, 80:60–61.

85. Del Busto to Ortiz and Vélez, Calamar, 18 September 1901, AGN, FGMD, 80:444; quoted from Palacio to General Jefe del Ejército, Calamar, 11 September 1901, AGN, FGMD, 79:731–32; quoted from Ramírez to Comandante General, Calamar, 24 September 1901, AGN, FGMD, 81:273.

86. Colombia, *Decretos legislativos expedidos durante la guerra*, 136–37; quoted from Barros to General Ortiz, Calamar, 19 September 1901, AGN, FGMD, 80:613.

87. Colombia, *Leyes colombianas* (1892–96), 377–80; Informe de Comisión, 26 December 1896; Palacio and Ayala to Camara, 23 October 1896, AC, Leyes Autógrafas, 15:7, 22–23.

88. Governor to Gobierno, 18 December 1899, AGN, Gobernaciones (Bolívar), 5:484–87.

89. Governor to Gobierno, 30 May 1895, Cartagena, AGN, Gobernaciones (Bolívar), 3:138–39; quoted from Governor to Cisneros, Cartagena, 26 May 1895, ibid., 123–24; quoted from Palacio, note in *El Porvenir*, 14 March 1895. See also Massey, "The Late Revolution in Colombia," 301.

90. See documents in AGN, Gobernaciones (Bolívar), 3:115–22, quoted from 122.

91. "Servicio militar obligatorio," *El Porvenir*, 19 February 1899; "Miscelánea," *Diario Comercial*, 3 April 1900; quoted from "Nuevos horizontes," *El Porvenir*, 31 December 1899; "Observación familiar," *Diario Comercial*, 9 February 1900.

92. "Página para el pueblo," *Diario Comercial*, 7 February 1900.

93. "Un buen empleado," *El Porvenir*, 20 October 1899.

94. "Grave situación," *El Porvenir*, 27 October 1899; Palacio, *Historia de mi vida* (1980), 65.

95. "Miscelánea," *Diario Comercial*, 20 April 1900; quoted from "Policía," *Diario Comercial*, 19 April 1900.

96. "Decreto 124 de 1899," *El Porvenir*, 12 January 1900; "Sección oficial," *Diario Comercial*, 27 April 1900.

97. Boletin Oficial No. 14, Barranquilla, 26 December 1899, AGN, Gobernaciones (Bolívar), 5:520.

98. "Miscelánea," *Diario Comercial*, 15 August 1900.

99. "La conspiración," *El Porvenir*, 31 March 1895; "La conspiración de Barranquilla," *El Porvenir*, 9 June 1895; Socarrás, *Recuerdos*, 44, 46, 68–69, 86; Jaramillo, *Los guerrilleros del novecientos*, 62–64; Bravo Páez, *Comportamientos ilícitos y mecanismos de control social en el Bolívar grande*, 81–82; quoted from "Las noticias falsas," *El Porvenir*, 17 March 1895.

100. Delpar, *Red against Blue*, 143.

101. Uribe Uribe, *Documentos militares*, 143, 200, 287, quoted from 226.

102. Orden General, Barranquilla, 26 December 1899, AGN, FGMD, 341:22; Palacio, *Historia de mi vida* (1980), 65; Jaramillo, *Los guerrilleros del novecientos*, 64–67; quoted from Socarrás, *Recuerdos*, 68.

103. Colombia, *Código militar* (1883), 1:135, 198, quoted from 132, 281.

104. "Respuesta," *El Porvenir*, 6 October 1898; quoted from "Infelices mujeres," *El Porvenir*, 29 September 1898. For women in the war, see Palacio, *Historia de mi vida* (1980), 65; and Jaramillo, *Los guerrilleros del novecientos*, 60–79.

105. Socarrás, *Recuerdos*, 83; cf. Bergquist, *Coffee and Conflict in Colombia*, 186–87; quoted from Dawson, *The South American Republics*, 485.

106. Uribe Uribe, *Documentos militares*, 398.

107. Colombia, *Decretos legislativos expedidos durante la guerra*, 314–15; Carrero Becerra, *Guerra de los Mil Días*, 53–55.

108. Pérez Escobar, *El negro Robles*, xxiii–xxiv; quoted from Socarrás, *Recuerdos*, 86.

109. Recolector de Armas to Ministerio, Cartagena, 4 December 1904, AGN, Gobernaciones (Bolívar), 5:797–800; Bravo Páez, *Comportamientos ilícitos y mecanismos de control social de control social en el Bolívar grande*, 82–83; Memoriales de Varios Vecinos, Cartagena, [May] 1904, AGN, Gobierno, Cuarta (Varios), 29:146, 182–86, quoted from 184.

110. "Sobre tráfico fluvial," *El Estandarte*, 11 December 1904.

111. Correa Uribe, *Republicanismo y reforma constitucional*, 120–22; Bergquist, *Coffee and Conflict in Colombia*, 219–23.

112. The official record of the trip is Pedraza, *República de Colombia*, quoted from 9, 35; see also Posada-Carbó, *The Colombian Caribbean*, 51; Bergquist, *Coffee and Conflict in Colombia*, 238–39.

113. For other novels about the war, see Escobar Mesa et al., *Narrativa de las guerras civiles colombianas*.

114. Marroquín and Rivas Groot, *Pax*, 377, 336, 464, quoted from 472; see also Pineda Botero, *La fábula y el desastre*, 424.

Epilogue

1. Archila, *Cultura e identidad obrera*, 222; Torres Giraldo, *Los inconformes*, 3:69–74; Poveda Ramos, *Vapores fluviales en Colombia*, 206.

2. Correa Uribe, *Republicanismo y reforma constitucional*, 142, 144; Gibson, *The Constitutions of Colombia*, 356; Bergquist, *Coffee and Conflict in Colombia*, 251–52; Posada-Carbó, "Limits of Power," 260.

3. Holt, *The Problem of Freedom*, 396–97. For the 1910 reforms, see Correa Uribe, *Republicanismo y reforma constitucional*, 142, 144; Bergquist, *Coffee and Conflict in Colombia*, 251–52. For links between labor militancy and national politics, see LeGrand, "El conflicto de las bananeras."

4. Briceño Jáuregui, *Los jesuitas en el Magdalena*, 50; and Catholic Church, *Las misiones católicas en Colombia*, 193, 194.

5. Pérez Gómez, *Apuntes históricos de las misiones agustinianas*, 315; Colombia, *Las misiones católicas en Colombia*, 7–14.

6. Pérez Gómez, *Apuntes históricos de las misiones agustinianas*, 311–17; Catholic Church, *Las misiones católicas en Colombia*, 196, 198–200; Colombia, *Las misiones católicas en Colombia*, 11; Colombia, *Informes de las misiones católicas de Colombia*, 9.

7. Uribe, *El fomento de las misiones y la colonización*, v.

8. Sowell, *The Early Colombian Labor Movement*, 135; Urrutia, *The Development of the Colombian Labor Movement*, 54; Bergquist, *Labor in Latin America*, 275–77, 280, 298; quoted from Uribe, *El fomento de las misiones y la colonización*, vii and 36.

9. "Puerto Colombia," *Revista Moderna*, March 1915.

10. "Meliorismo," *Cultura*, October 1915.

11. "Por telégrafo," *El Tiempo*, 21 January 1918.

12. Jiménez López, *Nuestras razas decaen*; see also Helg, "Los intelectuales frente a la cuestión racial"; McGraw, "Purificar la nación."

13. Jiménez López, *Los problemas de la raza en Colombia*, 129–30.

14. Naranjo, *Páginas sueltas*, 149, 150, 151, 152.

15. See, for instance, Vega Cantor, *Gente muy rebelde*; and Greene, "Vibrations of the Collective." For the gendered status of labor, see Farnsworth-Alvear, *Dulcinea in the Factory*, esp. 73ff.

16. Stanley, *From Bondage to Contract*; Ferrer, *Insurgent Cuba*; DuBois, *A Colony of Citizens*; Holt, *The Problem of Freedom*.

17. Cooper, Holt, and Scott, *Beyond Slavery*.

18. Rebecca Scott, *Degrees of Freedom*, 258.

19. Taussig, *The Devil and Commodity Fetishism in South America*; Sanders, "Contentious Republicans"; Leal, "Landscapes of Freedom."

20. Childs, *The 1812 Aponte Rebellion*; Rebecca Scott, *Degrees of Freedom*; Schmidt-Nowara, *Slavery, Freedom, and Abolition in Latin America*; DuBois, *A Colony of Citizens*.

21. Holt, *The Problem of Freedom*, xx. For nineteenth-century Atlantic Creoles, see Rebecca Scott, "Public Rights and Private Commerce."

22. Hoffman and Centeno, "The Lopsided Continent," 366; Vargas, "State, *Esprit Mafioso*, and Armed Conflict in Colombia," 112–13.

23. LeGrand, *Frontier Colonization and Peasant Protest in Colombia*, 167; see also de la Fuente, *A Nation for All*.

24. Holt, "Marking"; Appelbaum, Macpherson, and Rosemblatt, "Introduction: Racial Nations."

25. Wade, *Blackness and Race Mixture*; quoted from Morales Benítez, *Testimonio de un pueblo*, 46, 182; and Morales Benítez, *Muchedumbres y banderas*, 38.

26. Wade, *Race and Ethnicity in Latin America*, 25–39; quoted from Wade, *Blackness and Race Mixture*, 36.

27. Cunin, *Identidades a flor de piel*, 187–91, 319–20; Fals Borda, *Historia doble de la costa*, quoted from 1:150B; see also Wade, *Blackness and Race Mixture*, 82–92.

28. Colombia, *Constitución de Colombia*, 1991, quoted from Artículo Transitorio 55 and Artículo 7, respectively; see also Wade, "The Cultural Politics of Blackness in Colombia," 347–49.

29. Fraser, "Rethinking Recognition," 107.

30. Zapata Olivella, *Chambacú*, 57; DANE, *Colombia, una nación multicultural*, 33; "Afro-Colombians," http://www.minorityrights.org/5373/colombia/afrocolombians.html, accessed 19 January 2013.

31. Osterling, *Democracy in Colombia*, 201–36; Otis, "Targeting Teachers."

32. Arocha, "Inclusion of Afro-Colombians"; Bocarejo, "Deceptive Utopias."

Bibliography

Primary Sources

Archives

COLOMBIA
Archivo del Arzobispado de Cartagena
Archivo del Concejo Municipal de Barranquilla
Archivo del Congreso, Bogotá
Archivo General de la Nación, Bogotá, Sección República
    Fondo Asambleas Legislativas y Gobernaciones
    Fondo Baldíos
    Fondo Correspondencia
    Fondo Enrique Ortega Ricaurte, Serie Negros y Esclavos
    Fondo Gobernaciones
    Fondo Gobernaciones Varias
    Fondo Gobierno
    Fondo Guerra de los Mil Días
    Fondo Guerra y Marina
    Fondo Interior y Relaciones Exteriores
    Fondo Juzgados y Tribunales
    Fondo Manumisión
    Fondo Obras Publicas
    Fondo Relaciones Exteriores
Archivo Histórico de Cartagena
    Alcaldía
    Documentos Relacionados con la Guerra de los Mil Días
    Gobernación
Archivo Histórico del Magdalena Grande, Santa Marta
Archivo Histórico Eclesiástico de Santa Marta
Biblioteca Luis Ángel Arango, Bogotá
    Sala de Libros Raros y Manuscritos
Biblioteca Nacional, Bogotá
    Fondo Antiguo

UNITED STATES
Duke University Rare Book, Manuscript, and Special Collections Library, Durham,
    N.C.
    Leslie O. Arbouin Diary
    John Bull Smith Dimitry Papers

National Archives and Records Administration, Washington, D.C., Navy Records,
    RG 45
    Subject File, 1775–1910
Southern Historical Collection, University of North Carolina, Chapel Hill
    Samuel Henry Lockett Papers
    Trist Wood Papers

Government Documents

Angarita, Manuel J. *Códigos de organización y judicial de la nación.* Bogotá: n.p., 1891.
Antioquia. *Código judicial del Estado Soberano de Antioquia.* Medellín: n.p., 1866.
Arboleda C., Henrique. *Código de aduanas de la República de Colombia: Recopilación.* Bogotá: Vapor, 1899.
Archivo General de la Nación. *La esclavitud en Colombia.* Bogotá: Archivo General de la Nación, 2002.
Banco de la República. *Biografía de los Constituyentes, 1886.* Vol. 4. Bogotá: Banco de la República, 1986.
Bolívar. *Código civil del Estado Soberano de Bolívar.* Cartagena: Ruiz e Hijo, 1862.
———. *Leyes expedidas por la Asamblea Lejislativa del Estado s. de Bolívar.* Cartagena: Prins & Hernández, 1895.
———. *Procedimiento civil del Estado Soberano de Bolívar.* Cartagena: Antonio Araújo L., 1882.
Cauca. *Código de enjuiciamiento civil.* Popayán: Imprenta del Estado, 1884.
Colombia. *Actos oficiales del gobierno provisorio de los Estados Unidos de Colombia.* Bogotá: Echeverría Hermanos, 1862.
———. *Anales diplomáticos y consulares de Colombia.* 2 vols. Bogotá: Imprenta Nacional, 1901.
———. *Causa contra el presidente de los Estados Unidos de Colombia.* Vol. 1. Bogotá: Imprenta de la Nación, 1867.
———. *Causa de responsabilidad contra el ciudadano presidente de la república.* Vol. 1. Bogotá: Neo-Granadino, 1855.
———. *Codificación nacional de todas las leyes de Colombia desde el año de 1821.* Vol. 14– Bogotá: Imprenta Nacional, 1928–.
———. *Código civil nacional.* Bogotá: Gaitán, 1873.
———. *Código fiscal de la República de Colombia.* Bogotá: Imprenta Nacional, 1905.
———.*Código militar de los Estados Unidos de Colombia.* Bogotá: T. Uribe Zapata, 1883.
———. *Código penal colombiano con anotaciones y leyes reformatorias.* Medellín: Imprenta Departamento, 1899.
———. *Compilación de las disposiciones ejecutivas vigentes.* Bogotá: Medardo Rivas, 1881.
———. *Constitución i leyes de los Estados Unidos de Colombia, espedidas en los años de 1863 a 1875.* 2 vols. Bogotá: Medardo Rivas, 1875.
———. *Constitución de Colombia.* 1991.
———. *Decretos legislativos expedidos durante la guerra 1899 a 1902.* Bogotá: Vapor, 1902.

———. *Esposición sobre la hacienda nacional de la Confederación Granadina.* Bogotá: Imprenta de la Nación, 1860.

———. *Historia electoral colombiana.* Bogotá: Imprenta Nacional, 1991.

———. *Informes de las misiones católicas de Colombia relativos a los años de 1925 y 1926.* Bogotá, Imprenta Nacional, 1926.

———. *Informe del Director General de Instrucción Primaria de la Unión.* Bogotá: Medardo Rivas, 1876.

———. *Informe del Ministerio de Guerra al Congreso.* Vol. 2. Bogotá: Imprenta Nacional, 1896.

———. *Informe que el Ministro de Instrucción Pública presenta al Congreso de Colombia.* Bogotá: La Luz, 1894.

———. *Informe que el Ministro de Instrucción Pública presenta al Congreso de Colombia.* Bogotá: Imprenta Nacional, 1896.

———. *Informe que el Ministro de Instrucción Pública presenta al Congreso de Colombia.* Bogotá: Zalamea Hermanos, 1898.

———. *Jurisprudencia colombiana extractada y concordada por el relator de la Corte Suprema.* Vol. 1. Bogotá: Imprenta Nacional, 1903.

———. *Leyes i decretos.* Bogotá: Neo-Granadino, 1851, 1853, 1856.

———. *Leyes.* Bogotá: H. Andrade, 1877.

———. *Leyes.* Bogotá: Gerardo A. Nuñez, 1879, 1880.

———. *Memoria del Ministro de Instrucción Pública al Congreso.* Bogotá: Medardo Rivas, 1881.

———. *Memoria del Secretario de Guerra i Marina.* Bogotá: El Progreso, 1878.

———. *Memoria del Secretario de Hacienda i Fomento de Colombia.* Bogotá: Imprenta Nacional, 1867.

———. *Memoria del Secretario de Hacienda i Fomento.* Bogotá: Imprenta Gaitán, 1871.

———. *Memoria del Secretario del Tesoro.* Bogotá: Echeverría Hermanos, 1875.

———. *Memoria del Secretario del Tesoro.* Bogotá: Medardo Rivas, 1876, 1877.

———. *Memoria del Secretario del Tesoro i Crédito Nacional.* Bogotá: Echeverría Hermanos, 1878.

———. *Memoria que el Ministro del Tesoro presenta al Congreso.* Bogotá: Imprenta Nacional, 1904.

———. *Las misiones católicas en Colombia: Informes años de 1922 y 1923.* Bogotá: Imprenta Nacional, 1922.

———. *Noticias de la guerra.* Bogotá: La Luz, 1885.

———. *Ordenanzas para el réjimen, disciplina, subordinación i servicio de la Guardia Colombiana.* Bogotá: M. Rívas, 1876.

———. *Recopilación de las leyes y disposiciones vigentes sobre tierras baldías.* Bogotá: Medardo Rivas, 1884.

———. *Recopilación de leyes de la Nueva Granada.* Bogotá: Imprenta Nacional, 1845.

———. *Resoluciones del Senado de la Unión, fictadas en los años de 1875 a 1878.* 2 vols. Bogotá: Agustin Núñez, 1878.

Departamento Administrativo Nacional de Estadística (DANE). *Colombia, una nación multicultural: Su diversidad étnica.* Bogotá: DANE, 2007.

Department of State. *Special Consular Reports*. Washington, D.C.: Government Printing Office, 1891.

García y García, José Antonio. *Código de instrucción pública, presentado en proyecto a la Honorable Cámara*. Bogotá: Imprenta de la Nación, 1862.

Magdalena. *Código penal del Estado Soberano del Magdalena*. Santa Marta: Ferrocarril del Magdalena, 1874.

———. *Leyes adicionales i reformatorias del código judicial*. Santa Marta: Imprenta del Magdalena, 1878.

———. *Mensaje que el presidente del Estado S. de Magdalena dirije a la asemblea lejislativa*. Santa Marta: Tipografía Mercantil, 1872.

Pedraza, Pedro A. *República de Colombia: Excursiones presidenciales, apuntes de un diario de viaje*. Norwood, Mass.: Plimpton, 1909.

United States. *Foreign Relations of the United States*. Vol. 3. Washington, D.C.: Government Printing Office, 1867.

———. *Report upon the Commercial Relations of the United States with Foreign Countries*. Washington, D.C.: Government Printing Office, 1876.

United States Bureau of Foreign Commerce. *Labor in America, Asia, Africa, Australasia, and Polynesia*. Washington, D.C.: Government Printing Office, 1885.

Published Works

Academia Colombiana de Historia. *Antecedentes de la Constitución de Colombia de 1886*. Bogotá: Plaza & Janés, 1983.

Acosta de Samper, Soledad. *Biografía del general Joaquín Acosta*. Bogotá: Librería Colombiana, 1901.

———. *Una holandesa en América*. Curazao: A. Bethencourt, 1888.

———. *Novelas y cuadros de la vida sur-americana*. Gante: Eug. Vanderhaegan, 1869.

———. *Los piratas de Cartagena*. Bogotá: Silvestre, 1884.

Acosta H., Julio. *Manual del navegante*. Barranquilla: Empresa Litográfica, 1945.

Aguilar, Federico Cornelio. *Colombia en presencia de las repúblicas hispano-americanas*. Bogotá: Ignacio Borda, 1884.

———. *Ultimo año de residencia en México*. Bogotá: Ignacio Borda, 1885.

Alarcón, José C. *Compendio de historia del departamento del Magdalena*. Bogotá: Voto Nacional, 1963 [1900].

Ancízar, Manuel. *Peregrinación de Alpha*. Bogotá: Biblioteca Popular de Cultura Colombiana, 1942 [1853].

Añez, Julio. *Parnaso colombiano*. Vol. 2. Bogotá: Medardo Rivas, 1887.

Araújo, D. H. *Tratado de geografía física i política del Estado de Bolívar*. Cartagena: Ruiz e Hijo, 1871.

Arboleda, Sergio. *La constitución política*. Bogotá: Biblioteca de Autores Colombianos, 1952.

Arosemena, Justo. *Estudios constitucionales sobre los gobiernos de la América Latina*. 2nd ed. Vol. 2. Paris: Española i Americana, 1878.

Balmaseda, Francisco Javier. *Obras*. Cartagena: Ruiz e hijo, 1874.

Baraya, José María. *Recuerdos de un viaje: campaña de Santa Marta*. Bogotá: Estado de Cundinamarca, 1861.

Battersby, Jenyns C. "New Granada." *Hunt's Merchants' Magazine* 37, nos. 3, 5 (1857): 289–94, 563–73.

Bennett, J. A. "My First Trip up the Magdalena." *Journal of the American Geographical Society of New York* 9 (1877): 126–41.

Bernadino, Obispo de Cartajena. *El Reverendo Obispo de Cartajena, en Corozal, Sincelejo i Morroa, en su santa visita pastoral*. Cartagena: E. Hernández, 1858.

Borda, Francisco de Paula. *Conversaciones con mis hijos*. Vol. 1. Bogotá: Biblioteca Banco Popular, 1974.

Borda, José Joaquín. *Cuadros de costumbres y descripciones locales de Colombia*. Bogotá: Garcia Rico, 1878.

Borda, José Joaquín, and José María Vergara y Vergara, eds. *La lira granadina: colección de poesías nacionales*. Bogotá: El Mosaico, 1860.

Briceño, Manuel. *La Revolución, 1876–1877*. Bogotá: Imprenta Nueva, 1878.

Brioschi, Pedro A. *Vida de San Pedro Claver: heroico apóstol de los negros*. Paris: Garnier Hermanos, 1889.

Camacho Roldán, Salvador. *Escritos varios*. Vol. 1. Bogotá: Librería Colombiana, 1892.

———. *Notas de viaje*. Vol. 1. Bogotá: Banco de la República, 1973 [1890].

Camargo Pérez, Gabriel. *Sergio Camargo: el Bayardo Colombiano*. Tunja: Academia Boyacense de Historia, 1987 [1923].

Cané, Miguel. *Notas de viaje sobre Venezuela y Colombia*. Bogotá: La Luz, 1907.

Capella Toledo, Luis. *Leyendas históricas*. Vol. 1. 3rd ed. Bogotá: La Luz, 1884.

Carnegie-Williams, Rosa. *A Year in the Andes*. London: London Literary Society, 1882.

Caro, José Eusebio. *Obras escogidas, en prosa y en verso, publicadas é inéditas*. Bogotá: El Tradicionista, 1873.

———. *Poesías de d. José Eusebio Caro*. Madrid: M. Tello, 1885.

Caro, Miguel Antonio. *Apuntes sobre crédito, deuda pública y papel moneda*. Bogotá: La Luz, 1892.

Caro, Miguel Antonio, ed. *Poesías de Julio Arboleda*. Bogotá: Americana y Española, 1883.

Carrasquilla, Francisco de P. *Tipos de Bogotá*. Bogotá: F. Pontón, 1886.

Catholic Church. *Las misiones católicas en Colombia: labor de los misioneros en el Caquetá y Putumayo, Magdalena y Arauca: informes, 1918–1919*. Bogotá: Imprenta Nacional, 1919.

Cochrane, Charles Stuart. *Journal of a Residence and Travels in Colombia, during the Years 1823 and 1824*. New York: AMS Press, 1971 [1825].

Codazzi, Agustín. *Resumen del diario histórico del ejército del Atlantico, istmo i Mompós*. Bogotá: Echeverría, 1854.

Corona funebre que la agradecida y heroica ciudad de Cartagena consagra a la memoria del general Manuel Briceño. Cartagena: Antonio Araújo, 1885.

Corrales, Manuel Ezequiel. *Efemérides y anales del Estado de Bolívar*. 4 vols. Bogotá: Medardo Rivas, 1892.

———. *Homenaje de Colombia al libertador Simón Bolívar en su primer centenario*. Bogotá: Medardo Rivas, 1884.

Cortés, Enrique. *Escritos varios*. Vol. 1. Paris: Sudamericana, 1896.

Cuervo, Ángel. *Cómo se evapora un ejército*. Paris: de Durand, 1900.

———. *Curiosidades de la vida americana en París*. Paris: n.p., 1893.

Dawson, Thomas Cleland. *The South American Republics*. Vol. 2. New York: G. P. Putnam Sons, 1910.

Dessalines d'Orbigny, Alcide. *Viaje pintoresco a las dos Américas, Asia y África*. Vol. 1. Barcelona: Juan Oliveres, 1842.

Díaz Castro, Eugenio. *Manuela: novela de costumbres colombianas*. 2 vols. Paris: Española, 1889.

Díaz Lemos, Angel María. *Compendio de geografía de la República de Colombia*. Medellín: del Departamento, 1887.

Duane, William. *A Visit to Colombia, in the Years 1823 and 1824*. Philadelphia: T. H. Palmer, 1826.

Dunton, Larkin. *The World and Its People*. Boston: Silver, Burdett, 1896.

d'Espagnat, Pierre. *Recuerdos de la Nueva Granada*. Bogotá: Biblioteca Popular de Cultura Colombiana, 1942 [1900].

Esguerra Ortiz, Joaquín. *Diccionario jeográfico de los Estados Unidos de Colombia*. Bogotá: J. B. Gaitán, 1879.

Eyzaguirre, José Ignacio Víctor. *Los intereses católicos en América*. Paris: Garnier Hermanos Salva, 1859.

Franco V., Constancio. *Apuntamientos para la historia: la guerra de 1876 i 1877*. Bogotá: La Época, 1877.

Friede, Juan. *Fuentes documentales para la historia del Nuevo Reino de Granada*. Vol. 8. Bogotá: Editorial Andes, 1976.

Galindo, Aníbal. *Estudios económicos i fiscales*. Bogotá: H. Andrade, 1880.

Grillo, Max. *Emociones de la guerra: relato de la Guerra de los Mil Días en el gran Santander*. Bucaramanga: Universidad Industrial de Santander, 2008 [1903].

Groot, José Manuel. *Cuadros de costumbres*. Bogotá: Minerva, 1936.

———. *La lira nueva*. Bogotá: Medardo Rivas, 1886.

Guzmán, Antonio Leocadio. *Datos históricos sur americanos*. Vol. 1. Brussels: Vanderauwera, 1878.

Hamilton, John Potter. *Travels through the Interior Provinces of Columbia*. Vol. 1. London: John Murray, 1827.

Herndon, William Lewis, and Lardner Gibbon. *Exploration of the Valley of the Amazon*. Vol. 1. Washington, D.C.: Robert Armstrong, 1853.

Hettner, Alfred. *Viajes por los Andes colombianos (1882-1884)*. Bogotá: Banco de la República, 1976 [1888].

Holton, Isaac. *New Granada: Twenty Months in the Andes*. New York: Harper & Brothers, 1857.

Isaacs, Jorge. *María*. 2nd ed. Buenos Aires: Igón Hermanos, 1879 [1867].

Jiménez, Domingo. *Geografía física i política de la ciudad de Corozal*. Mompós: La Industria, 1873.

Jiménez López, Miguel. *Nuestras razas decaen: Algunos signos de degeneración colectiva en Colombia y en los países similares*. Bogotá: Juan Casis, 1920.

———. *Los problemas de la raza en Colombia*. Bogotá: Biblioteca de "Cultura," 1920.

Kastos, Emiro [Juan de Dios Restrepo]. *Artículos escogidos*. London: Juan M. Fonnegra, 1885.

Laverde Amaya, Isidoro. *Apuntes sobre bibliografía colombiana*. Bogotá: Zalamea Hermanos, 1882.

Leay, William. *New Granada, Equatorial South America*. Bristol: I. E. Chillcott, 1869.

MacDouall, Roberto. *El joven Arturo: poema*. Bogotá: Medardo Rivas, 1883.

Madiedo, Manuel María. *Nuestro siglo XIX*. Bogotá: Nicolas Pontón, 1868.

———. *Tratado de crítica jeneral*. Bogotá: Gaitán, 1868.

Mantilla, Daniel. *Artículos escogidos de Abel-Karl*. Bogotá: Echeverría Hermanos, 1870.

Marroquín, José Manuel. *Obras escogidas en prosa y en verso, publicadas e inéditas*. Bogotá: El Tradicionista, 1875.

Marroquín, Lorenzo, and José María Rivas Groot. *Pax*. New York: Brentano, 1920 [1907].

Massey, S. F. "The Late Revolution in Colombia." *Journal of Military Service Institution* 22 (1898): 288–311.

Matute, Santiago. *Los padres candelarios en Colombia: o apuntes para la historia*. 6 vols. Bogotá: Eugenio Pardo, 1897–1903.

Millican, Albert. *Travels and Adventures of an Orchid Hunter*. London: Cassell, 1891.

Le Moyne, Auguste. *Viajes y estancias en América del Sur*. Bogotá: Biblioteca Popular de Cultura Colombiana, 1945.

Mollien, Gaspar. *Viaje por la República de Colombia en 1823*. Bogotá: Biblioteca Popular de Cultura Colombiana, 1944 [1825].

Montejo, Isaac. *Nuestro estado social*. Bogotá: J. B. Gaitán, 1878.

Morales Benítez, Otto. *Muchedumbres y banderas*. Bogotá: Plaza y Janés, 1980.

———. *Testimonio de un pueblo*. Bogotá: Banco de la República, 1962.

Mosquera, Tomás Cipriano de. *Discurso del presidente provisorio de los Estados Unidos de Colombia, en la instalación de la Convención Nacional*. Bogotá: Echeverría Hermanos, 1863.

———. *Memoir on the Physical and Political Geography of New Granada*. New York: T. Dwight, 1853.

Murillo Toro, Manuel. *Obras selectas*. Ed. Jorge Mario Eastman. Bogotá: Imprenta Nacional, 1979.

Museo de cuadros de costumbres. 4 vols. Bogotá: Banco Popular, 1973.

Naranjo, Enrique M. *Páginas sueltas (El gran Río de la Magdalena y otros asuntos)*. Cali: Imprenta Departamental, 1957.

Nieto, Juan José. "Bosquejo histórico de la revolución que regeneró el Estado de Bolívar." In Juan José Nieto, *Selección de textos políticos, geográficos e históricos*, ed. Gustavo Bell Lemus, 51–115. Barranquilla: Gobernación del Atlántico, 1993 [1862].

Nieto, Máximo A. *Recuerdos de la regeneración*. Bogotá: Marconi, 1924.

Noguera Mendoza, Aníbal, ed. *Crónica grande del Río Magdalena*. 2 vols. Bogotá: Fondo Cultural Cafetero, 1980.

"Notes on New Granada by an English Resident." *Bentley's Miscellany* 31 (1852): 23–32.

Núñez, Rafael. *La reforma política en Colombia.* 2nd ed. Bogotá: La Luz, 1886.

Obeso, Candelario. *Cantos populares de mi tierra.* Bogotá: Borda, 1877.

———. *Lecturas para ti.* Reprint in *Cantos populares de mi tierra.* Bogotá: Ministerio de Educación Nacional, 1950 [1878].

———. *Lucha de la vida.* Bogotá: Silvestre, 1882.

———. *Proyecto de lei sobre orden público.* Bogotá: Echeverría Hermanos, 1874.

———. *Secundino el Zapatero.* Reprint in *Cantos populares de mi tierra, Secundino el zapatero.* Cartagena: Universidad de Cartagena, 2009 [1880].

Ortiz, Nicolás. *Guía de la navegación del Bajo Magdalena.* Bogotá: Medardo Rivas, 1894.

Ortiz, Venancio. *Historia de la revolución del 17 de abril de 1854.* Bogotá: 1972 [1855].

Ospina Rodríguez, Mariano. *Antología del pensamiento de Mariano Ospina Rodríguez.* Bogotá: Banco de la República, 1990.

Páez, Adriano. *La patria.* Vol. 1. Bogotá: Medardo Rivas, 1878.

Palacio, Julio H. *La guerra de 85.* Bogotá: Librería Colombiana, 1936.

———. *Historia de mi vida.* N.p., 1980.

———. *La historia de mi vida: Crónicas inéditas.* Barranquilla: Uninorte, 1992.

Parra, Aquileo. *Memorias.* Bogotá: La Luz, 1912.

Pérez, Felipe. *Anales de la Revolución.* Bogotá: Estado de Cundinamarca, 1862.

———. *Episodios de un viaje.* Bogotá: Ministerio de Educación, 1946 [1865].

———. *Geografía general física y política de los Estados Unidos de Colombia.* Vol. 1. Bogotá: Echeverría Hermanos, 1883.

———. *Imina: novela orijinal.* Bogotá: Colunje & Vallarino, 1881.

Pérez, Lázaro María. *Obras poéticas y dramáticas.* Paris: Roger Chernoviz, 1884.

Pérez, Rafael. *La Compañia de Jesús en Colombia y Centro-América después de su restauración.* Vol. 1. Valladolid: L. N. de Gaviria, 1896.

Pérez Gómez, José. *Apuntes históricos de las misiones agustinianas en Colombia.* Bogotá: Cruzada, 1924.

Peérez i Soto, Juan B. *La curarina, antidoto contra el Montalvismo.* Guayaquil: Calov, 1886.

———. *El vértice del ángulo.* Guayaquil: Los Andes, 1887.

Pérez Triana, Santiago. *Down the Orinoco in a Canoe.* London: Heinemann, 1902.

Petre, F. Loraine. *The Republic of Colombia.* London: E. Stanford, 1906.

Pinzón, Cerbeleón. *Catecismo republicano para instrucción popular.* Bogotá: El Mosaico, 1865.

Pombo, Manuel Antonio, and José Joaquín Guerra. *Constituciones de Colombia: recopiladas y precedidas de una breve reseña histórica.* Bogotá: Echeverría Hermanos, 1892.

Posada, Eduardo. *Viajes y cuentos.* Bogotá: La Luz, 1896.

Posada Gutiérrez, Joaquín. *Memorias histórico-políticas.* Vols. 3–4. Bogotá: Imprenta Nacional, 1954.

Powles, J. D. *New Granada: Its Internal Resources.* London: A. H. Bailey, 1863.

Quijano, Arturo A. *Ensayo sobre la evolución del derecho penal en Colombia.* Bogotá: Medardo Rivas, 1898.

Quijano Otero, José María. *Diario de la guerra civil de 1860 y otros sucesos políticos.* Bogotá: Incunables, 1982.

Quintero C., Juan B., and Ignacio V. Espinosa. *Jurisprudencia de la Corte Suprema de Justicia.* Bogotá: La Luz, 1896.

Reclus, Élisée. *Viaje a la Sierra Nevada de Santa Marta.* Bogotá: Foción Mantilla, 1869 [1861].

Restrepo, Antonio José. *Poesías originales y traducciones poéticas.* Lausana: Georges Bridel, 1899.

Restrepo, José Manuel. *Diario político y militar.* Vol. 4. Bogotá: Imprenta Nacional, 1954.

Restrepo, Juan Pablo. *La iglesia y el estado en Colombia.* London: Emiliano Isaza, 1885.

Rivas, Medardo. *Obras.* Vol. 2. Bogotá: Medardo Rivas, 1885.

———. *Los trabajadores de la tierra caliente.* Bogotá: Medardo Rivas, 1899.

Robinson, Wirt. *A Flying Trip to the Tropics.* Cambridge: Riverside, 1895.

Röthlisberger, Ernst. *El Dorado.* Bogotá: Banco de la República, 1993 [1897].

Rudas, Juan Manuel. *La insurrección en el Magdalena en 1879.* Bogotá: Borda, 1880.

Sagher, Leéon de. *Nociones de táctica, de infantería, de caballería y de artillería.* Translated by Candelario Obeso. Bogotá: H. Andrade, 1878.

Samper, José María. *Derecho público interno de Colombia.* Vol. 2. Bogotá: La Luz, 1887.

———. *Ensayo sobre las revoluciones políticas.* Paris: E. Thunot, 1861.

———. *Filosofía en cartera.* Bogotá: La Luz, 1887.

———. *Historia de una alma.* Bogotá: Zalamea Hermanos, 1881.

———. *El sitio de Cartagena.* Bogotá: La Luz, 1885.

———. *Viajes de un colombiano en Europa.* Paris: E. Thunot, 1862.

Samper, Miguel. *Escritos político-económicos.* 3 vols. Bogotá: Banco de la República, 1977 [1925].

Scruggs, William. *The Colombian and Venezuelan Republics.* Boston: Little, Brown, 1900.

Serret, Félix. *Viaje a Colombia, 1911–1912.* Bogotá: Colcultura, 1994 [1912].

Silva, Ricardo. *Artículos de costumbre.* Bogotá: Silvestre, 1883.

Socarrás, Sabas S. *Recuerdos de la Guerra de los Mil Días.* Bogotá: Tercer Mundo, 1977 [1930].

Steuart, John. *Bogotá in 1836-7.* New York: Harper & Brothers, 1838.

Tamayo, Joaquín. *La Revolución de 1899.* Bogotá: Banco Popular, 1975 [1938].

Torres Caicedo, José María. *Mis ideas y mis principios.* Vol. 1. Paris: Imprenta Nueva, 1875.

Uribe, Antonio José. *El fomento de las misiones y la colonización.* Bogotá: Cruzada, 1924.

Uribe, Juan de D., and Antonio José Restrepo. *Candelario Obeso.* Bogotá: Zalamea Hermanos, 1886.

Uribe Uribe, Rafael. *Documentos militares y políticos relativos á las compañas del general Rafael Uribe Uribe.* Bogotá: Vapor, 1904.

Vallet y Piquer, José. *Ensayo sobre el matrimonio cristiano y el matrimonio civil.* Barcelona: Librería Religiosa, 1882.

Vargas Vila, José María. *Aura ó las violetas; Emma; Lo irreparable.* Paris: Bouret, 1898.

Vélez, Fernando. *Datos para la historia del derecho nacional.* Medellín: Imprenta del Departamento, 1891.

Vergara, José Ramón, and Fernando E. Baena. *Barranquilla: su pasado y su presente.* Vol. 1. Barranquilla: Banco Dugand, 1922.

Vergara y Velasco, Francisco Javier. *Nueva geografía de Colombia.* Primera Parte. Bogotá: Zalamea Hermanos, 1892.

Vergara y Vergara, José María. *Artículos literarios.* London: Juan M. Fonnegra, 1885.

———. *Museo de cuadros de costumbres.* Bogotá: Foción Mantilla, 1866.

Vincent, Frank. *Around and about South America.* New York: D. Appleton, 1897.

Wilson, Erastus. *A Ramble in New Granada.* New York: G. W. Carlton, 1878.

Zapata Olivella, Manuel. *Chambacú: Black Slum.* Translated by Jonathan Tittler. Pittsburgh: Latin American Literary Review, 1989 [1965].

Periodicals

La Alianza

American Mail and Export Journal

Anales del Senado de Plenipotenciarios

El Artesano

El Bogotano

El Chino

El Churiador

El Ciudadano

La Civilización

El Combate

El Comercio

El Correo

El Correo de la Costa

El Correo Nacional

La Crónica

Cultura

El Demócrata

El Día

Diario de Avisos

Diario Comercial

Diario de Bolívar

Diario Oficial

Diplomatic and Consular Reports (Great Britain)

El Eco de los Andes

El Eco del Magdalena

El Elector

El Elector Popular

Enciclopedia del Semanario de Cartagena

La Escuela Normal

El Estandarte

Evangelical Christendom

La Familia

El Fisgón

Gaceta de Bolívar

Gaceta Judicial

Gaceta Mercantil

Gaceta Municipal (Cartagena)

Gaceta Municipal (Santa Marta)

Gaceta Oficial del Estado de Bolívar

Gaceta Oficial del Estado Soberano de Bolívar

El Granadino

La Independencia

The Independent

El Iris

El Látigo

El Loco

Los Locos

Monthly Consular and Trade Reports

El Mosaico

Nueva Revista de Buenos Aires
El Nuevo Mundo
El Orden
La Palestra
El Palo de Ciego
Papel Periódico Ilustrado
El Parapote
El Pasatiempo
El Patriota
El Picol
El Pobre
El Porvenir

El Progreso
La Reforma
El Relator
El Repertorio Colombiano
La República
El Republicano
Revista Moderna
El Tiempo
La Tribuna
El Vapor
La Voz

Secondary Sources

Abel, Christopher. *Política, iglesia y partidos en Colombia, 1886–1953*. Bogotá: Universidad Nacional de Colombia, 1987.

Abello Vives, Alberto, ed. *Un Caribe sin plantación: Memorias de la Cátedra del Caribe colombiano*. San Andrés: Universidad Nacional de Colombia, 2006.

Adas, Michael. *Machines as the Measure of Men: Science, Technology, and Ideologies of Western Dominance*. Ithaca: Cornell University, 1990.

Aguilera, Miguel. *Lácides Segovia, un carácter*. Bogotá: ABC, 1959.

Aguilera Peña, Mario, and Renán Vega Cantor. *Ideal democrático y revuelta popular*. 2nd ed. Bogotá: CEREC, 1998.

Aguirre, Carlos. *Agentes de su propia libertad: Los esclavos de Lima y la desintegración de la esclavitud, 1821–1854*. Lima: Pontificia Universidad Católica del Perú, 1993.

———. "*Tinterillos*, Indians, and the State: Towards a History of Legal Intermediaries in Post-independence Peru." In *One Law for All? Western Models and Local Practices in (Post-)imperial Contexts*, ed. Stefan B. Kirmse, 119–51. Frankfurt: Campus, 2012.

Alzate, Carolina, and Montserrat Ordóñez. *Soledad Acosta de Samper: escritura, género y nación en el siglo XIX*. Madrid: Iberoamericana, 2005.

Andrews, George Reid. *Afro-Latin America, 1800–2000*. New York: Oxford University Press, 2004.

Appadurai, Arjun, et al. "Editorial Comment: On Thinking the Black Public Sphere." *Public Culture* 7 (Fall 1994): xi–xiv.

Appelbaum, Nancy. *Muddied Waters: Race, Region, and Local History in Colombia, 1846–1948*. Durham, N.C.: Duke University Press, 2003.

Appelbaum, Nancy, Anne S. Macpherson, and Karin Alejandra Rosemblatt. "Introduction: Racial Nations." In *Race and Nation in Modern Latin America*, ed. Nancy Appelbaum, Anne S. Macpherson, and Karin Alejandra Rosemblatt, 1–31. Chapel Hill: University of North Carolina Press, 2003.

Arango Loboguerrero, Leonidas. "Catarino Garza, un mexicano en la guerra civil colombiana de 1895." *Anuario colombiano de historia social y de la cultura* 36, no. 1 (2009): 251–82.

Archila Neira, Mauricio. "Aspectos comparativos en la formación de la clase obrera colombiana." In *Historia y cultura obrera, memorias del segundo seminario,* 67–84. Medellín: Litoarte, 1987.

———. "Barranquilla y el río: Una historia social de sus trabajadores." *Controversia* 142 (November 1987): 1–90.

———. "La clase obrera colombiana, 1886–1930." In *Nueva historia de Colombia,* ed. Álvaro Tirado Mejía, 3:219–44. Bogotá: Planeta, 1989.

———. *Cultura e identidad obrera: Colombia, 1910–1945.* Bogotá: CINEP, 1991.

Arcila Estrada, María Teresa. "Poblamiento y cultura en el sur de Bolívar." In *Costa atlántica colombiana: Etnología e historia,* ed. Sandra Turbay and Amparo Murillo, 73–98. Medellín: Universidad de Antioquia, 1994.

Arcos, Dr. (Camilo S. Delgado). "Manumisión de siervos." *Boletín Historial* 43/44 (November-December 1918).

Arias Vanegas, Julio. *Nación y diferencia en el siglo XIX colombiano.* Bogotá: Universidad de los Andes, 2005.

Arocha, Jaime. "Inclusion of Afro-Colombians: An Unreachable Goal?" *Latin American Perspectives* 25 (May 1998): 70–89.

Arocha, Jaime, and Nina S. de Friedemann. *De sol a sol: Génesis, transformación y presencia de los negros en Colombia.* Bogotá: Planeta, 1986.

Avelar, Idelber. *The Letter of Violence: Essays on Narrative, Ethics, and Politics.* New York: Palgrave MacMillan, 2004.

Baretta, Silvio Duncan, and John Markoff. "Civilization and Barbarism: Cattle Frontiers in Latin America." *Comparative Studies in Society and History* 20 (1978): 587–620.

Barkley Brown, Elsa. "To Catch the Vision of Freedom: Reconstructing Southern Black Women's Political History, 1865–1880." In *African American Women and the Vote, 1837–1960,* ed. Ann Gordon et al., 66–99. Amherst: University of Massachusetts Press, 1997.

Barona Becerra, Guido. "Ausencia y presencia del 'negro' en la historia colombiana." *Memoria y Sociedad* 1 (November 1995): 77–105.

Barón Rivera, Juan David. *Perfil socioeconómico de Tubará: población dormitorio y destino turístico del Atlántico.* Documento de Trabajo sobre Economía Regional No. 34. Cartagena: Banco de la República, 2002.

Becerra Jiménez, Jorge. *Historia de la diócesis de Barranquilla a través de la biografía del Padre Pedro María Revollo.* Bogotá: Banco de la República, 1993.

Bensusan, Guy. "Cartagena's Fandango Politics." *Studies in Latin American Popular Culture* 3 (1984): 127–34.

Bergad, Laird W. *The Comparative Histories of Slavery in Brazil, Cuba, and the United States.* New York: Cambridge University Press, 2007.

Bergquist, Charles. *Coffee and Conflict in Colombia, 1886–1910.* Durham, N.C.: Duke University Press, 1978.

———. "In the Name of History: A Disciplinary Critique of Orlando Fals Borda's *Historia doble de la costa.*" *Latin American Research Review* 25, no. 3 (1990): 156–76.

———. "Labor History and Its Challenges: Confessions of a Latin Americanist." *American Historical Review* 98, no. 3 (June 1993): 757–64.

————. *Labor in Latin America: Comparative Essays on Chile, Argentina, Venezuela, and Colombia*. Stanford, Calif.: Stanford University Press, 1986.

Berlin, Ira. *Many Thousands Gone: The First Two Centuries of Slavery in North America*. Cambridge: Belknap Press/Harvard University Press, 1998.

————. *Slaves without Masters: The Free Negro in the Antebellum South*. New York: Vintage, 1974.

Bermúdez Q., Suzy. *El bello sexo: la mujer y la familia durante el olimpo radical*. Bogotá: Uniandes, 1993.

Bierck, Harold. "The Struggle for Abolition in Gran Colombia." *Hispanic American Historical Review* 24, no. 3 (1944): 365–86.

Blackburn, Robin. *The Overthrow of Colonial Slavery, 1776–1848*. New York: Verso, 1988.

Blanchard, Peter. *Slavery and Abolition in Early Republican Peru*. Wilmington, Del.: Scholarly Resources, 1992.

————. *Under the Flags of Freedom: Slave Soldiers and the Wars of Independence in Spanish South America*. Pittsburgh: University of Pittsburgh Press, 2008.

Bocarejo, Diana. "Deceptive Utopias: Violence, Environmentalism, and the Regulation of Multiculturalism in Colombia." *Law & Policy* 31, no. 3 (July 2009): 307–29.

Bóhorquez Casallas, Luis Antonio. *La evolución educativa en Colombia*. Bogotá: Cultural Colombiana, 1956.

Bolland, O. Nigel. *The Politics of Labour in the British Caribbean*. Princeton, N.J.: Markus Weiner, 2001.

Bonilla, Victor. *Servants of God or Masters of Men? The Story of a Capuchin Mission in Amazonia*. Translated by Rosemary Sheed. Harmondsworth, U.K.: Penguin, 1972.

Borges, Dain. *The Family in Bahia, Brazil, 1870–1945*. Palo Alto, Calif.: Stanford University Press, 1992.

Bravo Páez, Ivonne. *Comportamientos ilícitos y mecanismos de control social en el Bolívar grande: 1886–1905*. Bogotaé: Ministerio de Cultura, 2002.

Briceño Jáuregui, Manuel. *Los jesuitas en el Magdalena*. Bogotá: D. C. Kelly, 1984.

Brown, Jonathan C. "The Genteel Tradition of Nineteenth-Century Colombian Culture." *The Americas* 36, no. 4 (April 1980): 445–64.

Buelvas, Mirtha. "Barranquilla, la migración y Joselito Carnaval." In *Primer encuentro de investigadores del Carnaval de Barranquilla*, ed. Martín Orozco Cantillo, 113–23. Barranquilla: Universidad del Atlántico, 1999.

Buscaglia-Salgado, José F. *Undoing Empire: Race and Nation in the Mulatto Caribbean*. Minneapolis: University of Minnesota Press, 2003.

Bushnell, David. "The Development of the Press in Great Colombia." *Hispanic American Historical Review* 30, no. 4 (November 1950): 432–52.

————. *The Making of Modern Colombia*. Berkeley: University of California Press, 1993.

————. "Politics and Violence in Nineteenth-Century Colombia." In *Violence in Colombia: The Contemporary Crisis in Historical Perspective*, ed. Charles Bergquist, Ricardo Peñaranda, and Gonzalo Sánchez, 11–30. Wilmington, Del.: SR Books, 1990.

————. "Voter Participation in the Colombian Election of 1856." *Hispanic American Historical Review* 51 (1971): 237–49.

Bushnell, David, and Neill Macauley. *The Emergence of Latin America in the Nineteenth Century.* New York: Oxford University Press, 1988.

Bustamante Roldán, Darío. *Efectos económicos del papel moneda durante la Regeneración.* 2nd ed. Bogotá: La Carreta, 1980.

Butler, Kim. *Freedoms Given, Freedoms Won: Afro-Brazilians in Post-abolition São Paulo and Salvador.* New Brunswick, N.J.: Rutgers University Press, 1998.

Camacho, Juana, and Eduardo Restrepo, eds. *De montes, ríos y ciudades: Territorios e identidades de la gente negra en Colombia.* Bogotá: Fundación Natura, 1999.

Caplan, Karen D. *Indigenous Citizens: Local Liberalism in Early National Oaxaca and Yucatán.* Palo Alto, Calif.: Stanford University Press, 2009.

Caraballo, Vicente. *El negro Obeso.* Bogotá: ABC, 1943.

Carrero Becerra, Manuel Waldo. *Guerra de los Mil Días.* Chinácota: La Opinión, 2002.

Castellanos, Jorge. *La abolición de la esclavitud en Popayán, 1832–1852.* Cali: Departamento de Publicaciones, 1980.

Casas Orrego, Álvaro León. "Agua y aseo en la formación de la salud pública en Cartagena, 1885–1930." *Historia y Cultura* 4, no. 4 (December 1996): 77–100.

————. "Expansión y modernidad en Cartagena de Indias, 1885–1930." *Historia y Cultura* 3, no. 2 (December 1994): 39–68.

Castellar, Manuel, ed. *Los capuchinos en Colombia, 1888–1970.* Bogotá: Custodia Provincial, 1970.

Castillo, Luis Carlos. *Etnicidad y nación: el desafío de la diversidad en Colombia.* Cali: Universidad del Valle, 2007.

Castillo Mathieu, Nicolás del. *Esclavos negros en Cartagena y sus aportes léxicos.* Bogotá: Instituto Caro y Cuervo, 1982.

Castro Carvajal, Beatriz. "Aspectos de la vida diaria en las ciudades republicanas." *Revista Credencial Historia* 55 (July 1994): 8–11.

Caufield, Sueann. "Interracial Courtship in the Rio de Janeiro Courts, 1918–1940." In *Race and Nation in Modern Latin America*, ed. Nancy Appelbaum, Anne S. Macpherson, and Karin Alejandra Rosemblatt. Chapel Hill: University of North Carolina Press, 2003.

Chambers, Sarah. *From Subjects to Citizens: Honor, Gender, and Politics in Arequipa, Peru, 1780–1854.* University Park: Pennsylvania State University Press, 1999.

Childs, Matthew D. *The 1812 Aponte Rebellion in Cuba and the Struggle against Atlantic Slavery.* Chapel Hill: University of North Carolina Press, 2006.

Colmenares, Germán. *Partidos políticos y clases sociales.* Bogotá: Comuneros, 1984.

La Compañía de Jesús: Los jesuitas colombianos en el IV centenario de la Compañía a sus amigos y bienechores. Bogotá: Corazón de Jesús, 1940.

Conde Calderón, Jorge. "Carnaval, sociedad y cultura." In *Carnaval en la Arenosa*, ed. Laurian Puerta, 77–85. Barranquilla: Universidad del Atlántico, 1999.

Consejo Regional de Planificación de la Costa Atlántica (CRPCA). *Mapa cultural del Caribe colombiano.* Santa Marta: CRPCA, 1993.

Cooper, Frederick, Thomas C. Holt, and Rebecca J. Scott. Introduction to *Beyond Slavery: Explorations of Race, Labor, and Citizenship in Postemancipation Societies*. Chapel Hill: University of North Carolina Press, 1999.

Correa, Ramón. *La convención de Ríonegro: paéginas histoéricas de Colombia*. Bogotaé: Imprenta Nacional, 1937.

Correa Uribe, Rafael. *Republicanismo y reforma constitucional, 1891-1910*. Medellín: Universidad de Antioquia, 1996.

Crawford, Sharika. "Politics of Belonging on a Caribbean Borderland: The Colombian Islands of San Andrés and Providencia." In *Crossing Boundaries: Ethnicity, Race, and National Belonging in a Transnational World*, ed. Brian D. Behnken and Simon Wendt, 19-37. Lanham, Md.: Lexington Books, 2013.

Cunin, Elisabeth. *Identidades a flor de piel: Lo negro entre apariencias y pertenencias: Mestizaje y categorías raciales en Cartagena*. Bogotá: ICAHN, 2003.

de la Fuente, Alejandro. *A Nation for All: Race, Inequality and Politics in Twentieth-Century Cuba*. Chapel Hill: University of North Carolina Press, 2000.

Deas, Malcolm. "Algunas notas sobre la historia del caciquismo en Colombia." *Revista de Occidente* 127 (October 1973): 118-40.

———. "Colombia, Venezuela and Ecuador, c. 1880-1930." In *The Cambridge History of Latin America*, ed. Leslie Bethell, 5:644-65. Cambridge: Cambridge University Press, 1986.

———. "The Fiscal Problems of Nineteenth-Century Colombia." *Journal of Latin American Studies* 14, no. 2 (November 1982): 287-328.

———. "The Man on Foot: Conscription and the Nation-State in Nineteenth-Century Latin America." In *Studies in the Formation of the Nation-State in Latin America*. ed. James Dunkerley, 77-93. London: ILAS, 2001.

———. "Miguel Antonio Caro and Friends: Grammar and Power in Colombia." *History Workshop Journal* 34 (1992): 47-70.

———. *Del poder y la gramática: y otros ensayos sobre historia, política y literatura colombianas*. Bogotá: Tercer Mundo, 1993.

———. "Poverty, Civil War and Politics: Ricardo Gaitán Obeso and His Magdalena River Campaign in Colombia, 1885." *Nova Americana* 2 (1979): 263-303.

———. "La presencia de la política nacional en la vida provinciana, pueblerina y rural de Colombia en el primer siglo de la república." In *La Unidad nacional en América Latina*, ed. Marco Palacios, 149-73. México: El Colegio de México, 1983.

———. "The Role of the Church, the Army and the Police in Colombian Elections, c. 1850-1930." In *Elections before Democracy: The History of Elections in Europe and Latin America*, ed. Eduardo Posada-Carbó, 163-80. London: ILAS, 1996.

———. "Venezuela, Colombia and Ecuador: The First Half-Century of Independence." In *The Cambridge History of Latin America*, ed. Leslie Bethell, 3:507-38. New York: Cambridge University Press, 1985.

Deere, Carmen Diana, and Magdalena León. "Liberalism and Married Women's Property Rights in Nineteenth-Century Latin America." *Hispanic American Historical Review* 85, no. 4 (November 2005): 627-78.

Delpar, Helen. "Aspects of Liberal Factionalism, 1875-1885." *Hispanic American Historical Review* 51, no. 2 (May 1971): 250-74.

------. "Colombian Liberalism and the Roman Catholic Church, 1863–1886." *Journal of Church and State* 22, no. 2 (November 1980): 271–93.

------. *Red against Blue: The Liberal Party in Colombian Politics, 1863–1899*. University: University of Alabama Press, 1981.

------. "Renegade or Regenerator?: Rafael Nunez as Seen by Colombian Historians." *Revista Interamericana de Bibliografía* 35, no. 1 (1985): 25–37.

Diacon, Todd. *Millenarian Vision, Capitalist Reality: Brazil's Contestado Rebellion, 1912–1916*. Durham, N.C.: Duke University Press, 1991.

Díaz Díaz, Fernando. "Estado, Iglesia y desamortización." In *Nueva historia de Colombia*, ed. Álvaro Tirado Mejía, 2:206–19. Bogotá: Planeta, 1989.

Díaz Díaz, Rafael. *Esclavitud, región y ciudad: El sistema esclavista urbano-regional de Santa Fe de Bogotá, 1700–1750*. Bogotá: Pontificia Universidad Javeriana, 2001.

DuBois, Laurent. *A Colony of Citizens: Revolution and Slave Emancipation in the French Caribbean, 1787–1804*. Chapel Hill: University of North Carolina Press, 2006.

Duffey, Frank M. *The Early "Cuadros de Costumbres" in Colombia*. Chapel Hill: University of North Carolina Press, 1956.

Earle, Rebecca. "The War of the Supremes: Border Conflict, Religious Crusade or Simply Politics by Other Means?" In *Rumours of War: Civil Conflict in Nineteenth-Century Latin America*, ed. Rebecca Earle, 119–34. London: University of London Press, 2000.

Eley, Geoff. "Nations, Publics, and Political Cultures: Placing Habermas in the Nineteenth Century." In *Habermas and the Public Sphere*, ed. Craig J. Calhoun, 289–339. Cambridge: MIT Press, 1992.

Escalantes, Aquiles. *El negro en Colombia*. Bogotá: Universidad Nacional de Colombia, 1964.

Escobar Mesa, Augusto, et al., eds. *Narrativa de las guerras civiles colombianas*. Vol. 3. Bucaramanga: Universidad Industrial de Santander, 2005.

Escobar Ramírez, María. "Impuestos y reglamentos para el Carnaval de Barranquilla, 1930–1970." In *Primer encuentro de investigadores del Carnaval de Barranquilla*, ed. Ubaldo Meza Ricardo et al., 125–34. Barranquilla: Universidad del Atlántico, 1999.

Escobar Rodríguez, Carmen. *La revolución liberal y la protesta del artesanado*. Bogotá: Fundación Universitaria Autónoma de Colombia, 1990.

España, Gonzalo. *La guerra civil de 1885: Núñez y la derrota del radicalismo*. Bogotá: Áncora, 1985.

Etzioni, Amitai. "Toward a Theory of Public Ritual." *Sociological Theory* 18 (March 2000): 40–59.

Fals Borda, Orlando. *Historia doble de la costa*. 4 vols. Bogotá: Carlos Valencia, 1979–86.

Farnsworth-Alvear, Ann. *Dulcinea in the Factory: Myths, Morals, Men, and Women in Colombia's Industrial Experiment, 1905–1960*. Durham, N.C.: Duke University Press, 1999.

Ferrer, Ada. *Insurgent Cuba: Race, Nation and Revolution, 1868–1898*. Chapel Hill: University of North Carolina Press, 1999.

Fick, Carolyn. *The Making of Haiti: The Saint Domingue Revolution from Below.* Knoxville: University of Tennessee Press, 1990.

Figueroa, Luis A. *Sugar, Slavery, and Freedom in Nineteenth-Century Puerto Rico.* Chapel Hill: University of North Carolina Press, 2005.

Flórez, Iveth, and José Ramón Llanos. *Barranquilla y Sabanilla durante el siglo XIX, 1852-1898.* Barranquilla: Clio Caribe, 1995.

Flórez Bolívar, Roicer. "La borrosa línea de lo público y lo privado en el Estado Soberano de Bolívar." *Amauta* no. 14 (2009): 75-97.

Flórez Bolívar, Roicer, and Sergio Paolo Solano. *Infancia de la nación: Colombia durante el primer siglo de la República.* Cartagena: Pluma de Mompox, 2011.

Fraser, Nancy. "Rethinking the Public Sphere: A Contribution to the Critique of Actually Existing Democracy." *Social Text* 25/26 (1990): 56-80.

———. "Rethinking Recognition." *New Left Review* 3 (May-June 2000): 107-20.

Friedemann, Nina S. de, and Mónica Espinosa Arango. "Las mujeres negras en la historia de Colombia." In *Las mujeres en la historia de Colombia*, ed. Magdala Velásquez Toro, 2:32-76. Bogotá: Norma, 1995.

Galvis Noyes, Antonio José. "La abolición de la esclavitud en la Nueva Granada." *Revista Colegio Mayor Nuestra Señora Rosario* 515 (August-October 1981): 51-60.

García, Julio César. *Himnos y símbolos de nuestra Colombia.* Bogotá: Camer, 2000.

García Benítez, Luis. *Reseña histórica de los obispos que han regentado la diócesis de Santa Marta: primera parte, 1534-1891.* Bogotá: Editorial Pax, 1953.

Gibson, William. *The Constitutions of Colombia.* Chapel Hill: University of North Carolina Press, 1948.

Gilmore, Robert L. "Federalism in Colombia, 1810-1858." Ph.D. diss., University of California, Berkeley, 1949.

———. "Nueva Granada's Socialist Mirage." *Hispanic American Historical Review* 36, no. 2 (May 1956): 190-210.

Goenaga, Miguel. *Lecturas locales.* Barranquilla: Imprenta Departamental, 1953.

Gómez Olaciregui, Aureliano. *Prensa y periodismo en Barranquilla.* Barranquilla: Departamento del Atlántico, 1967.

Gómez Picón, Alirio. *El golpe militar del 17 de abril de 1854.* Bogotá: Kelly, 1954.

Gómez Picón, Rafael. *Magdalena, río de Colombia.* 6th ed. Bogotá: Biblioteca Colombiana de Cultura, 1973.

González, Margarita. "El proceso de manumisión en Colombia." *Cuadernos Colombianos* 2 (II Trimester 1974): 145-240.

González Echevarría, Roberto, and Enrique Pupo-Walker, eds. *The Cambridge History of Latin American Literature.* Vol. 1. Cambridge: Cambridge University Press, 1996.

González-Jácome, Jorge. "The Assault on Classical Legal Thought in Colombia (1886-1920)." Unpublished ms. Bogotá, January 2009.

González Rojas, Jorge Enrique. *Legitimidad y cultura: educación, cultura y política en los Estados Unidos de Colombia, 1863-1886.* Bogotá: Universidad Nacional/ CES, 2005.

Gould, Jeffrey. *To Die in This Way: Nicaraguan Indians and the Myth of Mestizaje, 1880-1965.* Durham, N.C.: Duke University Press, 1996.

Greene, W. John. "Vibrations of the Collective: The Popular Ideology of Gaitanismo on Colombia's Atlantic Coast, 1944–1948." *Hispanic American Historical Review* 76, no. 2 (May 1996): 283–311.

Grusin, Jay. "The Revolution of 1848 in Colombia." Ph.D. diss., University of Arizona, 1978.

Guardino, Peter F. *Peasants, Politics, and the Formation of Mexico's National State: Guerrero, 1810–1857.* Palo Alto, Calif.: Stanford University Press, 1996.

———. *The Time of Liberty: Popular Political Culture in Oaxaca, 1870–1850.* Durham, N.C.: Duke University Press, 2005.

Gudmundson, Lowell, and Justin Wolfe, eds. *Blacks and Blackness in Central America: Between Race and Place.* Durham, N.C.: Duke University Press, 2011.

Guerra, Francois-Xavier. "The Spanish-American Tradition of Representation and Its European Roots." *Journal of Latin American Studies* 26 (February 1994): 1–35.

Gutiérrez Sanín, Francisco. *Curso y discurso en el movimiento plebeyo (1849–1854).* Bogotá: Áncora, 1995.

Gutiérrez Azopardo, Ildefonso. *Historia del negro en Colombia: Sumisión o rebeldía?* Bogotá: Nueva América, 1980.

Gutiérrez de Pineda, Virginia. *Familia y cultura en Colombia.* Bogotá: Tercer Mundo, 1968.

Gutiérrez de Pineda, Virginia, and Roberto Pineda Giraldo. *Miscegenación y cultura en la Colombia colonial, 1750–1810.* Vol. 2. Bogotá: Uniandes, 1999.

Habermas, Jürgen. "The Public Sphere: An Encyclopedia Article (1964)." *New German Critique* 3 (Autumn 1974): 49–55.

Harrison, John P. "The Evolution of the Colombian Tobacco Trade, to 1875." *Hispanic American Historical Review* 32 (May 1952): 163–74.

Helg, Aline. *La educación en Colombia: Una historia social, económica y política, 1918–1957.* Bogotá: Fondo Editorial CEREC, 1987.

———. *Liberty and Equality in Caribbean Colombia, 1770–1835.* Chapel Hill: University of North Carolina Press, 2004.

———. "The Limits of Equality: Free People of Colour and Slaves during the First Independence of Cartagena, Colombia, 1810–1815." *Slavery and Abolition* 20 (August 1999): 1–30.

———. "Los intelectuales frente a la cuestión racial en el decenio de 1920." *Estudios Sociales* 4 (March 1989): 39–53.

Helguera, Joseph León. "The First Mosquera Administration in New Granada, 1845–1849." Ph.D. diss., University of North Carolina, Chapel Hill, 1958.

———. "The Problem of Liberalism versus Conservatism in Colombia, 1849–1885." In *Latin American History: Select Problems,* ed. Frederick B. Pike, 224–58. Chicago: Harcourt Brace, 1969.

Henderson, James D. *Modernization in Colombia: The Laureano Gómez Years, 1889–1965.* Gainesville: University of Florida Press, 2001.

———. *When Colombia Bled: A History of the "Violencia" in Tolima.* University: University of Alabama Press, 1985.

Hernández de Alba, Gregorio. *Libertad de los esclavos en Colombia.* Bogotá: ABD, 1950.

Hernández Gamarra, Antonio. *A Monetary History of Colombia.* Bogotá: Villegas, 2002.

Herzog, Tamar. *Defining Nations: Immigrants and Citizens in Early Modern Spain and Spanish America*. New Haven: Yale University Press, 2003.

Heuman, Gad. *Between Black and White: Race, Politics, and the Free Coloreds in Jamaica, 1792-1865*. Westport, Conn.: Greenwood, 1981.

Higginbotham, Evelyn Brooks. "African-American Women's History and the Metalanguage of Race." *Signs* 17 (Winter 1992): 251-74.

Hobsbawm, Eric. *Labouring Men*. New York: Basic Books, 1964.

———. "Peasant Land Occupation." *Past & Present* 62 (1974): 120-52.

———. *Primitive Rebels*. New York, 1959.

Hoffman, Kelly, and Miguel Ángel Centeno. "The Lopsided Continent: Inequality in Latin America." *Annual Review of Sociology* 29 (August 2003): 363-90.

Holt, Thomas C. "The Essence of the Contract: The Articulation of Race, Gender and Political Economy in British Emancipation Policy, 1838-1866." In *Beyond Slavery: Explorations of Race, Labor, and Citizenship in Postemancipation Societies*, ed. Frederick Cooper, Thomas C. Holt, and Rebecca J. Scott, 33-59. Chapel Hill: University of North Carolina Press, 1999.

———. "First New Nations." Forward to *Race and Nation in Latin America*, ed. Nancy Appelbaum, Anne S. MacPherson, and Karin Alejandra Rosemblatt, vii-xiv. Chapel Hill: University of North Carolina Press, 2003.

———. "Marking: Race, Race-making, and the Writing of History." *American Historical Review* 100, no. 1 (February 1995): 1-20.

———. *The Problem of Freedom: Race, Labor and Politics in Jamaica and Britain, 1832-1936*. Baltimore: Johns Hopkins University Press, 1992.

Horna, Hernán. "Transportation Modernization and Entrepreneurship in Nineteenth-Century Colombia." *Journal of Latin American Studies* 14 (1982): 33-54.

———. *Transport Modernization and Entrepreneurship in Nineteenth-Century Colombia*. Uppsala: Uppsala University, 1992.

Hudson, Randall. "The Status of the Negro in Northern South America, 1820-1860." *Journal of Negro History* 49, no. 4 (October 1964): 225-39.

Humphreys, Norman. "Race, Caste, and Class in Colombia." *Phylon* 13 (1952): 161-6.

Hunt, Lynn. *Politics, Culture, and Class in the French Revolution*. Berkeley and Los Angeles: University of California Press, 1984.

Jaramillo, Carlos Eduardo. "Antecedentes generales de la Guerra de los Mil Días y golpe de Estado del 31 de julio de 1900." *Nueva historia de Colombia*, ed. Álvaro Tirado Mejía, 1:65-88. Bogotá: Planeta, 1989.

———. *Los guerrilleros del novecientos*. Bogotá: Fondo Editorial CEREC, 1991.

Jaramillo Uribe, Jaime. "Cambios demográficos y aspectos de la política social español en el Nuevo Reino de Granada durante la segunda mitad del siglo XVIII." In *La personalidad histórica de Colombia*, 167-79. Bogotá: Instituto Colombiano de Cultura, 1977.

———. *Ensayos sobre historia social colombiana*. Bogotá: Universidad Nacional, 1968.

———. "Nación y región en los orígenes del Estado nacional en Colombia." In *Ensayos de historia social*, ed. Álvaro Tirado Mejía, 2:105-29. Bogotá: Planeta, 1989.

———. *El pensamiento colombiano en el siglo XIX*. 3rd ed. Bogotá: Temis, 1982.

———. "El proceso de la educación del virreinato a la época contemporánea." In *Manual de historia de Colombia*, ed. Jaime Jaramillo Uribe, 3:249–342. Bogotá: Círculo de Lectores, 1980.

———. "El proceso de la educación en la República (1830–1886)." In *Nueva historia de Colombia*, ed. Álvaro Tirado Mejía, 2:223–50. Bogotá: Planeta, 1989.

———. "Las sociedades democráticas de artesanos en la coyuntura política y social colombiana de 1848." *Anuario colombiano de historia social y de la cultura*, no. 8 (1976): 5–18.

Jiménez, Gustavo. "The Institutionalized Church as a Supporter of External Structural Arrangements." In *Internal Colonialism and Structural Change in Colombia*, ed. A. Eugene Havens and William L. Flinn, 53–80. New York: Praeger, 1970.

Joseph, Gilbert M. "On the Trail of Latin American Bandits: A Reexamination of Peasant Resistance." *Latin American Research Review* 25, no. 3 (1990): 7–53.

Kalmanovitz, Salomón. *Economía y nación: Una breve historia de Colombia*. 4th ed. Bogotá: 1994.

Kaplan, Steven L. *Provisioning Paris: Merchants and Millers in the Grain and Flour Trade during the Eighteenth Century*. Ithaca: Cornell University Press, 1984.

Kerr-Ritchie, Jeffrey. *Rites of August First: Emancipation Day in the Black Atlantic World*. Baton Rouge: Louisiana State University Press, 2007.

Keuthe, Alan. "The Status of the Free Pardo in the Disciplined Militia of New Granada." *Journal of Negro History* 56 (1971): 105–17.

Larson, Brooke. "Forging the Unlettered Indian: The Pedagogy of Race in the Bolivian Andes." In *Histories of Race and Racism: The Andes and Mesoamerica from Colonial Times to the Present*, ed. Laura Gotkowitz, 134–56. Durham, N.C.: Duke University Press, 2011.

Lasso, Marixa. *Myths of Harmony: Race and Republicanism during the Age of Revolution, Colombia, 1795–1831*. Pittsburgh: University of Pittsburgh Press, 2007.

Lauria-Santiago, Aldo. *An Agrarian Republic: Commercial Agriculture and the Politics of Peasant Communities in El Salvador, 1823–1914*. Pittsburgh: University of Pittsburgh Press, 1999.

Leal, Claudia. "Landscapes of Freedom: The Pacific Coast of Colombia, 1850–1930." Unpublished ms. Bogotá, 2014.

———. "Recordando a Saturio: Memorias del racismo en el Choco." *Revista Estudios Sociales* 27 (August 2007): 76–93.

LeGrand, Catherine. "El conflicto de las bananeras." *Nueva historia de Colombia*, ed. Álvaro Tirado Mejía, 3:183–217. Bogotá: Planeta, 1989.

———. *Frontier Colonization and Peasant Protest in Colombia, 1850–1936*. Albuquerque: University of New Mexico Press, 1986.

———. "Living in Macondo: Economy and Culture in a United Fruit Company Banana Enclave in Colombia." In *Close Encounters of Empire*, ed. Gilbert Joseph, Catherine LeGrand, and Ricardo Salvatore, 333–68. Durham, N.C.: Duke University Press, 1994.

Lemaitre, Eduardo. *Historia general de Cartagena*. Vols. 3-4. Bogotá: Banco de la República, 1983.

———. *Rafael Reyes: Biografía de un gran colombiano*. 3rd ed. Bogotá: 1967.

Levine, Daniel H. "Church Elites in Venezuela and Colombia: Context, Background, and Beliefs." *Latin American Research Review* 14, no. 1 (1979): 51-79.

Levine, Lawrence W. *Black Culture and Black Consciousness*. New York: Oxford University Press, 1977.

———. *Highbrow/Lowbrow: The Emergence of Cultural Hierarchy in America*. Cambridge: Harvard University Press, 1990.

Levine, Robert M. "'Mud-Hut Jerusalem': Canudos Revisited." *Hispanic American Historical Review* 68, no. 3 (August 1988): 525-72.

Liévano Aguirre, Indalecio. *Rafael Núñez y su época*. Bogotá: Áncora, 1985 [1944].

Loaiza Cano, Gilberto. "El maestro de escuela o el ideal liberal de ciudadano en la reforma educativa de 1870." *Historia Crítica* 34 (July-December 2007): 62-91.

———. "*El Neogranadino* y la organización de las hegemonías: contribución a la historia del periodismo colombiano." *Historia Crítica* 18 (December 1999): 65-86.

Lohse, Russell. "Reconciling Freedom with the Rights of Property: Slave Emancipation in Colombia, 1821-1852, with Special Reference to La Plata." *Journal of Negro History* 86 (Summer 2001): 203-27.

Lombardi, John. *The Decline and Abolition of Negro Slavery in Venezuela, 1820-1854*. Westport, Conn.: Greenwood, 1971.

Lomnitz, Claudio. "Nationalism as a Practical System: Benedict Anderson's Theory of Nationalism from the Vantage Point of Spanish America." In *The Other Mirror: Grand Theory through the Lens of Latin America*, ed. Miguel Ángel Centeno and Fernando López-Alves, 329-59. Princeton, N.J.: Princeton University Press, 2000.

Londoño Tamayo, Alejandro. "El juicio por jurados en el proceso de construcción de la justicia en Colombia (1821-1862)." *Historia 2.0* 2, no. 1 (January-June 2012): 57-71.

Londoño-Vega, Patricia. *Religion, Culture, and Society in Colombia: Medellín and Antioquia, 1850-1930*. Oxford: Clarendon, 2002.

Loy, Jane Meyer. "Modernization and Educational Reform in Colombia, 1863-1886." Ph.D. diss., University of Wisconsin, 1969.

———. "Primary Education during the Colombian Federation: The School Reform of 1870," *Hispanic American Historical Review* 51, no. 2 (1971): 275-94.

Maingot, Anthony. "Social Structure, Social Status, and Civil-Military Conflict in Urban Colombia, 1810-1858." In *Nineteenth-Century Cities*, ed. Stephan Thompson and Richard Sennett, 297-355. New Haven,: Yale University Press, 1969.

Mallon, Florencia. *Peasant and Nation: The Making of Postcolonial Mexico and Peru*. Berkeley: University of California Press, 1995.

Marín Tamayo, John Jairo. "La convocatoria del Primer Concilio Neogranadino (1868): un esfuerzo de la jerarquía católica para restablecer la disciplina eclesiástica." *Historia Crítica*, no. 36 (July-December 2008): 201-7.

Martínez, Frédéric. "Las desilusiones del orden público: Los comienzos de la Policía Nacional en Colombia, 1891-1898." In *In Search of a New Order: Essays on the Politics and Society of Nineteenth-Century Latin America*, ed. Eduardo Posada-Carbó, 153-75. London: ILAS, 1998.

———. *El nacionalismo cosmopólitano: la referencia europea en la construcción nacional en Colombia, 1845–1900.* Bogotá: Banco de la República, 2001.

Martínez Carreño, Aída. *La Guerra de los Mil Días.* Bogotá: Planeta, 1999.

Martinez-Alier, Verena. *Marriage, Class and Colour in Nineteenth Century Cuba.* 2nd ed. Ann Arbor: University of Michigan Press, 1989.

Maya Restrepo, Luz Adriana, ed. *Geografía humana de Colombia.* Vol. 6, *Los afrocolombianos.* Bogotá: Instituto Colombiano de Cultura Hispánica, 1998.

McClintock, Ann. "No Longer in a Future Heaven: Women and Nationalism in South Africa." *Transition* 51 (1991): 104–23.

McFarlane, Anthony. "*Cimarrones* and *Palenques*: Runaways and Resistance in Colonial Colombia." *Slavery and Abolition* 6, no. 3 (1985): 131–51.

———. *Colombia before Independence: Economy, Society and Politics under Bourbon Rule.* Cambridge: Cambridge University Press, 1993.

McGerr, Michael E. *The Decline of Popular Politics: The American North, 1865–1928.* New York: Oxford University Press, 1986.

McGraw, Jason. "Purificar la nación: Eugenesia, higiene y renovación moral-racial de la periferia del Caribe colombiano, 1900–1930." *Revista de Estudios Sociales* 27 (August 2007): 62–75.

———. "Spectacles of Freedom: Public Manumissions, Political Rhetoric, and Citizen Mobilisation in Mid-Nineteenth-Century Colombia." *Slavery and Abolition* 32 (June 2011): 269–88.

McGreevey, William. *An Economic History of Colombia, 1845–1930.* Cambridge: Cambridge University Press, 1970.

Mehta, Uday S. "Liberal Strategies of Exclusion." *Politics and Society* 18 (1990): 427–54.

Meisel Roca, Adolfo. "Esclavitud, mestizaje y haciendas en la provincia de Cartagena: 1533–1851." *Desarrollo y sociedad* 4 (July 1980): 227–79.

Meisel Roca, Aldolfo, ed. *Historia económica y social del Caribe colombiano.* Bogotá: Uninorte, 1994.

Melo, Jorge Orlando. "La constitución de 1886." In *Nueva historia de Colombia,* ed. Álvaro Tirado Mejía, 1:43–64. Bogotá: Planeta, 1989.

———. "Del federalismo a la constitución de 1886." In *Nueva historia de Colombia,* ed. Álvaro Tirado Mejía, 1:17–42. Bogotá: Planeta, 1989.

———. "La República conservadora." In *Colombia hoy: Perspectivas hacia el siglo XXI,* 15th ed., ed. Jorge Orlando Melo, 57–101. Bogotá: Tercer Mundo, 1995.

Meza Ricardo, Ubaldo et al., eds. *Primer encuentro de investigadores del Carnaval de Barranquilla.* Barranquilla: Universidad del Atlántico, 1999.

Miller, Raymond C. "The Dockworker Subculture and Problems in Cross-Cultural and Cross-Time Generalizations." *Comparative Studies in Society and History* 11 (1969): 302–14.

Minority Rights Group, ed. *No Longer Invisible: Afro-Latin Americans Today.* London: Minority Rights Report, 1995.

Mintz, Sidney. *Caribbean Transformations.* New York: Columbia University Press, 1989.

Miranda Salcedo, Dalín. "Familia, matrimonio y mujer: el discurso de la iglesia Católica en Barranquilla (1863–1930)." *Historia Crítica* 23 (December 2003): 21–50.

Molina, Gerardo. *Las ideas liberales en Colombia, 1849–1914*. Bogotá: 1974.

Montgomery, David. *Citizen Worker: The Experience of Workers in the United States with Democracy and the Free Market during the Nineteenth Century*. New York: Cambridge University Press, 1993.

Moscarella Varela, Javier, and Julio Barragán. "Hacia una historia ambiental de la subregión Ciénaga Grande de Santa Marta." In *Costa atlántica colombiana: etnología e historia*, ed. Sandra Turbay and Ampara Murillo, 17–40. Medellín: Universidad de Antioquia, 1994.

Mosquera, Claudia, Mauricio Pardo, and Odile Hoffman, eds. *Afrodescendientes en las Américas: Trayectorias sociales e identitárias: 150 años de la abolición de la esclavitud en Colombia*. Bogotá: Universidad Nacional de Colombia, 2002.

Múnera, Alfonso. *El fracaso de la nación: Región, clase y raza en el Caribe colombiano (1717–1810)*. Bogotá: Banco de la República, 1998.

Murillo, Amparo. "Poblamiento y sociedad en el sur de Bolívar." In *Costa atlántica colombiana: Etnología e historia*, ed. Sandra Turbay and Ampara Murillo, 73–98. Medellín: Universidad de Antioquia, 1994.

Neiberg, Michael S. *The Nineteenth Century*. Westport, Conn.: Greenwood, 2006.

Nichols, Theodore E. "The Rise of Barranquilla." *Hispanic American Historical Review* 34, no. 2 (May 1954): 158–74.

———. *Tres puertos de Colombia*. Bogotá: Biblio Banco Popular, 1973.

Nieto Arteta, Luis A. *Economía y cultura en la historia de Colombia*. 2 vols. 3rd ed. Bogotá: Oveja Negra, 1970.

Ortega Ricaurte, Carmen. *Negros, mulatos y zambos en Santafé de Bogotá*. Bogotá: Archivo General de la Nación, 2002.

Ortiz, Lucía, ed. *"Chambacú, la historia la escribes tú": Escritores afrocolombianos*. Madrid/Frankfurt: Iberoamericana/Vervuert, 2007.

Ospina, Joaquín. *Diccionario biográfico y bibliográfico de Colombia*. Vol. 2. Bogotá: Cromos, 1937.

Ospina Vásquez, Luis. *Industria y protección en Colombia, 1810–1930*. Bogotá: Santafé, 1955.

Osterling, Jorge Pablo. *Democracy in Colombia: Clientelist Politics and Guerrilla Warfare*. New Brunswick: Transaction Books, 1989.

Otis, John. "Targeting Teachers: The 'Dirty War' against Colombia's Unions." *GlobalPost*, 9 February 2012, http://www.globalpost.com/dispatch/news/regions/americas/colombia/120207/colombia-unions-teachers-violence, accessed 22 January 2014.

Pachón, Álvaro, and María Teresa Ramírez. *La infraestructura de transporte en Colombia durante el siglo XX*. Bogotá: Banco de la República, 2006.

Palacios, Marco. *Coffee in Colombia, 1850–1970: An Economic, Social and Political History*. Cambridge: Cambridge University Press, 1980.

———. *Estado y clases sociales en Colombia*. Bogotá: Procultura, 1986.

Palacios Prediado, Jorge. *La trata de negros por Cartagena de Indias*. Tunja: Universidad Pedagógica y Tecnológica de Colombia, 1973.

Pardo Rojas, Mauricio, Claudia Mosquera, and María Clemencia Ramírez, eds. *Panorámica afrocolombiana*. Bogotá: ICANH, 2004.

Pardo Rueda, Rafael. *La historia de las guerras*. Bogotá: Ediciones B, 2004.
Park, James W. *Rafael Núñez and the Politics of Colombian Regionalism, 1863–1886*. Baton Rouge: Louisiana University Press, 1986.
Patterson, Orlando. *Slavery and Social Death: A Comparative Study*. Cambridge: Harvard University Press, 1982.
———. "Three Notes on Freedom." In *Paths to Freedom: Manumission in the Atlantic World*, ed. Rosemary Brana-Shute and Randy J. Sparks, 15–30. Columbia: University of South Carolina Press, 2009.
Pérez Escobar, Jacobo. *El negro Robles y su época*. Bogotá: Centro para la Investigación de la Cultura Negra, 2000.
Pineda Botero, Álvaro. *La fábula y el desastre: Estudios críticos sobre la novela colombiana, 1650–1931*. Medellín: Universidad EAFIT, 1999.
Pineda Camacho, Roberto. *El derecho a la lengua: una historia de la política lingüística en Colombia*. Bogotá: Uniandes, 2000.
Pinzón de Lewin, Patricia. *El ejército y las elecciones: ensayo histórico*. Bogotá: CEREC, 1994.
Plazas Olarte, Guillermo. *La Guerra Civil de los Mil Días: estudio militar*. Tunja: Academia Boyacense de Historia, 1985.
Pocock, J. G. A. *The Machiavellian Moment*. Princeton: Princeton University Press, 1975.
Posada-Carbó, Eduardo. "Bongos, champanes y vapores en la navegación fluvial colombiana del siglo XIX." *Boletín Cultural y Bibliográfico* 26 (1989): 2–14.
———. *The Colombian Caribbean: A Regional History, 1870–1950*. Oxford: Oxford University Press, 1996.
———. "Elections before Democracy: Some Considerations on Electoral History from a Comparative Approach." In *Elections before Democracy: The History of Elections in Europe and Latin America*, ed. Eduardo Posada-Carbó, 1–12. London: ILAS, 1996.
———. "Elections and Civil Wars in Nineteenth-Century Colombia: The 1875 Presidential Campaign." *Journal of Latin American Studies* 26, no. 4 (October 1994): 621–49.
———. "Electoral Juggling: A Comparative History of the Corruption of Suffrage in Latin America." *Journal of Latin American Studies* 32, no. 3 (October 2000): 611–44.
———. *Una invitación a la historia de Barranquilla*. Bogotá: CEREC, 1987.
———. "¿Libertad, libertinaje, tiranía? La prensa bajo el Olimpo Radical en Colombia, 1863–1885." Unpublished ms. 2003.
———. "Limits of Power: Elections under the Conservative Hegemony in Colombia, 1886–1930." *Hispanic American Historical Review* 77, no. 2 (1997): 245–79.
———. "New Granada and the European Revolutions of 1848." In *The European Revolutions of 1848 and the Americas*, ed. Guy Thomson, 217–40. London: ILAS, 2002.
———. "Popular and Labour Participation in Colombian Electoral Politics, 1836–1930." In *Workers and "Subalterns": A Comparative Study of Labour in Africa, Asia, and Latin America*, ed. Colin M. Lewis, 9–24. Economic History Working Papers, 73/03. London: London School of Economics and Political Science, 2003.

———. "El puerto de Barranquilla: Entre el auge exportador y el aislamiento, 1850–1950." *Caravelle*, no. 69 (1997): 119–32.

———. "El regionalismo político en la costa caribe." In *El rezago de la costa caribe colombiana*, ed. Haroldo Stevenson and Adolfo Meisel Roca, 331–57. Bogotá: Banco de la República, 1999.

Poveda Ramos, Gabriel. *Vapores fluviales en Colombia*. Bogotá: Tercer Mundo, 1998.

Prescott, Laurence. *Candelario Obeso y la iniciación de la poesía negra en Colombia*. Bogotá: Instituto Caro y Cuerco, 1985.

———. "'*Negro Nací*': Authorship and Voice in Verses Attributed to Candelario Obeso." *Afro-Hispanic Review* 12, no. 1 (Spring 1993): 3–15.

———. *Without Hatred or Fears: Jorge Artel and the Struggle for Black Literary Expression in Colombia*. Detroit: Wayne State University Press, 2000.

Rama, Ángel. *The Lettered City*. Translated by John C. Chasteen. Durham, N.C.: Duke University Press, 1996.

Ramírez, María Teresa, and Irene Salazar. "The Emergence of Education in the Republic of Colombia in the Nineteenth Century: Where Did We Go Wrong?" Unpublished ms. Bogotá, 2008.

Rausch, Jane. *The Llanos Frontier in Colombian History, 1830–1930*. Albuquerque: University of New Mexico Press, 1993.

Rediker, Marcus. *Between the Devil and the Deep Blue Sea*. Cambridge: Cambridge University Press, 1988.

Reinhardt, Nola. "The Consolidation of the Import-Export Economy in Nineteenth-Century Colombia." *Latin American Perspectives* 48 (1986): 75–98.

Restrepo Arteaga, Juan Guillermo. "Educación y desarrollo en Barranquilla a finales del siglo XIX." In *Historia de Barranquilla*, ed. Jorge Villalón Donoso, 153–82. Barranquilla: Uninorte, 2000.

Restrepo Canal, Carlos. *La libertad de los esclavos en Colombia*. Bogotá: Imprenta Nacional, 1938.

Rey Sinning, Edgar. "El retorno eterno del Carnaval de Barranquilla." In *Fiesta y región en Colombia*, ed. Marcos González Pérez, 99–130. Bogotá: Aula Abierta, 1998.

Riascos, Álvaro José. "Two Hundred Years of Colombian Economic Growth." *Latin American Journal of Economics* 48, no. 2 (2011): 181–98.

Ripoll, María Teresa. "El Ingenio Central Colombiano: Un caso en los inicios de la industrialización en el Caribe colombiano." Unpublished ms. Cartagena: University of Cartagena, November 1997.

Rodríguez-Arenas, Flor María. *Bibliografía de la literatura colombiana del siglo XIX*. Vol. 2. Buenos Aires: Stockcero, 2006.

Rodríguez-Bobb, Arturo. *Exclusión e integración del sujeto negro en Cartagena de Indias en perspectiva histórica*. Frankfurt: Vervuert, 2002.

Rodríguez García, José María. "The Regime of Translation in Miguel Antonio Caro's Colombia." *diacritics* 34, nos. 3–4 (2004): 143–75.

Rodríguez Pimienta, José Manuel. *El negro Robles*. Santa Marta: Universidad del Magdalena, 1995.

Rodríguez Piñeres, Eduardo. *El Olimpo radical: ensayos conocidos e inéditos sobre su época*. Bogotá: Librería Voluntad, 1950.

Rojas, Cristina. *Civilization and Violence: Regimes of Representation in Nineteenth-Century Colombia*. Minneapolis: University of Minnesota Press, 2002.

Roldán, Mary. *Blood and Fire: "La Violencia" in Antioquia, Colombia, 1946–1953*. Durham, N.C.: Duke University Press, 2002.

Romero Jaramillo, Dolcey. "Aproximación a la historia de la comunidad negra en el departamento del Atlántico." Unpublished ms. Barranquilla, 1990.

———. "La discriminación racial en Barranquilla." In *Visión sociocultural del negro en Colombia*, ed. Amir Smith Córdoba, 269–76. Bogotá: Centro Investigación Cultural Negra, 1986.

———. *Esclavitud en la provincia de Santa Marta, 1771–1851*. Santa Marta: Fondo de Publicación de Autores Magdalenenses, 1997.

———. "Manumisión, ritualidad y fiesta liberal en la provincia de Cartagena durante el siglo XIX." *Revista Historia Crítica* 29 (January-June 2005): 125–47.

———. "La segunda liberación." In *50 días que cambiaron la historia de Colombia*, 101–5. Bogotá: Planeta, 2005.

Rout, Leslie. *The African Experience in Spanish America*. New York: Cambridge University Press, 1976.

Sabato, Hilda. *The Many and the Few: Political Participation in Republican Buenos Aires*. Stanford, Calif.: Stanford University Press, 2001.

———. "On Political Citizenship in Nineteenth-Century Latin America." *American Historical Review* 106, no. 4 (2001): 1290–315.

Safford, Frank. "Commerce and Enterprise in Central Colombia, 1821–1870." Ph.D. diss., Columbia University, 1965.

———. *The Ideal of the Practical: Colombia's Struggle to Form a Technical Elite*. Austin: University of Texas Press, 1976.

———. "Race, Integration, and Progress: Elite Attitudes and the Indian in Colombia, 1750–1870." *Hispanic American Historical Review* 71, no. 1 (February 1991): 1–33.

———. "Social Aspects of Politics in Nineteenth-Century Spanish America: New Granada, 1825–1850." *Journal of Social History* 5, no. 3 (Spring 1972): 344–70.

Safford, Frank, and Marco Palacios. *Colombia: Fragmented Land, Divided Society*. New York: Oxford University Press, 2002.

Samper, Diego. *Caribbean Carnival: An Exploration of the Barranquilla Carnival*. Bogotá: Andes Editores, 1994.

Samudio Trallero, Alberto. "El crecimiento urbano de Cartagena en el siglo XX: Manga y Bocagrande." In *Cartagena de Indias en el siglo XX*, ed. Haroldo Calvo Stevenson and Adolfo Meisel Roca, 139–74. Bogotá: Banco de la República, 2000.

Sánchez G., Gonzalo, and Mario Aguilera Peña, eds. *Memoria de un país en guerra: los mil días, 1899–1902*. Bogotá: Planeta, 2001.

Sanders, James. "Contentious Republicans: Popular Politics, Race, and Class in Nineteenth-Century Colombia." Ph.D. diss., University of Pittsburgh, 2000.

Santos, Adriana. "Formación de maestros, escuelas normales y misiones pedagógicas: Ejes de la reforma educativa de los radicales en el Estado Soberano del Magdalena." *Anuario de Historia Regional y de las Fronteras* 6 (2001): 295–301.

Saville, Julie. "Rites and Power: Reflections on Slavery, Freedom and Political Ritual."
Slavery and Abolition 20, no. 1 (1999): 81–102.

———. *The Work of Reconstruction: From Slave to Wage Laborer in South Carolina,
1860–1870.* New York: Cambridge University Press, 1996.

Scarano, Francisco A. "The *Jíbaro* Masquerade and the Subaltern Politics of Creole
Identity Formation in Puerto Rico, 1745–1823." *American Historical Review* 101,
no. 5 (December 1996): 1398–1431.

Schmidt-Nowara, Christopher. *Slavery, Freedom, and Abolition in Latin America and
the Atlantic World.* Albuquerque: University of New Mexico Press, 2011.

Scott, Joan W. "On Language, Gender, and Working-Class History." *International
Labor and Working-Class History* 31 (Spring 1987): 1–13.

Scott, Rebecca J. *Degrees of Freedom: Louisiana and Cuba after Slavery.* New York:
Cambridge University Press, 2005.

———. "Public Rights and Private Commerce: A Nineteenth-Century Atlantic Creole
Itinerary." *Current Anthropology* 48 (April 2007): 237–56.

———. *Slave Emancipation in Cuba.* Princeton, N.J.: Princeton University Press,
1988.

Scott, Rebecca J., et al. *Abolition of Slavery and the Aftermath of Emancipation in
Brazil.* Durham, N.C.: Duke University Press, 1988.

Serje, Margarita. *El revés de la nación: territorios salvajes, fronteras y tierras de
nadie.* Bogotá: Universidad de los Andes, 2005.

Sewell, William. "Toward a Post-materialist Rhetoric for Labor History." In
Rethinking Labor History: Essays on Discourse and Class Analysis, ed. Lernard
Berlanstein, 15–38. Urbana: University of Illinois Press, 1993.

Sexta Cátedra Anual de Historia Ernesto Restrepo Tirado. *150 años de la abolición de
la esclavización en Colombia.* Bogotá: Ministerio de Cultura, 2001.

Sharpe, William F. *Slavery on the Spanish Frontier: The Colombia Chocó, 1680–1810.*
Norman: University of Oklahoma Press, 1976.

Simposio sobre Bibliografía del Negro en Colombia. *El negro en la historia de
Colombia.* Bogotá: Fondo Interamericano, 1983.

Skidmore, Thomas. *Black into White: Race and Nationality in Brazilian Thought.*
Durham, N.C.: Duke University Press, 1993.

———. "Racial Ideas and Social Policy in Brazil, 1870–1940." In *The Idea of Race in
Latin America, 1870–1940,* ed. Richard Graham, 7–36. Austin: University of Texas
Press, 1990.

Smith Córdoba, Amir, ed. *Visión sociocultural del negro en Colombia.* Bogotá: Centro
Investigación Cultural Negra, 1986.

Solano, Sergio Paolo. "De bogas a navegantes: Trabajadores del transporte por el Río
Magdalena." *Historia Caribe* 2 (March 1998): 55–70.

———. "Protesta social y cultura política popular en el Caribe colombiano, 1850–
1900." Unpublished ms. Bogotá, 2010.

———. *Puertos, sociedad y conflictos en el Caribe colombiano, 1850–1930.* Cartagena:
Universidad de Cartagena, 2003.

———. "Trabajo y ocio en el Caribe colombiano, 1880–1930." *Historia y Cultura* 4
(1996): 61–76.

Solaún, Mauricio, and Sidney Kronus. *Discrimination without Violence: Miscegenation and Racial Conflict in Latin America*. New York: Wiley, 1973.

Sommer, Doris. *Foundational Fictions: The National Romances of Latin America*. Berkeley and Los Angeles: University of California Press, 1991.

Sourdis Nájera, Adelaida. "Ruptura del Estado colonial y tránsito hacia la República, 1800–1850." In *Historia económica y social del Caribe colombiano*, ed. Adolfo Meisel Roca, 155–228. Bogotá: Uninortes, 1994.

Sowell, David. "The 1893 *Bogotazo*: Artisans and Public Violence in Late Nineteenth-Century Bogotá." *Journal of Latin American Studies* 21, nos. 1–2 (June 1989): 267–82.

———. *The Early Colombian Labor Movement: Artisans and Politics in Bogotá, 1838–1919*. Philadelphia: Temple University Press, 1992.

Stanley, Amy Dru. *From Bondage to Contract: Wage Labor, Marriage, and the Market in the Age of Slave Emancipation*. New York: Cambridge University Press, 1998.

Stedman Jones, Gareth. *Languages of Class: Studies in English Working Class History, 1832–1982*. Cambridge: Cambridge University Press, 1984.

Steiner, Claudia. *Imaginación y poder: el encuentro del interior con la costa en Urabá, 1900–1960*. Medellín: Universidad de Antioquia, 2000.

Taussig, Michael. *The Devil and Commodity Fetishism in South America*. Chapel Hill: University of North Carolina Press, 1980.

Taylor, Charles. *Multiculturalism: Examining the Politics of Recognition*. Ed. Amy Guttman. Princeton, N.J.: Princeton University Press, 1994.

Thompson, Edward P. "Time, Work-Discipline and Industrial Capitalism." *Past and Present* 38 (December 1967): 56–97.

Tilly, Charles. "Citizenship, Identity and Social History." In *Citizenship, Identity and Social History*, ed. Charles Tilly, 1–17. Cambridge: Cambridge University Press, 1995.

Tirado Mejía, Álvaro. *Aspectos sociales de las guerras civiles en Colombia*. Bogotá, 1976.

———. "El Estado y la política en el siglo XIX." In *Nueva historia de Colombia*, ed. Álvaro Tirado Mejía, 2:155–83. Bogotá: Planeta, 1989.

Tirado Mejía, Álvaro, ed. *Nueva historia de Colombia*. 3 vols. Bogotá: Planeta, 1989.

Torres Almeida, Jesús C. *Manuel Murillo Toro: caudillo radical y reformador social*. Bogotá: El Tiempo, 1985.

Torres Giraldo, Ignacio. *Los inconformes: historia de la rebeldía de las masas en Colombia*. Vol. 3. Bogotá: Margen Izquierdo, 1973.

Tovar Pinzón, Hermes. "Los baldíos y el problema agrario en la costa caribe." *Fronteras* 1 (1998): 35–55.

Tovar Zambrano, Bernardo. "La economía colombiana (1886–1922)." *Nueva historia de Colombia*, ed. Álvaro Tirado Mejía, 5:37–49. Bogotá: Planeta, 1989.

Trouillot, Michel-Rolph. *Silencing the Past: Power and the Production of History*. Boston: Beacon, 1995.

Turner, Mary. *From Chattel Slaves to Wage Slaves: The Dynamics of Labour Bargaining in the Americas*. Bloomington: Indiana University Press, 1995.

Uribe de Hincapié, María Teresa, and Liliana María López Lopera. *La Guerra por las soberanías: memorias y relatos en la guerra civil de 1859-1862 en Colombia.* Medellín: La Carreta, 2008.

Urrutia, Miguel. *The Development of the Colombian Labor Movement.* New Haven, Conn.: Yale University Press, 1969.

Urrutia, Miguel, and Mario Arrubla. *Compendio de estadísticas históricas de Colombia.* Bogotá: Universidad Nacional de Colombia, 1970.

Valdelamar Sarabia, Lázaro, and Javier Ortiz Cassiani. Prologue. In *Cantos populares de mi tierra, secundino el zapatero,* by Candelario Obeso. Cartagena: Universidad de Cartagena, 2009.

Valdés, Dennis Nodin. "The Decline of Slavery in Mexico." *Americas* 44, no. 2 (1987): 167-94.

Valencia Llano, Alonso. "De los bandidos y políticos caucanos: el general Manuel María Victoria, 'El Negro.'" *Historia y Espacio* 19 (2002): 153-79.

Van Ausdal, Shawn. "The Logic of Livestock: An Historical Geography of Cattle Ranching in Colombia, 1850-1950." Ph.D. diss., University of California at Berkeley, 2009.

Van Young, Eric. *The Other Rebellion: Popular Violence, Ideology and the Mexican Struggle for Independence.* Stanford, Calif.: Stanford University Press, 2001.

Vargas, Ricardo. "State, *Esprit Mafioso,* and Armed Conflict in Colombia." In *Politics in the Andes: Identity, Conflict and Reform,* ed. Jo-Marie Burt and Philip Mauceri, 107-25. Pittsburgh: University of Pittsburgh Press, 2004.

Vega Cantor, Renán. *Gente muy rebelde: Protesta popular y modernización capitalista en Colombia (1909-1929).* 4 vols. Bogotá: Pensamiento Crítico, 2002.

Vélez, Humberto. "Rafael Reyes: Quinquenio, régimen político y capitalismo (1904-1909)." In *Nueva historia de Colombia,* ed. Álvaro Tirado Mejía, 1:187-214. Bogotá: Planeta, 1989.

Venture Young, Ann, ed. *The Image of Black Women in Twentieth-Century South American Poetry.* Washington, D.C.: Three Continents Press, 1987.

Villa, William, ed. *Comunidades negras: Territorio y desarrollo.* Medellín: Indymeión/SWISSAID, 1996.

Viloria de la Hoz, Joaquín. "Empresarios de Santa Marta: El caso de Joaquín y Manuel de Mier, 1800-1896." *Cuadernos de historia económica y empresarial,* no. 7. Cartagena: Banco de la República, November 2000.

Vos Obeso, Rafaela. *Mujer, cultura y sociedad: Barranquilla, 1900-1930.* Barranquilla: Universidad del Atlántico, 1999.

Wade, Peter. *Blackness and Race Mixture: The Dynamics of Racial Identity in Colombia.* Baltimore: Johns Hopkins University Press, 1993.

———. "The Cultural Politics of Blackness in Colombia." *American Ethnologist* 22 (May 1995): 341-57.

———. *Music, Race, and Nation: "Música Tropical" in Colombia.* Chicago: University of Chicago Press, 2000.

———. *Race and Sex in Latin America.* London: Pluto, 2009.

———. "Racial Identity and Nationalism: A Theoretical View from Latin America." *Ethnic and Racial Studies* 25 (September 2001): 845-65.

Walker, Charles. *Smoldering Ashes: Cuzco and the Creation of Republican Peru, 1780–1840*. Durham, N.C.: Duke University Press, 1999.

Weinstein, Barbara. *For Social Peace in Brazil: Industrialists and the Remaking of the Working Class in Sao Paulo, 1920–1964*. Chapel Hill: University of North Carolina Press, 1997.

Wheat, Valerie J. "Nineteenth Century Black Dialect Poetry and Racial Pride: Candelario Obeso's *Cantos populares de mi tierra* and Paul Laurence Dunbar's *Lyrics of Lowly Life*." *Afro-Hispanic Review* 15, no. 2 (Fall 1996): 26–36.

Wolfe, Justin. "'The Cruel Whip': Race and Place in Nineteenth-Century Nicaragua." In *Blacks and Blackness in Central America: Between Race and Place*, ed. Lowell Gudmundson and Justin Wolfe, 177–208. Durham: Duke University Press, 2011.

Wong Hiu, Alberto. "Sociedad y política en Barranquilla durante el periódo federal (1857–1886)." In *Historia de Barranquilla*, ed. Jorge Villalón Donoso, 135–52. Barranquilla: Uninorte, 2000.

Wrigley, Richard. *The Politics of Appearances: Representations of Dress in Revolutionary France*. New York: Bloomsbury Academic, 2002.

Zambrano, Fabio. *Colombia: País de regiones*. Vol. 1. Bogotá: CINEP, 1998.

Zambrano Pérez, Milton. *El desarrollo del empresariado en Barranquilla, 1880–1945*. Barranquilla: Universidad del Atlántico, 1998.

Zapata Olivella, Manuel. *El hombre colombiano*. Bogotá: Canal Ramírez-Antares, 1974.

Index

Acosta, Joaquín, 81–82
Acosta de Samper, Soledad, 114, 121, 127
Africa, 172
African American colonization, 113–14
African Diaspora: Colombia's place in, 3, 11, 14, 17
Afro-Colombians: population of, 2, 230; slavery conflated with, 2–3, 37, 114; and Obeso's vision of citizenship, 2–3, 118–22, 124, 229; histories of, 3; as *bogas*, 75; barbarism associated with, 112, 231; and popular politics, 137–40; and Catholic Church, 172; and triethnic amalgam, 222; and political culture, 223; and *mestizaje*, 228–29; recognition of, 229–31
Age of Revolution, 6, 224
Aguilar, Frederico, 171, 172, 176
Ancízar, Manuel, 80, 104, 112, 123
Antúñez, Manuel, 26
Apprenticeship system, 24
Araújo, D. H., 113
Arboleda, Julio, 47, 68, 69
Arboleda, Sergio, 47, 127, 152
Arhuaco people, 208, 228
Arosemena, Justo, 127
Arosemena, Pablo, 154
Artel, Jorge, 234 (n. 8)
Artisans: and emancipation, 21, 27, 40; and citizenship, 24; and democratic societies, 24–25; and equality, 34, 40; on free trade, 34, 44; and debtors' prison, 38; and jury trials, 38, 40–41, 43; and race mixing, 41–42; and size of army, 44; and military coup of 1854, 47; and Nieto, 57; and market economy, 73; and female labor, 78–79; and steamboats, 92; and Carnival, 137; and popular politics, 138;

and Catholic Church, 147–48; and Rafael Núñez, 155, 156, 165, 181, 208; and labor organizations, 180–81; and Thousand Days' War, 208, 209, 210
Authoritarian ethos, 164, 167
Authority: punishment for disrespect for, 38, 88, 166, 179, 183, 186, 206; of individual leaders, 72; in public opinion, 127; and popular politics, 132–33, 147, 150, 163; of Catholic Church, 167–68, 169; of Congress, 220
Azuero, Pedro Navas, 56–57

Ballestas, Benigno, 144
Banana industry, 16, 215, 217, 220, 221, 223
Barbarism: and *letrados*, 13, 100, 117; barbarian democracy, 47, 50; and education, 108, 109, 110; Afro-Colombians associated with, 112, 231; white civilization distinguished from, 112–13; Obeso on, 121, 126; and marriage and divorce rights, 152
Barranquilla, Colombia: demographic patterns of, 14, 16; and Liberal Party, 17, 150, 201–2; as commercially dynamic settlement, 22, 92; social class in, 26; manumission ceremonies in, 30; and cholera epidemics, 40, 49, 188; education in, 102, 110; and popular politics, 134; Carnival in, 137, 158, 167, 168, 210, 223–24; cemetery of, 147–48, 158; and San Roque church, 149, 168, 224; and Gaitán Obeso, 160–61; marketplace of, 183–84; and poor relief, 188; and Thousand Days' War, 208, 210
Barrera, Plácido, 82, 83

Belonging: means of, 1; universal sense of, 2, 6; and emancipation, 4, 5, 18; egalitarian modes of, 6, 34, 37; religious belonging, 7; vernacular sense of, 8; and public-private distinctions, 10; Obeso on, 101, 122; erudition and philology as markers of, 111; local boundaries of, 132; and inequality, 227

Black Atlantic: studies of, 19

Bogas: kinship relations of, 5, 78, 79, 85; and independence from wages, 8, 78, 79, 80, 81, 82, 85, 87, 96; strike of 1857, 10, 13, 74, 85–91, 98; as feminized, uncivilized labor force, 10, 80; as term, 11; commercial capital against, 13; and military coup of 1854, 45; and trade recession, 55; and *champanes*, 73, 75–78, 79, 82, 83, 91, 94, 158, 177; *inspección de bogas*, 74, 82–85, 94; and patrones, 75, 77, 79, 82, 83, 84, 86, 87–88, 89, 90; and free trade, 75, 78, 80; and merchants, 77, 78, 79–84, 85, 89; control of labor, 77–78, 80, 91, 173; anti-*boga* rhetoric, 80–81, 82, 89, 92–93, 98, 119, 176, 225, 226; and *boga* clause, 81, 88, 178; and postal service, 86–87, 88, 89, 90; and civil war of 1859–62, 89; and delays in wage payments, 90–91; and steamboats, 91–92; leisure strikes, 97; and labor policies, 99; Obeso on, 101; and *costumbrismo*, 115, 116; and taxation, 142, 158, 177; and sexual deviancy, 152; and Catholic Church, 168; diminishing presence of, 176–77; and Thousand Days' War, 205–6, 211, 214, 218

Bogotá, Colombia: and Obeso, 1, 104, 125, 129; artisans of, 24, 27, 34, 40, 138, 169, 181; and abolitionist petitions, 28; demographics of, 40; and military coup of 1854, 47; and 1861 conquest by Liberal armies, 60, 66–67, 129, 160; and women, 63, 125; and *letrados*, 99–100; and Thousand Days' War, 196; marketplaces of, 214

Bolívar, Simón, 44, 45–46, 65, 144, 157, 158, 224

Bolívar Railway, 143–44, 158, 178, 180, 182, 210, 212, 220

Borda, Francisco de Paula, 63, 217

Borda, Orlando Fals, 228

Brazil: slaves fleeing into New Granada, 24

Briceño, Manuel, 117, 127

Calamar, Colombia, 78, 86–88, 89, 92, 93, 142, 144, 211

Calvo, Juan Antonio: on municipal elections, 26; on egalitarian ethos, 40, 41; and military coup of 1854, 46–47; and civil war of 1859–62, 52; and pre-civil war protests, 53, 54; Nieto's coup against, 57–59, 60, 63, 65, 66, 89; and *bogas*, 86, 87–88, 90, 93

Calvo, Juan Bernardo, 46–47

Camacho, Plácido, 198

Camacho Roldán, Salvador, 38, 85–86, 145, 150, 177, 187

Campo Serrano, José M., 154, 217–18

La Candelaria, 146

Capital punishment, 38, 39, 55, 89–90, 161, 220

Caribbean Colombia: paradox of emancipatory citizenship in, 5–6; and military coup of 1854, 13, 21, 44–46, 47; geography of, 14; demographics of, 14, 16, 17; population centers of, 14, 16–17; slavery in, 17, 24, 28; and presidential election of 1856, 49, 54; and civil war of 1859–62, 70; highland peons compared to laborers of, 79; education in, 102, 172, 223; and Catholic Church, 165, 169, 171–73. *See also* Barranquilla, Colombia; Cartagena, Colombia; Magdalena River; Mompós, Colombia; Santa Marta, Colombia

Carmona, Francisco, 44, 46, 137

Carnival, 44, 95, 137, 157, 158, 167, 168, 210, 223–24

59–64, 69, 191, 197; and economic recession, 60; and race war, 64–68; and "Death to the Whites" slogan, 65; postwar analysis of, 68–72; political violence following, 71–72

Claver, Pedro, 18, 153, 167–68, 171, 172, 224

Coffee industry, 12, 91, 178, 179, 220

Colegio Militar, 104, 160

Colegio Ribón, 110

Colombia: population centers of, 14, 16–17; Claver as patron saint of, 18, 167–68, 172, 224; emancipation in, 22–29; formation of United States of Colombia, 52, 62, 64, 70, 72, 89; formation of Republic of Colombia, 164; social inequality in, 226–27; neoliberal reforms in, 230. *See also* Caribbean Colombia; Cauca Valley, Colombia; Congress; Constitutions; Magdalena River; Pacto de Unión

Colombian Academy of Language, 110, 116

Commercial interests: and public sphere, 19; and steamboats, 91–93, 178; and Regeneration, 176–79, 182–83. *See also* Market economy; Merchants

Compañía Colombiana de Transportes (CCT), 178–79, 180, 181, 182, 212–13

Compañia Fluvial de Cartagena, 189

Concordat (1887), 166–67, 169

Congress: and 1851 emancipation act, 21, 28–29; and López's legitimacy, 25; and abolition, 28; and letters of freedom for fugitive slaves, 33; and constitution of 1853, 35; and size of army, 44, 47–48; and Conservative Party, 47; and national intervention in state elections, 56; and 1867 coup, 72; and Piña Channel, 81; and education, 101, 102, 107; and Obeso, 126, 128; authority of, 220

Congress of Cúcuta, 23–24

Conservative Party: in Caribbean Colombia, 18, 25–28, 44; compromise with Liberals, 21, 47, 48, 127, 155;

popular societies of, 25; and emancipation, 28, 32, 39, 43; and egalitarian ethos, 36, 39, 43; and marriage and divorce rights, 36, 151–52, 153; and military coup of 1854, 45–46, 47; and presidential election of 1856, 49–50, 51; and civil war of 1859–62, 52–53, 64–68; and pre–civil war protests, 53–56; and language of democracy and emancipation, 68–69; uprising of 1876, 71, 109–11, 120, 126, 139, 158; and education, 101, 109–10, 111, 127; coalition with Independents, 127, 156, 161, 164; and Gaitán Obeso's movement, 160–61; alliances with Liberals (Radicals), 173, 175; and Thousand Days' War, 201, 206, 208

Constitution: of 1853, 8, 21, 35–37, 38, 42–43, 50, 81, 227; of 1863, 25, 81, 90, 112; of 1858, 81; of 1886, 161–63, 165, 166, 171, 177, 212, 224; constitutional reforms of 1910, 223; of 1991, 229, 230. *See also* Rionegro Constitution of 1863

Cortés, Enrique, 119

Costumbrismo: and citizenship, 7–8, 133; racial stereotypes in, 100, 174, 227; and *bogas*, 115, 116; and social types, 115–16; and women of color, 118–19; and national romances, 122; and barbarism, 126

Cotes, Miguel, 154

Criminal justice system, 37–41

Cuba, 10, 224, 226

Cuervo, Rufino, 115

Cunin, Elisabeth, 229

Debtors' prison, 27, 38–39, 55, 84

De Lesseps, Ferdinand, 138

De Mier, Joaquín, 23

De Mier, Manuel Julián, 144

Democratic culture: and social status, 6; egalitarian ethos, 9, 12, 21, 34–43, 52, 57, 62, 65, 106, 113, 152–53, 154; experiments in, 21; and emancipation,

29, 51; antidemocratic attitudes, 45–46, 49, 156, 158, 161

Democratic societies: and education, 24–25, 103; support for López administration, 25, 26, 27, 59, 136; as multiracial, 26; and Catholic Church, 27, 146; and manumission ceremonies, 30; and Obando, 47; and Rafael Núñez, 135

Díaz Castro, Eugenio, 84, 115, 116

Dique Canal, 86, 96, 189, 198, 217

Discrimination: and recognition, 6, 227; and public-private distinctions, 10, 37, 42; ethos against, 21, 34, 36, 37, 41, 42, 43, 106, 113, 136, 138; and Gólgota faction, 43; artisan critics of, 138; contested meanings of, 142; Catholic Church's disavowal of, 152–53

Disenfranchisement: consequences of, 13, 163, 164–65, 175, 189; and recognition, 14, 223; Claver as symbolic replacement for rights, 168, 224; and Thousand Days' War, 197, 205, 213, 218; persistence of, 221

Divorce: equal rights to, 35–36, 48, 150, 151–52; and Catholic Church, 36, 150, 151–52, 154, 156, 159, 166, 171, 187, 221; repeal of, 48, 150, 161, 166, 187

Doña Juana (Enviadista leader), 193

Dovale, Antenor, 33, 34

Durán, Justo, 202–3

Economic development, 74, 100

Economic privileges, 36

Economic recession of 1858–60: and social class, 55; and Conservative Party, 56; and civil war of 1859–62, 60; and tobacco exports, 88; and steamboats, 91–92

Economic recession of 1890s, 165, 179, 191

Education: and *letrados*, 8, 13, 100, 102, 111, 112, 169; and democratic societies, 24–25, 103; standards in, 36, 101–2, 105, 106; universal primary education, 100, 105–11, 112, 134;

and Catholic Church, 101, 109–10, 145, 149, 152, 157, 166, 169–71; and double freedom of learning, 101–2, 105, 109; and citizenship, 102, 105, 107, 112; national spending on, 105, 111, 170, 254 (n. 18); and teacher preparation programs, 107, 108, 109, 111; and Robles, 107–9; and enrollment, 108–9, 170; female education, 111, 114, 127, 138, 170; and urban and rural areas, 170

Elites: and cholera epidemic, 39–40; and social inclusion, 42; and military coup of 1854, 45; and race war, 65; and education, 102, 110–11, 127, 152, 169–70; Obeso's relationship with, 125; and Catholic Church, 168; and Thousand Days' War, 201

Emancipation: Obeso on, 2, 3, 19; sesquicentennial of, 3, 230; pessimism toward, 4; as expression of political affinity, 5; and rights of adult males, 7, 8; and racial difference, 11, 127, 228; democratic legacy of, 13, 49, 101, 127, 197, 224; and national antislavery consensus, 21; and race abolished as category in law, 34; and universal manhood suffrage, 35; and marriage and divorce rights, 35–36; and civil war of 1859–62, 52, 65, 69, 224; and labor and industry, 74; and monopolies, 80–81; legal reforms of, 81; and *bogas*, 84; and *letrados*, 99, 101, 110; and Rafael Núñez, 135. *See also* Freedom

Employment: rise in unemployment, 51, 55, 220, 221. *See also* Labor

Enviadistas, 190–94, 196, 198, 219, 221

El Enviado de Dios (The One Sent from God), 13, 18, 166, 190–94, 196, 221

Equality: and freedom, 4–5, 11, 13, 34; redefinitions of, 21; ethos of, 34–43, 51, 127, 136, 142, 146; antiegalitarian arguments, 42–43; Obeso's belief in, 125

Escalante, Aquiles, 234 (n. 8)
Esguerra, Nicolás, 217
Eugenics, 222, 227
Europe: revolutions in, 24; libertarian and revolutionary ideas from, 27; and ideas of progress, 100; eugenics studies, 222

Families, 5, 10, 11, 22, 40, 101, 106, 167; and legitimacy claims, 7, 133, 149–54, 163, 187, 192, 223; perceived threats to, 53, 66, 68, 200, 207; of elites, 66, 102, 110, 134, 137, 139, 144, 145, 146, 166; of *bogas*, 78–80, 87, 115; and private life, 110, 157, 169, 183; of color, 112, 143; Obeso on, 117–19, 126
Federal system, 51–52, 54, 56, 65, 105, 108, 127, 135
Female labor, 78, 79, 87, 98, 185; male dependence on, 35, 80; as artisanal, 78–79; and politics, 135–36
Feminism, 111, 114, 121
Fifa, Pedro, 86
Fishermen, 16, 141, 142, 143–44, 146, 167, 173, 205, 213
Fraser, Nancy, 6, 229
Freedom: and citizenship, 2, 4, 5, 21; and equality, 4–5, 11, 13, 34; contested meanings of, 6, 19, 21, 74, 223, 225, 226, 227; vernacular understandings of, 7; rhetoric of, 32, 37, 81; and industry, 74, 81, 98, 101, 133, 155, 165; and labor, 74, 81, 98, 101, 155, 165; press freedom, 112, 114, 161, 175, 181, 220. *See also* Emancipation
Free people of African descent, 22–23, 26, 75
French Revolution, 31

Gaitán Obeso, Ricardo: movement of, 160–61, 171, 173, 174, 191, 197, 210, 218; remembrance of, 166; death of, 194
Galindo, Aníbal, 4–5, 11, 127
García, Eusebio "La Pulga," 20

García, Vicente, 31–32
Garizábalo, José, 198
Garrapata, Battle of, 120, 128
Gender: and race, 10, 11, 114, 122, 187, 227; and war, 14, 63; distinctions between men and women, 35; and political exclusion, 70; and social class, 110, 168, 223; and Catholic Church, 168. *See also* Market women; Men; White men; White women; Women of color
Gold standard: abandonment of, 165, 180
Gólgota faction, 41, 43, 47, 48, 53, 70, 134
Gómez, Ramón, 98, 154
González, Dionisio, 90
González, Florentino, 47, 48
González Carazo, Antonio, 61, 63, 154
Granadine Confederation, 51–52, 58, 59–60, 62, 68
Great Britain, 27
Guajiro (Wayúu) people, 54, 68, 208, 228
Guerrero, Casimira, 214
Guerrero, José María, 36
Guerrilla warfare. *See* Thousand Days' War
Gutiérrez, Pascual, 20
Gutiérrez de Piñeres, Juan A., 45, 64–65, 66

Haciendas, 42, 57, 158, 190, 216; and slavery, 17, 22, 23; Hacienda San Pedro Alejandrino, 144, 224
Haiti, 224
Hernández, D. G., 86
Hernández, Inocencia, 186
Hernández Cárdenas, Rafael, 198
Holt, Thomas, 225
Honda, Colombia, 76, 82, 83, 86, 91, 92, 93

Independent Liberal faction, 126, 127, 130, 155–58, 160, 161, 164. *See also* Núñez, Rafael

Indigenous Colombians: and perceived social exclusion, 50, 69, 152; as *bogas*, 75; as Andean peons, 79; claims of vanishing Indians, 176; and Thousand Days' War, 197, 208; civilization of, 221; and *mestizaje*, 228–29

Industry: and freedom, 74, 81, 98, 101, 133, 155, 165, 190

Isaacs, Jorge, 115, 116, 118, 128

Jamaica, 224

Jefes Civiles y Militares, 195, 204

Jesuits: expulsion of, 25, 145, 171; as missionaries, 165, 171–72, 173, 221, 222; and El Enviado de Dios, 193

Jews, 40, 148

Jiménez López, Miguel, 222

Jury trials, 38–41, 102, 105, 162

Kogui people, 228

Labor: defined as prerogative of state, 8, 74, 90; and citizenship, 8, 177–79, 212, 221; and inclusion and exclusion, 9; material conditions of, 11; discipline of, 13; obscurity of, 18; and public sphere, 19; and freedom, 74, 81, 98, 101, 155, 165; and wages, 82–83, 98, 165, 220; surveillance of, 84, 165, 210; social structure of skilled and unskilled labor, 93; and Regeneration redefinition of, 177–82, 212; organization of, 180–81, 222–23, 230; and strikes, 181–82, 220, 221, 222, 223; and Thousand Days' War, 209–15

Laborers: and voter registration, 25; alliance with prominent men, 27; and emancipation, 27; and Obando, 44; and military coup of 1854, 45; and economic recession, 55; and Nieto, 57; role in public life, 72; women as, 78–79, 185–87; and delays in wage payments, 90; and steamboats, 91–98, 161, 179, 180; as peons, 92, 96; and Carnival, 137; and taxation,

142–43; declining wages, 180–81, 182, 191, 209, 220; and Thousand Days' War, 205, 206, 209, 210–12

Land invasions, 144, 155, 158, 216. *See also* Peasants

Landless people: and Regeneration, 10; civil standing of, 37, 38; and military coup of 1854, 45; and economic recession, 55; and suffrage, 70, 72, 134, 162, 164, 167, 174, 178, 221

Landowners, 39, 141, 158

Language: and education, 107, 110, 111; vernacular language, 115–16, 117

Lawmaking, 7, 11, 20–21, 23–24, 29, 34–40, 48, 56, 63, 154, 212

Legitimacy of children, 7, 149–54, 163

Letrados: Obeso as *letrado*, 1, 101, 122, 128, 138; on freedom, 4; and print culture, 7, 99, 100; and citizenship, 8, 9–10, 100, 127; and education, 8, 13, 100, 102, 111, 112, 169; and public sphere, 9, 13, 19, 42, 99, 112, 114; and literacy, 13, 100, 102, 113, 134; and Conservatives, 39; and social class, 43, 44; and foreign trade, 43–44; and size of army, 43–44; and universal manhood suffrage, 48, 134; and López administration, 52; and civil war of 1859–62, 64, 70; and race war, 65; and Mosquera, 72; and *bogas*, 74, 177, 225, 226; on steamboats, 93; and emancipation, 99, 101; and plebeian citizens, 99, 102–3, 157; and civil service positions, 112; and racial etiquette, 113–15, 129; folk culture interpreted by, 116–17; Obeso's ambivalence toward, 125–27; and Carnival, 137; and Catholic Church, 145; and marriage law, 154; on Claver, 167–68; and Hispanic descent claims, 172; and black personae, 173–74; and labor, 177; on prostitution, 187; and Thousand Days' War, 196, 201, 218

Liberal Party: rise of, 12; and intra-Liberal rivalries, 18, 134–35, 138–40,

155–57, 158, 160–61, 173; compromise with Conservatives, 21, 47, 48, 127, 155; and egalitarian ethos, 39; and election of 1856, 48–49; and election of 1862, 52; and civil war of 1859–62, 52–53, 60, 61, 62, 63, 64, 65, 224; and pre–civil war protests, 53–55; and coup against Calvo, 57–58; and proclamations, 58–59, 60; and secessionist movement, 59; and popular politics, 60, 133–45; and *bogas*, 88–89; and education, 100, 109, 111, 155; alliances with Conservatives, 127, 156, 161, 164, 173, 175; and Rafael Núñez, 133; and racial etiquette, 137; and Catholic Church, 145–49, 151–52, 155, 156, 158, 159, 207–8; and marriage, 149–54; and constitution of 1886, 162–63; political base of, 165; and antigovernment demonstrations, 166; breakdown of organization, 173, 174; uprising of 1895, 191, 196, 200, 217; and Thousand Days' War, 195, 196, 197, 198, 199, 200, 201–4, 205, 206, 207–8, 210, 211, 214, 215, 218; return to power in 1930, 223

Literacy: and preliterate society, 7; illiteracy as trope for postemancipation citizenship, 8; as standard for political inclusion, 8, 70, 72, 134; and racial marking, 10; and social class, 11; and *letrados*, 13, 100, 102, 113, 134; and egalitarian ethos, 35; and jury trials, 38; as suffrage qualification, 70, 72, 134, 162, 164, 167, 174, 178, 221; and citizenship, 105, 106; and morality, 106; illiteracy as defect, 117; Obeso on, 123; illiteracy rates, 170; and racial ideology, 227

Locke, John, 121

López, José Hilario: reforms under, 20–21, 37; and democratic societies, 25, 26, 27, 59, 136; and emancipation, 27, 28, 29, 31, 32; and manumission ceremonies, 29, 32, 33, 43; and equality, 34; and jury trials, 38, 39; appointees of, 41; and military coup of 1854, 44; and compromise with Conservatives, 47; and decentralization of governmental powers, 48; and *letrados*, 52; and education, 101; and Rafael Núñez, 135; and Catholic Church, 145

López de Mesa, Luis, 222

Lugo, José María, 198

Macheteros (machete wielders), 53, 64, 66, 67, 71, 72, 201

Macías, Agustín, 221

Madiedo, Manuel María, 69–70, 84, 113, 115

Magangué, Colombia, 14, 16, 77, 92, 135, 142; trade fair, 73, 79, 177

Magdalena River, 46, 73–86; geography of, 14; and trade, 16, 75; and smallholders, 78, 87; and communications, 81, 85–87; and Catholic Church, 171; and Thousand Days' War, 210–11; and race mixing, 222. See also *Bogas*

Mallarino, Manuel María, 47, 135

Manrique, Venancio G., 118, 125, 128

Mantaño, José, 82

Manumission: public ceremonies for, 21, 29–34, 36, 39, 42, 43, 136; manumission juntas, 23–24, 27, 28, 29, 30, 32; and liberty caps, 31; rate of, 32; perspectives on, 224–25

Marco, Rudecindo, 86

Marín, Ramón "El Negro," 197

Market economy: labor in, 8; and rights and duties, 9; of Caribbean Colombia, 16; role of *bogas* in, 73, 74, 75, 82, 88; state-led economic reforms, 74–75

Marketplaces: control of, 183–88; and Thousand Days' War, 214

Market women: kinship relations of, 5, 79; and independence from wages, 8; and steamboats, 96; and Catholic Church, 168; and education, 173;

protests of, 184–85; regulation of, 186–88; and El Enviado de Dios, 193; and Thousand Days' War, 213–14; freedom of, 224; occupation of public places, 226

Marriage: equal rights to, 35–36, 48; rights to civil marriage, 48, 150, 151–52, 153, 154, 159, 161; and legitimacy, 149–54, 163; and Regeneration, 187–88

Marroquín, José Manuel, 91, 107, 110, 115, 200, 203, 215

Marroquín, Lorenzo, 218–19

Marx, Karl, 224

Melista coup. *See* Military coup of 1854

Melo, José María: military coup of, 44–46, 47, 48, 50, 52, 54, 55, 59, 61, 65; and democratic societies, 53; and civil war of 1859–62, 67; and Rafael Núñez, 135

Men: equal rights to marriage and divorce, 35–36; Obeso on white men, 118, 119–21, 123–24, 126. *See also* Gender; Universal manhood suffrage

Mendoza, Ignacio, 132–33, 138, 163

Meneses (*champán patrón*), 198

Mercado Robles, Joaquín, 198

Merchants: and lack of social control, 8–9, 77, 95, 212–13; and Conservatives, 39; and military coup of 1854, 45; and *bogas*, 77, 78, 79–84, 85, 89; and taxation, 141, 182

Mestizaje, 3, 176, 222, 228–29, 230

Military: military conscription, 9, 63, 212, 213; military service, 13, 58, 60, 70, 71, 203, 208, 212, 218; Obeso on, 120, 129

Military coup of 1854 (Melista coup): and Caribbean Colombia, 13, 21, 44–46, 47; and postcoup political order, 47–50, 52, 54, 55, 61, 65

Mina, José Cinecio, 197

Miranda, Ensermo, 79

Miranda, Juan, 77, 79

Mompós, Colombia: demography of, 14, 16; and outmigration, 22; artisans of, 27; and 1851 emancipation act, 29; and manumission juntas, 30; pre–civil war protest in, 53, 54, 55; antigovernment demonstrations in, 166

Money inflation, 55, 165, 179–83, 189–90, 204; in wartime, 199, 205, 209, 213, 217

Monopolies: and Regeneration, 20, 165, 178, 179, 182, 188–89; abolition of, 74; and *bogas*, 80–82, 91, 153; political monopoly of Bogotá, 155

Morales Benítez, Otto, 228

Morality: and labor, 11; and emancipation, 12; and egalitarian ethos, 39, 40; and gender, 63; and literacy, 106; and education, 106–7, 110; and *costumbrismo*, 115; Obeso on, 128; and Catholic Church, 150, 152, 153, 161–62, 167, 176; and sex, 152; and marriage and divorce law, 153; and citizenship, 167

Moreno Pupo, Pedro, 86

Mosquera, Tomás C.: seizure of manumission process, 31; and cholera epidemic, 40, 49; and military coup of 1854, 44, 45, 46, 59; and presidential election of 1856, 48–49; Nieto's alliance with, 52, 59, 134, 218; and Pacto de Unión, 60, 70; and civil war of 1859–62, 61, 62–63, 66–67, 68, 129, 201; deposing of, 72; and *inspección de bogas*, 82; and *bogas*, 84, 89; and steamboats, 91; and Colegio Militar, 104, 160; and African American colonization, 114; and Rafael Núñez, 135, 154; and Liberal Party, 135, 155, 161; and salt tax, 140; and poor relief, 141; and Catholic Church, 145

Multiculturalism, 229, 230–31

Murillo Toro, Manuel: on equality, 34–35, 43; on universal manhood suffrage, 35; and compromise with Conservatives, 47; and presidential election of 1856, 48–50; and emancipation, 49; and Ospina, 49–50, 57; and *letrados*, 52; and Rionegro Constitution of 1863, 71; on industrial technology, 93, 98; and Obeso, 105, 107, 108; language used by, 107; and Robles, 107–8; and African American colonization, 114; and Liberal Party, 135; and poor relief, 141; and taxation, 142; and land reform, 145; and popular politics, 161

Naranjo Martínez, Enrique, 222

National identity, 6, 228

Nationalist (Núñez) Party: in Caribbean Colombia, 18; and Catholic Church, 164–65, 167, 176; and economic policies, 165–66, 179–80, 204–5; Liberal concessions to, 173, 175; paranoia of, 173, 193; and whiteness of ruling class, 175–76; election fraud of, 191; and Thousand Days' War, 195, 196, 201, 204–5, 206, 208, 210; coup of July 1900, 200

National (Mosquera) faction, 134–35, 139–40, 155

National unity, 3

National University, 104, 111

New Granada. *See* Colombia

Newspapers: and emancipation, 29; access to, 30; and fictionalized narratives of race mixing, 41; and popular vote, 48; and race war, 65, 66; and civil war of 1859–62, 69; and *bogas*, 81–82, 84; and education, 100, 112; racist language barred in, 113; and rhetoric of popular politics, 136–37; and Rafael Núñez, 156; and labor, 181, 182; and Thousand Days' War, 213

Nieto, Juan José: political speeches of, 25, 41; people of color appointed by, 26; and emancipation, 28, 30; and manumission, 31, 32; and discrimination, 36–37, 42; and criminal justice

system, 39, 41; and egalitarian ethos, 40; and military coup of 1854, 44–45, 46, 59; and federal system, 48; Mosquera's alliance with, 52, 59, 134, 218; and Glorious Battalion, 57, 64; coup against Calvo, 57–59, 60, 63, 65, 66, 89; and Pacto de Unión, 60, 70; and wartime propaganda, 61; and civil war of 1859–62, 61, 62–64, 66–69, 103, 195, 201; overthrow of state government, 72; and *bogas*, 89–90; and Rafael Núñez, 126, 135, 154; and popular politics, 137, 138, 161; and taxation, 142; and land reform, 145

Núñez, Agustín, 28

Núñez, Rafael: and military coup of 1854, 46; and civil war of 1859–62, 69; and free trade, 98; and Obeso, 126, 128; and Conservative Party, 127, 156; and Liberal Party, 133, 135, 139–40, 163; as *letrado*, 135; and taxation, 142; and Ballestas, 144; as bigamist, 152; and regional base of support, 154–55; and trade, 155, 156, 165; and artisans, 155, 156, 165, 181, 208; and Independence Day festivals, 155, 157; and Catholic Church, 156, 158–59; Bolívar celebrations, 158; and Gaitán Obeso, 160–61, 218; on suffrage, 162; coalition with Caro, 164; funeral procession of, 167; and Claver, 168; and Spencer's theories, 175; nationalization of public lands, 182

Núñez, Ricardo, 88

Obando, José María: political speeches of, 25; support for candidates of color, 26; on universal manhood suffrage, 35, 48; and egalitarian ethos, 40; and presidential election of 1852, 43; and laborers, 44; and military coup of 1854, 47; propaganda used by, 68; and Madiedo, 69; and Rafael Núñez, 135; and popular politics, 137; and Catholic Church, 145

Obeso, Candelario: and Caribbean region, 1, 5, 18; as *letrado*, 1, 101, 122, 128, 138; identification as *negro*, 1, 101, 125; *Cantos populares di mi tierra*, 1–2, 4, 8, 117–24, 125, 126, 128, 129, 130, 224; on emancipation, 2, 3; on citizenship, 2–3, 8, 18, 19, 225–26, 227, 229; on freedom, 4; and recognition, 6; on orality, 8, 13; on racism, 101; and sex, 101, 117, 118, 119, 122, 125, 130; on *bogas*, 101, 119; education of, 102, 103–4, 131; and Colegio Militar, 104, 160; and Murillo Toro, 105, 107, 108; careers of, 105, 128; and promotion of popular learning, 108–9; and racial etiquette, 114, 115, 117; vernacular language in writing of, 117–18, 122–24, 125; political critique of, 118, 124, 129; on status of girls and women, 118–19, 121, 126–27; on social relationships, 118–20; and Robles, 120, 128, 139; *Proposed Law over Public Order*, 121; on partisan commotions, 121, 133; and racial allegories, 122; intentional misspelling of title, 123, 257 (n. 83); expropriation of, 124, 125; eulogies to, 124, 129–30, 175; *Lecturas para ti*, 124–26; *Secundino el zapatero*, 126, 258 (n. 94); *Lucha de la vida*, 128; nostalgia in writing of, 128; critics of, 128–29; funeral of, 130–31; on marriage, 150; and Catholic Church, 159; Posada on, 174; on racial violence, 231
Obeso, Eugenio, 103, 104
Office of River Inspection, 177, 179, 181, 216, 222
Orality, 8, 13, 100, 117
Organic Decree on Public Instruction (1870): Conservative movement against, 71, 109–10, 120, 127, 128; and educational policy, 100, 105–11, 112, 118, 134, 154; criticism of, 116, 158; and compulsory attendance, 145, 170; and Catholic Church, 169

Ortiz, José María, 84
Ospina, Pastor, 61, 62, 146
Ospina Camacho, José, 162
Ospina Rodríguez, Mariano: and Conservative caucus, 39; and Murillo Toro, 48–49, 57; and presidential election of 1856, 48–50; protests against, 51; and emancipation, 52; and interim appointment powers, 54; and Azuero, 56; and Nieto, 59; and civil war of 1859–62, 60, 62, 64, 66–67, 68; and *bogas*, 88
Otero, José María, 30

Pacto de Unión, 52, 60, 62, 70. *See also* Colombia
Páez, Adriano, 115
Páez, José Antonio, 44
Palacio, Francisco J., 206–7, 211
Palacio, Julio H., 97, 211
Palacio clan, 134
La Palestra, 156
Panama, 32, 68, 139, 156, 158, 161, 163, 194, 217, 220, 225
Parra, Aquileo: and *bogas*, 73, 75, 83–84, 139; and education, 110; concessions to Conservatives and Nationalists, 110, 173; and Robles, 138, 140; and Rafael Núñez, 139, 154, 160; and Catholic Church, 145, 158; and marriage law, 153–54
Pax (novel), 218
Peasants, 16, 76, 136, 143–45, 153, 155, 158, 162, 180, 191, 193, 196, 197, 199, 201, 212, 224; in literature, 116, 121, 122–23, 124, 126. *See also* Smallholdings
Pereira Castro, Francisco, 198
Pérez, Felipe, 52, 56, 66, 67, 79, 96, 114, 115, 119
Pérez, Juan Manuel, 44–45, 46
Pérez, Santiago, 173
Pérez Triana, Santiago, 174, 270 (n. 44)
Petitions, 28, 29, 36, 56, 69, 82, 86, 87, 88, 102, 140, 142, 143, 146–47, 149,

153, 159, 169, 173, 182, 183, 185, 186, 188, 189

Piña Channel, 81

Pino, Simón, 86

Plebeian citizens: formal participation of, 7; enfranchisement of, 21; political appointments of, 26; and jury trials, 38; demands for political change, 44; and military coup of 1854, 45; and postcoup political order, 47; and civil war of 1859–62, 52–53, 61, 64–65; and martial civic practices, 57, 64, 136; and authority of individual leaders, 72; and *letrados*, 99, 102–3, 157; and education, 111; and *costumbrismo*, 116; and recognition, 133, 222–23, 226; and Carnival, 137; protest of arbitrary policies, 142–43; and land reform, 143–45, 158; and Catholic Church, 146, 152, 159, 168; and marriage and divorce law, 150–51, 153, 154; and Rafael Núñez, 156; and Liberal Party, 165; antigovernment demonstrations of, 166; and Thousand Days' War, 197, 200, 213, 214

Pluralism, 127, 148, 149, 229, 230

Political culture: and vernacular citizenship, 7; and democratic societies, 26–27; and emancipation, 27, 32; and civil war of 1859–62, 52, 71, 136, 164; and Rionegro Constitution, 104, 132, 136, 137, 139; fragmentation of, 131; and universal manhood suffrage, 162; and passive citizenship, 164–65; of Regeneration, 173–74; and Thousand Days' War, 207; and Afro-Colombians, 223; and violence, 230–31

Ponce, Julián, 38, 138, 154

Popular politics: struggles within, 9; and freedom, 12; and Liberal Party, 60, 133–45; and suffrage, 127, 134; and authority, 132–33, 147, 150, 163; and festivities, 135–36, 137, 146; and social class, 135–38, 140–45; rhetoric of, 136–37; and Carnival,

137; and racism, 139–40; and Catholic Church, 145–49; and marriage and legitimacy, 149–54; and Rafael Núñez, 154–59; collapse of, 159–63; and Gaitán Obeso, 160–61

Popular societies: of Conservative Party, 25

El Porvenir, 156, 185, 189, 213

Posada, Eduardo, 174

Posada Gutiérrez, Joaquín, 84

Positivism, 108, 176, 228

Postal service, 85–87, 88, 89, 93

Poverty and the poor: and egalitarian ethos, 35, 38, 39, 40, 43; and antipoor sentiments, 39–40; and cholera epidemics, 39–40, 44; and education, 102, 106, 107, 110, 172–73; and women, 107; and taxation, 140, 141, 142–43; deserving poor, 141, 142; and Catholic Church, 148, 172; and marriage, 151; paternalism toward, 188–90; and contemporary Caribbean, 226–27

Presidential election: of 1848, 39; of 1852, 43; of 1856, 33, 48–50, 51, 54; of 1862, 52; of 1876, 135, 139–40, 154, 155, 156, 157; of 1880, 155–56; of 1904, 217

Press freedom, 112, 114, 161, 175, 181, 220

Print culture: and contentious public sphere, 7; and *letrados*, 7, 99, 100; expansion of, 99, 112; racism in, 113–15

Property crimes, 38–39

Prostitution, 152, 185–88

Protestants, 148, 150, 169–70

Public opinion, 27–28, 39, 127

Public-private distinctions: and race, 9–10, 37, 42, 113, 132, 137, 138, 227; and belonging, 10

Public sphere: and print culture, 7; boundaries of inclusion and exclusion, 8–9, 10, 42–43, 164–65; and *letrados*, 9, 13, 19, 42, 99, 112, 114; racial marking in, 11; and manumission ceremonies, 21, 36; and race mixing, 36–37, 41; and egalitarian ethos, 40, 42–43;

and Regeneration, 166; representations of Afro-Colombians in, 231

Puerto Colombia, 176, 179, 180, 212–13, 221–22

Puerto Rico, 116

Queto, Francisco, 86

Race mixing: and public sphere, 36–37, 41; fictionalized narratives of, 41; Reclus on, 50; José María Samper on, 112–13; Obeso on, 121, 122, 130; and civil marriage, 150; Jiménez López on, 222

Race war: and civil war of 1859–62, 64–68

Racial difference: and citizenship, 2, 9; and national unity, 3; and postemancipation civil equality, 9–10, 36–37; historicizing race, 10–11, 228; and emancipation, 11, 127, 228; and social class, 26; and military coup of 1854, 45; public legitimacy of, 227; and multiculturalism, 229

Racial etiquette: and antiblack racism, 10, 113; and public-private distinctions, 113, 132, 137, 138; and *letrados*, 113–15, 129; and Obeso, 114, 115, 117. *See also* Democratic culture

Racial ideology: and public-private distinctions, 10, 11; and market economy, 12; in *costumbrismo*, 100, 174, 227; and debate over racial decline, 222–23; political shaping of, 227; and *mestizaje*, 228–29

Racialization studies, 227

Racism: and Conservative Party, 67; and Liberal Party, 68; Obeso on, 101; and racial hierarchy, 112–13, 125; in print culture, 113–15; and popular politics, 139–40; and Thousand Days' War, 200; in premises of nonracist liberalism, 225

Radical faction. *See* Gólgota faction; Liberal Party

Railroads, 75, 98, 176, 178–79, 180, 183, 189, 204, 212

Ramírez, Hermógenes, 192–94. *See also* El Enviado de Dios

Rape: black or plebeian men accused of, 10, 65–67, 121, 122, 200, 215

Reclus, Élisée, 50

Recognition: articulation of demands for, 2; as essence of contested citizenship, 6–7, 11; and metalanguages of race and class, 11; and disenfranchisement, 14, 223; and market economy, 16; and Caribbean Colombia, 18; historicizing of, 19; and military coup of 1854, 22; and *bogas*, 88, 98; and racial etiquette, 115; and plebeian citizens, 133, 222–23, 226; and Thousand Days' War, 218–19; and Regeneration, 223; and national symbols, 223–24; national scope of, 226; of Afro-Colombians, 229–31

La Reforma, 66

Regeneration: and rights of landless majority, 10; state-building during, 12; and state-church relations, 13, 164–73, 176, 207; and authoritarian ethos, 164, 167; economic policies of, 165–66, 179–81, 189–90, 191; El Enviado de Dios challenging, 166, 190–94; and *letrados*, 173–74; and commercial interests, 176–79, 182–83; and labor, 177–82, 212; and marketplace regulation, 183–85; and women laborers, 185–87; and marriage and divorce laws, 187–88; and poverty and the poor, 188–90; and recognition, 223

El Relator, 114

Religious freedom, 166

Rerum Novarum encyclical, 221

Restrepo, Antonio José, 125, 129–30, 175

Restrepo, José Manuel, 55, 102

Restrepo, Juan de Dios, 74, 79–80, 92

Restrepo Canal, Carlos, 3

Revista Moderna, 222

Reyes, Rafael, 216–18, 220–21
Riascos, Joaquín, 154
Ribón, Isaac, 136
Riohacha, Colombia: artisans of, 27
Rionegro Constitution of 1863: and states' sovereignty, 70, 155, 157; and suffrage, 70–71, 133–34; and political culture, 104, 132, 136, 137, 139; and Rafael Núñez, 156, 161; reform of, 160, 163; and divorce, 166; civic traditions of, 173
Rivas, Medardo, 95, 112, 174–77, 190, 218
Rivas Groot, José María, 129, 130, 218–19
Rivera, Jacinto, 84
Roa, Bernardo, 36, 37
Robles, Luis A.: as *letrado*, 101, 138, 175; education of, 102, 103–4, 131; as director of public instruction, 107–9, 134, 138, 140; and racial etiquette, 114, 115; and Obeso, 120, 128, 139; Caribbean cliques led by, 133; and Parra, 138, 140; and stamp tax, 140, 141; and land reform, 144–45; and popular politics, 155–56, 157; concessions to Nationalists, 173; and economic reforms, 182; and rebellion plots, 202; hagiographies of, 216; as icon of Afro-Colombia, 229
Rodríguez, José del Rosario, 84
Rojas Garrido, José María, 28, 34
Ruiz, Rafael, 149, 150

Samper, José María: on social class, 26; and military coup of 1854, 45; on *macheteros*, 71; on *bogas*, 80, 89, 92–93, 115; on steamboats, 92–93; on *marineros*, 94; on *letrados*, 100, 106; on mulattoes, 112–13; and Conservatives, 127, 156; on suffrage, 162; on race mixing, 176
Samper, Miguel, 156, 189–90
Santa Marta, Colombia: demography of, 14, 16; and Liberal Party, 17, 175; and outmigration, 22; slave population of, 24; democratic societies in, 25, 27;

social class in, 26, 54; and 1851 emancipation act, 29; pre–civil war protest in, 53–55; municipal government in, 56; and Robles, 107, 155
Sarmiento, Domingo, 126
Savannas of Bolívar, 14, 24, 58, 143, 199
Scott, Rebecca, 7, 225
Sears, Henry, 36–37, 41
Sex: and honor, 10, 152; sexual relations, 13, 67, 118–19, 149–54; and people of color, 67, 118–19, 121, 122, 130, 153, 187; as allegory of inclusion, 101, 117, 118–19, 121, 122, 125; and deviancy, 152, 200. *See also* Families; Gender; Legitimacy of children; Prostitution
Sierra Nevada de Santa Marta, 14, 22, 196, 215, 228
Slaveholders: compensation for, 28, 29; and seizure of manumission process, 31; legend of *zurriago*, 42
Slavery: Afro-Colombians conflated with, 2–3, 37, 114; abolition of, 12–13, 21, 23, 27–28, 35, 84, 146; in Caribbean Colombia, 17, 24, 28; and self-purchase, 22; slave resistance, 22–23, 24, 32, 33. *See also* Emancipation
Slave societies, 4, 224
Smallholdings: in coastal backlands, 22, 23; and *bogas*, 78, 87; and land reform, 145; and Thousand Days' War, 213. *See also* Peasants
Smith Córdoba, Amir, 234 (n. 8)
Socarrás, Sabas, 196, 197, 198, 199, 201, 202–3, 207–8, 215–16
Social class: and recognition, 6; multiclass interaction in politics, 9; and race, 10; language of, 11; and democratic societies, 26; and egalitarian ethos, 34, 35, 41, 42–43; and contravention of informal social barriers, 36; and Conservative Party, 39; and social deference, 42; and military coup of 1854, 45; and pre–civil war protests, 53, 54; and education, 101, 169–70; and popular politics, 135–38,

140–45; and Catholic Church, 146, 168; and Thousand Days' War, 196, 197, 200–201, 202, 212–13; and racial ideology, 227. *See also* Elites; Plebeian citizens; Poverty and the poor

Social Darwinism, 175, 176

Sociedad Filantrópica, 28

Societies-with-slaves: emancipation in, 4, 5, 11–12, 224–25

Society for the Daughters of the Sacred Heart, 152

Sovereignty: national, 5; parishioner, 13, 145–49, 169; popular, 46, 57, 120, 150; of federal states, 70, 155, 157; of labor, 81

Spanish America: emancipation in, 4, 11–12; democracy in, 45–46

Spencer, Herbert, 175

Steamboats: *bogas*' opposition to, 74; and commercial interests, 91–93, 178; and laborers, 91–98, 161, 179, 180; social structure on, 93–95; and *marineros*, 94–95, 96, 97; work-related deaths on, 96; inefficiencies of, 96–97; and taxation, 158; and labor organizations, 180–81, 182; and Thousand Days' War, 204, 210

Strikes, 10, 13, 18, 73, 74, 77, 85–89, 91, 93, 97, 137, 181–82, 189, 190, 211, 212–13, 220–21, 223

Suffrage: rules of indirect and restricted suffrage, 39; expansion of, 39, 43, 48; literacy and property qualifications for, 70, 72, 134, 162, 164, 167, 174, 178, 221; popular suffrage, 127, 134, 136; and Thousand Days' War, 202; adult male suffrage, 228; of women, 228. *See also* Disenfranchisement; Universal manhood suffrage

Taxation: and rights and duties, 9; and popular politics, 140–45, 158; and fishermen, 141, 142, 143; and merchants, 141, 182; and *bogas*, 142, 158, 177

Taylor, Charles, 6

Thousand Days' War (1899–1902): and Regeneration, 12; as partisan conflict, 13–14; and Liberal Party, 195, 196, 197, 198, 199, 200, 201–4, 205, 206, 207–8, 210, 211, 213, 214, 215, 218; and militarization of civil functions, 195, 196, 200, 202, 204–9, 211; and limits of peace, 195–96, 200, 203, 209, 215–19; and guerrilla warfare, 196, 197–204, 207, 209, 210, 211, 212, 213, 214, 216, 219; and banditry, 199, 200, 201, 202, 203, 204, 207, 216; propaganda of, 200–201, 207–8; and labor, 209–15; Treaty of Neerlandia, 215–16; and *convivencia*, 216–18; and limitations of political reform, 220

Tithing: and rights and duties, 9, 147, 148; and democratic societies, 27, 146; protests against, 169

Titles of honor and address, 36

Trabajadores de la tierra caliente (novel), 174–75, 176, 218

Trade: and Caribbean Colombia, 16; recessions in, 51, 55, 144, 179, 191; free-trade era, 74, 80; and tobacco exports, 74–75, 87, 88, 144; and steamboats, 91–92; and Rafael Núñez, 155, 156, 165; and coffee industry, 178, 179, 220

Treaty of Neerlandia, 215–16

Troncoso, Francisco, 25, 26, 28

United Fruit Company, 217, 223. *See also* Banana industry

United States: and abolitionism, 27; as slavocracy, 29, 37, 65; federal system of, 48, 65; bank panic in, 55; civil war of, 69, 113–14; and African American colonization, 113–14; Reyes's treaty with, 220; and slave emancipation, 224

Universal liberal individualism, 34

Universal manhood suffrage: rules of, 13, 21–22, 25, 33, 47, 228; and presidential election of 1856, 33, 48–50; and constitution of 1853, 35–36, 39, 42–43; and Rionegro Constitution of 1863, 70–71, 133–34; and popular politics, 136, 140; and Conservative Party, 162; repeal of, 163

Uribe, Antonio José, 221

Uribe, Juan de Dios, 129–30

Uribe Uribe, Rafael: and Robles, 175; on economic policies, 189–90; call for rebellion, 191, 203; and Thousand Days' War, 197, 198–99, 201, 202–3, 210, 214, 215–17

Valencia, Casimir, 132, 163

El Vapor, 80–81, 89, 93

Vargas Vila, José María, 173–74

Velásquez, Rogerio, 234 (n. 8)

Vélez, Joaquín, 195, 202, 204, 208, 210, 212, 217

Vera, Manuel "El Indio," 198, 201

Veterans' pension law, 153, 154, 163

Victoria, Manuel María "El Negro," 61

Wade, Peter, 6, 228, 229

War of the Supremes (1839–42), 43

Wars of independence: social disruptions of, 22

White men: Obeso on, 118, 119–21, 123–24, 126

White women: rumors of black Liberals raping, 10, 65–67, 121, 122, 200, 215; and manumission ceremonies, 31; and egalitarian ethos, 42; role of, 42; and education, 114; Acosta de Samper on, 114, 121; Obeso on, 121–22, 130

Wiwa people, 228

Women of color: and vernacular citizenship, 7; active and visible role in marketplace, 22; and manumission ceremonies, 30, 31; and marriage and divorce rights, 35–36, 48, 151–52; and civil war of 1859–62, 61, 63, 67, 70; and *bogas*, 78, 80, 85, 87; as laborers, 78–79, 185–87; as vendors on steamboats, 92; and education, 106, 107, 108, 110–11; Obeso on, 118–19; and baptism of children, 151, 192; and Catholic Church, 168; declining wages, 180; and Thousand Days' War, 214–15, 219. *See also* Female labor; Gender; Market women; White women

Woodcutters, 92, 95, 210–11

World War I, 220

Zapata Olivella, Delia, 234 (n. 8)

Zapata Olivella, Manuel, 229, 234 (n. 8)

Zuleta, Saúl, 197

Zurriago: legend of, 42